DEFAULT

DEFAULT

The Landmark Court Battle over
Argentina's $100 Billion Debt Restructuring

GREGORY MAKOFF
With a Foreword by LEE C. BUCHHEIT

Georgetown University Press / Washington, DC

The publisher is not responsible for third-party websites or their content. URL links were active at time of publication.

Library of Congress Cataloging-in-Publication Data

Names: Makoff, Gregory, author.
Title: Default : the landmark court battle over Argentina's $100 billion debt
    restructuring / Gregory Makoff ; with a foreword by Lee C. Buchheit.
Description: Washington, DC : Georgetown University Press, 2024. | Includes
    bibliographical references and index.
Identifiers: LCCN 2023008304 (print) | LCCN 2023008305 (ebook) | ISBN
    9781647123970 (hardcover) | ISBN 9781647123987 (ebook)
Subjects: LCSH: Default (Finance) —Law and legislation. | Debts, External—
    Law and legislation. | Debts, Public—Law and legislation. | State bankruptcy.
    | Debts, Public—Argentina. | Foreign bonds—United States. | Conflict of
    laws—Debts, External—United States—Cases. | Argentina—Trials, litigation,
    etc. | Elliott Investment Management—Trials, litigation, etc. | International
    Monetary Fund. | United States. District Court (New York : Southern District)
Classification: LCC K4449 .M35 2024 (print) | LCC K4449 (ebook) | DDC
    343.82/037—dc23/eng/20230928
LC record available at https://lccn.loc.gov/2023008304
LC ebook record available at https://lccn.loc.gov/2023008305

∞ This paper meets the requirements of ANSI/NISO Z39.48-1992 (Permanence of Paper).

25 24   9 8 7 6 5 4 3 2 First printing

Printed in the United States of America

Cover design by Faceout Studio, Spencer Fuller
Interior design by Paul Hotvedt

For Eileen

The idea in life is to try to be a judge, never a partisan.
—Nassim Nicholas Taleb, TWITTER, April 25, 2023

Contents

Foreword

The facts of life are this. . . . We do not have a normal situation.
　　　　　　　　　　　—*Judge Thomas P. Griesa, February 23, 2012*

Even a decade later, it is hard to discern whether Judge Thomas P. Griesa ever fully realized that he was presiding over a protracted Kobayashi Maru scenario.[1] Judge Griesa, the senior U.S. federal district court judge before whom all lawsuits involving Argentina's defaulted bonds were consolidated, believed in his soul that court judgments—particularly his judgments—should be paid or settled by the defendant. When the Republic of Argentina openly defied those judgments for more than a decade, the U.S. federal judiciary branded the country a "uniquely recalcitrant debtor."

But what appeared as willful defiance to U.S. judges was, in the view of Argentine authorities, the only rational policy that could be followed. The country had experienced a devastating economic crisis starting in 2001. That crisis forced a default on nearly $100 billion of Republic of Argentina bonds. Every one of those instruments was a legal, valid, and binding obligation under New York law, enforceable in a New York court at the absolute discretion of the holder. Every single holder was thus, from a legal perspective, armed and dangerous. Like all sovereign debtors, however, Argentina lacked a bankruptcy-style mechanism to force any of those bondholders to accept an offer to restructure the securities. Sovereign borrowers in this situation have only one effective weapon to induce holdout creditor participation in a workout: the threat that any who decline to join the restructuring will be consigned to the outer darkness of perpetual payment default. Most sovereign debtors in this situation convey that message with at least a modicum of subtlety. Argentina elected to deliver the message brutally, repeatedly, and inflexibly, a tactical decision that later turned out to be the country's undoing (see chapter 8).

For obvious reasons, no sovereign debtor can offer its creditors a choice between accepting a debt restructuring in which, by definition, they will lose money or obtaining a court judgment on their claims that will be paid in full or, at the worst, settled on terms better than those offered in the restructuring. Such an offer would inevitably result in the entirety of the country's creditors electing to become judgment creditors. Nothing would be resolved. The Argentine authorities therefore felt that they had no choice other than obstinately to defy Judge Griesa's orders, and Griesa felt that he had no choice other than to insist that Argentina pay or settle his judgments.[2]

The result? A no-win, no-escape, no-alternative standoff.

In the entire history of sovereign debt workouts and sovereign debt disputes, there has never been anything like the events Gregory Makoff recounts in this book. He takes us into the negotiating rooms, the backrooms, the courtrooms, and the settlement rooms where this fifteen-year struggle agonizingly unfolded. The main dramatis personae in this story—Argentina, the holdout creditors, and Judge Griesa—were all convinced that they had both the moral and legal right to behave in the way they did. Indeed, each felt that they were duty-bound to behave in no other way.

Some readers of this book may conclude that we shall not have peace in the sovereign debt markets until the last avaricious hedge fund manager is strangled in the entrails of the last boastful debtor country politician. Perhaps. But largely as a result of the events described in this book, the sovereign debt community has focused most of its intellectual energies over the last twenty years on finding mechanisms that will prevent maverick creditors from using the courts to extract preferential recoveries from financially distressed sovereign debtors, recoveries made possible only by the willingness of their fellow creditors to provide debt relief to the afflicted country. Contractual provisions (collective action clauses) that bind dissident lenders to the restructuring decisions of the supermajority of their colleagues have since 2003 become widespread in sovereign bonds governed by New York law. A variety of other proposals, including possible changes in law to facilitate sovereign debt restructurings, are also being debated. The hope is that one or more of these mechanisms will save sovereign debtors from being forced into a situation in which they must either accept preferential settlements with their more litigious creditors or incur the judicial moniker of "uniquely recalcitrant."

Lee C. Buchheit
Millbrook, New York, November 2022

Introduction

On the evening of November 26, 2001, Anne Krueger stepped up to the microphone at the annual dinner of the National Economists Club and spoke about a festering problem in the area of sovereign debt restructuring. Already a distinguished academic and policy maker, as First Deputy Managing Director Krueger was the top-ranked American at the International Monetary Fund (IMF) and second-in-command after the managing director, a role by tradition given to a European. As such, her words came with added authority. The title of her speech was "A New Approach to Sovereign Debt Restructuring," and it was timely because everyone in the audience knew that Argentina was teetering on the brink of a $100 billion default.[1]

Krueger got straight down to business. In her fabulously clear speaking voice, she boomed that there's a "gaping hole" in the international financial architecture for resolving sovereign debt crises. She said, "We lack incentives to help countries with unsustainable debts resolve them promptly and in an orderly way. At present the only available mechanism requires the international community to bail out the private creditors. It is high time this hole was filled."[2]

Krueger's essential observation was that while households and corporations around the world benefit from bankruptcy laws to shield them from creditors when insolvent, countries lack access to this basic protection.

If it strikes you as odd that it was an economist, not a lawyer, giving a keynote speech on the topic of bankruptcy, here's why nobody in the audience batted an eye: from the 1980s, the IMF had been an important player in virtually all sovereign debt restructurings around the world, a role stemming from its business of lending to and advising countries in distress. What did capture their attention that night was what Krueger

1

had to say. She was proposing that the IMF would not just have an important role in future sovereign debt restructurings but instead that it would run the show.

Krueger's idea was for the IMF to set up a new international facility—what she called a sovereign debt restructuring mechanism (SDRM)—to administer future sovereign debt restructurings and under which the IMF would gain extraordinary new legal powers, including the authority to decide when countries could default and enjoy protection from litigation while they worked out their debts.[3]

The world urgently needed an SDRM, Krueger explained, because countries had changed how they borrowed from the market over the prior decade. In the 1970s, developing countries took out large loans from major international banks such as Citibank and Chase Manhattan. After a wave of defaults in the 1980s banks stopped lending to sovereigns, so developing countries went to the international bond market for all their new borrowings. By the end of the 1990s, most sovereign debt was in bond format. This shift created a problem. In the past, a financially troubled country could sit down with a dozen or so of its leading banks and negotiate a workable repayment schedule. Now that sovereign debt was owned by thousands—if not tens or hundreds of thousands—of bond investors spread out all over the world, that was no longer possible. The problem, Krueger observed, was that private creditors had become "increasingly numerous, anonymous, and difficult to coordinate."[4]

In addition to its coordination problem, sovereign debt restructuring had a legal problem as well, Krueger said. She pointed out that just the year before, a Belgian court had forced Peru to repay one investor in full even though the country's other lenders had all voluntarily accepted a significant loss. Krueger called out the name of the investor who'd won special treatment through litigation: "A vulture company called Elliott Associates."[5]

Yet Krueger's new idea would do nothing for Argentina's exposure to these two problems. She admitted in her speech that her SDRM idea would take a few years to implement and therefore could not be used to resolve Argentina's rapidly deteriorating situation.

Just ten days later on December 6, 2001, the IMF pulled the plug on Argentina, which led over the following four weeks to the freezing of the country's financial system, the fall of the government, a steep devaluation of Argentina's currency, and default on about $100 billion of bonds.

Thus began a fifteen-year chain of events that proved Krueger right. There was a gaping hole in the system of restructuring sovereign debt, and just as she had warned, when Argentina moved to restructure its debt, it was beset by problems coordinating its many creditors and was hit by a massive wave of litigation. To top it off, the litigation was led by the same hedge fund Krueger had flagged in her speech: Elliott Associates.

The Story

This book follows Argentina as it fought a fifteen-year battle to restructure its debt after its default on about $100 billion of bonds in December 2001. It is a disaster story with multiple problems besieging the restructuring, some stemming from inadequacies of law and contract, some political, and some that were homegrown. Without a doubt, what Argentina went through was worse than any worst-case scenario that any audience member could have imagined when listening to Anne Krueger's speech on November 26, 2001.

The first third of the book covers the period from Argentina's 2001 default through June 2005, when it restructured 76% of its defaulted debt. Chapter 1 features bitter fights between Argentina and the IMF over the terms of a new lending program during 2002. Covering the period of 2003 through 2005, chapters 2 and 3 detail Argentina's bond restructuring process and feature a three-way battle between Argentina, the IMF, and creditor activists about how the negotiations should be handled. Argentina's deal was marketed without the support of the IMF and under attack from creditor activists, so the country's transaction was not entirely successful. Holders of $19.6 billion of bonds rejected the deal, opting instead to sue and setting the stage for the latter two-thirds of the story.

Chapter 4 details Elliott's lawsuits against Peru between 1996 and 2000, the same litigation Anne Krueger flagged in her 2001 speech.

Although a break in the chronology, this detailed analysis of the earlier litigation is essential background for understanding the Argentina cases, particularly in terms of how Elliott used the pari passu clause in Peru's loans to convince a Belgian court to rule in its favor in September 2000. The chronology also provides a convenient way to introduce Elliott's sovereign debt investment team and the firm's business model.

Chapters 5 and 6 dive into the almost three hundred lawsuits that holdout investors brought against Argentina in the U.S. District Court for the Southern District of New York (the Southern District). These chapters feature dozens of assorted plaintiffs making ad hoc, uncoordinated efforts to attach Argentina's assets via court order. They went after bank accounts, bond holdings, diplomatic properties, a presidential plane, satellite parts, and a ship carrying a cargo of liquified natural gas on the high seas. Yet with two small exceptions these efforts failed, it being nearly impossible to collect from a defaulting sovereign. Frustrated by the lack of recovery through litigation, two-thirds of Argentina's holdouts capitulated and accepted Argentina's reopening of its offer in 2010, even though the terms were no better than the country's prior offer. Their participation brought Argentina's aggregate success rate in restructuring its defaulted debt to 92%.

Chapters 8, 9, and 10 cover the litigation the holders of the remaining 8% of defaulted debt continued to bring. Elliott brought its long-anticipated pari passu claim against Argentina in October 2010. The matter came to a head at a February 2012 hearing when the hedge fund's lawyer, former solicitor general Theodore Olson, argued to Judge Thomas P. Griesa that the judge should use his judicial power to compel Argentina to pay Elliott and its co-plaintiffs in full by blocking payments to the 92% of bondholders who had settled with the country in 2005 and 2010. Despite pleas from debt restructuring experts to not favor the holdouts, Judge Griesa imposed the injunction, which gave Argentina two choices: pay Elliott in full and be permitted to pay all its other bondholders or refuse to pay Elliott and be forced into default because the court would block payments to the other creditors. Pausing the pari passu story, chapter 9 provides an overview of litigation taking place in other states and around the world, including Elliott's attachment of Argentina's tall ship ARA *Libertad* in Ghana in 2012. The chapter also covers economic and political developments in Argentina after 2010 as well as Elliott's intensive lobbying efforts in Washington and elsewhere. Returning to the pari passu story, chapter 10 discusses Argentina's decision in July 2014 to default rather than pay Elliott, which leads to even more bitter litigation. However, just weeks after Argentina's 2014 default, the sovereign debt market accepts powerful new clauses in their bonds to prevent holdouts from profiting at their expense in the future.

Chapter 11 brings the story to a close with a play-by-play description of the settlement that Argentina and its holdout investors reached in early 2016 following the election of Mauricio Macri as the president of Argentina in November 2015. President Macri makes settling the country's legal dispute with the holdouts the first priority of his new government, and his team inks a surprisingly good deal by persuading the court-appointed arbitrator, Special Master Daniel Pollack, to help the country turn the tables on Elliott.

Approach

All the events described above are fairly well known to regular readers of the *Financial Times*, the *Wall Street Journal*, or the business section of the *New York Times* over the last twenty years. What is less known are the root causes, the reasons, the answer to the question of why. Why did these events occur? How were the people, institutions, and ideas interconnected? Why was Argentina's 2005 debt restructuring so contentious? And, most important of all, why did Judge Griesa make his famous— some would say infamous—decision to impose the injunction on Argentina in 2012? These are the questions this book strives to answer, while at the same time teaching readers how the world of sovereign debt restructuring really works.

To answer these questions, I take readers into the room as the events play out, telling the story almost as a historical drama. I allow the characters to speak for themselves as much as possible, relying heavily on verbatim quotes taken from primary sources, such as court transcripts and IMF Executive Board meeting minutes. I took this approach to make the book more fun to read and to make the topic of sovereign debt restructuring accessible to a broader audience, but this approach also yields a more authentic product, as each event was truly the consequence of choices made by human beings, governments, and institutions, some wise and some less so. However, scholars will find in the endnotes sources backing every claim the book makes, including legal citations in the level of detail and in the format conventionally found in law review articles.

One challenge with Argentina's story is that it involves many characters, institutions, and events. To help readers keep track, I repeat the year of the action and the full title and affiliations of characters in every chapter subsection except where it would be excessively repetitive. I also provide a glossary and, in the appendixes, a character list and a timeline of events.

Now, on to Argentina's default.

1

Argentina Defaults and Then Fights with the IMF

(December 2001–March 2003)

On December 6, 2001, the IMF pulled the plug, announcing that it was refusing to disburse a pending $1.24 billion loan installment to Argentina.[1] The reason? The IMF had determined that Argentina's finances were unsustainable. This withdrawal of official support pushed Argentina, which had already been teetering on the brink, over the edge.

Within weeks, in response to draconian measures to stabilize the country's banking system in the absence of IMF support, Argentines filled the streets screaming "they should all go,"[2] Argentina's minister of economy resigned,[3] and on December 20 President Fernando de la Rúa dramatically fled, departing from the roof of the presidential palace via helicopter.[4]

Default followed on December 23 when Adolfo Rodríguez Saá, one of the country's three interim presidents that month, announced a moratorium on the repayment of the country's external debt to the Argentine Congress.[5] Lawmakers rose to their feet and cheered "Argentina! Argentina!"[6]

If at the time of the default the country's economy was in a deep freeze reminiscent of the darkest days of the Great Depression in the United States, in the new year the situation worsened. Argentina suffered from a sharp drop in economic activity, recurrent banking holidays, and sky-high unemployment.

The social dimension of the crisis was enormous. Over half the Argentine population slipped below the poverty line. Crime was way up. Rioting and lawlessness ruled the streets. Those in the middle class experienced social disorder that left them shocked and disoriented. There were pickets everywhere, massive and multisectorial strikes, and no-notice raids on local supermarkets, with crowds coming out of nowhere to strip the shelves bare. An important trigger of this disorder was a breakdown of the payments system. To deal with the lack of foreign currency liquidity after the withdrawal of IMF support, the government cut access to bank accounts, which meant that middle-class families could not withdraw enough money to meet regular expenses, and there was no money to pay workers in the cash economy. The result was lines of angry depositors at banks and lines of poor people at city halls looking for handouts so they could feed their families. In a spontaneous mid-December eruption, people all over Argentina started banging pots and pans in anger, a subsequently regular form of mass protest the press called *cacerolazos*. And late at night Buenos Aires, the country's beautiful capital, came to be haunted by an army of thirty thousand "cartoneros," poor men, women, and children who collected discarded boxes just to earn enough money to buy maybe a pizza.[7] All this was happening in a country that had long enjoyed a relatively high standard of living.

Washington policy makers did not pull the plug on Argentina without a lot of thought. They knew that ordinary Argentines would suffer, and they knew that bondholders would experience deep losses. All that said, Argentina's economy was broken beyond repair.[8] For a decade the country had relied on its "convertibility plan," which featured a one-for-one peg of the peso to the U.S. dollar, a scheme adopted to bring an end to the hyper-inflation of the 1980s. The one-for-one peg tamed inflation but created other problems over time, including an unsustainable buildup of external debt by the government and the private sector. After all, dollar-based debt appeared much cheaper to service than its peso-based equivalent: investors demanded a lower coupon for dollar bonds since they would be protected if Argentina's one-for-one peg broke someday.

Unfortunately, Argentina's pegged-currency regime also made the

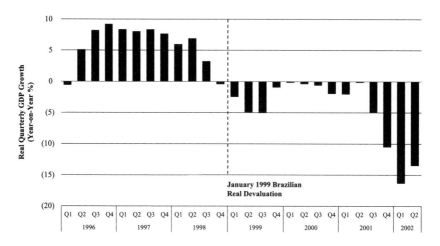

Figure 1.1. Argentina real quarterly GDP growth (1996–2002)

Source: República Argentina, Instituto Nacional de Estadística y Censos
(INDEC), https://www.indec.gob.ar/indec/web/Institucional-Indec-Informacion
DeArchivo-5, supplemented by author's calculations.

country vulnerable to external shocks, including global credit market volatility and competitive currency devaluations by its neighbors. Argentina was hit hard by a series of such events in the late 1990s, including the Asian financial crisis, Russia's August 1998 default, and in January 1999 the steep devaluation of the Brazilian real. Figure 1.1 shows that Argentina's economy never recovered from these shocks, with the country falling into a multiyear recession, which led to shrinking revenues, rising expenditures, increasing government debt, extraordinarily high unemployment, and extreme political polarization.

The IMF's judgment in December 2001 was that lending more to Argentina would only make matters worse.[9] It was time to let the country fail. The IMF does not speak so directly about countries in harm's way, however. What IMF chief economist Kenneth Rogoff did say that month was, "It's clear that the mix of fiscal policy, debt, and exchange rate regime is not sustainable," which in plain English meant there would be no more money from Washington until Argentina started dealing with its debt overhang and fixed exchange rate.[10]

No More Bailouts

There was more than math at work in the decision to let Argentina fail; there was also an idea. George W. Bush's administration firmly believed that it was time to stop bailing out troubled countries, even if this led to bond defaults. This was a relatively new idea but one that had picked up steam in the second half of the 1990s. Conservatives, led by Carnegie Mellon professor Allan Meltzer, bemoaned the $10 billion–plus rescue packages that Mexico, Thailand, Indonesia, South Korea, and Russia had received during the Clinton administration. They believed that bailouts created a moral hazard.[11] They believed that when investors lent to countries with lax economic controls, those governments were incentivized to start making risky economic decisions under the expectation that they would get an IMF bailout if their bets didn't work out as expected. This prospect irked conservatives. They didn't want U.S. taxpayer money to be handed over to foreign governments and bondholders who had made bad choices. It was time, they said, to start letting countries fail to teach them and their lenders a lesson. Argentina's bad luck was that it was first in line.

U.S. treasury secretary Paul O'Neill expressed the Bush administration's view at a World Economic Forum event held in New York about a month after Argentina defaulted: "Over the last 15 years the temptation has been to rush in with a fire-station crew and dump money on the rest of the world. I don't think that's O.K." O'Neill said that the United States should not send cash to countries that make "mistake after mistake," adding that it was ridiculous for America's "plumbers and carpenters to pay for someone's bad decisions."[12]

Secretary O'Neill wasn't insensitive to the situation on the ground in Buenos Aires, noting that he was pained to see the images of rioting in the streets. Nonetheless, he was adamant that fresh funding would be provided to Argentina only after it put comprehensive reforms in place. It would have to be reform, then money, not bailouts based on promises of reforms that might never be delivered. The United States was wary of Argentina's past failures to deliver on promises. In this the Bush administration was of one voice, for over the next few months Secretary O'Neill, National Security Advisor Condoleezza Rice,[13] and Secretary of State Colin Powell[14] all used the same talking point when the topic of Argentina came up: reform then money, reform then money, reform then money.[15] It was tough love for both Argentina and the market.

No Contagion

While some savvy investors found ways to bet against Argentine bonds, the market as a whole suffered tens of billions of dollars of losses when Argentina defaulted. Asset managers, mutual funds, pension funds, banks, and retail investors all over the world lost huge sums on their Argentine bonds. Some market participants blamed policy makers for not bailing out the country. Walter Molano, a frequent commentator on Argentine debt at BCP Securities, called it an "engineered default" and said that the country was "pushed over the edge by the U.S. Treasury."[16]

The team at the U.S. Treasury was ready to take the heat. They knew that bondholders would lose enormous sums, and they knew there would be complaints—hence the effort to articulate the Bush administration's no-more-bailouts policy. Contagion, however, would be another matter. While there was no doubt that the price of Argentine bonds would plunge when the IMF cut off funding, it would not be okay if a general panic in the market ensued, one that would hurt innocent countries and harm the global economy.

Ultimately, the U.S. Treasury determined that the best way to prevent contagion from Argentina's approaching default was to warn the market that it was coming. This message was inserted into a September 2001 press release announcing a small top-up of Argentina's program, the last money Argentina would get from the IMF before the country's crash. The warning was that $3 billion of the new funds to be provided to Argentina were earmarked for supporting a restructuring of the country's debt.[17] Since restructuring debt is a form of default, it was now on paper in black and white that Argentina's bonds were about to be pushed over the edge.

Argentina's subsequent default wasn't all that surprising since investors had been warned, and the market yawned. In sum, the U.S. Treasury's strategy worked, as detailed in John Taylor's fascinating memoir *Global Financial Warriors*.[18]

Argentina was the poster child for the Bush administration's new no-more-bailouts policy, and the U.S. Treasury didn't shy away from its role in the default. Deputy Treasury Secretary Kenneth Dam crowed to an audience at the World Affairs Council in Washington in January 2002 that there was "little evidence of contagion in the Argentine crisis, particularly not worldwide contagion."[19] The U.S. Treasury, which typically plays things close to the vest, was proud of this result.

Duhalde and Remes Lenicov Try to Pick Up the Pieces in Buenos Aires

Back in Argentina, it was time to pick up the pieces.

The process began on January 1, 2002, when Congress appointed Eduardo Duhalde, a member of the Argentine Senate, to serve out the remainder of former president de la Rúa's term.[20] Duhalde was the fourth person to assume the post in the wake of the prior president's departure; Rodríguez Saá and two others had not lasted more than a few days or hours each. Such was the chaos of that time.[21]

President Duhalde headed a unity government that made policy in close coordination with the governors of the Argentine provinces, the power brokers in the country's political system. It was agreed that Duhalde would not run for president in the upcoming election; he was there to fix the country, not to consolidate his personal power, a worry since he was one of the most powerful politicians in the country, having served as vice president under Carlos Menem for two years and as governor of the province of Buenos Aires for eight years and having run unsuccessfully for president in 1999.

With Argentines experiencing the worst living conditions of their lives, Duhalde wasn't popular.[22] His presidency didn't play well abroad either.[23] Some in Washington doubted his legitimacy because he had been appointed rather than elected. It didn't help that in his first days in office he talked about building a "home-field advantage" for local manufacturers, which was a big affront in the era of peak globalization.[24]

January through April 2002 was an absolute disaster, with Argentina in the depths of simultaneous currency, debt, banking, and humanitarian crises. President Duhalde and his minister of economy, Jorge Remes Lenicov, imposed harsh measures to stabilize the situation. They devalued the currency, froze utility tariffs, restructured bank assets and liabilities, increased taxes, cut spending, and imposed capital controls to conserve foreign reserves.[25] Yet the economy remained in free fall. Confidence was near zero, and money was continuing to flow out of the system despite the imposition of capital controls. Outside support was needed.

Economy Minister Remes Lenicov went to Washington in early February 2002 to ask for a new loan of $20 billion to stabilize the economy; however, the meetings didn't go well. His most important counterpart in Washington, IMF managing director Horst Köhler, a German, was in a sour mood over Argentina's recently failed program. His reputation at stake for having supported Argentina before the collapse, Köhler delivered a harsh message to the new minister: "You will only succeed with fiscal austerity and with reforms that you have not done during all this period, but if you do not take hard decisions do not expect anything from us, because I will not repeat again with you the error that is costing us so dearly."[26] Remes Lenicov came away empty-handed, as he subsequently did in March and April.

Remes Lenicov didn't last much longer. He resigned his role as minister of economy in late April 2002 after failing to implement a measure that the IMF insisted was essential for unlocking a new loan: a politically unpopular swap of bank deposits for medium-term bonds. This swap was designed to stop depositors from withdrawing pesos from their current accounts and selling them for dollars, which was depressing the value of the currency and draining the country's foreign reserves. While a deposit swap was a good idea in theory, it was met with insurmountable opposition in practice. Argentina had implemented a similar swap in the early 1990s that cost the middle class billions, so critics attacked

Remes Lenicov's proposal as soon as it was floated. Surrounded by an angry mob, the Argentine Congress shot down the proposed measure. Having staked his credibility at home and with the IMF on getting the measure passed, Remes Lenicov resigned, and Argentina was left in the middle of the deepest economic and financial crisis in its history without a minister of economy.[27]

President Duhalde quickly moved to fill the post. One candidate was Roberto Lavagna, the sixty-year-old economist who was serving as Argentina's ambassador to the European Union and as its representative at the World Trade Organization. Duhalde called Lavagna in Geneva to ask him to come back to Buenos Aires immediately to talk to him.[28] Another call went to Guillermo Calvo, a respected Yale-trained economist who was the head of research at the Inter-American Development Bank in Washington.[29]

In contrast to Calvo, Lavagna was not known to Washington policy makers. In Buenos Aires, however, the powers that be had a pretty good feel for the man, who was known as a skeptic of foreign debt and for his work on trade.[30] In the 1990s Lavagna had regularly criticized Argentina's IMF-backed one-for-one currency arrangement, saying it was killing growth and generating sky-high unemployment. In 1987 he quit the government of President Raúl Alfonsín for issuing what Lavagna called a "festival of bonds."[31]

Lavagna's Arrival

Returning to Buenos Aires to meet with President Duhalde, Lavagna arrived at the capital's international airport early on the morning of Friday, April 26, 2002. When he appeared in the arrivals area, reporters shouted, "Have you been offered the job of minister of economy?" Lavagna denied the rumor. The truth is he didn't know. When the president had called him two days earlier, Duhalde hadn't specifically offered him the job. Moreover, he and the reporters knew that Guillermo Calvo was also in the running.

That said, Lavagna had prepared a statement: "Any plan must contemplate and balance the international framework and their demands with the internal needs of the people, the Argentine citizens."[32] While this quote wasn't a headline grabber, its meaning was clear: Lavagna was going to resist demands from the IMF for more austerity.

After a quick stop at home, Lavagna made his way to meet with the president at Olivos, the presidential residence located north of the Buenos Aires city center. After preliminaries, Duhalde and Lavagna sat and talked about the options for solving the country's crisis. Sensing a commonality, Lavagna put his cards on the table: "Yes, Mr. President, if you are offering me the Ministry of Economy, my answer is yes."[33]

A Harder Line

Tall, thin, and with a statesman's posture, Roberto Lavagna was sworn in as minister of economy of the Republic of Argentina on the morning of Saturday, April 27, 2002, at the Casa Rosada—the Pink House—the presidential office building.[34] After the ceremony Lavagna made his way to the presidential residence, where he was due to meet with the crème de la crème of the Argentine political establishment: the president, the full cabinet, all the governors, and the leading deputies and senators. When offered the floor, Lavagna presented his two main policy ideas. First, social policy would be an integral part of economic policy, not an afterthought, as he believed it had been in the 1990s. Second, the provinces were not to blame for the crisis despite repeated claims in both Buenos Aires and Washington to the contrary.[35]

At a press conference that afternoon, Lavagna outlined his agenda for normalizing the Argentine economy: open the banks, maintain a floating peso, use foreign reserves selectively to prevent the currency from dropping below its fair value (which would risk stimulating inflation), force banks to subsidize the cost of loans temporarily to help struggling borrowers, and drop Remes Lenicov's mandatory deposit swap idea.[36] As to the negotiations with the IMF, Lavagna said that he didn't plan to rush to Washington for help. Instead, he would reengage with the country's international counterparts after initiating his program at home. Getting on his knees to beg for money from abroad wasn't his style.

Building the Team

The following day, Minister of Economy Roberto Lavagna started to build his team. It was tough going. Many people wished him well but said that they'd prefer to "help from the outside," which wasn't much use in a war zone.[37]

One acquaintance was willing to join Lavagna in the trenches, however: fifty-one-year-old economist Guillermo Nielsen. Nielsen was a good fit for the role of secretary of finance, the minister of economy's most important deputy.[38] For one, Nielsen had the technical skills needed to lead the restructuring of the country's almost $100 billion of defaulted bonds. Not only had he trained at Boston University, but he also spoke flawless English and had significant private-sector experience.[39] Moreover, he was media savvy, exemplified by his weekly gig talking on the radio in Spain about the Argentine economy.

To complete the team that would later restructure Argentina's debt, Nielsen brought in Leonardo Madcur and Sebastian Palla, both of whom had worked with him in the private sector, and Hugo Medina, a friend from high school and a lawyer by training. Medina was an important addition to the team because he had been serving as a top manager of the Buenos Aires Stock Exchange and was very knowledgeable about debt issuances. A young lawyer named Sergio Chodos joined the team in 2003.[40]

Archbishop Bergoglio Asks for a Contribution

On the morning of Monday, April 29, 2002, Minister of Economy Roberto Lavagna slipped out of his office to meet privately with the head of Argentina's Roman Catholic Church, archbishop of Buenos Aires Jorge Mario Bergoglio,[41] who had been working closely with President Duhalde since the beginning of the year on an initiative called Argentine Dialogue,[42] a series of sit-downs with civil society leaders from all over the country to build consensus on the way forward. Meeting with the archbishop was a way for Lavagna to follow up on his promise that social policy would not be "an afterthought."

While there is no public record of what the minister and the archbishop discussed that day, it is unlikely that their discussion strayed far from Archbishop Bergoglio's message during the following month's Revolution Day mass. This mass, given each year on May 25, is an annual tradition that celebrates the mutual respect in Argentina between the church and the state. This year per tradition, the president and his entire cabinet attended the mass, and it was broadcast on television on all the channels. Archbishop Bergoglio's message was stark. He warned that the country was in "danger of dissolution," he spoke of the many impoverished Argentines, and he urged all sectors of Argentine society to work together as partners to heal the broken country.[43]

Archbishop Bergoglio—the future Pope Francis—also told a story from Luke 19 in which Jesus prompted Zacchaeus, a hated tax collector, to let Jesus spend the night in his home, inspiring Zacchaeus to donate half of his wealth to the poor as a sign of repentance and repair.[44] The archbishop's message wasn't subtle. It was a clear call for Argentina's wealthy to make a big contribution toward the recovery of the nation. He and Lavagna were singing from the same hymnal, for when the minister's proposal to restructure the country's foreign bonds came out, he didn't ask creditors to give up half their claims. He asked them to give up three-quarters.

Lavagna, Taylor, Krueger, and CACs versus SDRM

Minister Roberto Lavagna knew he had his work cut out for him when he went to Washington, D.C., in May 2002 to start rebuilding Argentina's relationship with the IMF. It would be an uphill battle against U.S. treasury secretary Paul O'Neill's and IMF managing director Horst Köhler's anti-Argentina sentiments. Ultimately, however, Lavagna's quest for financial support would succeed or fail based on his ability to convince their deputies, Undersecretary for International Affairs John Taylor and First Deputy Managing Director Anne Krueger, to support a new IMF program.

A new IMF program was key. In addition to providing Argentina with much-needed financial support, it would signal to the world that Argentina was on the mend. The IMF's "seal of approval" would, in turn, convince investors to hold its beat-up currency or even put new money to work in the country, where assets could now be purchased for a song. The hope when the IMF gives a loan to a distressed country is that its effect will be catalytic, the benefit many times the amount of money lent. With the people devoid of confidence in the government and the economy, its leaders understood the symbolic importance of winning a new IMF program. The question, however, was what conditions would be attached, and that's what Minister Lavagna went to Washington to negotiate.

The road to IMF support was far from straightforward. One issue was that while Taylor and Krueger were, in effect, partners in bringing the IMF's resources to bear in solving Argentina's economic problems, they were at odds on the topic of Krueger's SDRM proposal from the year before. In April 2002, Taylor had attacked Krueger's proposal by counterproposing a slimmed-down alternative called Collective Action Clauses (CACs), which would have the sole purpose of preventing potential holdouts such as Elliott Associates from gaming future sovereign debt restructurings.[45]

At the time, countries were carrying out sovereign debt restructurings without the benefit of any such tools. Countries would restructure their debt by proposing an exchange offer to their bondholders in the hope that almost all of them would be reasonable and accept a smaller amount of new performing bonds in exchange for their old defaulted bonds. Most bondholders voluntarily accepted such offers, but a few would hold out and seek better terms, often through litigation. John Taylor's CACs would remove that free option. When included in a bond contract, a CAC gives a supermajority the power to force all bondholders into the same deal, the voting threshold typically fixed at 75%.[46] Once this participation level is reached, holding out is no longer an option. There are no holdouts, and there is no holdout litigation.

Unfortunately, CACs, unlike Krueger's SDRM, couldn't be used on outstanding bonds with retroactive effect. This distinction mattered a great deal to Argentina when it began to work on its $100 billion restructuring. There was no way to force CACs into Argentina's bonds after the fact: CACs are not a matter of law but instead are a contractual feature that must be incorporated into bonds when they are issued. None of Argentina's U.S. dollar global bonds—the biggest part of its debt—had been issued with CACs, although some of its non-U.S. debt did have such clauses. Krueger's SDRM could have solved this problem. Changes in bankruptcy laws—which an SDRM would have required—can have retroactive effect. Under an SDRM, Argentina's many existing U.S. dollar bonds would have been restructured pursuant to a legal procedure whose outcome, as under a CAC, would have been based upon a vote of the majority of creditors, and holding out would not have been an option, but SDRM was not adopted.

For Argentina, this debate in Washington over CACs and SDRM was a distraction. Theoretically, it was a critically important topic, but since neither solution was available to restructure Argentina's defaulted bonds, the debate was a net negative because it pulled attention away from the country's need for an IMF program. In the longer term, it caused another ultimately more significant problem: in association with this 2002 policy debate, the IMF made a small tweak to its lending rules that enhanced creditors' bargaining power, a change that came back to haunt Argentina when it moved to restructure its debt the following year.

Lavagna Goes to Washington

Economy Minister Roberto Lavagna led with his diplomatic skills when approaching the IMF for a new program in May 2002. Not only did he need to capture policy makers' attention in the midst of the CAC-SDRM battle then under way, but he also needed to rebuild trust in his discredited nation. And so, instead of just showing up and asking for money as most of his predecessors had done, his first move was aimed at rebuilding support for Argentina in capitals around the world.

For one, Minister Lavagna placed a piece in the *Financial Times* under the title "Trust Argentina," which was published on May 2, 2002. In it, he explained that since his arrival in Buenos Aires, the country had pulled together and found a way forward. He wrote that while there was much work to be done—laws to be passed, regulations to be implemented, and policies to be carried out—the country now had the political will and the leadership to succeed. He concluded by saying that "Argentines have no illusions that there is an easy path forward. . . . We need to break this circle of doubt and restore our credibility as well as our credit. . . . Our goal is simple. We need to renew Argentina's faith in itself and the world's faith in Argentina. If we do that, we will succeed."[47]

Moreover, before going to Washington, Lavagna joined President Eduardo Duhalde in Madrid, where they met with Spanish prime minister José María Aznar, a key ally, to solicit advice on their upcoming negotiations with the IMF.[48] At an earlier meeting, Prime Minister Aznar had recommended they face IMF managing director Horst Köhler in an honest talk "a cara de perro" (with the face of a dog), implying that Argentina should use a tough face and negotiate hard.[49]

Lavagna's visit to Washington started on a friendly note. On his first night he enjoyed a pleasant dinner with First Deputy Managing Director Krueger and her deputy Anoop Singh. They spent the meal discussing economics at the Aquarelle restaurant in the Watergate building, a few blocks down the street from IMF headquarters.[50] The business meeting the next day went well and was capped off by an impromptu meeting with Managing Director Köhler.

According to Lavagna, Köhler was overjoyed when he revealed that he was withdrawing former minister Remes Lenicov's request for $20 billion in new money.[51] Focused on gaining a quick confidence boost and mindful of the prevailing no-more-bailouts, tough-love philosophy, Lavagna said that all that he wanted was the ability to refinance maturing payments owed to the IMF and a program that was relatively light on conditions. Köhler asked for clarification. He thought he had misunderstood Lavagna's lightly accented English. Lavagna repeated that Argentina was not asking for new money. Köhler now understood, and it was music to his ears and would be to the IMF's shareholders too. Shortly after Lavagna left, the IMF issued a positive news release about the meeting, stating that "Minister Lavagna's visit provided a welcome opportunity to review the efforts of his new economic team."[52] Two weeks later, the G7 finance ministers followed with a statement saying that they were "encouraged by the significant progress" Argentina was making in stabilizing its economy.[53] This was the first positive press Argentina had received from the international community in a very long time. Minister Lavagna was off to a good start.

Standstill and Breakthrough

While Roberto Lavagna's May 2002 trip to Washington was a great success, the economy minister's quest to secure a quick program failed miserably. All the issues that had toppled his predecessor were still in play, including the politically unpopular mandatory deposit swap, which the IMF saw as a precondition to a deal but which Lavagna was dead set against, favoring instead a smaller voluntary swap. Despite an IMF mission to Buenos Aires and the generally positive atmosphere of the discussions, Argentina and the IMF team simply couldn't agree on the basic terms for a program. The heart of the matter was that the economy minister and the IMF were working with vastly different assumptions: Lavagna thought that Argentina's economy and balance of payments were beginning to stabilize,[54] while the IMF thought that the country's economy was still deteriorating and possibly on the brink of 1980s-style hyperinflation, necessitating tough measures.[55] It is hard for government officials and the IMF to agree on policy measures when they can't agree on the macroeconomic trajectory. Not surprisingly, negotiations on the terms of a new program soon came to a standstill.

With negotiations still stalled in the third week of June, Lavagna flew to Washington to expedite matters. On this trip, he met with the IMF as well as with both Secretary Paul O'Neill and Undersecretary for International Affairs John Taylor at the U.S. Treasury. Lavagna's meeting with O'Neill went well, with the Treasury Secretary remarking, "That makes things easier" when he explained that the country wasn't seeking new cash, just the rollover of existing loans.[56] Lavagna's second meeting was critical because Taylor, the author of the famous Taylor Rule for setting interest rates, understood that the fundamental difference between Argentina and the IMF concerned monetary policy. Shortly thereafter, a compromise was brokered in which the IMF agreed to the unprecedented step of forming an independent committee of former and current central bankers to weigh in on the dispute over the deposit swap and monetary policy.[57]

The committee was chaired by Hans Tietmeyer, the highly regarded former German Central Bank president, and its ranks were filled with similarly distinguished experts.[58] Working quickly, the committee made a trip to Argentina to meet with officials in early July and released a report by the end of the month.[59] The report and the process of preparing it fostered a spirit of compromise and marked a much-needed success. On a technical level, the report validated positions held by Argentina and the IMF, and so it was time for both sides to show flexibility in the ongoing negotiations. In addition, the report was released at an auspicious moment, because while the committee was working in July 2002, the Argentine peso had finally stabilized, and the country's foreign reserves had started to increase for the first time in years.[60]

Shifting Political Winds in Buenos Aires and Washington

While Hans Tietmeyer's committee of central bankers was sorting through Argentina's dispute with the IMF over monetary policy in July 2002, consequential political and financial events were taking place in Argentina, in the region, and in Washington.

In Buenos Aires, the presidential election that had been slated for the following year was moved up by six months.[61] This shift was a big blow to President Duhalde's credibility but was necessary after the shocking killing of two protestors at the hands of police during a massive organized demonstration in Buenos Aires in late June. Scarred by a decade of abuse under military governments in the 1970s and early 1980s, Argentines have zero tolerance for any form of police repression or human rights abuse.

In Washington, the big development was serious backpedaling on the U.S. Treasury's no-more-bailouts policy. After pulling the plug so dramatically on Argentina in December 2001, the IMF, with U.S. support, was shoveling big new loans to Brazil[62] and Uruguay.[63] The United States even made a $1.5 billion direct loan to Uruguay to tide the country over while it negotiated a new program with the IMF.[64] So, why the change of heart? Contagion. While not initially an issue in the bond markets, events in Argentina were infecting its neighbors through other channels. Brazil was suffering from a sharp drop in exports to Argentina, and Uruguay's banks were collapsing as their Argentine customers were rushing to withdraw funds, the doors to their Argentine banks shut. An infusion of cash was needed to stop the crisis from spreading even further.

It was in this context that U.S. treasury secretary Paul O'Neill visited South America the first week of August 2002, making stops in Argentina, Brazil, and Uruguay.[65] In Argentina, Secretary O'Neill and his team from the U.S. Treasury met with President Duhalde and with Minister of Economy Roberto Lavagna and his team. Participants say that the meetings went well, with the United States supporting Argentina's final push to reach an agreement with the IMF. O'Neill's skepticism of Argentina was thawing, although at the close of the meetings all he had to offer was a fairly bland statement: "With the right policies in place, the people of Argentina will succeed."[66] Nonetheless, this was progress compared to what O'Neill had been saying about the country over the prior year, and a visit by a U.S. treasury secretary was big news in Argentina. To grumbling that O'Neill had offered only words to Argentina while the United States had just loaned $1.5 billion to Uruguay, an Argentine government spokesman retorted, "We were visited by a senior US official, not by Father Christmas."[67]

Following this meeting, the outlook for Argentina closing a new program with the IMF was promising. One very positive sign was that in early September the IMF agreed to wait a year on an upcoming $2.8 billion payment due from Argentina.[68] All that said, policy differences and lack of trust soon brought progress to a standstill yet again.

Lack of Trust Leads to a New Default

While there was movement toward the development of a program during August 2002, there were also problems. At a technical level, the IMF and Argentina were still at odds over monetary policy despite the work of Hans Tietmeyer's committee. And there was a gulf between the parties over the reform of the country's utility sector and state-owned banks. The electric, gas, and water utilities were a big concern. Argentina had privatized many of these companies in the 1990s, and they were now owned by U.S., French, and Spanish companies, which were desperate for Argentina to lift a January 2002 freeze on utility rates in peso terms. Most of the utilities had borrowed vast sums in dollars, so they had become insolvent overnight with the rate freeze. IMF board members and staff economists had another reason to be concerned, however. It is nearly impossible to raise utility prices once a population grows used to paying below-market rates. When a government fails to deal with the problem, the next government inevitably faces the painful trade-off between continuing to subsidize rates at great fiscal cost or paying the political cost at the ballot box. Argentina's state-owned banks were also a big concern. Many in Washington thought that Banco de la Provincia de Buenos Aires in particular should be privatized, as all of Argentina's other provincial banks had been in the 1990s.[69]

More fundamentally, there was a growing sense of alarm in Washington about Argentina's ability to deliver on a program if one were signed, since Argentina's Congress and courts were proving hard to control. The Argentine legislative branch had recently reinstated a freeze on mortgage foreclosures, even though President Duhalde's team had promised the IMF that the country would not do so.[70] In addition, the Argentine Supreme Court struck down a 13% cut in public-sector wages and pensions that the prior administration had put in place, while local courts were letting depositors circumvent capital controls that were put in place to protect the country's scarce foreign reserves. The Argentine Supreme Court was also threatening to strike down a reform of the country's banking system that the Duhalde administration had implemented earlier in the year, specifically a conversion of the assets and liabilities of banks' balance sheets into Argentine pesos, a measure introduced to prevent widespread corporate and household bankruptcies in the wake of the January 2002 devaluation. If the Supreme Court had gone through with its threat, the fiscal cost would have been so many billions of dollars that it would have undermined any agreement that might have been reached with the IMF. With the court packed with supporters of former president Carlos Menem, who was expected to run in the upcoming election, the IMF's worry about Argentina's Supreme Court was no idle concern.[71]

In this context, Economy Minister Roberto Lavagna's quest to get the world to "trust Argentina" was a tough sell in Washington in the fall of 2002. With the IMF queasy about signing a program with Duhalde's administration and technical talks barely inching forward, tensions spiked and soon spilled over into the international press.

On September 5, IMF managing director Horst Köhler fired the opening salvo of a bitter and damaging exchange of words. About Argentina's economic program, he said that the IMF's directors were "concerned that it was taking much longer than had been anticipated to formulate a coherent and comprehensive policy package."[72]

On September 23 at an IMF press conference, IMF first deputy managing director Anne Krueger joined the fray, stating, "We can't help unless Argentina will do at least a minimum to help itself." Köhler said, "We have asked for some minimum consensus in the society, also including institutions like a judicial system, Congress, and so on." Undiplomatically, Köhler also related a German children's story about a dishonest schoolboy, ending the story by suggesting that Argentina was behaving in the same way. This was not the usual fare at an IMF press conference.[73]

The next day, September 24, Lavagna fired back that Argentina was "not going to sign any old agreement. . . . We will maintain social programs and ensure the financing of provincial economies."[74]

On September 26 during an IMF press conference, Krueger responded, "I don't think it would be the end of the world if negotiations broke down."[75]

Behind this bitter public exchange of words was an initially private threat. Playing hardball, Argentine officials had told IMF management that they would default on a $600 million payment to the World Bank due in mid-November if the IMF did not yield on program conditions. This was no conventional threat; it was a breach of the golden rule of Washington lending that all countries always repay their loans from official lenders such as the IMF and the World Bank. These organizations are said to have "preferred creditor status," which protects their shareholders and gives them the capacity to borrow huge sums cheaply so they can be reloaned to poor countries at a far below market cost.[76] If Argentina defaulted on the World Bank, it could theoretically jeopardize the institution's AAA credit rating, the loss of which would surely lead to an increase in the borrowing costs of its clients, not an outcome anyone wanted. Washington policy makers were infuriated by Argentina's threat, and with good cause.

It was a tough situation on both sides, however. Argentina's leaders felt that they were backed into a corner and had no choice but to threaten to default on the country's next large upcoming payment to a Washington lender (the IMF, the World Bank, or the Inter-American Development Bank). If the country made all scheduled payments to its official lenders between November 2002 and May 2003 and failed to obtain a new IMF program to replenish its foreign reserves, it would have none left when its next president took office, an unacceptable scenario. What's more, Argentina was being asked to sign a program that its economists didn't believe was in the best interests of the country, something Minister Lavagna and his team were unwilling to do following the failure the year before of the country's IMF-backed economic program of the 1990s. Ultimately, the stalemate came down to a lack of trust: the IMF didn't trust that Argentina would deliver, and Argentina didn't trust the IMF's advice.[77]

With disaster imminent, the U.S. Treasury stepped in and asked both sides to tone down the rhetoric and resume negotiations, which relieved tensions for a while.

On October 10, the IMF told the press that "some progress" had been made.[78] Nine days later Lavagna said that the IMF and the government "have made important progress in the past two weeks in an atmosphere of greater understanding of the Argentine political and economic situation."[79] Perhaps a deal could be reached.

On October 29, however, the threats returned. Lavagna told the press that if Argentina were forced to choose between continuing to make social security payments to its citizens and paying the World Bank, he would choose the former. The IMF hit back, indicating that it would not be pressured into signing a weak agreement, fearing the loss of credibility if it were to give in to Argentina's threats.[80]

With no agreement in sight, Argentina defaulted on its World Bank loan payment on November 15, 2002, although in a conciliatory gesture the country made a partial payment of $79.2 million to cover interest due.[81]

Cleaning Up the Mess

The biggest shock of November 15, 2002, was that Argentina's strategic default on its World Bank loan payment was presented as a nonevent. The IMF told the press that "we have made further progress with Mr. Lavagna and his team this week"[82] and that "we expect discussions will continue in the coming days."[83] Argentina chimed in: "Our impression is that we moved forward a great deal on technical issues."[84] U.S. treasury secretary Paul O'Neill added, "If anything has changed in Argentina in the last six months, it has been for the better."[85] A few days later, the IMF Executive Board agreed to let Argentina push back a $141 million loan payment that was approaching its due date.[86]

Ultimately, it was in everyone's interest to play down Argentina's failure to make its World Bank loan payment. Making a big deal about it could worry the agencies that rated the World Bank's debt and, in the longer term, give other countries the idea that it was okay to occasionally default on their official lenders. Terming it a negotiating delay was a clever way to sweep under the rug the ugly truth that Argentina had deliberately defaulted on the World Bank to gain leverage over the IMF on program conditions.

Also being papered over that month was the fact that Argentina's default on its World Bank payment caught many in Washington off guard. Some key officials had been told that Argentina would pay with its foreign reserves, despite Argentina's repeated insistence that it wouldn't.[87] In effect, the debate on program terms had become a game of chicken, one that ended in a splat because neither driver swerved at the last minute. With damage all around, the IMF's Group of Seven (G7) shareholders intervened to make sure that Argentina obtained a new program and quickly repaid the World Bank, with the severity of a default for the institution rising if it persisted for more than 180 days. Despite continuing protests from IMF senior management, in January 2003 the IMF Executive Board approved a new program for Argentina along the lines of the one Minister of Economy Lavagna had proposed, one without new cash but also light on conditions. It was termed a "transitional" program, however, and it had a term of only eight months.[88] If Argentina was looking for a seal of approval, this was a weak one, because a normal IMF program for a deeply distressed country would have a term of three years and would entail comprehensive reforms. Still, it brought stability to Argentina's official finances for the first time since the country's 2001 default and would cover the period through the upcoming presidential election. In fact, the program's eight-month term was chosen to give the country just enough time to elect a new president and come back to the IMF to negotiate the terms of a new program.

Tensions Persist, Then Ease

In the first half of 2003 Argentina's economy was on an upswing, and the country was meeting all the fiscal and monetary targets set out in its new IMF program, a welcome change since the country had gone off track as soon as the ink had dried on its immediately preceding programs. Yet neither Argentina nor the IMF would easily forget the bitter events of the fall of 2002.

For one, in Argentina Roberto Lavagna's victory made him a household name.[89] One periodical even started calling him "the Satanic Dr. No" for refusing to give in to the IMF's demands.[90] Political insiders asked Lavagna if he would run for president in the upcoming election, but he demurred, his mind focused on fixing the economy.[91] Others surely noticed, however, that being tough with the IMF paid political dividends.

The flipside was bitterness in Washington. The *Financial Times* reported in January 2003 that "there is a deep sense of resentment and even anger in the normally sedate beige-carpeted corridors of the IMF" that Argentina had played chicken with the IMF and won.[92] Bitterness extended to the board of directors, where five member countries with a total voting share of about 25% had abstained from supporting Argentina's interim program.[93]

Despite these obstacles, tensions had eased by the time the spring blossoms appeared in Washington in 2003. Argentina's strong economic performance and the absence of new policy fights allowed for a reset of the relationship. It helped that a senior IMF staffer privately admitted to Argentina that the IMF had been too slow to understand the difficult social situation in the country.[94] Then during a visit in June, IMF managing director Köhler magnanimously admitted in public "that the IMF may have underestimated the recovery of this economy."[95]

The good feelings wouldn't last.

2

The Three-Way War

Argentina Battles with Creditors and the IMF over the Debt Deal (January 2003–April 2004)

On January 24, 2003, the same day the IMF Executive Board approved its eight-month transitional program, Argentina floated a trial balloon with respect to its foreign bondholders who hadn't been paid since the country's December 2001 default. On its website, the government stated for the first time that the country's bond debt would have to be cut by 70%, implying a recovery value of about thirty cents on the dollar for Argentina's defaulted bonds; before this date the government had only said that creditors would have to suffer a "substantial" debt cut.[1] Buenos Aires–based reporter David Haskel stuck this news into an article written for the Bureau of National Affairs announcing the terms of Argentina's new IMF program; other than that, this announcement didn't elicit much comment. With an election pending, it was easy to dismiss announcements from an economic team that could be on its way out. Furthermore, many investors probably thought that the aggressive terms being floated by the government were not a serious reflection of its intentions. Typical creditor losses had only been half as much in the 1990s, with Argentina, Brazil, and Mexico obtaining debt relief of only 35% in their Brady programs.[2]

Roberto Lavagna's team at Argentina's Ministry of Economy was deadly serious, however. They had run scenarios over the previous year, some alongside IMF staff, and government officials were convinced that if the country didn't obtain such extraordinary debt relief, it would find itself in a crisis again in another five or ten years. They were on a mission to put a permanent end to the country's repeated boom, bust, and default cycles of the previous hundred years.

Argentina's January 2003 announcement that it needed a 70% reduction in its debt was the opening move of what would be even in the best case a long, drawn-out process. For one, negotiations with creditors couldn't begin for months. The country had an election to carry out. After that, the new presidential administration had to agree to a conventional three-year program with the IMF. Only then would Argentina be in a position to make a specific proposal to creditors, after which serious negotiations could begin, negotiations that would take an incalculable amount of time. No other country in history had defaulted on close to $100 billion of bonds comprising 152 different instruments denominated in seven different currencies, documented under the laws of eight different countries, and owned by investors all over the world, including more than half a million retail investors in Italy, Germany, Austria, Japan, and elsewhere.[3]

Everyone knew that it was going to be a nightmare to restructure Argentina's defaulted bonds, from the amount of debt to the many owners, the required losses, and the risk of holdout activity. The remainder of 2003 saw hints of just how difficult this restructuring would be, as Argentina's pending transaction became the subject of fresh fights in Washington, bitter derision in the international press, and disputes in court. It was the year that set the stage for all that followed.

Passing the Baton

With the nation and the world watching, on May 25, 2003, Eduardo Duhalde handed Argentina's presidential baton to former Santa Cruz governor Néstor Kirchner. In a country with a long history of military coups and disorderly leadership transitions, this was a moment to celebrate.

In his inaugural speech, President Kirchner, who was elected with the support of Duhalde and Minister of Economy Roberto Lavagna, set out his plan to fix his broken country. In economics, he promised to accelerate growth, increase upward mobility, and distribute revenues more fairly. About public finances, he said that the "fiscal balance must be respected." On debt, he promised a tough negotiation with international creditors. Kirchner also said respect for human rights is fundamental and that he would not leave his values at the door to the presidential palace. Famous for his human rights activism in the 1990s, Kirchner was touching on the nation's deep wound, the abusive military dictatorship of 1976–1983, during which torture facilities were set up all over the nation and many thousands of people "disappeared." His message was conciliatory. He said, "We arrived without rancor but with memory. Memory not only of mistakes and horrors of the other. But it is also memory about our own mistakes."[4]

Kirchner's speech was well received by diplomatic services, and when U.S. president George W. Bush called to congratulate him, Argentina's new president promised a "normal and united" Argentina.[5]

After this promising start, Kirchner moved quickly to consolidate power. The weekend after the election he purged the army, navy, and air force of aging generals and admirals and gave top posts to Santa Cruz loyalists.[6] A few days later, he attacked the members of the Supreme Court who had undercut his predecessor's reforms.[7] Though coming from a Patagonian province with far more sheep than people, it didn't take long for Kirchner to leave his mark on Buenos Aires. Perhaps that's because, coming from a small province, he was used to getting his way.[8]

The Argentina–U.S. Relationship Enjoys a New Beginning

The change in government brought a new focus on the Argentina–U.S. relationship. Not only was it expected that the new administration would make a fresh start with its foreign counterparts, but President Kirchner, leading the first elected postcollapse government, had the mandate to set his own direction. He made a bold start by announcing that under his foreign policy there would be no "automatic alignments," a sharp cut at Carlos Menem, Argentina's president during the 1990s who had said he'd follow the lead of the United States in matters of foreign policy.[9] Underlining the point, Kirchner invited Fidel Castro to his inauguration, the

Cuban leader's second trip to Buenos Aires since 1959.[10] In response, the United States sent Mel Martínez, Bush's anti-Castro secretary of housing and urban development, to attend the ceremony on behalf of the U.S. government.[11]

Still, Secretary of State Colin Powell visited Argentina two weeks later with goodwill in hand. He told reporters on his flight that "the U.S. stands ready to help. I really want to listen to President Kirchner as he tells me about his plans, his aspirations, what he hopes to do in his administration."[12] Reciprocating, Kirchner told the press, "I am going to listen to what he has come to talk about."[13]

The mutual interests were clear. The United States wanted help with fighting terrorism, the pending Free Trade Area of the Americas, and blunting the regional influence of Venezuela's firebrand leader Hugo Chávez. Argentina, in turn, needed help with the IMF, especially on the topic of the country's upcoming debt restructuring.

The Powell meeting went well, and a date was made for Kirchner to visit the White House. In the meantime, the wheels were beginning to turn on Argentina's plan to restructure its debt, a plan that would have a deep effect on the Argentina–U.S. relationship.

Argentina's Ministry of Economy Circles the Globe

In early 2003, Argentina's Ministry of Economy released a road map of its plan to restructure the country's defaulted sovereign bonds. The main phases were (1) negotiate a medium-term deal with the IMF, (2) present an indicative proposal to bondholders, (3) meet with investors to discuss the proposal, and (4) launch a public offer that would give each investor the chance to accept or reject the offer.[14]

Going into the process, Argentina aimed to establish consultative working groups around the world to facilitate the discussion of terms, one per country or major geographic area. Already before year end 2002, the Ministry of Economy team, including Secretary of Finance Guillermo Nielsen, Sebastian Palla, and Leonardo Madcur, started circling the globe and talking to investors, meetings that continued during 2003.[15] Investment bank Lazard Frères had also been hired to develop a database of bondholders.[16]

Investors welcomed these visits, but they were frustrated, too. Argentine officials provided ample details of their country's economic crisis but none on the terms of the upcoming debt restructuring. Bondholders wanted a deal, wanted one quickly, and wanted assurances that Argentina would be reasonable when it came time to agree on terms. The Ministry of Economy team was vague, however, and reminded investors that they'd only be able to provide details after they had worked out the terms of its new IMF program. When asked about the projection that bondholders stood to see their investments' face value slashed by 70%, the team told investors that the number wasn't carved in stone and that it was subject to further discussions with the IMF. These assurances placated investors, and there wasn't much noise in the financial press.

Things Get Testy at the IMF Executive Board

Argentina's negotiations with the IMF over its soon-expiring program were more than just a way station for investors waiting for the deal to commence; they were a critical component of the restructuring process itself.[17] Lenders would rely on the IMF's seal of approval as a way of getting comfortable with the country's economic program. They knew from history that countries often fall back into default if they don't overhaul their fiscal policies and economies at the same time that they restructure their debt. They could rely on the IMF because its staff would send teams of experts to the country to collect data, build models, and negotiate a set of reforms with the government that would provide a path to economic and fiscal stability. Moreover, after the program was finalized, the IMF staff would monitor compliance, keeping a sharp eye on a constant stream of data, while the IMF Executive Board would hold quarterly reviews, cutting off funding if a country's performance was unsatisfactory. Less exciting to creditors, the IMF would also weigh in on the terms of the sovereign debt restructuring, a concern because the IMF had been increasingly siding with borrowers instead of their creditors in negotiations since the mid-1990s. Ironically, the IMF had only about $10 billion of loans outstanding to Argentina at the time versus the country's almost $100 billion in outstanding bonds. No matter; the IMF's imprimatur was the key to unlocking all forms of support: refinancing of amounts owed to the IMF, new World Bank loans, and debt relief from private creditors. Hence, in the Northern Hemisphere summer of 2003, the market eagerly awaited news of Argentina's negotiations with the IMF.

For its part, the IMF was tasked with the thankless and sometimes impossible job of helping a deeply troubled country out of a profound crisis. As an emergency lender, the IMF almost by definition has to ask countries to undertake painful reforms, which more often than not threaten powerful vested interests and are deeply unpopular with the masses. The consequence is that the IMF often ends up as a political target within countries, even though its advice, if followed, typically leads to higher structural growth and fairer outcomes. As a result, the IMF does its best to manage the public perception of its missions and the rationale for recommended measures, making frequent statements to the press and releasing the terms of its agreements with countries. That said, IMF management (its top executives) and its staff (the team of economists who develop and negotiate the programs with countries) have another challenge: managing the IMF Executive Board. As in any organization, IMF management reports to its board of directors. The control of the board, in turn, rests in the hands of the executive directors, the critical majority of whom are appointed by the G7 countries. The problem is that board dynamics sometimes make the job of management and staff more difficult than it otherwise would be, as is also true in any organization. This dynamic would be at work in Argentina's upcoming bond restructuring.

At the July 28, 2003, board meeting to review progress on Argentina's existing transitional program, for example, several executive directors attacked the country's draft successor program as being too soft on Argentina and too hard on creditors. At issue was Argentina's proposal to repay bondholders at a rate of thirty cents for every dollar of outstanding bonds. At the board meeting, Germany's executive director asked that the draft program be amended to force Argentina to raise taxes and cut social spending so it could pay more to the holders of its defaulted bonds, including the many thousands of retail bondholders in Germany caught holding defaulted Argentine bonds who were undoubtedly a concern. In macroeconomic terms, the German director asserted that Argentina needed to deliver a primary surplus of at least 4.5% of GDP to allow "the early presentation of a credible proposal" to creditors, versus the 3% area primary surplus target being mooted by Argentina.[18] In plain English, a country's primary surplus is its net cash flow before debt service, which makes it a good proxy for how much a country can pay to service its debt on an annual basis. Since a higher primary surplus means a higher capacity to pay debt service, asking a country to generate a higher primary surplus is synonymous with asking it to tighten its belt to allow it to pay more to its creditors. Directors from Italy and Japan, two other countries with extensive retail ownership of defaulted Argentine bonds, shared the German director's concerns, although directors from a handful of other countries without similar concentrations of bondholders also joined them.[19]

These statements at the July 28, 2003, board meeting had a strong political edge that undercut the IMF's intended role as a technocratic organization. Operating in deeply distressed countries, which inevitably need to carry out extremely painful reforms, the IMF staff, management, and board must always be seen as insisting on conditions that are grounded in economic fundamentals and arrived at in an unbiased process. Debt restructuring recommendations, specifically, were not supposed to be dictated by the board but instead were to be grounded in a debt sustainability analysis (DSA) performed by IMF staff, a new practice just being formalized at the IMF after 2000. A DSA sets the amount of debt relief required. Leaving a country with too much debt inevitably results in no sustained growth, a repeat crisis, more emergency loans from the IMF, and another debt restructuring.[20] The IMF staff's DSA is its most important analytical contribution to a debt restructuring process.

The question then became how well IMF staff and management would navigate this pressure coming from the board. The answer, as it turned out, was not very well. Complicating the situation, the U.S. Treasury, the IMF, and Argentina itself all had new ideas about how to restructure sovereign debt. Applying these new ideas resulted in the conventional staff DSA-driven process falling by the wayside, which in turn made it much harder for staff and management to contain the evolving conflict over the depth of losses to be suffered by creditors.

The GDP Warrant Solution to Argentina's Deep Haircut Problem

Argentina knew that asking bondholders to accept a 70% loss on their bonds—a 70% haircut in restructuring parlance—would be a hard sell. Among the biggest losses creditors accepted in the 1990s was about 50% on their Poland loans, which they did under pressure from a U.S. government eager to cement Poland's move to the West.[21] A more typical loss was the 35% that creditors had suffered on their loans to Mexico, Brazil, and Argentina. Well aware of this history, Secretary of Finance Guillermo Nielsen's team at the Ministry of Economy looked for ways to make the country's offer more palatable. What they hit on was a financial instrument called a GDP warrant, an idea based on a paper by two IMF economists who promoted the use of GDP-indexed bonds.[22] These bonds pay investors more when a country's gross domestic product (GDP) rises and less when it falls. Economists love the idea because debt crises are correlated with economic slowdowns. What could be better than debt that becomes less expensive to service when economies weaken but more expensive when economies strengthen? A GDP warrant is similar, but it has an asymmetrical *payoff*: holders earn nothing if a country's GDP remains flat or falls but can win big if it rises above a preset threshold. A GDP warrant, the Argentine finance team thought, would take some of the sting out of the country's harsh 70% haircut. With this instrument, investors might earn back much of their losses if Argentina's economy bounced back. In the end, Argentina's GDP warrants did pay out hugely—reducing investor haircuts by a whopping 18% of the face value of their original holdings[23]—although Argentina's critics derided them as worthless at the time.

Critics notwithstanding, both the IMF and the U.S. Treasury liked Argentina's idea of adding a GDP warrant to soften the blow of the deal.[24] It made a lot of sense in the context: if the U.S. government was against creditor bailouts, which implied less IMF lending and much deeper debt restructurings, why not add in a mechanism to give some money back to creditors if things turned out better than expected? IMF management was so supportive that it sent staff economist Eduardo Borensztein to Argentina for six months to help develop the idea.[25] This assignment closed a circle, as Borensztein was one of the authors of the paper that had stimulated Nielsen's interest in GDP-linked securities in the first place.

The U.S. Approach to Argentina's Debt Restructuring

As Argentina finalized the terms of its deal with the IMF and worked to develop a bond restructuring proposal for the market, it enjoyed strong support from the George W. Bush administration. In July, President Bush welcomed President Kirchner to the White House, the two leaders sharing a cozy photo op.[26]

What's more, the U.S. Treasury backed Argentina's drive for deep debt relief, despite strong opposition from some IMF board members, although the same officials also warned their Argentine counterparts that U.S. support for the transaction would be limited once Argentina's IMF program was in place. An element of its new no-more-bailouts policy was that the U.S. Treasury did not want to wade into the middle of countries' negotiations with their private creditors.

This hands-off approach was something new: the United States had been neck deep in all the sovereign debt restructuring deals of the prior two decades. Indeed, during the 1980s and 1990s the U.S. government was the single most important player in sovereign debt restructurings around the world. One could almost say that the Federal Reserve and the U.S. Treasury cooked up the sovereign debt deals of the 1980s and 1990s and force-fed them to the IMF, the banks, and distressed countries. The United States openly claimed the territory: The debt restructuring plans of the 1990s were called "Brady Plans" after Treasury Secretary Nicholas

Brady, and a predecessor plan was called the "Baker Plan" after Treasury Secretary James Baker. Paul Volcker, chairman of the board of the Federal Reserve between 1979 and 1987, also took credit. He told the *New York Times,* "I don't know who you thought was making all those deals; I was,"[27] when asked if he was ready for the deal-making side of Wall Street after announcing that he was going to work at a boutique investment bank in New York a few months after stepping down from the Fed.

In contrast, the George W. Bush Treasury wanted the United States to step back. As a matter of principle, Undersecretary for International Affairs John Taylor thought that the market—not the government—should handle commercial matters, an idea George Shultz had put into practice when he served as Richard Nixon's secretary of labor.[28] Taylor's deputy, Randal Quarles, who later served as vice chairman of supervision for the Federal Reserve,[29] wrote in a 2010 paper about his work at the Treasury that it was Shultz's handling of a messy longshoreman's strike in 1969 that animated the Treasury's new approach toward sovereign debt negotiations. As Quarles explained, U.S. policy during labor disputes before Shultz was to provide "extensive and athletic mediation." As secretary of labor, however, Shultz refused to get involved. He thought that too much government involvement subverted private bargaining, that potential crises from strikes were overrated and overdramatized, and that the willingness of high administration officials to become involved resulted in their exploitation by one side or the other. Shultz was right, Quarles concluded, because in the 1969 strike, "when the parties saw they could not draw the federal government into their conflict, they realized they would have to solve it on their own and turned to doing that."[30]

Quarles's boss, Undersecretary Taylor, thought the same logic should apply to sovereign debt restructuring, arguing that the U.S. Treasury should be less involved in these deals. Instead, sovereign debt restructurings should be market-based operations employing CACs to deter holdouts. During a keynote speech on the importance of adopting CACs at the 2002 Emerging Markets Traders Association's (EMTA) annual meeting, Taylor said that the United States supported a new "decentralized" approach to debt restructurings in which "the sovereign government and its creditors would work out the terms on their own." He also said that restructurings should be "guided by the clauses" and carried out "without the involvement of a central group or panel."[31] This assertion was fairly close to a direct statement that the IMF and the United States—the IMF's biggest shareholder—would stand back from future negotiations. This was the policy that Taylor and his team were seeking to put into practice when Argentina moved to restructure its debt in 2003.

Argentina's officials had no problem with the U.S. Treasury's new approach. They were more than happy to duke it out with their creditors: it was their country and their debt, and they wanted to handle their restructuring themselves.

Argentina's Unusual IMF Program

Not surprisingly given the turbulence that had long plagued the relationship between Argentina and the IMF, the announcement of the country's new three-year program on September 10, 2003, was not without drama.[32] The United States had to use a lot of elbow grease to convince the board to sign on, and as part of the negotiation's endgame, Argentina purposefully missed a $3 billion payment to the IMF, albeit for less than a day.[33] While the process left many board members feeling bitter, the program announcement was a major milestone in Argentina's recovery. Finally, nineteen months after its collapse, Argentina had a conventional IMF program and could start grappling with its defaulted bonds.[34]

The first days after the announcement went well. On September 12, President George W. Bush called President Kirchner from Air Force One to congratulate him on the IMF program.[35] And according to an article that Buenos Aires–based reporter David Haskel wrote for the Bureau of National Affairs, when Bush and Kirchner ran into each other on the floor of the United Nations later that month, Bush called out, "Here comes the conqueror of the IMF." The same article reports that in a sidebar meeting Bush said, "Congratulations again for the agreement with the IMF; now you must keep negotiating firmly with private creditors."[36] To all appearances—at least in Buenos Aires—the United States had Argentina's back as it moved forward with its plan to obtain deep debt relief from its international bondholders.

While U.S. presidential support was a big positive, the U.S. Treasury's new noninterference policy soon led to controversy. IMF programs traditionally included annual primary surplus targets, but Argentina's September 2003 program specified a surplus target only for 2004; targets for future years were left blank.[37] Leaving out these key parameters was intended to give Argentina room to negotiate the terms of its debt deal with its creditors, as per the U.S. Treasury's new policy. The standard operating procedure, in contrast, was for IMF staff economists to run their DSA models to determine how much debt a country could safely incur and fix future-year primary surplus targets to be consistent with those levels. These targets, in turn, determined the haircut creditors would need to withstand.[38] Leaving out the targets was like letting the tail wag the dog and quickly proved problematic, inviting a bitter dispute over not just the terms of the deal and the primary surplus but also the negotiating process itself.

On the surface, the IMF was at one with its newly reduced role. At the press conference announcing Argentina's new program, IMF managing director Köhler explained, "The IMF will not interfere in the talks between Argentina and private creditors. That is our guideline, that is our principle, and we stick to this principle."[39] While it went unremarked, this was a truly shocking statement to come from the head of the institution that just the year before had been promoting its expansive SDRM initiative. It was also not a principle that was adhered to for very long: the IMF was soon deeply embroiled in a controversy over how Argentina was negotiating with its creditors, as decentralizing sovereign debt restructuring operations was proving harder in practice than it was in theory.

The lack of future-year primary surplus targets in Argentina's IMF program soon led to a bitter dispute with bondholders over what level of surplus the country should aim to achieve. Argentina's view was that it was only obliged to set aside cash to pay creditors in the amount of 3% of GDP per year, which was the baseline level assumed in its IMF program, the one approved by the board in September.[40] Creditor activists, with the support of some IMF board members, countered that the 3% level in Argentina's program was meant as a floor and complained that Argentina was treating it as a ceiling.[41] Bitterness and contention followed.

Argentina knew there would be a battle to achieve the debt relief it was certain it needed. Economy Minister Roberto Lavagna prepared the country for contention. On national TV the week before Argentina presented its proposal to investors, he said, "There will be lots of long faces in many languages. In Italian, in German, in Japanese, and certainly in English." About the coming negotiations, he told his Argentine audience, "We have to prepare to see creditors adamantly rejecting our first offer. That's when the to-ing and fro-ing will begin."[42]

Argentina's "Shock" Dubai Offer

On September 22, 2003, Economy Minister Roberto Lavagna and Finance Secretary Guillermo Nielsen unveiled the "guidelines" of the country's upcoming debt restructuring to a large audience of bondholders gathered in Dubai to attend that year's World Bank–IMF Annual Meetings, held outside the United States every third year. Some investors traveled to Dubai just to see Argentina unveil its proposal. The news wasn't good.

Lavagna gave the economic background to Argentina's proposal, while Nielsen explained the technical terms. The deal was harsh on four parameters: holdings of old bonds would be replaced with new bonds worth 75% less in terms of face value, new bonds' coupon rates would be small, new maturities would be very long, and the country would not make up the almost $20 billion of interest payments missed since December 2001.[43] The one bright spot was that investors could potentially earn back some of their losses through the GDP warrants to be issued alongside the new bonds. These terms are commonly referred to as Argentina's "Dubai Offer" even though Argentina was careful to present them as indicative guidelines.

Bondholders were appalled. As soon as Argentina's presentation was over, creditor dissatisfaction zipped to all corners of the world. The *New York Times* reported investor reactions. An Italian banker called the 75%

haircut "unreasonable and not an option." BCP Securities' Walter Molano said, "The tough talk in Dubai appears to be a ploy by the government to buy time, trim down expectations and feed the populist rhetoric in Argentina. In the end, we don't believe the Argentine government will scalp investors." Fernando Losada, an analyst from ABN Amro in New York, said, "This is just the first move in what is going to be a prolonged chess game." And Stefan Engelsberger, a German debt activist representing 250 small investors, observed that "I can't say it was a surprise for us, but it's certainly completely unrealistic." Engelsberger also tossed in a threat: "I will not give up; I will keep my bonds. I have legal claims, and I will fight for my rights in the courts, and I think most other investors will do the same."[44]

This coverage was just the beginning of a steady stream of attacks in the international press on Argentina's deal that emanated, more often than not, from three highly organized groups of investors that were braced for a fight: a U.S. group called the Argentina Bondholders Committee (ABC), an Italian group called Task Force Argentina (TFA), and a German Group called the Argentine Bond Restructuring Agency PLC (ABRA), all of which formed well before Dubai and were therefore poised and ready to go.

The members of the American group ABC, which formed shortly after Argentina's default in 2002, included hedge funds, a few conventional money managers, and a number of European banks. Membership overlapped with that of the Emerging Markets Creditors Association (EMCA), which used its website to post information about the new committee.[45] The ABC's members were genuinely shocked at the offer Argentina put on the table in Dubai. They had met with Nielsen over the summer and were under the impression that Argentina's 70% debt relief target was not "fixed in stone" and that it might be reduced when the terms of the IMF program were finalized. Instead, Argentina had raised its target to 75% and was indicating very little flexibility. The ABC quickly put out a press release stating that "these terms are not reflected in secondary market prices of Argentina's bonds" and calling Argentina's 3% primary surplus target assumption "overly pessimistic and self-serving."[46] The ABC was prepared for the long haul. Its marketing documents stated that it would not only press Argentina for improved terms but would also engage with the IMF, the World Bank, the Inter-American Development Bank, and the G7 to the same end.[47] And after Dubai, that's exactly what the group did.

Creditors outside the United States also lined up to do battle in response to the Dubai offer. In Italy, which was home to about 450,000 retail holders of the defaulted bonds, the banking community had long been preparing for the fight. TFA was not the only investor group that formed in Italy, but it was the largest, the loudest, and the best resourced, established in September 2002 by Italy's eight largest banks acting as a committee of the Association of Italian Banks.[48] TFA was headed by Nicola Stock, a seasoned international banker and former general manager of Banco di Roma. Stock, in turn, was backed up by a five-person staff. Legally, TFA was an informal organization, although it followed formal processes, holding regular board meetings and the like. TFA was as vocally opposed to Argentina's Dubai announcement as the ABC, and, as an organ of the Italian banking system with close ties to the government, powerful consumer organizations, and the press, it could make its position known. For example, Italy's *La Repubblica* ran a story on Argentina's Dubai proposal under the headline "Argentina Bonds, Shock Offer," par for the course for the Italian media coverage that would follow, with Argentina's offer later called a "rip-off" and a "scam." With that said, Stock was highly diplomatic when making public statements about the Argentina situation and in this case said, "This is not going to work, but we will negotiate."[49]

Germany-focused ABRA, formed in early 2003, was the brainchild of Adam Lerrick, a Carnegie Mellon professor and former investment banker. Lerrick, who was later a senior Treasury official in the Trump administration, was well connected and could bring in Angel Gurría, a former Mexican finance minister and subsequently the secretary-general of the Organisation for Economic Co-operation and Development, as a partner as well as former German Central Bank governor Hans Tietmeyer to head ABRA's supervisory board.[50] ABRA's mission was to give European retail investors professional representation so they wouldn't receive a worse deal than institutional investors, as many of them feared. Registered as a corporation in Ireland, ABRA arranged to sell instruments listed on the Luxembourg Stock Exchange to retail investors in exchange for taking physical control of their bonds.[51] The idea was that Lerrick and his team would have the power to bind all of ABRA's members to a deal with Argentina. These investors, in turn, would receive professional representation in the negotiations in exchange for a relatively small fee that would be deducted from any settlement, an idea Lerrick came up with in 2002 when visiting Europe after the default. It was a for-profit idea, with Lerrick and his team eventually earning an estimated $16 million by selling this vehicle to holders of more than $1 billion of Argentine bonds, mostly small investors in Germany, Austria, and elsewhere in Europe.[52] Lerrick's words carried extra weight back in Washington because he was a protégé and colleague of Allan Meltzer, the conservative economist associated with the Bush administration's no-more-bailouts policy. About Argentina's deal announced in Dubai, Lerrick complained, "Not even poor African countries have ever received debt relief of this magnitude."[53]

The Early Argentina Cases

Unlike the ABC, TFA, and ABRA, which were positioning for a negotiation with Argentina after it had put an IMF program in place, a handful of small investors didn't wait for a negotiation and filed lawsuits against Argentina shortly after its default. While common wisdom has it that large sophisticated investors, not small investors, sue sovereigns that assumption didn't hold in this case. The lack of large investors among the first plaintiffs was because most bond funds have a strong distaste for litigation. The professional investors at the time had little experience in it, and they didn't want Jubilee 2000 debt activists to start protesting in front of their offices.[54] ABC member Hans Humes perfectly captured the attitude of this cadre in 2002 when he told the *International Financing Review*, "We would prefer to wait to see whether there's room to have a constructive dialogue with Argentina."[55] And so, the earliest plaintiffs were all retail investors.

Just months after the default and more than a year before Dubai, the first plaintiff in the Argentina bond cases was seventy-year-old Allan Applestein, a businessman and Harvard Law grad from Aventura, Florida, who had gotten rich by developing an automated chicken feeder.[56] In March and May 2002, Applestein brought a pair of claims in the U.S. District Court for the Southern District of New York (the Southern District) against Argentina and the Province of Buenos Aires with respect to two bonds he owned, one with a face value of $1.02 million and another with a value of $245,000.[57] He was represented by Marc Dreier, the head and sole owner of Dreier LLP, a rapidly growing law firm.[58]

In May 2002, lawyers from Moss & Kalish followed with a pair of suits on behalf of Lightwater Corporation and Old Castle Holdings with respect to $7.7 million in bonds.[59] Since both corporations were set up in the Bahamas, it's impossible to know who was behind them. One might guess that they were owned by rich Argentines who wanted to hide their identities to avoid retribution from the government.

In July 2002, the Macrotecnic International Corporation, a Uruguayan company holding $452,000 of defaulted bonds, also sued Argentina in the Southern District.[60] Macrotecnic's suit was filed by Guillermo Ariel Gleizer, an Argentine lawyer who would also come to represent about a dozen other clients in similar cases.

The first large investor to jump into the fray was Kenneth Dart, a billionaire and the scion of the family that had previously owned Dart Container Corp., a company known for its foam and plastic cups. On April 10, 2003, five months before Dubai, Dart's EM Ltd. filed a complaint in the Southern District with respect to its holdings of $595 million of defaulted Argentina bonds.[61] Dart was a savvy player, and he had attracted media attention in the 1990s for two things. First, he gave up his U.S. citizenship, took up Belizean citizenship, and moved to the Cayman Islands to lower his taxes.[62] Second, he sued Brazil over its Brady restructuring, complaining that the country had switched up the bonds that he would receive in the deal, a deal he was initially positioned to support.[63] Dart later supported Ecuador's bond restructuring of 2000.[64] Given Dart's notoriety and the large size of his position, the financial press eagerly covered the news of his suit against Argentina.

Hearing these cases in the Southern District court was seventy-three-year-old senior judge Thomas P. Griesa, who was known in the judicial community for two of his rulings.[65]

First, he had held U.S. attorney general Griffin Bell in contempt of court in 1978 for refusing to release the files of eighteen informers who had spied on the Socialist Workers Party for the Federal Bureau of Investigation. Though politically conservative, Judge Griesa—who was nominated by President Richard Nixon in 1972—sided with the socialists out of a strong distaste for abusive governments.[66]

Second, in the 1980s Judge Griesa had sided with environmental activists and the Hudson River's striped bass population against the New York political establishment over the proposed Westway Highway that would have been sunk just off the west side of Manhattan.[67] Developers liked the proposed highway because it would have opened up significant amounts of land for parks and housing. Environmentalists countered that the highway would destroy the breeding grounds of the Hudson River's striped bass population and that the money would be better spent on mass transit. In a series of rulings, Griesa held up federal funding for the road project because he didn't like the aggressive and dishonest way in which New York State was pressing for the project. In particular, he found that the environmental impact statement the state submitted lacked credibility. Griesa killed the road project by putting a stay on federal funding pending the delivery of a new environmental impact report. This ruling, in turn, put New York into a use-it-or-lose-it position with respect to the money Washington had allocated for the project, to which a time limit applied. The upshot was that the money went to mass transit, and the striped bass were left in peace.

The *New York Times* wrote glowingly about Judge Griesa during the Westway saga, noting that he looked "years younger than his age" and calling his adjudicating style "arduous and almost philosophical." Yet the paper also reported that while Griesa was "personable off the bench," he had a "stern approach in court," had "been known to criticize witnesses sharply when he felt they were less than candid," and "rebuked lawyers he felt were being dilatory."[68]

Judge Griesa's stern approach ended up being a double-edged sword for Argentina. At first it was the investors who felt the sharp edge of his justice; over time, however, his sword would swing the other way.

Judge Griesa in Court

On October 31, 2003, just about six weeks after the country's presentation in Dubai, Judge Griesa held a hearing on a motion brought by Argentina's lawyers for a ninety-day stay of enforcement actions against the country. In prior months, he had issued a series of such stays that applied to all the pending cases against Argentina, and now it was time for him to decide if the facts and circumstances warranted granting another one. Stays block a creditor's ability to obtain a court order to seize a defaulting debtor's assets. With the country in disarray and stays in sovereign debt cases permitted by precedent, Griesa had no trouble with the stays he had approved over the prior year. Time was dragging on, however, and he was running out of leeway because such stays are not meant to be open-ended.

Argentina's lawyer, Jonathan Blackman from Cleary Gottlieb Steen & Hamilton (Cleary Gottlieb), argued that the additional stay was warranted given that the debt negotiations had just begun.[69] Creditors' lawyers countered that the Dubai offer was so derisory that it wasn't relevant. They also complained that Argentina was being high-handed in its meetings with bondholders. One lawyer said, "These aren't meetings. There is a presentation being made, creditors responding they aren't happy and then walking out." He also said that President Kirchner was making an ultimatum, stating, "We offer this and nothing else."[70]

Judge Griesa ruled for extending the stay, although he added that it was the last one he would be willing to grant. He also encouraged the creditors gathered in his courtroom to take a serious look at Argentina's offer. He said, "I have never heard of anything indicating that there is much of anything to recover on. . . . What it could be is that the exchange offer looks better realistically than getting judgments and going around and trying to recover with very little result. I don't know the answer to that, but I also know that there are times that relatively low percentage of recovery is better than nothing."[71]

Argentina couldn't have hoped for a more supportive judge.

The Conflict Comes to a Head in December 2003

Argentina's September proposal in Dubai was highly controversial, and organized creditors immediately set about to derail it. It took until December for the conflict to come to a head, however.

Indeed, October was relatively peaceful. Following its announcement of indicative terms in Dubai, Argentina went on a global roadshow, using much of the month to present its proposal to investors. The first meetings were held in Buenos Aires in mid-October. After that, teams from the Ministry of Economy headed to Frankfurt on October 21, Tokyo and Rome on October 22, Los Angeles on October 23, Zurich on October 24, and New York on October 28.[72]

Organized creditors made their first wholesale attack on Argentina's deal in the *Financial Times* article "Creditors Lose Faith in Argentina's Plans over Debt," published on November 2, 2003. The paper reported that "Suspicions have grown that the Argentines are stringing out the negotiations in order to prolong the time that they do not have to service their defaulted debt."[73] The article went on to quote EMCA chairman and ABC steering committee member Abigail McKenna,[74] who said, just ahead of the October 31 court hearing described above, that "a cynical view of the administration's intentions right now is that they are trying to create the appearance of a dialogue as evidence to present to the judge that they are negotiating with creditors. An objective look at the discussions would make it difficult to conclude that they have been negotiating in good faith."

This could be read as an attack at the heart of the matter, which was how Argentina was conducting its negotiation process, and presaged a massive power struggle over the terms of the deal. While nominally directed at the court proceedings, McKenna's accusation that Argentina was not negotiating in good faith spoke to a 2002 change in IMF lending policy, which required countries undertaking debt restructurings to prenegotiate the terms of their deals with creditor committees "in good faith." Good faith, in turn, meant that countries were "expected" to negotiate the terms of their offers with a "representative creditor committee" if one formed.[75]

Calling out a breach of good faith suggests that the ABC believed that it met the definition of a representative creditor committee and deserved to prenegotiate the terms of the deal with Argentina in a traditional face-to-face bargaining session similar to those carried out during the bank loan restructurings of the 1980s and 1990s. Instead, Argentina was running around the world talking at its creditors (i.e., giving one-sided lectures) rather than negotiating (i.e., participating in bargaining sessions). Reading McKenna's assertion broadly would imply that Argentina was out of compliance with the IMF's newly updated good faith negotiations policy, which might be cause for it to fail its upcoming quarterly review with the IMF, the country's first review since its September 2003 program was so painstakingly put in place.

What ensued was a three-way power struggle of epic proportion over who would control the terms of Argentina's upcoming transaction: the IMF, Argentina, or organized creditors. Each of these parties had a reason to claim that they should control the process. The IMF was an international organization, the lender of last resort, and its staff was uniquely qualified to objectively determine the amount of debt a country could safely sustain. In the last quarter of 2003, however, the U.S. Treasury had knocked the IMF out of contention by insisting that it not intervene in the negotiations. It looked like this was going to be a two-way, Argentina versus creditor face-off, but the organized creditors brought the IMF back into the dispute by complaining that Argentina was in breach of its good faith negotiations rule. By doing so, the creditors hoped to use the IMF to gain leverage: if the IMF threatened to cut off the money spigot to Argentina based on a breach of this rule, the country would soften up on process and terms. The effect of bringing the IMF back into play, however, was that the IMF was soon a full participant in the power struggle, with creditors pressuring it to enforce its new rule and the IMF pressuring Argentina to ease up on its approach to the deal.

While the complaints voiced by the organized creditor groups were deeply felt, the process Argentina was undertaking in the fall of 2003 was not particularly unusual for the time. Pakistan in 1999, Ukraine in 2000, Ecuador also in 2000, and Uruguay earlier in 2003 had done exactly what Argentina was now doing, using a consult-and-launch approach—talking to various creditors but not engaging in a centralized, formal face-to-face negotiation—and those transactions were all highly successful. Argentina taking this approach rankled the creditor activists, however, because it was out of anger over these other transactions—particularly Ecuador's—that they had lobbied the IMF to adopt the new good faith negotiations rule in the first place. One investor told *Euromoney* in April 2001—before Argentina defaulted—that once the EMCA was formed, debtors would have to work with bondholder committees: "The country will have to make a tactical decision how it wishes to approach its creditors. If a significant group of creditors says this is a situation where we think a negotiation is appropriate, and we will refrain from accepting an offer that isn't preceded by a negotiation, obviously that's a factor the sovereign has got to take into account."[76] Why the EMCA's creditor rights activists wanted this rule was apparent, but why the IMF agreed to implement it is not entirely clear from the record. Perhaps one important factor in 2002 was that its SDRM initiative—then still alive—strongly favored the use of formal committee processes in sovereign debt restructuring negotiations.[77]

Regardless of how the good faith rule came to be, the question in late 2003 was how—and when—the IMF should enforce its new rule. Should Argentina fail its first review as creditor activists seemed to be suggesting? Or was Argentina making a fair start in its compliance, presenting an offer and having a first set of meetings with investors all over the world? There was also another issue, one of exclusivity: Could Argentina work with the many different consultative groups that it had set up, or did it have to negotiate with a single, consolidated committee of creditors as the creditor activists wanted? The success of Argentina's transaction would soon hang on the answers to these questions.

Events came to a head in December 2003 when Argentine finance secretary Guillermo Nielsen came to New York to address EMTA's annual meeting. First on his agenda, however, was a private meeting on December 3 with representatives from the ABC. At this meeting the creditor group's leaders proposed that Argentina slash the debt relief it was requesting by more than half, to 35% from 75%, and make up the nearly $20 billion of interest payments it had missed over the preceding two years.[78] In total, the ABC was asking for a recovery of three times what Argentina had offered in Dubai.[79] Part of the ABC's rationale, as it set out in its written proposal, was that it was just asking Argentina for the average terms that other countries had agreed to in their (mostly Brady) restructurings of the prior decade,[80] although the ABC also included calculations suggesting that Argentina had the economic capacity to pay this much higher sum. Nielsen listened politely; there were no reports of fireworks going off at the meeting.

The next day, Nielsen was the keynote speaker at EMTA's annual meeting. Nielsen started with a frank discussion of Argentina's need for deep debt relief. Nevertheless, he said, the country was committed to working with creditors through the consultative working groups it had set up around the world. He also said, "We do not intend to impose a unilateral offer," which was the term creditor activists used to describe the scenario in which a country makes a legal offer before reaching a consensus with leading bondholders on the terms of the deal.[81] The *Financial Times* printed an upbeat account of the event.[82]

Behind the scenes, however, a total breakdown was in the works. While in New York to attend the EMTA meeting, U.S.-based ABC, Italy-based TFA, and Germany-based ABRA formed a union to enhance their collective bargaining power. The collective called itself the Global Committee of Argentina Bondholders (GCAB).[83] As a global group representing many thousands of retail and institutional investors, GCAB thought that it met the definition of the type of "representative creditor group" with which the IMF "expected" countries to negotiate pursuant to its September 2002 rule. As such, GCAB asked Argentina to recognize it and requested a formal negotiation. Threatened, Argentina answered that it did not intend to negotiate with this new group and would instead continue to work with the many consultative groups it had set up over the prior year. This exchange marks the beginning of the war over Argentina's debt restructuring, a war that took until 2016 to truly resolve.

The *Financial Times* broke the story of the evolving conflict on December 9, 2003, reporting that "Argentina's creditors are joining forces to press for improved terms."[84] Argentine cabinet chief Alberto Fernández—who would be elected president of Argentina in 2019—warned in the same article that the country did not plan to alter its proposal and told creditors to prepare for a "complicated, difficult and drawn-out process." The battle lines were drawn.

On December 12, Minister of Economy Roberto Lavagna and Finance Secretary Guillermo Nielsen upped the ante. Lavagna said, "We have to take the tough decisions we have been making in the area of the debt so that we don't start another lost decade in which we are always running behind the game." Playing the bad cop in the same article, Nielsen called the ABC's proposal "not serious" and added that the group's financial analysis "falls to pieces and they know it." He rubbed salt into the wound by saying that recovering money from Argentina through the courts was "practically impossible" and that the country had carried out "adequate financial engineering" to protect its assets from legal attacks.[85] These were fighting words, and they would later be used many times in court as evidence of Argentina's ill intentions.

In this evolving battle the IMF sided with GCAB, telling Argentina that it had yanked the first quarterly review of the country's program off the December board meeting agenda for its breach of the IMF's good faith negotiations rule.[86] Argentina was outraged: The debt negotiations were at their most sensitive point, and now the IMF was in the middle of them and siding with a group of creditors with very aggressive expectations. This is not what Argentina had expected, since the U.S. Treasury had told the country to work out its deal directly with its creditors, and the IMF's Köhler had said that the IMF would not interfere.

President Néstor Kirchner lashed out. He told the press that he would not accept "pressures of any kind" and that "we are no longer able to be chased by the Fund or by the friends of the Fund." Kirchner also talked in the local press about "defenestration of the 'usual prophets of doom' who intended to impose foreign remedies" on the country.[87]

There was no doubt that the poison was back in the Argentina-IMF relationship.

The United States Brokers a Truce, but the War Rages On

The new rift between Argentina and the IMF threatened to undermine recent progress in the Argentina–U.S. relationship. On January 7, 2004, President Néstor Kirchner attacked President George W. Bush in the press even though the two were due to meet in Mexico the following week.[88] The pretext of President Kirchner's attack was a critical statement a U.S. State Department official had made about the failure of Argentina's foreign minister to meet with dissidents on a recent trip to Cuba. Bitterness flowed both ways, as Argentina soon learned that an anticipated $5 billion loan from the World Bank was now delayed because its approval hinged on Argentina passing its first IMF review, which was now delayed indefinitely.[89]

Two days later on January 9, IMF managing director Köhler called President Kirchner to inform him that the country's first review had been put back on the calendar for the January board meeting. First Deputy Managing Director Anne Krueger followed with a letter to Economy Minister Lavagna with the same message. Behind the shift were "several days of intense negotiations" between Paul O'Neill's successor U.S. treasury secretary John Snow, Undersecretary for International Affairs John Taylor, Minister Lavagna, and Managing Director Köhler, according to Buenos Aires–based reporter David Haskel of the Bureau of National Affairs.[90] As a result, by the time Kirchner and Bush met in Mexico, the tensions had eased. In Monterrey they shared a photo op, their second in six months.[91]

This rapprochement would not last.

The IMF Executive Board's first review of Argentina's program, on January 28, 2004, was a grueling three-and-a-half-hour affair in which Argentina faced off against skeptical executive directors from around the world, many of whom were agitated by the status of the debt restructuring and sympathetic to creditor demands for a "good faith negotiation."[92]

The setup was per tradition: The executive directors representing the United States, Germany, Japan, the United Kingdom, China, Russia, Saudi Arabia, and France sat around the oval board table in high-backed leather armchairs, as did voting members who represented groups of countries aggregated on a quasi-regional basis. Behind the executive directors sat their top advisers, and behind them were arrayed staffers from all of the IMF's departments whose technical teams helped design, monitor, and administer the program, including professionals from the Western Hemisphere, policy development and review, fiscal affairs, monetary and financial systems, legal, research, finance, statistics, international capital markets, and external relations departments. Observers from the World Bank also sat in, as did representatives from countries not seated at the board table. In all, about 125 people attended the meeting, spread out in the sizable, well-appointed room designed exactly for this purpose.[93]

According to the official minutes, Argentina took heavy fire. The hottest topic was the country's approach to its debt restructuring, particularly its refusal to pay more and its refusal to negotiate with GCAB. Debt restructuring was not the only issue, however; virtually every executive director complained that Argentina was not delivering quickly enough on promised structural reforms, even though all the directors admitted that Argentina had met or exceeded all the macroeconomic targets set out in the program.

The heaviest criticism poured in from the directors from Europe, Australia, and Japan. They complained about the debt deal and the lack of progress in cleaning up the country's utility sector and state-owned banks. Some also complained that Argentina wasn't doing enough to help its private banking system recover from the crisis. Directors from eight countries abstained from supporting Argentina's first review, their votes representing about 35% of the voting power of the IMF.[94] This percentage wasn't large enough to scupper Argentina's review, but it was a notable display of dissent from a board that decides most matters unanimously.

During the meeting, on the topic of debt the Japanese executive director said that good faith in negotiations "should go beyond mere formalities, such as holding a few meetings."[95] He also said, "They must demonstrate their 'good faith' in substance by making their utmost efforts toward more ambitious fiscal consolidation," adding that if the IMF didn't firmly enforce its new rule it could "ultimately undermine the Fund's credibility as the guardian of the international financial system."[96] The Italian director chipped in that Argentina's behavior was putting the entire asset class of emerging markets debt at risk.[97]

Rather than expressing an opinion, some executive directors asked IMF management for their position on the state of Argentina's ongoing discussions with its creditors, a timely topic to say the least. What was extraordinary was the level of focus on GCAB, some of which was the product of outside lobbying. As it emerged later in a Wikileaks cable, GCAB had lobbied IMF executive directors in advance of the meeting asking them to abstain from supporting Argentina's first review.[98] In addition, Charles Dallara, managing director of the Washington-based bank lobby group Institute of International Finance (IIF), had held a press conference several days before the board meeting at which he criticized IMF management for putting Argentina's first review back on the calendar, a strong indicator that the country would pass the review despite the ongoing standoff with GCAB. Dallara said, "The IMF's corporate conduct is not consistent with its own stated policies."[99]

One comment made at the meeting stands out for its balanced take on the situation. Indonesian executive director Sri Mulyani Indrawati said, "It is crucial to frame the negotiation to be conducted in a fair and transparent manner, taking into account the social and economic impact on all the parties concerned."[100] Even this voice of moderation was far from a raging endorsement of Argentina's position.

The United States left no doubt as to what it wanted Argentina to do. Not mincing words, U.S. executive director Nancy Jacklin said, "We are deeply concerned by Argentina's poor performance on the structural aspects of the program, particularly banking, debt restructuring, and utilities."[101] On debt restructuring, she indicated that Argentina needed to show more flexibility on terms. While not suggesting that the United States embroil itself in the negotiations, she said the United States believed that Argentina had agreed to an "upward trend" in the path of the country's primary surplus, which can be read as a suggestion to boost the payout to creditors to get a deal done.[102]

Argentina Recognizes GCAB, but as One of Many

Argentina got the memo. After the contentious January 2004 board meeting, it started analyzing how much it could increase its offer to bondholders without jeopardizing its economic plan. In early February, Argentina and IMF management met at the Ritz-Carlton Coconut Grove in Florida on the heels of a G7 meeting held in Boca Raton.[103] In a hotel meeting room they talked for five hours about the way forward for the program, including options for increasing the value of the deal.

Yet the friction over GCAB was unresolved. The IMF thought that Argentina was obliged to negotiate with the group, while Argentina countered that GCAB was not a valid representative group because it was grossly exaggerating the number of creditors it represented. In particular, Argentina complained that TFA was not a bona fide representative of the 450,000 mom-and-pop Italian investors who collectively owned $15 billion in bonds; instead, Argentina said it was an organ of the Italian banks looking out for their own self-interest. According to Argentina, TFA was pushing for better settlement terms in the hope of heading off billions of dollars of lawsuits from retail customers to whom they had sold Argentine bonds as safe investments.[104] Argentina's attack on TFA, however, was falling on deaf ears at the IMF, which thought the group was a legitimate representative of retail Italian bondholders. TFA's response to Argentina's criticism was that TFA had been formed to protect half a million retail customers who were owed around $15 billion and that without TFA's support they would have been helpless in addressing the pending loss of a large portion of their personal savings. In a recent interview, TFA's Stock said, "Helping Italian retail investors deal with Argentina's default was a humanitarian necessity, not a scheme for the banks to protect themselves."[105]

Argentina's arguments against GCAB didn't cut the mustard with the IMF's G7 shareholders, and a new press war soon broke out. In early February 2004, the G7 itself called for Argentina to "engage constructively with its creditors to achieve a high participation rate in its restructuring."[106] Italian prime minister Silvio Berlusconi said, "We are working fervently with our diplomacy to reach a new solution, since we find Argentina's proposal unacceptable."[107] Minister of Economy Roberto Lavagna countered, "The days of big, publicly financed rescue packages are over, which means that private creditors must accept bigger losses than during the past." Linking the Bush administration's no-more-bailouts policy and large bondholder losses when countries fall into crisis, Minister Lavagna said, "I agree that you must not use the money of American plumbers and carpenters or German dentists to bail out Argentina, Turkey or any other country. . . . But if you take that decision many other things have to happen too."[108] In other words, since the corollary of no more bailouts was deep creditor losses, policy makers couldn't squirm away from the latter when creditors started complaining.

Despite these very public squabbles, Argentina passed its second IMF review in March 2004, and the vote was unanimous.[109] In the face of yet another breakdown, the U.S. Treasury forged a compromise under which Argentina would formally recognize GCAB as a representative creditor group, although its purview would not be exclusive. Argentina would also negotiate the terms of its deal with the dozen or so other consultative creditor groups it had set up around the world whose members were not affiliated with GCAB. In addition, the compromise required Argentina to sign its much-delayed engagement letter with the three international investment banks it had lined up to lead the restructuring deal and, as a sign of good faith, invite all its representative creditor groups to Buenos Aires for talks in April.[110]

To the relief of everyone involved, as March 2004 drew to a close, Argentina's bond restructuring was moving forward again.

The Gaping Gulf Signals Danger Ahead

While First Deputy Managing Director Anne Krueger posited in her famous speech of November 2001 that there was a "gaping hole" in the legal rules for restructuring sovereign debt, the reality was that by March 2004 the more important problem was the gaping gulf between Argentina and GCAB on the terms of the deal. The gap was enormous: tens of billions of dollars between the amount of new bonds Argentina wanted to issue to settle the default and the amount of new bonds that the bondholders affiliated with GCAB were demanding.[111] This difference was so great that it was in neither side's interest to start giving concessions.

In the first quarter of 2004, this gaping gulf and the lack of motion toward closing it had experts worried. Michael Chamberlin, executive director of EMTA, told the *New York Times* that "the two sides seem to be talking past each other. And as long as they continue talking past each other, the chances for progress are slim."[112] In Washington, Michael Mussa, a senior fellow at the Institute of International Economics and former IMF chief economist, testified in Congress that Argentina's IMF program was in deep trouble. Noting the lack of progress, he argued that the U.S. Treasury and the IMF would have to get involved before it was too late. Attacking the new hands-off philosophy being applied to the transaction, Mussa said, "The international community cannot avoid responsibility for establishing broad parameters for what is fair and reasonable—both for Argentina and its creditors"; that is, the IMF should use its debt sustainability models to bridge the difference between the parties. He also warned that Argentina would break with the IMF if there was no change in course. He said, "If the gap remains this large, negotiations between the Argentine government and its disgruntled private creditors are unlikely to get very far very fast. In this event, the international community, operating through the IMF, needs to be prepared for a breach in its relations with Argentina."[113] Despite this warning, no course correction followed.

Left unstated was that from a strictly commercial perspective, what was taking place in Argentina's debt restructuring was entirely normal. One side offered too little, and the other asked for too much; that's how most debt restructuring negotiations begin. The rhetoric was also standard, with Argentina announcing "we have no capacity to move our offer" and creditors saying "the country has far more capacity to pay than it is letting on." What was highly abnormal was the amount of time wasted on the process. It took six months—from Argentina's Dubai presentation in September 2003 to the IMF's March 2004 board meeting—for the IMF, Argentina, and creditors to agree on a reasonable process. That time would have been better spent discussing the deal's commercial terms. This delay proved costly because Argentina's final consultation with its creditors was squeezed into two months, with the country announcing its final terms in early June. Argentina didn't give GCAB much time in this two-month period and certainly didn't sit down for the prolonged face-to-face bargaining sessions the group wanted, which left the organization unsatisfied even though Argentina substantially increased its offer. The cry that Argentina was not offering enough value and was not negotiating in good faith was raised again, and Argentina's IMF program soon fell by the wayside. It was exactly the scenario that Michael Mussa had warned Congress about.

3

Kirchner's Triumph

Argentina's 2005 Debt Restructuring
(April 2004–June 2005)

With the IMF Executive Board unanimously approving Argentina's second review late the month before, April 2004 saw the first normal moment in the country's debt restructuring process. Finally, after months of stagnation, activity hit a frenetic pace as the government consulted with creditors and worked with its bankers to prepare a revised offer. Since the fundamental issues separating the main parties remained unresolved, however, there was more drama to come.

Creditor Consultations and the Bankers Model the Deal

In April 2004, Argentina met with all its creditor groups and some individual investment firms in Buenos Aires at the Ministry of Economy. Visitors included five Italian investor organizations, five Japanese banks, two German banks, a German retail investor organization, the Swiss Bankers Association, two Argentine investor groups, Nicola Stock and Hans Humes from GCAB, and individuals from Alliance Capital Management, Capital Research Global Investors, Fintech Advisory, and JPMorgan Fleming.[1] With Argentina during these meetings were team members from its recently hired international financial advisers, Barclays Capital, UBS Investment Bank, and Merrill Lynch & Co., and its local advisers, BBVA Banco Francés, Banco de Galicia y Buenos Aires, and Banco de la Nación Argentina.[2]

Argentina and its bankers recounted that the discussions were orderly. During most of the meetings the country presented its proposal and then answered questions, although some investors brought discussion materials of their own. At the encouragement of the Ministry of Economy, while in town most investors also met with Argentine Dialogue, the church-based civil society organization set up in the early days of the Duhalde administration.[3]

The April meetings were designed to show the world that Argentina was consulting with its creditors ahead of launching its transaction. Some investors were skeptical, however, including Stefan Engelsberger, who headed the German retail investor group that visited that month. He recalls that Argentina sent cars to the airport to pick up investors and that when they arrived at the Ministry of Economy, reporters were ready to welcome them with lights flashing and TV cameras rolling. He felt that the setup was designed to leave the impression that Argentina was actually "negotiating" with creditors, but he found his meeting more performative than substantial.[4]

Argentina's meeting with GCAB took place on April 16, 2004, and was both contentious and unproductive.[5] Attendees say that it started with Finance Secretary Guillermo Nielsen yelling, "Why are you attacking my country?" at GCAB cochairs Nicola Stock and Hans Humes, who had traveled across the world for the meeting.[6] In response, Stock and a GCAB attendee from Japan stood to leave, but Humes reportedly calmed them down, and a business discussion ensued. Talks didn't touch on the terms of the deal, however, but were instead about process: GCAB's leaders wanted Argentina to share confidential information with them and visit New York to negotiate the terms of the deal across the table from the group's negotiating team. Argentina promised to follow up, although no date was set, and no such information sharing or meeting ever occurred.

In tandem with these meetings, Argentina's newly hired banks developed an independent analysis of the country's debt sustainability to advise how much more the country could safely pay investors. While their analysis validated Argentina's conclusion that it would be patently unsafe for the country to pay the large amount that GCAB and some of its backers on the IMF Executive Board were demanding, their models showed less onerous options that might be sufficiently attractive to creditors to ensure an adequate success rate. Together with the Ministry of Economy, the bankers generated several options to present to President Néstor Kirchner for approval.[7]

Stefan Engelsberger Hits a Nerve

A debt default and currency devaluation typically trigger the worst years in the lives of a country's people, and this was certainly the case for Argentina. On par with the U.S. Great Depression and Weimar Germany's hyperinflation, the economic crisis leading up to and following Argentina's default clobbered the population. In addition to political turmoil and a decline in public safety, Argentines suffered substantially reduced purchasing power, higher taxes, and an inability to obtain imported goods. And the crisis never ended: TV sets and newspapers constantly bombarded Argentines with news about the country's negotiations with the IMF and its creditors. Still, sovereign debt restructurings are not exactly relatable, even for people living through one. Stefan Engelsberger, organizer of the German retail investor group, found a way to bring it home.[8]

Engelsberger started purchasing Argentine bonds after seeing the IMF's top-up of Argentina's program in September 2001. With the IMF supporting Argentina and the bonds trading at a deep discount, he felt he'd made a clever move. He'd recently made a small fortune off Russian bonds and thought he would repeat his success in Argentina. Just three months later, however, the IMF pulled the plug on Argentina, and the country defaulted. Now, Engelsberger's Argentine bonds were trading at twenty-five cents on the dollar, and he was mad, having paid forty-five cents on average. His response was to organize like-minded investors to demand redress.

While hailing from the small picturesque Bavarian village of Inzell, the thirty-four-year old Engelsberger was far from provincial. An intellectual and a savvy financial player, he had a background in banking, political science, and journalism, and he had worked in a number of businesses.

He was able to bring many of these areas of expertise to bear in dealing with Argentina. His first step was to launch a website—in several different languages—to bring small European investors together to fight for a good recovery. The response was immediate. Soon thereafter, he represented 250 mostly small investors who were organized into a group called Interessengemeinschaft Argentinien e.V, which Engelsberger registered as a nongovernmental organization and from whose members he raised a small amount of money to support its operations.

Engelsberger first met with Argentine finance secretary Guillermo Nielsen on November 6, 2002, in Düsseldorf but didn't hit his stride as a debt activist until he attended the conference in Dubai the following year. Engelsberger went to Dubai after a German couple who lived there begged him to attend; they had put much of their life savings into Argentine bonds and were desperate for him to help them and others in the same predicament. They said they would pick him up at the airport, and he could sleep on their couch. After arriving in Dubai, Engelsberger went to the conference center where, to his joy, he learned that as a representative of a nongovernmental organization, he had full access to the facilities. He used the copy machines to make hundreds of copies of a flyer about his initiative, complete with his contact details. Engelsberger placed this leaflet in all the conference center's offices and handed it out at events. His phone soon started ringing; the next day he was quoted in the *New York Times* and the German press.

Engelsberger followed up his success in Dubai with a trip to Buenos Aires in February 2004. In a flash of marketing genius, he bought a bicycle to travel from his cheap hotel to the Ministry of Economy, where he had an appointment to meet with Guillermo Nielsen. Engelsberger told the press what he was about to do, and they jumped on the story. The next day all the major newspapers ran the story about the German bondholder who rode his bike across town to meet with the Ministry of Economy.[9] These articles, in turn, caught the attention of cartoonists Rubén Mira and Sergio Langer, who added him as a character to their crisis-era comic strip *La Nelly*. The comic featured Nelly, a struggling Argentine spinster. After sketching him in the newspaper's offices, Mira and Langer wrote Engelsberger into the story as Klaus, a lederhosen-wearing Austrian bondholder who moved into Nelly's house in partial payment for his bond losses.[10]

Néstor Kirchner Decides the Debt Relief Amount

While it is unlikely that the general population of a country will ever understand the ins and outs of a sovereign debt restructuring, it is certain that its leaders will be highly sensitive to the headlines it generates. Politicians need their people to think the government inked a good deal, although the degree to which a country's political leadership becomes involved with its ministry's operations differs between countries.

In Argentina's case, President Néstor Kirchner took a particularly strong interest in what his Ministry of Economy was doing with foreign debt. In fact, it was Kirchner who decided that Argentina come out with the hardest of several options under consideration, insisting on proposing 75% debt relief in Dubai at the beginning of the negotiations, much to the chagrin of Finance Secretary Guillermo Nielsen, who would have to deliver the bad news.[11] What happened in Dubai was now water under the bridge, though. What mattered was whether Argentina's political leadership would support the revised terms, terms that would balance the sustainability of the country's debt against the need to achieve an adequate success rate in the transaction.

The meeting to finalize the proposal that Argentina would offer the market took place during the last days of May 2004, with First Lady Cristina Fernández de Kirchner also attending. During the meeting, the ministry team presented the options for increasing the value of the country's offer they had prepared with the country's advisers. President Kirchner approved the lowest increase in value, that is, the option that would be the least costly for Argentina. Scarred by the deep crisis just then resolving, neither the president nor the Ministry of Economy wanted to overpay at the risk of falling into crisis again, and as such they were of one mind in going forward with the least costly option. They knew that the market wouldn't find it a generous offer, but they also knew that the market would value it in the vicinity of the prevailing market price of the defaulted bonds. The GDP warrants would also offer investors the potential for significant additional recovery if all went well. The team would do everything in their power to make the deal work on these terms.[12]

Argentina Sweetens the Deal and Leaves GCAB by the Wayside

On June 1, 2004, Argentina presented what became known as its Buenos Aires Offer in the microcinema room at the Ministry of Economy, the usual location for ministry press conferences. While the room was seldom filled, this time it was hard for reporters to even find a spot in the hallway. Kicking off the event, Economy Minister Roberto Lavagna staked out the center ground. He said, "The conservative sectors will think that we will not pay enough. The sectors of the left will say that any arrangement is a bad arrangement."[13] The revised offer, Lavagna's team explained, decreased the nominal cut investors would see in their holdings to 66% from 75%.[14] Small investors would also have the option to take no loss of principal, although to compensate they would receive bonds with extra-low coupons, starting around 2% and stepping up to 5.25% over twenty-five years. All participants would receive an amount of GDP-linked warrants proportional to their holdings of old defaulted bonds. These warrants would pay off handsomely if Argentina's economy subsequently grew at a rate in excess of 3% per annum. Leaving no room for discussion, Lavagna concluded, saying that "obviously, this is our final offer."[15]

The market's response to Argentina's revised offer was mixed. For the first time, some investors were admitting in public that the deal was marginally adequate in light of the situation. For example, the leader of a group representing small Italian investors—which operated separately from Nicola Stock's TFA—told *La Nación* that while he was not happy with the new proposal, he understood that it is a plan in accordance with the reality of the Argentine economy.[16] Yet the more active creditor groups were still aggrieved. German debt activist Stefan Engelsberger, for example, was angry, frustrated, and at the end of his rope. He had one last meeting with Finance Secretary Nielsen, sent out a press release with the title "Adiós, Argentina," and flew home.[17] Once there, Engelsberger sold his bonds, although he continued to lead the creditor organization he had set up.

GCAB came out swinging. Cochair Hans Humes told the *New York Times*, "Clearly, there is a political issue here between what they want to pay and what they can pay. Come on, they can afford to pay more."[18] Behind this public attack was anger that Argentina had never negotiated with the group. After the April meeting in Buenos Aires, GCAB had repeatedly requested information from Argentina and a negotiation session. On May 4, GCAB sent a letter to Lavagna saying, "GCAB is prepared to initiate direct and good faith negotiations with the Argentine government." On May 13, the group sent a letter stating that "GCAB is still waiting to be invited for the agreed technical meeting with the Argentine government." And on May 26, GCAB sent a letter to Lavagna requesting the proposed agenda and timing for the "previously discussed technical meeting and productive negotiations leading to an acceptable deal." Even after the country had announced its revised final terms, GCAB wrote a letter to Lavagna stating that "it is now essential to initiate the good faith negotiation process to which the government committed in order to reach an acceptable deal."[19]

Still receiving no response from Argentina, GCAB announced on June 21, 2004, that it had hired the investment bank Bear Stearns to help it negotiate. In the press release announcing the new hire, Humes and fellow GCAB cochair Nicola Stock reverted to the claim that Argentina was in breach of the IMF's good faith negotiations standard. They wrote, "Any filing by Argentina or the commencement of an exchange offer that does not take into account the forthcoming GCAB response through good faith negotiations is inconsistent with Argentina's agreement with the IMF and greatly compromises the restructuring process."[20]

Following this announcement, Bear Stearns reached out to Finance Secretary Guillermo Nielsen to start a dialogue, but the firm was as unsuccessful as Stock and Humes had been over the prior months. Asked about it, Nielsen recently said that he talked to the Bear Stearns team after they were hired but that the conversations were not constructive.[21] Soon thereafter on July 5, 2004, Argentina sent a letter to GCAB in which it said that the appointment of Bear Stearns came "too late in the process" and that "at this point, your advisors will have to wait until the SEC approves our filing and we are again in a position to meet again with our creditors."[22] It was a polite and legalistic way of saying "Adiós, GCAB."

A Remarkably Quiet Lapse in Argentina's IMF Program

Argentina's jilting of GCAB didn't play well in Washington. The IMF's newly revised good faith negotiations rule stated that Argentina was expected to "negotiate" with its creditors, not just consult. Argentina had effectively done the latter when it met with its bondholders in Buenos Aires in April 2004. In a comment directed at Argentina, U.S. Treasury undersecretary for international affairs John Taylor told a crowd at the American Enterprise Institute on June 9, 2004, that he thought a negotiation was supposed to include "give and take."[23] The IMF staff was also convinced that Argentina was in violation of its new rule.

Under these circumstances Argentina's program with the IMF was untenable, particularly in light of the country's lack of progress in cleaning up its utility sector and state-owned banks. To focus its resources on its debt deal and perhaps anticipating failure at its upcoming third review, Argentina asked the IMF to pause, or lapse, its program while it worked to get its debt deal done.[24]

Nobody was surprised by the lapse, but they were surprised at the relatively harmonious way in which it was handled. Argentina stopped all threats to miss payments to its official lenders, the IMF gave the country a clear runway to restructure its debt by agreeing to defer $1.1 billion in loan payments due to the IMF through the end of January 2005,[25] and both sides spoke of the lapse in muted tones.

The immediate positive effect of the lapse was that Argentina's Ministry of Economy team would no longer be pinned down by nonstop interactions with the IMF staff, nor would the country be subject to quarterly reviews by the IMF Executive Board. The downside was that it would be blocked from obtaining new financial support from the IMF or its other official lenders outside of the payment deferrals noted above. Nonetheless, Argentina's Ministry of Economy intended to continue to manage the country's economy according to the general plan agreed to with the IMF. Careful control of fiscal and monetary policy was necessary to keep the recovery on track, and Argentina intended to restart the program once the debt deal was done.

Jilted GCAB Gets Threatening

GCAB took Argentina's refusal to deal with it as a declaration of war. In July 2004, the group's top brass set out on a global roadshow with stops in Washington, D.C., as well as Los Angeles, New York, Boston, Paris, London, Zurich, Frankfurt, Rome, and Tokyo.[26] Their purpose was to criticize Argentina's Buenos Aires offer and to present a new counterproposal, one that was substantially similar to the ABC's proposal to Argentina the December before but with one important exception: it reduced the debt relief the group was willing to offer to Argentina. In December, the group had offered 35% debt relief. Now it was offering 20–30%. Conditions in Argentina were improving, so GCAB's leaders felt that Argentina could pay more. GCAB's presentation indicated that its offer would force Argentina to pay $25 billion more in value to bondholders and detailed how Argentina would fund the increase: $17 billion from "increased fiscal effort" (i.e., spending cuts and higher taxes), $5 billion from "enhanced GDP growth," and $3 billion from alternative macroeconomic assumptions.[27] As a result, the gaping gulf between Argentina and GCAB remained unchanged, for the group had increased its demands by the same amount that the country had sweetened its offer.

Now, however, the press, analysts, and experts at think tanks were starting to take Argentina's side. On July 21, the *Financial Times* quoted an unnamed expert who said, "GCAB's proposal is about as ridiculous as the original offer Argentina made in Dubai last year, and that was a laughing stock."[28] Professional investors, Wall Street analysts, and third-party commentators had their doubts about GCAB's demands too. One critic was JPMorgan's Vladimir Werning, the firm's head of economic research for Latin America. Werning, who later worked in the government of Argentine president Mauricio Macri, told the firm's clients that Argentina's offer was in the right area.[29] Werning showed them a graph of past sovereign debt haircuts against corresponding economic crises; it showed that Argentina's proposal was in line with precedent when adjusted for the depth of its crisis. He even thought that Argentina's offer was too generous when the value of the GDP warrant was factored in. Months later, Council on Foreign Relations fellow Brad Setser published a similar conclusion but with an argument centered on Argentina's foreign debt ratio.[30]

Argentina's lapse of its IMF program seriously undercut GCAB's leverage in pushing for changes to the terms of the deal. Claudio Loser, a fellow at Inter-American Dialogue and a former head of the IMF's Western Hemisphere division, told the *Financial Times* that "investors were using the IMF and the Group of Seven industrialized countries to apply a lot of pressure on the Argentine authorities and they will not be able to do that any more."[31] In the same article Lacey Gallagher, head of Latin American research at Credit Suisse First Boston, called Argentina's choice to pause its IMF program a "clever short-term move." She explained, "The idea was that the Fund could tighten the screws in the third and fourth reviews, but now Argentina has a breathing space and can launch whatever offer it wants."

GCAB's initial response was denial. When the news came out, GCAB cochair Hans Humes told the *Financial Times* that there was zero chance that Argentina could finalize the deal without his organization's support. "This is a complete joke," he said. "Argentina's offer had no chance of success before and now it has less than no chance."[32] This tone persisted into mid-September, when well-connected *Financial Times* columnist John Dizard quoted an involved party who told him that "the official sector is so f***ing on our side, it's unreal. . . . They aren't going to support this [the Argentines' 75 per cent writedown]."[33]

Yet GCAB soon received the memo, and its talking points switched from denial to threats. On September 30, Humes told the *Financial Times* "If Argentina forces us to use litigation, the scale will be unprecedented."[34]

GCAB's marquee event in the fall of 2004 was a meeting held on October 4 in Washington, D.C., during the World Bank–IMF Annual Meetings. After the event the group announced that more than 150 people had attended the meeting, and the group claimed that it controlled $38 billion in Argentine bonds. GCAB also said that Argentina's revised offer did not "reasonably reflect the ability of the country to pay" and that without the group's support, the results of the deal would fall "well short of an acceptable level of participation."[35]

In a companion presentation, GCAB provided details on its claim that the group, through its member organizations in the United States, Italy, Switzerland, Germany, and Japan, controlled $38 billion in face amount of bonds, just under half of the $82 billion nominal bonds due to be included in the deal; the much-discussed $100 billion restructured debt amount consisted of $82 billion of defaulted principal plus $20 billion of accrued and unpaid interest.[36]

Argentina didn't believe GCAB's numbers and doubted that Italian retail bondholders would follow the group's advice, since GCAB's Italian member group, TFA, was an organization created by the banks, not by the bondholders themselves. Nor had GCAB provided convincing evidence that the majority of the U.S., Swiss, and Japanese investors that it identified as members would take the group's advice. According to its internal analysis of the available information, Argentina would easily achieve a participation rate of at least 60%. GCAB, they believed, was full of hot air and could be beaten through an intensive global marketing effort.

Ultimately the proof of the mix would be in the pudding. Soon Argentina would launch its transaction, and individual holders of its defaulted bonds would choose to accept or reject its offer. The percentage of investors who accepted the deal would determine if GCAB really held a blocking stake or if Argentina was right in believing that the group was wildly exaggerating its influence. Commentators decided to draw the victory line at 70%. If the deal reached this participation rate, Argentina would be deemed the victor.[37] If the acceptance rate fell short of this mark, however, Argentina would not only suffer embarrassment in the press but would also have to crawl back to GCAB to negotiate terms that the group would accept, and the group would inevitably force the country to hand over billions of dollars more of new bonds than it was planning to issue. The stakes were very high.

Argentina Improvises as It Approaches the Starting Line

Putting Argentina's offer into the market was an amazingly complex undertaking given the number of bonds, the number of jurisdictions involved, and the need to disclose the economic situation in the country. The offer document was several inches thick and had to be thoroughly reviewed by regulators in Argentina, Japan, Luxembourg, the United States, Germany, and Italy, a process that took much longer than anticipated.[38] Regulatory delays, first in the United States and then in Italy, forced Argentina to postpone the launch to January 2005 instead of November 2004, which was very embarrassing for the Ministry of Economy.[39] Besides dealing with conventional delays from regulators, Argentina also had to fight to retain the agent it had lined up to handle the submission and settlements process. The complexity of the operation and the risk of getting embroiled in litigation had given their provider pause.[40]

Further complicating matters, Adam Lerrick, head of ABRA, a GCAB member group, reached out to Argentina to suggest an addition to the transaction. Specifically, he asked Argentina to add a price-match guarantee to the deal.[41] It would work like this: if Argentina settled with creditors at thirty-four cents on the dollar in the transaction but subsequently offered holdout investors fifty cents on the dollar, the country would pay the sixteen-cent difference to the investors who had accepted the initial thirty-four cents. This feature would cleverly protect Lerrick's retail clients from getting a worse deal than professional investors who chose to hold out for better terms. As an ancillary benefit, the price-match guarantee would protect Lerrick and his highly regarded partners from reputational damage—and possibly even legal claims—as ABRA was sold to investors on the basis that its managers would get retail investors the same deal as professional investors.[42] The price-match guarantee would be a win-win all around, even for Argentina, as it would most likely boost participation among all types of investors, particularly investors who were deeply dissatisfied with the terms of the deal but were also afraid to hold out.

Argentina liked Lerrick's idea and inserted it into the offer. It was dropped into the offer document under the heading "Rights Upon Future Offers" (RUFO).[43] The guarantee would run for ten years—quite a long time—possibly as a way of indicating to potential holdouts that a better deal wouldn't be forthcoming. It was a powerful statement, but it came at a price: a significant loss of flexibility in dealing with its holdouts, which would prove costly in the end.

The Argentina RUFO clause was also unique, for no other country had included such a provision in a sovereign debt restructuring transaction—at least in recent memory.

Argentina Markets Its Deal

Finally clearing all regulatory hurdles, Argentina launched its debt restructuring via a presentation at the Ministry of Economy, which was held on January 12, 2005.[44] Introducing the transaction, Minister Lavagna laid out the economic logic of the government's approach. While Argentina could have followed the "rapid and comfortable" path of offering creditors a much more attractive deal, any gains from following such a strategy would have been ephemeral because a second restructuring would have become inevitable. The chosen path, he continued, was intended to achieve "maximum acceptance in the markets within a framework of sustainability." He concluded that "most serious and objective foreign analysts recognize that this is the right path."[45]

After the Buenos Aires presentation, the Ministry of Economy split into two teams to meet with investors around the world. Team One included Finance Secretary Nielsen, Sergio Chodos, and two other officials. Their meetings were held on January 13–14 in Miami, January 17–18 in Rome, January 19–20 in Milan, January 21 in Verona, and January 25–28 in New York. Team Two included Ministry of Economy team members Sebastian Palla, Leonardo Madcur, and two other officials. Their meetings were held on January 13 in Buenos Aires; January 17 in Frankfurt; January 18 in Munich; January 19 in Geneva; January 20 in Lugano, Vaduz, and Zurich; January 21 in Zurich; January 24 in Rijswijk and Amsterdam; January 25 in Paris; January 26–28 in London; and January 31 in Boston.[46] There was also a one-on-one conference call with a European investor on February 2. Argentina's local law offer to Japanese investors was handled as a completely separate legal process, with several team members traveling from Europe to Japan to cover that part of the operation.

On the road, Argentina had eighty-three separate meetings with investors, presenting the terms of the offer, explaining the mechanics of participating, and answering questions. Investors were particularly interested in both the status of Argentina's relationship with the IMF and the criticisms that GCAB had leveled at the country.

According to meeting notes, the most frequently asked questions were as follows:

Why are the terms of the offer significantly worse than what
    creditors got in other transactions such as for Russia and Ecuador?
What is the IMF's position on the restructuring? What participation
    level do they expect/require?
What happens if enough investors do not tender?
How does the GDP warrant work?
What is Argentina's plan for holdouts?
Is it possible to negotiate a better offer?
How does the RUFO clause work?
Why do you think people will trust Argentina in the future?
Why is the offer period so short?
How do you avoid holdouts seizing payments on the new bonds?
What happens if we don't participate?

What do you think GCAB will do?

What participation rate will you consider to be successful?

What are private bankers recommending in Italy?

What happens if you get a 45% acceptance rate?

Holdouts expect the IMF to press you to improve the offer. Is this the case? [47]

GCAB and TFA Trash the Deal

While Argentina circled the globe trying to sell its deal, GCAB worked furiously to kill it.[48] The organization's ground operation started with an antideal roadshow in Europe, where the group held meetings in London, Geneva, Zurich, Frankfurt, Milan, Lugano, and Rome.[49] Then GCAB moved to the United States, with the group stopping in New York and Boston.[50]

GCAB's media operation was directed toward the pages of the *Financial Times* and Italy's financial press. Italy's *La Repubblica* ran stories reflective of GCAB's perspective, including "Offer of Argentinian Bonds, the Savers' Protest" on January 11;[51] "Argentine Proposal Is a Scam" on January 12;[52] "Revolt against Tango Bonds: The Offer Is a Big Rip-Off" on January 13;[53] and "The Refusal" on January 14.[54] *Financial Times* coverage was similar. Columnist John Dizard predicted on January 10 that Argentina would sweeten its deal because the coalition of creditor rights groups would force participation below the 70% threshold commentators had decided was necessary for success.[55] On January 11, GCAB cochair Hans Humes was quoted as saying that "Argentina is just trying to bully people into accepting an unacceptable offer. If Argentina's offer succeeds it will dramatically lower the cost of defaulting and strip power from creditors. All borrowers—not just sovereigns—will be much more tempted just to pull the plug."[56] Later that month on January 20 the paper covered GCAB member group ABRA's announcement of its intention to reject Argentina's "take-it-or-leave-it" offer.[57] On February 1 the *Financial Times* quoted Humes once again, this time as saying that participation in the deal would fall short and that "creditors have realized that there is much more risk going into the deal than staying out."[58]

In the meantime, the transaction's RUFO price-match guarantee had become a bone of contention. Just after the restructuring was launched, the *Financial Times* published an article claiming that Argentina could pay court judgments obtained after the deal closed without triggering the guarantee.[59] In other words, if holdouts sued, they could get a better deal without triggering the RUFO. GCAB made hay with this new claim, spreading the word that the RUFO lacked teeth. Argentine finance secretary Guillermo Nielsen countered this attack on the credibility of the deal, telling the press that "there is not going to be any improvement in the offer. This is the only one."[60] Yet questions about the clause and Argentina's intentions toward any holdouts persisted.

Two Striking Absences: No Exit Consents and No IMF Support Letter

While the RUFO clause triggered many questions and doubts about Argentina's deal, it wasn't the transaction's only deviation from sovereign debt restructuring norms. Two striking absences stood out: the lack of an exit consent and the lack of clear support from the IMF.

The "exit consent" topic came up at a January 28, 2005, roadshow meeting with Elliott Associates in New York.[61] In retrospect, it was somewhat surprising for Argentina to meet with Elliott, the famous holdout firm that was already engaged in litigation with it. Finance Secretary Guillermo Nielsen's team was willing to meet with anyone who asked for their time, however, Elliott included. By all reports, the meeting was civilized and technical. While most of Elliott's questions focused on how the deal was going and other conventional matters, one particular question stands out in light of subsequent events: Why didn't Argentina's deal include an exit consent as part of the transaction, a feature that both Ecuador and Uruguay had included in their recent sovereign debt restructuring deals?[62] Elliott undoubtedly had read Argentina's exchange offer prospectus and noted that it made no provision to seek any consent from bondholders as part of the process.

Corporate and sovereign bond restructurings, particularly in the

United States, regularly include exit consents to convince would-be hold-outs to play nice. Investors who take the offer of new bonds in an exchange offer with an exit consent simultaneously vote to strip protective covenants from the original bonds. Investors are thus compelled to take the issuer's transaction, because they otherwise risk being left holding a rump of old bonds whose protective covenants have been stripped.[63] From a game theory perspective, an exit consent is a stick. And it's legal. U.S. courts and regulators allow exit consents to be used even when doing so is commercially aggressive, causing great harm to bondholders who do not accept a deal. The only condition on their use is that the original bond documents permit an exit consent to take place, typically providing a specific list of covenants that may be stripped in a vote. Elliott's question that day was why Argentina did not put an exit consent into its bond exchange offer document when its original bond document permitted it to wield this particular stick.

Elliott's question about exit consents implied that they were thinking of holding out. The only question was which covenant in Argentina's bonds the firm cared about. It wasn't hard to guess, because sovereign bonds don't have many covenants. Without a doubt, what Elliott cared about was the pari passu clause, the one it had used against Peru in a Belgian court in 2000 and the one that was at the heart of its subsequent campaign against Argentina in New York.

While Elliott's reason for asking about exit consents is obvious, Argentina's decision not to include this preventative stick against potential holdouts is not very clear. Argentina's explanation at the time was that adding this measure was too complicated in the context of its already supercomplex transaction. It was a regrettable decision.

A second notable absence hobbled Argentina's transaction more immediately: the lack of a support letter from the IMF. Just as prior deals for Ukraine and Uruguay had included exit consents (or similar features), they had also had support letters from the IMF. Ukraine's February 2000 offering circular, for example, included a letter from IMF managing director Stanley Fischer,[64] while Uruguay's 2003 deal included a particularly strong one from Managing Director Horst Köhler, who wrote that "the Uruguayan authorities are aware of the substantial challenges ahead, and have reaffirmed their determination to address the economic imbalances and deepen structural reforms in order to put the economy on a path of sustained growth and financial stability. I believe that their program represents a strong and balanced effort to achieve these goals. The support of the financial community, including institutional and retail investors from the private sector, is essential to the success of this program."[65]

Such a letter could have been especially helpful to Argentina in Italy, where the press and the banks were telling retail investors that the deal was a "rip-off" and a "scam." All Argentina would have had to do to convince most doubters would have been to wave a letter from the head of the IMF stating that a deep debt reduction was economically necessary. With its program lapsed, however, such a letter was not forthcoming or, more likely, wasn't requested.

Argentina's Lock Law: The Feature Added on the Fly

While many sovereign debt restructurings include an exit consent, a letter of support from the IMF, or both, Argentina was alone in enacting a new law to scare potential holdouts into its deal. The law that the Argentine Congress enacted in early February 2005, which came to be known as the Lock Law, said that investors who held out would never be paid even if they held court judgments, at least as long as the law remained in effect.[66] This was a big stick to add, albeit late in the game, on February 9, 2005, to be precise.[67]

President Kirchner presented the Lock Law to the Argentine Congress as a way to ratchet up the pressure on indecisive bondholders,[68] while Economy Minister Lavagna told the *Financial Times* "We have turned to the highest legal instrument available, which is a law, so that nobody is left in any doubt that the possibility of reopening the exchange is closed forever."[69]

The Lock Law was a brilliant tactic to scare investors—particularly the 450,000 Italian retail investors—into the deal. They got the message, and they were frightened. The Lock Law, in turn, forced TFA to respond in kind. The Italian banks could hardly sit idly by and let Argentina scare all their customers into a deal they thought was wholly inadequate.

TFA's Counterpunch

TFA's response to the Lock Law came a few days later. It was an idea with money attached: Italian investors would jointly sue Argentina, and TFA would pick up the tab.[70] The money to cover legal expenses was a game changer because Italian retail investors on average held only €10,000–20,000 of defaulted bonds, which made it economically unfeasible for them to hold out individually and litigate on their own. TFA underwriting the cost changed their decision matrix; now they had the option to hold out.

The thinking behind TFA's offer to subsidize lawsuits on behalf of its mom-and-pop investors came from GCAB's lawyers at White & Case,[71] who thought that Argentina's Lock Law was akin to an expropriation of property. This parallel, in turn, opened up the possibility of bringing Argentina to binding arbitration at the International Centre for Settlement of Investment Disputes (ICSID) in Washington, D.C., using commitments Argentina had made to the Italian government under a bilateral investment treaty signed the decade before.[72] It was a clever idea, but nobody had brought a sovereign debt case to the ICSID before, so it was also a bit of an experiment. In the end, it took much longer to gain momentum than anyone could have imagined in February 2005. In the heat of the transaction, however, nobody was asking a lot of questions. Desperate for any source of leverage, TFA took the idea and ran with it.

It Comes Down to the Wire in Italy

As the deal ticked ever closer to its February 25 expiration,[73] an operation of massive complexity was being carried out all over the world. Processing the deal involved thousands of people, including government officials, lawyers, bankers, and, in particular, financial intermediaries who processed the physical and electronic instructions. It was a multistep process that connected every single individual investor directly to Argentina. For example, a mom-and-pop investor in a small town in Germany might sign a paper to instruct his local bank to accept the transaction on his behalf. That bank would then give an instruction to a larger German bank in Frankfurt that served as its custodian, after which the custodian bank would put an instruction through Clearstream, a European electronic clearing system, which would then put an instruction into the U.S.-based Depository Trust Company. The Depository Trust Company would, in turn, provide the country's transaction agent with a periodic update of the running tally of bonds tendered for each of Argentina's 152 issues; the agent would then inform Argentina and its lawyers and financial advisers of the aggregate and bond-by-bond results. And on the closing date of the transaction several months later, the same process would work in reverse, with the same chain of agents delivering new Argentine bonds to investors into the same accounts from which their old bonds were debited. At the end of February 2005, this massive global enterprise was under way, and its purpose was to allow investors to accept Argentina's offer. Rejecting the offer was easy; investors simply did nothing.

Most investors were inclined to accept the transaction. They were tired of all of the fighting and felt that it was time to turn their nonperforming assets into performing ones, even at a loss. They knew getting something was better than getting nothing and that Argentina had suffered a profoundly deep crisis, but many still thought that an offer of fifty cents on the dollar would have been fairer. In Italy, where Argentina's deal was said to be a scam, the calculus was more positional: the question was whether to sue Argentina with TFA or to capitulate to avoid the risk of getting nothing. It was a painful, horrible decision for individual investors to have to make about their personal savings and made the outcome in Italy hard to predict. With participation on $15 billion of bonds at stake, it was here that the battle would be won or lost.

The fighting continued to the bitter end. TFA's head Nicola Stock jumped on an opportunity that presented itself in the last two weeks: a report that Argentina had achieved outsize growth in the final quarter of the prior year. On February 17 he told the *Financial Times*, "GDP is much better, the primary surplus is much better, tax revenues are very high. I am very happy for the Argentines but these are important signals that Argentina could offer more." He also used the opportunity to attack Argentina's GDP warrants, calling them "a waste of time" because their performance depended "entirely on figures that could be manipulated at the discretion of the government."[74]

Despite TFA's barrage, many Italians had serious doubts about the organization's claims and turned to the internet for help making their decision. Chatrooms had been buzzing for months with alternative views of the pending deal. For example, some chatroom commentators encouraged investors to be realistic about their expectations,[75] while others warned of the risks of not participating.[76]

As it came down to the wire, all eyes were on Italy, and the 450,000-person question was which way would they jump. The Italians were mad at Argentina, but they were also mad at their banks. They were scared of the Lock Law, but TFA had said it would fund suing Argentina. Anything could happen, but in the end the results were divided. About 200,000 held out and joined TFA's lawsuit; the rest took the deal or later sold their holdings into the market. For Argentina, this outcome was good enough. Most Italian investors would have had to reject the deal for it to fail. Instead, enough accepted it for the transaction to make it across the 70% finish line.

With Italy a Draw, Argentina Wins the Game, Sort Of

On February 25, 2005, a few hours before the deal expired, Argentina announced that it had already achieved a 75% participation rate, a much more successful outcome than the country's detractors had said would be possible. A jubilant President Kirchner told the Argentine people that "thousands and thousands of millions were going to be plundered from Argentina's coffers, but they have been saved."[77] The victory became even sweeter when, in the final hours before the offer expired, Adam Lerrick's ABRA broke with GCAB and exchanged $1 billion or so of bonds, pushing the deal's success rate up to 76%.[78] There was no denying the magnitude of the victory. Even the conservative, Argentina-skeptical *Economist* acknowledged that "Argentina talked tough and won," although it tacked on "for now," pointing out it that would all be for naught if the country didn't complete needed reforms.[79]

Benchmarked against other sovereign debt restructuring transactions, Argentina's success was astounding in light of the large debt relief extracted from bondholders. Pakistan, Ukraine, Ecuador, and Uruguay had all achieved much less. In its 2003 transaction, Uruguay hadn't even reduced its bond principal and coupon; it just extended the maturity of its bonds by an average of about five years. Argentina's 76% participation rate was relatively low, however, with its peers achieving between 89% and 99% on their foreign law bonds.[80] The cost? Argentina was left with $19.6 billion of untendered, defaulted bonds.[81] Significant litigation was sure to follow.

Argentina could thank GCAB, particularly TFA, for this suboptimal result. While the transaction was 95% successful with respect to yen-denominated bonds and 84% successful with respect to U.S. dollar–denominated bonds, it was only 63% successful with respect to euro-denominated bonds, including bonds originally denominated in euro-area member currencies.[82] Of particular note, the uptake rate was only 57% among holders of bonds originally issued in Italian lira.[83] TFA clearly drew blood. With that said, GCAB was less successful in the United States. Only a handful of its institutional members rejected the deal alongside Elliott and Dart, which were never expected to take it in the first place. Most of the big U.S. and European asset managers simply didn't want to own nonperforming assets and didn't want to be in litigation with a foreign government, nor were they really equipped to litigate. The big hit to participation was in Europe, and ground zero was Italy, which suggests that if GCAB and its member groups had not attacked the deal so forcefully, Argentina's aggregate success rate would have been much higher, around 85% or even 90%. Not dealing with GCAB and its member organizations had left the country with a big contingent liability to manage, a $19.6 billion one. Time would tell how well the country would manage this potentially huge cost.

Holdout Investors Sue to Disrupt the Closing

Argentina didn't have much of a chance to savor its great victory before it was hit by motions in the Southern District court aimed at disrupting the deal's closing.

On March 21, 2005, less than a month after the transaction results were announced, Elliott Associates went to court with an action that could disrupt both the transaction's closing and its economic gains. Elliott asked Judge Griesa to attach the old bonds submitted into the exchange while still allowing the new bonds promised to participants to be issued.[84] If Griesa agreed, the net effect of the transaction would be to increase Argentina's debt, not reduce it, because the country's old bonds would remain outstanding (and in the hands of holdouts), and the new bonds would be in the hands of deal participants. Griesa, strongly committed to seeing the deal closed, would have none of it. On March 29 he ruled against Elliott and some other holdouts that had filed copycat motions,[85] although he stayed his ruling pending appeal, which held up the transaction's closing for a few months. In May 2005 the Second Circuit Court of Appeals affirmed his ruling, which cleared the way for the deal to settle in early June. In its opinion, the circuit court wrote that the completion of the restructuring "is obviously of critical importance to the economic health of a nation."[86]

Elliott wasn't the only investor challenging the transaction's closing, however. On April 25, a new disrupter showed up: Capital Ventures International (CVI),[87] an offshore affiliate of Philadelphia-based Susquehanna Advisors Group, Inc.[88] Working on its own, CVI planned to attempt to attach $1 billion of collateral held at the Federal Reserve Bank of New York on behalf of holders of Argentina's Brady bonds—bonds issued in 1993 in exchange for defaulted bank loans from the 1980s. CVI cleverly realized that while the collateral was pledged to Brady bondholders, Argentina had a reversionary interest. When the Brady bonds matured or were otherwise canceled, the collateral would revert to Argentina. CVI sought a second lien on the collateral, covering Argentina's reversionary interest. Because holders of about 75% of Argentina's collateralized Brady bonds, which were also in default, had accepted the country's 2005 restructuring transaction, the corresponding portion of the collateral held at the Fed would be affected. As part of the settlement process, 75% of the collateral would revert to Argentina's agents, who would sell it. The proceeds would be paid to the Brady bond participants who accepted the deal as part of the consideration they were set to receive. Grabbing the collateral would throw a major wrench in the process of settling the exchange of Argentina's Brady bonds, which undoubtedly is why Judge Griesa rejected CVI's motion.[89]

Despite Elliott's and CVI's best efforts, Argentina's deal settled on June 2, 2005.[90] The transaction was finally over. Argentina's old bonds were canceled, providing significant debt relief; the new exchange bonds were trading actively in the market; and Argentina commenced making regular payments on them when due. Argentina had finally achieved the fresh start it needed, and the investors that took the offer finally had a performing asset in their hands. The question that remained was what to do about the $19.6 billion of holdout bonds.

Storm in Italy and Pressure on Argentina from the G7

Argentina's success hit TFA like a bomb. Italy's *La Repubblica* reported that the hundreds of thousands of Italians who had rejected the offer were now worried that their bonds would "turn into waste paper," and they were angry at TFA for encouraging them to hold out.[91]

Moving quickly to avert a large-scale political disaster, Italy pushed its G7 partners to pressure Argentina to deal with the problem of the investors left behind.[92] Their threat was that Argentina would be unable to restart its program with the IMF if it were found to be in violation of the IMF's good faith negotiations rule for not working to settle with the holdouts of its recent transaction.

Argentina bristled at this new round of pressure. Economy Minister Roberto Lavagna told the press that the holdouts would be addressed "in due course" and that "there is absolutely nothing today, nor tomorrow nor in a month."[93] Until that time, he said, creditors were free to seek redress in the courts, and many did.

Elliott Associates Buys More Bonds and the FRAN Plaintiffs Sue

While this postexpiration political drama was playing out, Elliott Associates and two other smart money investors launched a trio of lawsuits with respect to a unique set of securities: floating-rate accrual notes (FRANs), an instrument issued by Argentina in 1998. As of 2005, there was only about $300 million in nominal value of these bonds outstanding; Elliott and these two other investors had managed to scoop up almost all of them.[94] Why the special interest in these bonds? An annual interest rate of 101.5% a year. Yes, 101.5% a year! Payment under the FRANs was based on a formula tied to the yield in the market of another Argentine bond. When Argentina defaulted, the yield of that reference bond shot up to 101.5%. Then, for some reason, the agent responsible for quoting the yield of the reference bond stopped publishing new market values, which left the FRANs running at a 101.5% coupon forever.[95] Of the 152 bonds Argentina had defaulted on, this one was the worst for the country. For investors the FRANs were a dream come true, and the smart money investors scavenged the market to buy them all. In time, these three investors (and affiliated funds) would obtain judgments of about $3 billion dollars on their $300 million of FRANs, ten times the bonds' face value.

The lawsuits these three firms filed with respect to their FRAN holdings were neatly spaced a month apart from each other. Elliott lodged its FRAN lawsuit on February 28, 2005, the first business day after Argentina announced the successful outcome of its transaction.[96] Boston-based Bracebridge followed on March 29, filing a suit on behalf of its vehicles, FFI Fund and FYI Ltd. (a fund wholly owned by Yale University).[97] On April 28, a fund called Montreux Partners, L.P., led by Michael Straus,[98] a lawyer who had represented Elliott and other plaintiffs involved in sovereign debt lawsuits during the 1990s, filed the third lawsuit.[99] For lack of a better term, we'll call Elliott, Bracebridge, and Montreux the FRAN plaintiffs when talking about their activity with respect to these lawsuits. While there is only indirect evidence that these investors were working together as a group in the early days of the litigation,[100] there is plenty of evidence of close coordination in the later stages of the litigation.[101]

Elliott also purchased over $50 million additional defaulted Argentine global bonds in the immediate post-announcement period.[102]

Post-transaction Commentary

In late February 2005, the closest thing the world had to leading experts in sovereign bond restructuring were NYU economist Nouriel Roubini and Council on Foreign Relations fellow Brad Setser. They had published their seminal book *Bailouts or Bail-ins? Responding to Financial Crises in Emerging Economies* the year before.[103] Both naturally took the time to comment on the result of Argentina's historic bond restructuring.

The day after the results were announced, Setser posted to his *Follow the Money* blog a thought piece with the title "Has Argentina Changed the Rules of the Sovereign Debt Game?" He argued that it hadn't: "Argentina does set a precedent. But it is not the only precedent out there, and it is a precedent that most countries won't find all that appealing."[104] He added that Argentina's haircut was justifiable considering the facts and circumstances, including how little foreign exchange the country's limited export base generated to service foreign debt. Yet Setser also said that Argentina would have been wise to make a slightly more generous offer to creditors to increase participation and reduce the risk of posttransaction litigation.

On March 2 on his EconoMonitor website, Roubini followed with a merciless takedown of the IMF, the U.S. Treasury, and GCAB. Regarding the uproar about "good faith negotiations," Roubini wrote that creditor committee prenegotiation of terms is not required and that countries should just put their deals into the market so that investors can decide individually whether to take or reject them. He labeled the U.S. Treasury's new "laissez-faire" approach to the deal an "utter failure." He called GCAB's criticism of the deal "shrill." And he accused the Italian banks of "aggravated deceit." Yet he also called on Argentina to maintain fiscal discipline, fix its utility sector, clean up its banking system, and correct problems in state-provincial fiscal transfers. Prescriptively, he called on Argentina to immediately reopen its offer to give "hapless retail creditors" a second chance to take the deal on the same terms.[105]

A wave of commentary is typical in the wake of a major sovereign debt restructuring, but it usually dries up after a few weeks. When the fights are over, the market moves on. In Argentina's case, however, with $19.6 billion of holdouts, the fights weren't over, and the market didn't move on. Instead of fading away into obscurity, Argentina's 2005 debt restructuring became the Energizer Bunny of sovereign debt restructurings because the fighting kept going, and going, and going.

Argentina Breaks with the IMF and the United States

All the controversy over Argentina's 2005 debt restructuring did huge damage to the country's relationship with the IMF and the United States, which was of great consequence. Two events before year end demonstrated the extent of the damage.

First, in November 2005, protests and a large anti-American rally headed by Venezuela's Hugo Chávez marred U.S. president George W. Bush's visit to Mar del Plata, Argentina, for a summit of American leaders.[106]

Second, in December 2005, two weeks after President Kirchner parted ways with Minister of Economy Roberto Lavagna,[107] Argentina announced it would repay in full the $9.9 billion it owed to the IMF to escape from the oversight that comes with having outstanding loans from the organization.[108] For the IMF and its G7 shareholders, this was a bad development. While their relationship with Argentina was difficult, they also knew that having a contentious relationship was better than having none at all. Indeed, after Argentina kicked out the IMF, progress on structural reforms halted. In time, fiscal and monetary policy would revert to historical norms, and Argentina would fall back into crisis.

That said, Argentina was in such a good place in 2005—with deep debt relief achieved and international prices for its commodity exports high—that it would take years for policy slippages to take a toll. Indeed, Argentina wasn't just in a good place; the country was on a roll, enjoying 8% growth as China was at the time. That, in turn, made President Kirchner a hero to his people: He was the president who had triumphantly battled the creditors, the president who had kicked out the IMF, and the president who was putting more money in their pockets. He was also the president who kept utility rates down by continuing to refuse to come to terms with the foreign owners of many of the country's water, electric, and gas utilities. His approval rating in 2006 was in the 60–80% range,[109] Argentina was Kirchner country, and a political dynasty was in the works. The plan was for Néstor and his wife, Senator Cristina Fernández de Kirchner, to alternate running for president so the family would control the country's political apparatus for the foreseeable future without running afoul of Argentina's term-limit rules. This plan was on its way to fruition when Cristina won the 2007 general election by a landslide. Néstor's death in October 2010 forced a change in plan, however, and Cristina ran again in 2011, winning reelection. As a result, she was Argentina's president throughout most of the holdout litigation that followed the 2005 debt restructuring. At a political level, Néstor Kirchner got the deal done, and Cristina Kirchner would deal with the holdouts.

4

Backstory

Elliott's War on Peru (1996–2000)

On the morning of March 25, 1998, more than three years before Argentina defaulted, Paul Singer, the president of Elliott Associates, a New York–based hedge fund, was where no plaintiff wants to be: on the witness stand being forced to defend his firm's behavior in pursuing its lawsuit against a defendant. The accusation against Elliott was that in early 1996 the firm had purchased defaulted Peruvian loans with a face value of $20.7 million with the "intent and purpose" of suing the country. Such activity—which is termed "champerty" in court—was proscribed under New York law. If the allegation were proven, Elliott would be at risk of losing the entire $11.4 million it had spent purchasing the defaulted loans.

The key moment that day was when Peru's counsel, Mark Cymrot of Baker & Hostetler, asked a pair of questions designed to force Singer to admit that Elliott's purpose from day one was to sue Peru.

"One of your possibilities that you saw before you purchased Peruvian debt was that the debt would be paid in full to Elliott, isn't that correct?" Cymrot asked.

"Yes," Singer replied.

"And you believed that would come about either by Peru paying in full or you would sue Peru, isn't that correct?" Cymrot asked.

"Or a negotiation," he answered.[1]

It was a simple yes or no question, but Singer, a Harvard Law School grad, dodged.

His answer was a good one because an intention to sue or negotiate would defuse the champerty allegation. To make a champerty claim stick, Cymrot would have to prove that suing Peru was Elliott's sole or primary intent. Yet Cymrot had a powerful weapon in his pocket found in a year of invasive discovery against Elliott.

Brandishing the transcript from an earlier deposition, Cymrot said,

> "If you look at page 193, line 4, it says, 'Q. How did it come about? How did they anticipate it would come about that they would get paid in full? A. Peru would either pay people in full or pay us in full or be sued.'"
>
> "Is that your testimony?" Cymrot asked.
>
> "Yes," Singer answered.[2]

In the wake of this testimony, Judge Robert Workman Sweet, who heard the case, ruled against Elliott on August 6, 1998.[3] It was a stinging loss, and Singer's team would have to work hard to reverse the ruling on appeal.

Elliott's Strategy and the Challenges of Holding Out

Elliott's litigation against Peru was to its litigation against Argentina as the Spanish Civil War was to World War II: it was a place to test the new technology, in this case of legal rather than actual warfare. As such, studying *Elliott v. Peru* is an essential prerequisite for understanding the Argentina litigation that followed. *Elliott v. Peru* is also worthy of a chapter-length detour because it provides a unique opportunity to understand Elliott's press-shy team. In the Peru case, unlike in the Argentina case, they were all deposed or put on the witness stand and forced to reveal their view of the world and their role in it.

The path to Elliott versus Peru started in late 1995 when Elliott Associates first assembled its sovereign debt investment team, a team built around the unflinching belief that sovereign borrowers should always repay their debts. This is not an uncommon position in the market, because if borrowers didn't repay their debts, bond markets would close, countries would be unable to borrow to invest in infrastructure, and economies would not grow. Where Elliott stood out, however, was just how far it would go to enforce this belief in court.

Elliott's strategy, as court records of its lawsuits against developing countries suggest, had three elements. First, scoop up a country's defaulted debt at bargain-bin prices. Second, stand by as other investors accept the restructuring terms offered by the country, which typically entailed a significant loss of value. Finally, demand that the debtor country repay the firm's still-defaulted debt in full, using the threat of litigation, or litigation itself, to get its way. Usually, the end result was outsize profits. It was a pretty simple idea: let other investors take a big loss so you can get repaid in full, and sometimes profits came easily. For example, Vietnam rolled over without a fight in 1997, unwilling to be subjected to the humiliation of a lawsuit.[4]

While some profits came easily, holdout investing attracted many critics and exposed those pursuing it to substantial financial risks. The high up-front cost of litigating meant a big loss if a holdout's lawsuits couldn't be converted into an attractive settlement. In the mid-1990s when Elliott entered the business, victory in holdout lawsuits was not a sure bet, and not all would-be holdout firms were successful in turning a profit. Not only was sovereign debt law tricky to use, but the law was also too underdeveloped for investors to tell how far the courts would go in helping them pursue their claims.

One example of a failed holdout investor was Pravin Banker, a former IBM executive.[5] Banker picked up $1.4 million face amount of defaulted Peruvian loans when brokering a trade in the secondary market.[6] He sued Peru in 1993 to obtain full repayment, a suit that ran for five years, but Peru's lawyers outsmarted him every time he came close to collecting. For example, in June 1996 after obtaining a judgment, Banker tried to attach the $1 billion in proceeds from Peru's telephone company privatization, but Peru's lawyers structured the cash flows of the privatization deal so that they flowed offshore, preventing Banker from getting his hands on them.[7] Frustrated by half a decade of failure, he threw in the towel in 1998 and settled on terms equivalent to those that the participants in the country's 1997 Brady restructuring had accepted.[8] It was not easy to win special treatment from a sovereign in distress in a U.S. federal court, he learned.

Being a holdout also brought notoriety. The press routinely called holdouts "rogues" and "vultures." And the big banks hated the holdouts because they threatened to undermine the process that had been put in place to resolve the debt crisis of the 1980s in less developed countries, in which distressed countries, the big international banks, the IMF, the U.S. Treasury, and the Federal Reserve worked together to help get the countries back on track. The banks voluntarily agreed to debt reduction, the official sector lent money, and the countries undertook ambitious economic and fiscal reforms. Holdouts were most unwelcome, because they in effect were trying to get repaid in full out of cash flows freed up by the big banks' losses. The banks called them "free riders," and they became very anxious whenever a holdout showed up in a transaction.

In the mid-1990s, the banks were worried not just about holdouts profiting off of their losses; like unruly party crashers, the holdouts also threatened to disrupt the proceedings. At that time the big banks were facing a structural problem within their community. A handful of big international banks owned 80% of the defaulted debt, while the other 20% was spread among hundreds of small and medium-sized banks all over the world. The big banks were increasingly having trouble keeping the smaller banks in line. From the beginning of the 1980s debt crisis, small banks complained about accepting the deals negotiated by the big banks. They also balked at the commitments the big banks made to provide new money to the countries as part of the deals. The smaller banks eventually fell into line, but only after various government officials, regulators, and the big banks put them under considerable pressure. Over time, however, there was leakage, with some small banks insisting on being bought out. In that context, the big banks were terrified that if Pravin Banker or Elliott won in court, the trickle of small banks declining to cooperate with deals they had cut would turn into a flood—what they called the "nightmare scenario" in which so many creditors tried to hold out of a sovereign debt restructuring deal that it would fail for lack of adequate participation.[9] While a debt restructuring could close without much harm done if 0.5%

of creditors snuck out in secret, 10%, 20%, or 30% holding out could scupper a deal. The majority of creditors would not want to absorb the cost of such a big holdout fraction if they had to give extra debt relief to compensate or, even worse, suffer the embarrassment of seeing a large number of competitors getting a much better deal. Because of these concerns, the big banks extracted a verbal promise from Peru at the closing of its Brady restructuring that it would fight the holdouts in court. And Peru was good to its word: it fought Elliott for years and years, although the country eventually ran out of steam, as we shall see.

Elliott's Sovereign Debt Team and Their Philosophy

Elliott's debt team was composed of legal crack shots. To win at holdout investing, they had to be. The team was headed by Paul Singer, the firm's head; Jay Newman, the firm's portfolio manager for sovereign debt; and Michael Straus, an outside legal adviser.

Paul Singer bankrolled the effort and made all key investment decisions. He founded Elliott in 1977 after a brief career as a lawyer. Little was known about the firm for many years because Singer shunned the press. Once his firm hit a critical size, however, he developed a public persona. In a 2004 interview with *Euromoney*, he presented himself as a modest and thoughtful professional.[10] He explained in neutral language that his firm focused on generating a moderate return at low risk, often by hedging the ancillary risks associated with a specific investment. He also said that the firm specialized in situations in which it could play a leadership role in defending creditors' rights. Paul Singer was a big contributor to George W. Bush's reelection campaign, the article also noted. In photos, with gray hair, a trim beard, and a mustache, Singer looks like a Harvard professor, not a top hedge fund manager.

Elliott's portfolio manager for sovereign debt was Jay Newman. The head of day-to-day operations, Newman was the guy who made things happen. Like Singer, Newman was a lawyer by training. He started trading sovereign loans at Lehman Brothers at the birth of the market in the early 1980s. Later he headed a team at Morgan Stanley.[11]

The third member of Elliott's team was Michael Straus, a Wall Street lawyer who happened upon sovereign debt early in his career at Sullivan & Cromwell. In May 1984, Straus coauthored a brief to the Second Circuit Court of Appeals on behalf of the New York Clearing House Association, an association of large New York banks.[12] The brief was in favor of the court rehearing and reversing a ruling the Second Circuit had made in April 1984 in the Allied Bank case, the first important holdout lawsuit to hit the court of appeals since the enactment of the Foreign Sovereign Immunities Act in 1976.

Once Singer, Newman, and Straus came together as a team in late 1995, they lost no time getting into the mix. Within months, the Elliott team bought Panamanian and Peruvian debt and asked the countries for repayment outside of the terms of the Brady restructurings then under way. It wasn't the nicest of business models, but if challenged by critics, including in court, they justified what they were doing by saying that the repayment of debt was the best option for the people of the affected country. They were, in effect, creditor rights activists protecting the world from defaulters. The distinctive thing about Singer, Newman, and Straus wasn't their philosophy, however, but rather their competence in litigating. They knew everything that could be known about sovereign debt law, and they excelled at pushing judges to the limit. They were smart, they were systematic, and they were relentless. But before they came together to form an unbeatable litigating machine, there was an idea: sovereign debt must always be enforceable in the U.S. courts, an idea first articulated in the 1985 Allied Bank opinion by the Second Circuit Court of Appeals handed down after a rehearing, the case in which Straus had played a role.

The Allied Bank Case

The Allied Bank case involved Costa Rica, which was in the process of rescheduling the debt it owed to 170 different lenders.[13] The dispute arose because a bank in a 39-bank subgroup of these lenders didn't want to take the restructuring terms the country proffered. While the total amount lent by the 39-bank syndicate was less than $5 million, the case became a cause célèbre in the banking community because the district court judge, Thomas P. Griesa, ruled for Costa Rica against the holdout investor in July 1983.[14] Then in April 1984 the Second Circuit Court of Appeals did too, albeit on different grounds. These rulings implied that sovereign debt was not always enforceable.

The Second Circuit's 1984 ruling was a disaster for the international banks whose portfolios were chock-full of loans to insolvent, less developed countries. These countries, in aggregate, owed the banks so much money relative to their capital bases that the banks could not afford for there to be any doubt that all the loans would eventually be repaid in full. From an economic perspective, the Allied Bank ruling was an existential threat. It was also a legal threat because aside from keeping a large amount of these loans on their own balance sheets, large banks had sold billions of dollars of these loans to small and medium-sized banks. If the big banks were found to have sold unenforceable debt to the small banks, they could be on the hook for the losses.

Michael Straus was an attorney at Sullivan & Cromwell. The firm appeared in the Allied Bank case on May 21, 1984, with the delivery of a brief to the Second Circuit on behalf of the New York Clearing House Association, an association of New York banks. In technical parlance this was an amicus brief, a "friend of the court" brief presented, with the permission of the court, by a third party with an interest in the legal issues at hand. This particular brief was submitted because of the strong interest the New York banking community had in seeing a reversal of the appeal court's April ruling. Straus and other lawyers from Sullivan & Cromwell argued that the Second Circuit needed to rehear the Allied Bank case and reverse its opinion, which jeopardized the enforceability of sovereign debt and New York as a financial center:

> The April 23 decision has created uncertainty as to the enforceability
> in United States courts of United States dollar obligations of foreign
> borrowers payable in New York City. Prior to the decision, any lender
> could expect to obtain a prompt judgment in his favor upon default
> in payment. . . . Now the lender must regard such relief as question-

able. . . . Unless set aside, the decision may have the following effects
on international banking: Defaults may be encouraged. . . . Banks
may reevaluate the desirability of participation in syndicated dollar
loans arranged in and payable in New York City in comparison with
the arrangement and payment of loans in other jurisdictions where
the banks expect prompt payments can be obtained as of right in the
event of default. . . . Were a substantial part of international dollar
lending to move from New York to Europe, the effects upon the public and commercial interests of this City and the United States would
be material and adverse. In addition to the diminution of New York's
importance as a financial capital and with the concomitant loss of
employment and taxes—the established role of New York law as the
law of choice in international finance may be compromised.[15]

The U.S. government also stepped in with a holdout-friendly amicus brief.
Arguing that the court's earlier opinion had been based on a faulty understanding of the U.S. policy toward Costa Rica's restructuring transaction,
the U.S. government echoed Sullivan & Cromwell's brief on behalf of the
New York banks, saying that sovereign debt must always be enforceable
while also asserting that creditor participation in a restructuring had to be
voluntary.[16] In other words, every single creditor should have the right to
accept or reject a restructuring offer from a defaulted country regardless
of what other creditors did. It was a holdout-friendly policy.

The Second Circuit reheard the case on October 17, 1984. The U.S.
government and Sullivan & Cromwell briefs did the trick, and the court
reversed its earlier ruling, finding now in favor of the banks.[17] As of March
18, 1985, sovereign debt was unambiguously enforceable in the United
States, and the government was on record as saying that all offers must
be voluntary. It was a perfect outcome for potential holdouts, although nobody would succeed in making a regular business of it until Elliott's team
came together and started buying Panama's and Peru's defaulted loans.

In retrospect, this rehearing of the case begs the question as to just
why the U.S. government and the major banks supported the holdout
lender the way they did. Holdouts would, after all, come to greatly annoy
the large banks and cause great disruption in the sovereign bond market.

At the time, however, sovereign debt was still relatively narrowly held within the international banking community, and most loans contained clauses to deter holdout behavior.[18] Ultimately, the Allied Bank ruling and the government's holdout-friendly policy would increase that risk, but that possibility didn't emerge for some time and it only occurred because of the evolution in the structure of the sovereign debt market. First, in the late 1980s sovereign loans started trading in the secondary market, and nonbank investors, including hedge funds, began to buy them; and, second, countries started issuing bonds, which for operational reasons lacked the antiholdout features commonly embedded in loans.

Elliott Accused of Champerty by Peru

Elliott v. Peru was heard by Judge Robert Workman Sweet of the U.S. District Court for the Southern District of New York. Judge Sweet was a man of the world. Not only did he serve as a commander of a submarine chaser in the Atlantic during World War II, but from late 1966 through 1969 he was the deputy mayor of New York City under John Lindsay, his law school roommate.[19] While working for the city government, Sweet represented the mayor in contentious labor disputes with teachers and sanitation workers. Having gotten down and dirty in these big fights, Sweet was well prepared to adjudicate thorny money fights from the bench.

Judge Sweet was not a lucky draw for Elliott. Many judges on the federal bench take an instant dislike to countries in default. Certainly, the first words out of the mouth of many a judge in the history of sovereign debt have been, "Well, why aren't you paying your debts?" Sweet showed equanimity on the topic, however, as best illustrated when he dropped a quote by French philosopher Simone Weil into a ruling in the Pravin Banker case in 1994: "The payment of debts is necessary for social order. The non-payment is quite equally necessary for social order. For centuries humanity has oscillated, serenely unaware, between these two contradictory necessities."[20] This was not a promising philosophical inclination for the judge tasked with helping Elliott collect on an unpaid debt from an impoverished country.

Judge Sweet's philosophical inclination came to the fore in his willingness to consider a champerty argument in Peru's defense. Other judges had nipped similar efforts in the bud, as his colleague Judge Denny Chin had done in an earlier case against Panama. Judge Chin opined, "Even assuming Elliott had no intention of participating in [Panama's Brady restructuring] no reasonable factfinder could conclude that it spent $8 million just to enjoy the pleasures of litigation."[21] In contrast, in the Peru case Sweet allowed Peru's lawyer, Mark Cymrot, to pursue extensive discovery in his effort to prove that Elliott had, in fact, committed champerty.

Still, Judge Sweet warned Cymrot that he was fighting an uphill battle, stating that "application of the 'medieval' defense of champerty in the secondary market for foreign debt raises daunting questions."[22] In other words, it would be hard for Cymrot to prove that suing Peru was Elliott's sole or primary intent when it purchased defaulted Peruvian loans. Sweet gave him leeway, however, once Cymrot pointed out that Michael Straus, Elliott's lawyer, had been part of many sovereign debt lawsuits, including a series of cases brought in the Southern District on behalf of a mysterious Cook Island entity called Water Street Bank & Trust that had sued several countries in rapid succession in 1994 and 1995.[23]

Cymrot was relentless in pursuing discovery. He deposed or received statements from Paul Singer, Jay Newman,[24] Michael Straus,[25] Newman's subordinates, and Newman's former coworkers at Morgan Stanley.[26] Cymrot also deposed professionals from the international banks from which Elliott had bought the defaulted loans as well as from the JPMorgan manager responsible for administering Peru's loans.[27] In addition, Cymrot sought (but apparently failed) to depose one of Newman's counterparts in the market, an expert in African debt named Eric Hermann who ran an outfit called FH International and was later involved in the Argentina bond cases in partnership with Michael Straus.[28] Cymrot collected thousands of pages of depositions and documents out of which he developed a step-by-step narrative of how Singer, Newman, and Straus had met and what they did once they came together as a team.

Peru's champerty allegation was tried from the bench the week of March 17–25, 1998, in a series of hearings, the transcript of which runs about eight hundred pages long.[29] The hearings included live testimony from many witnesses, which was unusual because in most sovereign debt cases the facts are not in dispute; instead, the parties state the facts to the court in written declarations. Since Peru's allegation had to do with Elliott's "intentions," however, there was no alternative but to put the firm's investment team on the stand to ask them what they were thinking when the firm bought defaulted Peruvian loans.

During the trial, Cymrot squared off against former U.S. attorney for the Southern District of New York Otto G. Obermaier, a partner at Weil, Gotshal & Manges.[30] On-stand testimony by Elliott team members Paul Singer and Jay Newman was the highlight of the case.

Paul Singer on the Stand

On the morning of March 17, 1998, Paul Singer, the lead-off witness, was questioned by his own counsel, Otto Obermaier. Their exchange that morning provides an excellent introduction to Singer and his firm. It also establishes that all of Elliott's investment decisions ran through Singer, so when it came to champerty, the most important thing to judge would be what Singer intended when he decided the firm would purchase Peru's defaulted loans:

> Q. Mr. Singer, how old are you?
> A. 53.
> Q. Are you affiliated in any way with Elliott Associates, L.P., the plaintiff in this case?
> A. I'm the general partner of Elliott Associates.
> Q. How long have you been the general partner of Elliott Associates?
> A. Since 1977 when it was formed.
> * * *
> Q. What is the business of Elliott Associates, L.P.?
> A. Trading and investing in securities.
> Q. What are your duties as the general partner of Elliott Associates?
> A. I make all the investment decisions. I run the firm and manage the people. I speak to investors and potential investors.
> Q. How much money is under management by Elliott Associates?

A. Approximately $700 million right now.

Q. What did you do before forming Elliott Associates in 1977?

A. I graduated Harvard law school in 1969 with a J.D. degree. I clerked for a New Jersey superior court Appellate Division judge for one year. I was an attorney with Kaye Scholer, a firm in New York, for two years, with Fried Frank, a law firm in New York, for two years. I had a job for a short time as a financial writer for a publication called *Indicator Digest* and spent from 1974 to 1976 as a lawyer for DLJ Real Estate, an affiliate of Donaldson, Lufkin & Jenrette. I formed Elliott in January 1977.

Q. Who decides what the investment strategy of Elliott Associates is?

A. I do.

Q. Who decides what specific investments Elliott Associates make?

A. I do.

Q. What was Elliott Associates' investment strategy for the years 1994 through 1996?

A. Elliott's overall goal is to achieve a moderate return with low overall risk. In pursuance of that goal, Elliott pursues a number of strategies. It's an eclectic approach. The primary strategy is and has been and was in that period investing in distressed securities. . . .

* * *

Q. What investment analysis does Elliott typically make when it considers investment in distressed securities?

A. Each situation is different, but typically the . . . analysis would cover the fundamental situation in the company or issuer, the context and negotiating context, that is to say who owns the instrument, the debt, who else owns it, who else owns other claims on the issuer. It also could cover the particular terms of the instrument, the legal terms. It could also cover the particular process, the mechanical process of the—the contextual process, that is to say whether it's in a proceeding, what is the nature of the proceeding, what are the rules in the particular jurisdiction. And an analysis of the price of the instrument in relation to its current and prospective value is also done.

Q. Does Elliott in fulfillment of its investment strategies on occasion become a holdout in certain of the distressed securities?

A. Yes.

* * *

Q. When did Elliott first consider purchasing the debt of the Republic of Peru or its instrumentalities?

A. I believe sometime in late 1995 or early 1996.

Q. Who, if anyone, assisted you in making the investment analysis with respect to the debt of the Republic of Peru or its instrumentalities?

A. We had retained Jay Newman as a consultant. In-house, the team was Andrew Kurtz, one of my senior analysts, and Ralph Dellacamera, my head trader.

Q. Who at Elliott ultimately decided to make the decision to purchase the debt of the Republic of Peru or its instrumentalities?

A. I did.[31]

Jay Newman on the Stand

Following Singer's testimony, Peru's counsel called Elliott's Jay Newman to the stand with the primary objective of tying Newman to Water Street's litigation against foreign countries. This was essential. Cymrot had used Elliott lawyer Michael Straus's involvement in the Water Street cases in arguing for the leeway to perform discovery. To prove a champerty violation, however, he would need to prove a pattern of behavior at the investment firm itself, and to do that he had to tie an Elliott investment professional to Water Street's litigious activities.

Cymrot used the hearings and prior depositions to document Newman's career path up to the time he joined Elliott, although some of Newman's story was already in the public domain. In 1990, for example, the *New York Times* reported that Newman had just been appointed to head a new emerging markets debt trading unit at Morgan Stanley and explained that he had "pioneered the development of the secondary market for such debt at Shearson Lehman Hutton Inc. in the early 1980s."[32] The article noted that Newman's former Shearson colleagues R. Fogerty, Pierre Biraben, John J. Foley, Peter J. Grossman, and Gordon R. Wood would also be part of the team. Cymrot used depositions to nail down Newman's career path after leaving Morgan Stanley in 1993. Newman, with his former coworker Pierre Biraben, set up the Percheron Fund, which invested in sovereign debt,[33] and also set up a group of firms that originated leases across Eastern Europe, also with Biraben,[34] and Biraben set up Water Street Bank & Trust, the focus of the investigation.[35] Yet in depositions Newman explained that he had no formal role with Water Street. He was friends with Pierre Biraben and Water Street CEO Christian Veilleux, and that was it.[36]

Cymrot didn't have to work hard to prove that Water Street had carried out a rapid series of lawsuits against countries in 1994 and 1995, as they had all been filed in the Southern District court, and the records for each were readily available in the clerk's office. The defendants and filing dates were as follows: People's Republic of the Congo on March 18, 1994; Ivory Coast on April 4, 1994; Poland on April 6; 1994, Panama on April 12, 1994; and Ecuador on July 14, 1995.[37]

Cymrot tried to tie Newman to Water Street using two tactics. First, Cymrot established a sequence of events in which Newman had moved to Elliott after both Water Street and Newman's own Percheron Fund had failed in 1995. Bad market conditions in the wake of Mexico's shock 1994 devaluation roiled the market and both entities. The fatal blow came when Judge Harold Baer Jr. dismissed Water Street's case against Panama on February 15, 1995, because the firm refused to disclose the name of its investors. Presumably the wealthy people who invested in Water Street didn't want their names associated with lawsuits against poor countries.[38] Water Street subsequently went into liquidation—one can guess for failing to succeed at its evident buy-and-sue investment strategy.[39] Cymrot's second tactic to link Newman to Water Street was to put the portfolio manager on the stand to prove he was in regular contact with both Straus and his friends at Water Street about the firm's investments and its lawsuits.

Cymrot started by establishing the background of how Newman and Straus met:

> Q. You joined Elliott Associates in approximately September of 1995, is that correct?
>
> A. Yes, September or October.

* * *

Q. And then you introduced Michael Straus to Elliott, is that correct?

A. Yes, that's right.

Q. And you had met Michael Straus in 1993 when he was conducting litigation against Paraguay, is that correct?

A. '92 or '93. And I believe the litigation was over because I think it was as a result of seeing a reported case that I met him.

Q. But you knew him as a trial lawyer?

A. Initially, yes.

Q. And while you knew him he was plaintiff's counsel against Ecuador on behalf of Banque de Gestion Privee, correct?

A. I'm aware of that case, but I don't know anything about it.

Q. But you just knew that he was the plaintiff's lawyer, correct?

A. I know that, yes.

Q. And he was the plaintiff's lawyer on behalf of Water Street?

A. I know that as well, yes.

Q. And so you knew him essentially as a trial lawyer, is that correct?

A. Initially as a trial lawyer. But I came to know him as someone who was very knowledgeable about foreign debt generally. Michael Straus was a lawyer for the Iranian claims tribunal in the Hague and he had a lot of experience dealing in various issues, not just related to litigation.[40]

After this, Cymrot pivoted to asking Newman about when he joined Elliott and their purchases of sovereign debt:

Q. Now, Mr. Newman, isn't it correct that you discussed litigation with Paul Singer in the very first meeting in discussing purchases of Emerging Market debt?

A. No, I don't recall doing that.

Q. You say it didn't occur?

A. Yes, did not occur.

* * *

Q. When Elliott purchased Peruvian debt was one of your strategies that Elliott would demand full payment?

A. No.

Q. When Elliott purchased Peruvian debt was one of your strategies that Elliott would sue Peru and attain full payment?

A. No.[41]

After that, Cymrot asked Newman about his relationship with Water Street's Christian Veilleux and Water Street's lawyer Michael Straus:

Q. Did you give advice to Mr. Veilleux concerning sovereign debt?

A. Yes.

Q. In connection with Water Street?

A. It was—well, yes. It was the time he was running Water Street.

* * *

Q. Did you give Mr. Veilleux advice about purchasing Polish People's Republic debt?

A. I'm pretty sure we discussed Polish debt, yes.

Q. Did you give Mr. Veilleux advice about purchasing Congo debt?

A. I think we discussed virtually every kind of debt that was available in the market, including Congo debt, yes.

Q. And you came to learn that Water Street made investments in Polish debt?

A. I did.

Q. And in Congo debt?

A. I did.

Q. And in Panama debt?

A. Yes.

Q. And in Ivory Coast debt?

A. Yes.

Q. And you gave advice to Mr. Veilleux about Ivory Coast debt?

A. I think we discussed all of those, yes.

Q. And Ecuador debt? Did you give advice to Mr. Veilleux about Ecuador debt?

A. I don't remember specifically, but it's very likely we discussed it, yes.

* * *

Q. You knew that Mr. Straus worked for Water Street?

A. Yes.

Q. As its lawyer?

A. Yes.

Q. You met Mr. Straus in about 1992 or 1993, is that correct?

A. Yes.

Q. And that was shortly before Water Street was created, isn't that correct?

A. Yes.

Q. And over the time that Water Street existed, you spoke to Mr. Straus about Water Street's investments in developing country debt?

A. Yes, from time to time we did.

Q. And you and Mr. Straus also talked about lawsuits that Water Street brought against Ivory Coast, Panama, Ecuador, Poland, is that true?

A. I was certainly aware of them. I don't recall having much detail about them, but I knew about them.

Q. And did you talk to Mr. Straus about those lawsuits?

A. Yes.[42]

Paul Singer Defends Elliott's Business Model

It was during the closing day of the trial that Mark Cymrot recalled Paul Singer to the stand to nail him on the issue of whether his firm "intended" to sue Peru from day one, the testimony that opens this chapter. After that exchange, Cymrot took a swing at Singer's morality by forcing him to admit that he didn't know that 50% of Peruvians had income below the poverty line and that 20% of Peruvians had insufficient resources to meet their daily nutritional requirements. While almost monosyllabic on the topic of why his firm had bought Peruvian debt, Singer responded with a full-throated defense of his reputation and his firm's business:

> As in any country, there are poor people, and without attempting to appear insensitive, obviously in any emerging country it is part of the aggregates. Of course, that is true. When I focused on Peru's poverty, the thing that I mostly thought about it is that when a country like Peru enters or

reenters . . . the world financial community, that the cycle, the virtuous cycle of paying debts, encouraging outside capital to think it can come in, lend
money, invest money, get it back under a system in which the constitution
is not suspended whenever people want it to be suspended, that I thought
that that would be—my general thinking about these matters is that that is
helpful to the people, even the poor people.[43]

Elliott Loses in the District Court but Wins on Appeal

Ultimately Mark Cymrot persuaded Judge Sweet, who ruled that Elliott
purchased Peruvian debt "with the intent and purpose to sue" on August
6, 1998. Sweet also opined that Elliott's intention to sue was "primary"
and not "contingent" or "incidental" to its purpose.

In his ruling, Judge Sweet cited the history of Straus and Newman's
involvement with Water Street. The judge also noted that Straus had set
up a fund called Red Mountain Finance, which sued the Democratic Republic of the Congo in 1997. Sweet said, "Newman and Straus have a long
history of suing sovereigns."[44]

To Elliott's assertion that it had tried to negotiate a settlement with
Peru, Judge Sweet wrote that its efforts were "pretextual and never demonstrated a good faith negotiating position."[45]

Elliott Associates filed an appeal of Judge Sweet's ruling in the Second Circuit Court of Appeals on September 18, 1998,[46] after which it left
no stone unturned in building up its case for reversal. The firm based its
case on an encyclopedic analysis of every champerty case in New York
State history. The firm also made the public policy argument that allowing countries to use a champerty defense to avoid paying sovereign
debt claims would hurt New York as a business center. In support of its
position, Elliott obtained amicus briefs from trade associations and investors, including EMTA, the Bond Market Association, the Commercial
Law League of America, the Loan Syndications and Trading Association,
the firm Angelo Gordon, the Baupost Group, Contrarian Capital Management, Franklin Mutual Advisers, and the Van Eck Associates Corporation.

The Second Circuit's hearing of Elliott's appeal was a lively affair.
During the hearing, Cymrot sparred with Elliott's counsel Otto Obermaier,

Second Circuit judges Joseph McLaughlin and Pierre Leval, and Paul Michel, a judge from the U.S. Court of Appeals for the Federal Circuit who was invited to sit on the panel. All three judges mercilessly attacked Cymrot's reading of the New York State precedents. They were also openly sympathetic to the plaintiff's argument that allowing a champerty defense in a sovereign debt case would be bad for the market.[47]

Just as in the Allied Bank case, the court ruled that sovereign debt must be enforceable. Handing Elliott the victory on October 20, 1999, the court declared that "we hold that, in light of the pertinent New York precedent and compelling policy considerations, the district court erroneously interpreted [the applicable law]. . . . We hold that [New York's champerty statute] is not violated when, as here, the accused party's 'primary goal' is found to be satisfaction of a valid debt and its intent is only to sue absent full performance."[48] The Second Circuit reached the same conclusion that Judge Denny Chin had reached several years before in the Panama case: they did not believe that Elliott had purchased defaulted sovereign loans just for the pleasure of litigation.

The Peru appeal was a great victory for Elliott Associates, particularly after its humiliating defeat in the district court. Moreover, it was a ruling with ancillary benefits. It effectively killed the champerty defense in New York State in all kinds of debt litigation, which would help Elliott's business generally, since the threat of champerty defenses must have often been a worry. From a lemon, Elliott had made lemonade.

The story of *Elliott v. Peru* was far from over, however, as a dispute soon broke out over exactly how much Peru owed the firm.

Peru's $12 Million Surprise

After the Second Circuit's ruling, Elliott Associates submitted to the district court its calculation of how much it was owed: $52 million. This amount shocked Peru, which was expecting the bill to be $40 million, $20 million of unpaid principal and $20 million of past due interest. Elliott was claiming an additional $12 million to cover interest on interest, the time value lost since the missed payments. Peru had thought it was safe from paying interest on interest because Judge Sweet had ruled against Pravin Banker's claim for a similar component in a judgment a few years earlier. In the meantime, however, New York State law had been altered to make it a required component of a debt settlement. Nonetheless, Peru's lawyer Mark Cymrot challenged the extra $12 million on the allegation that Elliott had non-transparently lobbied the New York State Legislature to change the law governing interest on interest in its favor.

Judge Sweet took great interest in Mark Cymrot's allegation. The judge devoted a large chunk of a June 1, 2000, opinion to describing the facts and circumstances as Cymrot had presented them to the court.[49] Sweet ruled, however, that Peru had to pay the extra money: the law was the law, and it had to be obeyed. And on June 22, 2000, Sweet granted Elliott a $55 million judgment against Peru: the $52 million discussed in court plus another $3 million for subsequent accruals of past due interest and interest on interest.[50]

Elliott now moved to collect.

Blitzkrieg on the Brady Bonds

On September 6, 2000, Elliott launched an international blitzkrieg with the aim of forcing Peru to pay its $55 million judgment. Elliott's tactic was to try to block Peru's ability to complete an $80 million payment due on September 7 to the holders of the country's $4 billion in Brady bonds, the bonds issued in 1997 to the holders of its 1980s-era defaulted loans. Elliott simultaneously filed papers in New York, England, Belgium, and Luxembourg asking the courts to grab or block the payment.[51] One can assume that Elliott hit these four jurisdictions because Chase Manhattan Bank, the paying agent for Peru's Brady bonds, had offices in New York and London, and payments were due to go through clearing systems in Belgium and Luxembourg. It was a clever strategy, because Elliott needed to frustrate only a part of Peru's payment to force the country into a corner. Missing even a portion of the amount due would be a default event under the terms of Peru's Brady bonds. This legal strategy gave the firm four ways to win.

Shrewd though this multiprong strategy might have been, Elliott did not enjoy an overnight victory. Peru got wind of the attack and called off the payment, giving the country a month to fight Elliott in court.[52] Like most bonds, Peru's Brady bonds incorporated an automatic thirty-day grace period on interest payments, which would buy the country's lawyers enough time to persuade the relevant courts to dismiss the motions or, in the worst case, time to post a bond with the court to cover amounts due while litigating and appealing the validity of the motion. The odds were that Elliott was looking at either a quick loss or a two-year victory, the time it would take for its case to work its way through the courts.

Victory came quickly for Elliott, however. Peru folded after a Belgian appeals court blocked $47 million of the $80 million due to pass through the country in a ruling made on September 26, 2000.[53] On September 29, 2000, Peru agreed to pay Elliott $58,450,000 in return for the cessation of the litigation,[54] the final payment amount adjusted upward for further accruals of interest and interest on interest (but excluding about $9 million in legal expenses that Elliott had been claiming).

And that was the end of *Elliott v. Peru*.

Muted Aftershocks and the Dispute over the Latin Term "Pari Passu"

Elliott's attack on Peru was big news in the market for a few weeks, but interest faded once the settlement was reached. The ruling vexed legal scholars, however, who wrote articles in law journals warning of trouble ahead. Duke University professor Mitu Gulati wrote, "What the Brussels Opinion does is to put a large hammer in the hands of holdout creditors."[55] At the same time, Gulati and others argued that the Belgian ruling was simply wrong. A Belgian appeals court wasn't the right court to interpret a New York law contract, the ruling was approved following an ex parte hearing (one to which Peru's lawyers were not invited), and the court had misread Peru's loan contract. In particular, the scholars argued, the Belgian court's ruling on the pari passu clause in Peru's loans was incorrect. Because almost all sovereign bonds (and loans) have such a clause, pretty much all sovereign debt issuers could be at risk to such holdout-favorable rulings if the Belgian interpretation became accepted in courts around the world. That's what had the scholars worried, that the Belgian ruling they disagreed with might not end up being a one-off event. And they were right to worry.

The meaning of the Latin phrase "pari passu" was the crux of the matter. In English, it translates as "in equal step," which Elliott took to mean equal payment in its argument to the Belgian court. In other words, whenever Peru made a payment to any of its bondholders, it would have to pay all its bondholders any amounts that were due, regardless of whether they had accepted a restructuring deal or held out. By this logic, if Peru made a payment on its performing Brady bonds, it would also be obliged to pay any amounts due on the defaulted Peruvian loans Elliott held. As the firm's expert witness, New York University professor Andreas Lowenfeld, told the court, "A borrower from Tom, Dick, and Harry can't say 'I will pay Tom and Dick in full, and if there is anything left over I'll pay Harry.' If there is not enough money to go around, the borrower faced with a pari passu provision must pay all three of them on the same basis."[56]

The genius of Elliott's pari passu argument was that it linked the equal payments interpretation of the clause to the demand for a blockade on Peru's payments to its Brady bond holders. If the court accepted the equal payments interpretation, they would be almost obliged to impose the blockade to prevent further selective nonpayment of holdout creditors. The legal scholars countered that pari passu was about equal ranking, not equal payment, and so the blockade remedy was not justified.[57] Ranking obligations and payment obligations are two distinct contractual features of credit instruments, the scholars argued, and should not be conflated. An equal ranking clause, they pointed out, prohibits a country from issuing a new bond that is higher ranked than an old bond if that old bond has a pari passu clause protecting its holders. Such a higher-ranking bond issuance would cause an instantaneous violation of the clause. According to the scholars, the pari passu clause covered only this specific scenario and had nothing to do with unequal payments. The meaning of the clause hadn't been litigated in the United States, however, and the language of the clauses found in various loan and bond agreements were not entirely clear on their intended meaning. Pari passu in any particular instance could mean equal ranking or could mean equal payments. It would depend on the wording of a particular country's clause. This ambiguity gave Elliott room to argue that the equal payments interpretation applied to Peru's and Argentina's debt. Scholars derided Elliott's reading of the pari passu clause as a "novel interpretation" in academic articles and court papers. The ambiguity did not go away, however, and the courts in the Argentina litigation used this lack of clarity to justify ruling against Argentina even though the market, if asked at the time of issuance, probably would have said the equal ranking interpretation should be the one to apply.[58]

Legal scholars were not the only ones who were vexed by the Peru ruling. Policy makers in Washington were concerned about it too. The IMF kept its eye on sovereign debt litigation, which was on a worrying upward trend. First Deputy Managing Director Anne Krueger even used the events in Peru as an argument in favor of the SDRM in her famous "gaping hole" speech, the one that starts off this book.[59] The market was skeptical, however, with creditor organizations arguing that Peru was a one-off, not a sign of things to come.[60] That said, Argentina was somewhat worried in 2003 as it inched closer to bringing its deal to the market. Although Argentine government officials agreed with the legal scholars that it was a bad ruling in the wrong court, a U.S. court could theoretically rule a similar way. Argentina's team thought that Elliott's interpretation of the pari passu clause was a "black swan," that is, an unpredictable event that is beyond what is normally expected of a situation and that has severe consequences. Nonetheless, it was a black swan that had to be killed, and two weeks after Argentina first presented its debt restructuring proposal in Dubai, Argentina's lawyers put in motion a plan to do just that.

Argentina Tries and Fails to Kill the Pari Passu Black Swan

On October 2, 2003, in an effort to head off a potential pari passu attack, Argentina's lawyer Jonathan Blackman wrote a letter to Kenneth Dart's lawyer:

I am writing because I have heard reports that EM Ltd/Dart is planning to attempt to disrupt payment streams on restructured debt of
the Republic of Argentina and/or performing debt to multilateral
institutions (e.g., the I.M.F.) and others. These reports indicate that
EM/Dart will attempt to enjoin payment by the Republic to other
creditors on the ground that any such payment while EM remains
unpaid would violate the "pari passu" clause in [Argentina's bonds].
The Republic believes this interpretation of [the clause] is without
merit under New York law because, inter alia, the pari passu clause
addresses the creation of legal priorities, and not the order of payment of the Republic's general unsecured debt.[61]

Dart's lawyers shot back the next day. On October 3, David Rivkin wrote
to Jonathan Blackman:

I write in brief response to your letter of yesterday. You refer to "reports" you have heard about various means that EM Ltd. may employ
to collect on the judgment it recently obtained. I am not sure what
reports you are referring to, and we are certainly not going to accept
your invitation to reveal our litigation strategy to you. However, I can
assure you that we intend to take whatever steps are necessary and
appropriate to collect on the judgment.[62]

On October 14, Argentina's lawyers escalated the pari passu issue to Judge
Griesa, who held a preliminary hearing on the topic later that month.[63] In
December, he called a second hearing on the matter for January 15, 2004.
All the early plaintiffs attended this hearing, including Dart and clients
represented by Guillermo Gleizer, Moss & Kalish, and Marc Dreier.[64]

    Three days before the hearing, Argentina delivered what should have
been a knockout blow to pari passu: amicus briefs from the U.S. government, the New York Clearing House Association, and the Federal Reserve
Bank of New York, all in favor of the equal-ranking interpretation of the
clause.[65] Argentina's hope was that these briefs would do for pari passu
what the amicus brief from the New York Clearing House Association
had done in the Allied Bank case: drive the decision of the court to its

favor. Argentina was in a very strong position going into the January 15 hearing.

The day before the hearing, however, a relatively new plaintiff showed up to spoil the party, its lawyers delivering a letter to Judge Griesa detailing why he shouldn't rule on pari passu the next day.[66] The entity was NML Capital, Ltd., a Cayman Islands corporation that owned about $172 million in defaulted Argentine bonds and had filed its complaint against Argentina on November 7, 2003.[67] Elliott's name was not disclosed in NML's filing, but since the letter its lawyers delivered to Griesa repeated all the arguments that Elliott had used against Peru in Belgium, it wasn't hard to guess the author.

The substantial legal argument in NML's January 14, 2004, letter was that Argentina was bringing forward the pari passu issue, not the plaintiffs. Under the U.S. Constitution, judges are only empowered to decide live "cases and controversies." Argentina was fishing for an "advisory opinion" to head off a possible claim under the clause, and pursuant to the Constitution, U.S. judges do not give advisory opinions. In legal language, NML—that is, Elliott— argued that the issue was not "ripe" for adjudication. At the hearing the next day Judge Griesa agreed, putting a stop to Argentina's effort to kill the pari passu black swan in advance of its debt restructuring transaction.

Argentina didn't get what it asked for that day, but it did get something important. After listening to the country's lawyer, Jonathan Blackman, recite the entire history of the Peru saga, Judge Griesa said in open court that he thought that the Belgian court had used a "very odd interpretation" of the pari passu clause in making its ruling.[68] This statement dealt a big blow to investors hoping that Griesa would lean toward Elliott on the matter. Investor research reports for more than a year had been openly talking about the possibility of holding out and using Elliott's pari passu strategy against Argentina. Griesa's "very odd interpretation" remark must have quashed such thinking for all but the die-hard believers, that is, those working on Elliott's team and some closely affiliated funds. Nonetheless, Griesa did leave the issue open. Argentina's pari passu black swan was only wounded and lived to fly another day.

5

Raid on the Argentine Central Bank

(December 2005–January 2007)

Asked why he robbed banks, Willie Sutton apocryphally told a reporter "because that's where the money is."[1] For the same reason, a common target in sovereign debt litigation is a country's central bank, especially since most central banks hold deposits with the Federal Reserve Bank of New York (the New York Fed), which is just a short walk down the street from the District Court for the Southern District of New York (the Southern District).[2] That said, it's significantly harder to break into a country's central bank with a court order than it is to rob a downtown bank with a handgun and a note: the Foreign Sovereign Immunities Act (FSIA) gives foreign central bank reserves nearly bulletproof immunity.

Thanks to this statutory protection, the Central Bank of Argentina should not have been at the top of creditors' lists of potential attachment targets. President Néstor Kirchner put it there in December 2005, however, when he announced that Argentina had decided to escape from IMF oversight by repaying the IMF in full.[3] At the time a strong economy had bolstered the country's ability to build up its foreign reserves, so President Kirchner signed two decrees ordering the Central Bank of Argentina to pay $9.9 billion of its assets to the IMF.[4] The opportunity for creditors was that these two decrees were written in a way that appeared to blow the central bank's special immunity.

Under the FSIA, protection of a country's foreign reserves is limited to property of a foreign central bank held for its own account. But Argentina's two decrees split its reserves into two parts, one to be used by the central bank for its own account and the other to be used to repay the IMF.

Just fifteen days after President Kirchner triumphantly announced the repayment of the IMF, creditors claimed in court that the funds earmarked for repaying the IMF were attachable. Specifically, they argued that the "excess reserves"—the part Kirchner set aside to repay the IMF—were no longer property of the Central Bank of Argentina but were instead property of the Republic of Argentina and thus subject to attachment under the law.

Freezing Order

On December 30, 2005, lawyers for Elliott Associates' NML Capital, Ltd. and Dart's EM Ltd. asked for an emergency hearing with a judge, which was granted. It was an ex parte hearing, so Argentina's lawyers were not invited. At the hearing, NML's and EM's lawyers asked Judge Barbara Jones to attach Argentina's central bank money held at the New York Fed or in New York commercial banks or both on the theory that Kirchner's recent decrees compromised the central bank's immunity. As is conventional when asking for ex parte orders, they argued for an immediate attachment of the funds on the grounds that if Argentina heard about it, the country would take the targeted funds out of the United States. Judge Jones signed the orders.[5]

These papers were served on the Federal Reserve Bank of New York and the top international banks with offices in New York City probably within the hour. Argentina's foreign reserves in New York were now frozen. The catch, however, was meager: only $105 million at the New York Fed and nothing at the commercial banks, for a total of just 0.38% of Argentina's $27 billion of foreign reserves.[6] Fearing such an order, the central bank had long since moved virtually all the country's foreign reserves to the Bank for International Settlements (BIS) in Switzerland, a bankers' bank that enjoys strict immunity under Swiss law.[7] Moving funds to the BIS is what countries do before they default; it's standard operating procedure. Argentina was hardly the first to move its assets preemptively to the BIS, nor would it be the last, but this shift was treated as anything but ordinary in the litigation that followed.

Furthermore, the attachment order freezing the $105 million at the New York Fed was only temporary. It would have to be confirmed at a hearing that would include two-way argument about whether the attachment was legally valid, and that hearing would have to take place within about two weeks.

The Confirmation Hearing at the District Court

The battle over whether NML and EM could keep their attachment on the $105 million at the New York Fed commenced at 4:00 p.m. on January 12, 2006. On the creditors' side were David Rivkin from Debevoise & Plimpton for EM and Robert Cohen from Dechert for NML. Taking Argentina's side were Jonathan Blackman from Cleary Gottlieb for the republic and Joseph Neuhaus from Sullivan & Cromwell for Banco Central de la República Argentina (the Central Bank of Argentina).

The hearing was contentious from the moment it began. Triggering the first tussle of the day, Judge Griesa asked, "Who wants to lead off?"

Rivkin, for EM, signaled that the creditors should go first by shouting out "Since it's our attachment!"

Neuhaus, for Argentina, simultaneously challenged with "It's our motion!"

"Let's hear the affirmative in favor of the attachment,"[8] Judge Griesa ruled.

Before allowing Rivkin to commence, the judge warned the lawyers from both sides that he'd read their briefs and would cut off their arguments if he found them redundant.

Rivkin waved a certified translation of President Kirchner's two December 15 decrees in the air. He read them out loud, explaining that they split the country's foreign reserves into two parts: a portion necessary for protecting the country's currency and "excess reserves" that would be used to repay the IMF. Rivkin argued that the excess reserves portion had lost its immunity because it was no longer property of the central bank being used for central banking purposes but was instead the government's money being used to pay off competing creditors.[9]

The exact wording of Kirchner's decrees supported Rivkin's interpretation, although to win the attorney would have to jump through two additional hoops. First, he would have to prove that the $105 million caught in New York was part of Argentina's "excess" reserves and thus property of the government and not being retained for normal central banking purposes. Second, he'd have to prove that Argentina's planned repayment of the IMF was a "commercial activity," a requirement for the funds to be attachable under the FSIA.

Shortly after Rivkin launched into his argument, Judge Griesa cut him short, jumping in when the lawyer asserted that the repayment of the IMF was a "textbook example" of a commercial activity.

"Why is that a textbook example?" Judge Griesa challenged.

"Because the Supreme Court said so in the *Weltover* case," Rivkin responded, referring to a U.S. Supreme Court ruling from the early 1990s in which the court opined that the repayment of commercial debts is an attachable activity.

"Really?" Judge Griesa said, questioning the applicability of *Weltover*. Rivkin explained:

There's no difference, your Honor, between the debt which they, Argentina, owed to us and the debt which Argentina owed to the IMF. In both cases they borrowed money, which is the same that a private person can do. . . . So, your Honor, we think we have properly attached funds which are the government of Argentina's. We don't think any basis for immunity applies to the funds we have attached, and we would ask you to confirm the attachment in place.

Judge Griesa responded, "Look, the $105 million in the Federal Reserve Bank here deposited by the central bank was not actually used to pay the IMF, right?" He thus suggested that the money hadn't been used for a commercial activity, which is what would have made it attachable.

"That is what they say. That is their assertion," [10] Rivkin answered.

After Rivkin finished, NML's lawyer Robert Cohen presented a second reason as to why Argentina's $105 million was not immune, arguing that the country had waived its sovereign immunity in its bond contracts. Reading from the bond documents, Cohen said that Argentina had "irrevocably agreed not to claim and has irrevocably waived such immunity to the fullest extent permitted."[11] This argument, it seems, was tailored to aggravate Judge Griesa. It was well known—and backed by Supreme Court precedent—that such a waiver must specifically list the country's central bank for its immunity to be compromised, which was not the case here. Cohen also tacked on a completely specious argument that a different part of the bond document, referring to local law matters, provided a specific waiver.

Taking the bait, Argentina's Jonathan Blackman shot up to speak.

"Your Honor," he said, "I was not planning on taking the floor . . . but I am going to take it because what Mr. Cohen just said is so radically wrong as to almost be beyond belief."

"Mr. Cohen, you're beyond belief—" Judge Griesa mimicked, evidently annoyed with Blackman's rhetoric.

Blackman persisted:

> The reason I say that, your Honor, and I try not to indulge in hyperbole, is this is the Republic's waiver and the Republic's bond. It's not a waiver of the central bank's immunity. . . . There's no piece of paper in which the Republic says I hereby waive the central bank's immunity. . . . What is clear on this record is that there was no intention to use the money at the Fed for this payment for the IMF, nor was it used.[12]

Blackman added that while the funds in New York had "ebbed and flowed" over the years, they had always been used for central banking activities such as buying and selling currencies and receiving reserve deposits of Argentine banks.[13]

After Blackman finished, the Central Bank of Argentina's lawyer, Joseph Neuhaus, reiterated that the waiver of sovereign immunity had been given by the Republic of Argentina, not the Central Bank of Argentina, explaining to Judge Griesa that the Supreme Court had ruled that waivers of sovereign immunity by central banks must be explicit if they are to have force.[14] Neuhaus used the bulk of his time explaining that Argentina's central bank assets were not attachable because of the special immunity provided to central bank assets under the FSIA.

On rebuttal, Rivkin lobbed a gently worded stinker at Argentina: "I found it amusing when Mr. Blackman talked about the ebb and flow of central bank money" in the New York account. "They have clearly taken $2 billion out of the country, and if—"

"What about that?" Judge Griesa interrupted.

Rivkin explained:

Last February . . . we found a press report that showed that they had removed money from the U.S. to the BIS, Bank for International Settlements in Switzerland. . . . And at the time . . . they had more than $2 billion in the central bank accounts in the United States. And we know now that on December 30th when we served the order of attachment they had only [$105] million. So, we know that's not an ebb and flow, your Honor, that is taking money out of the country to take it out of the reach of creditors like ourselves, to take it out of your jurisdiction, despite your order to Argentina not to do so.

Blackman shot up: "Could I respond for two seconds to that, your Honor?"[15]

A lengthy exchange between Blackman, Rivkin, and Judge Griesa followed. At issue was when and why Argentina had moved money out of the United States. Animating the conversation was Griesa's prior order to the Republic of Argentina not to remove assets from the country. Accusing Argentina of systematically moving central bank assets from the New York Fed to the BIS was an accusation that Argentina had violated a specific court order. To this emotive accusation, Blackman argued that the Central Bank of Argentina was a separate legal entity from the Republic of Argentina and thus not subject to Griesa's order. Furthermore, Blackman added, the country's foreign reserves were immune, regardless.

Blackman's defense of Argentina's actions was on point, but Rivkin's allegation hit home with Judge Griesa's sense of fair play.

"What do you want to do about that?" Judge Griesa asked Rivkin.

"That's past history," Rivkin said. "What I want to do, your Honor, is keep the $105 million that we have now attached and not lose benefit of that."[16]

A Rant and a Ruling

The arguments from both sides completed, it was time for Judge Griesa to decide what to do about the $105 million frozen down the street at the New York Fed. His options were to make a ruling ("decide the matter"), announce that he needed more time to think about how to rule ("reserve"), or kick the can down the road by asking for additional briefs, further argument, or more information.

Judge Griesa chose to rule. The facts and the law were clear, and Argentina had the better argument: the central bank reserves were immune under the black letter of the law, that is, the text of the FSIA. Griesa had something on his mind, however. He was angry at Argentina, and he didn't want to give the country an unblemished victory. For one, Rivkin's and Cohen's arguments had resonated with him. Griesa was perturbed that Argentina was using sovereign immunity to avoid paying debts, and he was upset at the allegation that it had moved money out of his jurisdiction to avoid attachment.

Judge Griesa was also annoyed that Argentina seemed to be playing games with retail investors' right to sue, which grated on his sense of fair play. The country had recently appealed two of his rulings that found that plaintiffs' brokerage statements were sufficient proof of ownership to sue.[17] Argentina also wanted these plaintiffs to provide confirmation of ownership from the top-level bond depository, the Depository Trust Corporation, that its lawyers said was needed to prevent fraud—which actually occurred in three cases as was uncovered many years later.[18] Griesa thought the issue should have been settled in his courtroom, not on appeal, and he thought it was being used as a delaying tactic and to curtail the rights of small investors.

Demonstrating his agitation, Judge Griesa let loose a lengthy rant that not only spoke to the topics of the day but also indicated—for the first time—a marked change in his sympathies. He was now showing more affinity with the investors who had opted out of Argentina's transaction.

Let me put something on the record. Part of the big picture to me is that we have lawsuits in this Court based on bonds and related agreements in which the Republic, in order to induce investors to buy the bonds, made very broad waivers of sovereign immunity, agreed to the jurisdiction in this Court, and presumably that was supposed to mean something.

What has been demonstrated by these lawsuits is how little it means. The Republic has done everything possible to avoid the fruition of the lawsuits it agreed to have brought. The Republic at one point made arguments about the standing of [some retail plaintiffs to sue] and then went up to the Court of Appeals and there was a remand. After the remand the issue dissolved completely because it was never a substantial issue.

The Republic has done everything possible to prevent the collection of these debts in these lawsuits. Of course, there [was] an offer of an agreement to bondholders; if they [would] take a certain cut, they [could] have new bonds and so forth. That's fine. But the Republic originally agreed to be sued. There's no question about the right of these plaintiffs, if they establish ownership of the bond, to get judgments.

Now the next question is: Can there be any recovery on the judgments? So far it looks as if it is virtually hopeless. There's not a whimper of an idea that the Republic might pay the judgments which they really should pay. There was an absolute agreement permitting suit and it was certainly implicit that those lawsuits would be handled in a way that, if the lawsuits were valid, which they are, [and] it was implicit that there could be collection, and the Republic is doing everything possible to frustrate that.

Now when I say everything possible, the Republic is represented by very good lawyers and very honorable lawyers who are representing their clients. The Republic has a right to raise all legal defenses. But what it illustrates is that these lawsuits may ultimately be illusory. The agreement for jurisdiction and to waive sovereign immunity may be ultimately totally illusory. And that's quite unfortunate.[19]

On the issue at hand, however, Judge Griesa sided with Argentina:

> I regret to say that I do not think that the attachment can stand. And I very much regret that because it simply illustrates the fact that despite all this high sounding waiver of sovereign immunity and so forth in connection with the bonds, when it comes down to it, so far it's an illusion, and I regret that. . . . But the law is the law, and what we have here is an attachment and a restraint relating to $105 million deposited by the Central Bank of Argentina in the Federal Reserve Bank in New York City.[20]

Now, in rapid fire, Judge Griesa rattled off his legal conclusions about what had been argued that day: Argentina's waiver of sovereign immunity did not compromise the central bank assets, repaying the IMF was not a commercial activity, and Argentina's $105 million at the Fed was property of the Argentine central bank and was being used for central banking functions. In short, he granted the central bank's motion to terminate the attachment.

Argentina won, though only in part, because on a motion from the creditors, Judge Griesa stayed the release of the $105 million at the New York Fed pending an appeal of his ruling to the Second Circuit Court of Appeals. Argentina's money was still frozen, although by virtue of a stipulation signed by the parties the week before, the funds could be used to process day-to-day transactions, provided the balance was maintained.

The Foreign Sovereign Immunities Act §1609, §1610, and §1611

The discussion was more technical when Elliott and Dart's appeal reached the Second Circuit. Instead of discussing the issues in plain English as the lawyers did in Judge Griesa's court, the circuit court judges referred to the section numbers in the FSIA as shorthand for the legal concepts under discussion. As such, it is necessary to review the text of the FSIA before proceeding to the circuit court. The key issues, as before, were whether repaying the IMF was a "commercial activity" and whether an extra layer of immunity applied to central bank assets.

The FSIA begins with the presumption that all sovereign assets are immune from attachment unless a specific exception applies. Creditors typically claim that an asset is being "used for a commercial activity," which compromises its immunity, rendering it attachable. These two principles are codified in 28 U.S. Code §1609, which specifies that foreign government property in the United States is generally immune from attachment, and §1610, which states that sovereign assets "used for a commercial activity in the United States" lose their immunity from attachment.[21]

According to the courts, a commercial activity is one that any player in the market can undertake.[22] If a country buys a tank of oil located in the United States, for example, that purchase is a commercial activity and is therefore attachable. On the other hand, if the country holds funds at a U.S. bank for the exclusive purpose of paying the salaries of its diplomats, that money is being used for a governmental activity, because paying diplomats is something that only governments do. That embassy account is not attachable.

Complicating matters, another layer of immunity applies to assets controlled by a foreign country's central bank or military authorities, a stipulation Congress added to prevent the diplomatic problems that would result if creditors could attach such assets. Section 28 U.S. Code §1611 grants this special immunity, with §1611 part (b)(1) stating that property of a foreign central bank is immune if it is "held for its own account" and §1611(b)(2) adding that foreign sovereign property is immune if it "is, or is intended to be, used in connection with a military activity and A) is of a military character, or B) is under the control of a military authority or defense agency."

Enter the Second Circuit

The Second Circuit Court of Appeals Thurgood Marshall U.S. Courthouse is located just about forty feet from the back door of the Daniel Patrick Moynihan Federal Courthouse that houses the Southern District. Yet, in terms of how they dispense justice, these two courts couldn't be further apart.

While district court hearings are often scrappy and raucous, the atmosphere at the Second Circuit is usually hushed and scholarly. It's also
a place where every word and every second matters. Because of the high
volume of cases handled by the appeals courts, hearings usually last only
about half an hour. Time is doled out ungenerously: each side typically
gets about ten minutes to argue, with the appellant able to reserve two or
three of its minutes for rebuttal. These limits are strictly enforced with
the help of a bar of lights: a green one for when a lawyer starts arguing,
a yellow one for when there are two minutes left, and a red one when
time's up.

Proceedings at the Second Circuit are also quite formal. It is not the
place for an attorney to rant or spew rhetoric at opposing counsel, although it's possible to get in a jab here or there. The lawyers are also
particularly formal in addressing the judges. Argentina's lawyer Jonathan
Blackman often used the phrase "with all due respect, your Honor" when
countering an argument made by one of the circuit court judges, for example. Reinforcing the formality, the judges' bench is so high off the floor
that the lawyers at the podium have to crane their necks to see the judges.
It's humbling just to watch.

The Central Bank Case at the Second Circuit

At 12:50 p.m. on August 29, 2006, the Second Circuit commenced its
hearing of NML and EM's appeal of Judge Griesa's January 12 ruling vacating the attachment on the $105 million of Argentine central bank money
held at the New York Fed. Judge José Cabranes chaired the session, with
Judge Rosemary Pooler at his side and senior judge Ralph Winter dialing
in from the New Haven courthouse.[23] The hearing clocked in at around
120 minutes.[24]

During the hearing, Judge Cabranes and Judge Pooler tag-teamed
the lawyers arguing below them. Cabranes played the scholar, analytically
dissecting NML's and EM's legal arguments as if out of purely intellectual
interest, while Pooler needled the soft spots in Argentina's case.

Since they represented the appellants, counsel for NML and EM argued first, with David Rivkin talking for EM and Roy Englert from Robbins Russell speaking for NML. Englert was a ringer, an appellate specialist brought in to increase the odds of victory. A judo enthusiast, he boasts a math degree from Princeton (1978) and a JD cum laude from Harvard (1981). He was the executive editor of the *Harvard Law Review*, and as of the time of publication, he had enjoyed eighteen wins at the Supreme Court.[25] When it came to hiring lawyers for a hearing, Elliott always brought in the best of the best.

From the start, Judge Cabranes and Judge Pooler showed that they were not convinced by Rivkin's and Englert's arguments. Englert got only about ten sentences out before Judge Cabranes, channeling Socrates, started peppering him with a series of questions about the logic of his case.

Judge Cabranes asked, "The account at issue was in the name of the Banco Central de la República Argentina, right?"

Englert replied, "Correct."

"Why isn't that the end of the issue?" Judge Cabranes asked, suggesting that the creditors had no recourse to the central bank's property because the suit was against the Republic of Argentina, the obligor of the bonds, not against the central bank.

When Englert tried to press his argument, Judge Cabranes interrupted him again and, pointing to the amicus brief the New York Fed wrote in favor of Argentina's position, asked, "Why wouldn't we as a court of the United States, if we had any question at all about the statutory situation, why couldn't we simply defer to the judgment of the Federal Reserve Bank of New York?"[26]

Shortly after that, Judge Cabranes said, "Why don't you turn to the commercial activity issue. Your second issue."[27]

Englert now tried to assert that the repayment of debt was a commercial activity and thus subject to seizure under §1610 of the FSIA.

Judge Cabranes interrupted yet again. "Why isn't Argentina transacting business with the International Monetary Fund a sovereign act as opposed to a commercial act?"[28]

Englert reiterated that paying the IMF was a commercial act, but he got no traction.

When it was his turn, Rivkin tried to make the same point, but Judge Cabranes cut him off: "Don't you think that the proposition you're asserting would come as something of a shock to Central Bankers?"[29]

Judge Cabranes finished him off, saying that the plaintiffs' legal brief had failed to cite even one legal precedent to prove its assertions.

At the halfway mark, NML and EM's case was all but dead.

Argentina and the Central Bank of Argentina fielded the same team it had in the district court: Jonathan Blackman for the republic and Joseph Neuhaus for the central bank. On this day they were also joined by Serrin Turner, an assistant U.S. attorney for the Southern District of New York, who weighed in for Argentina on behalf of the U.S. government as amicus curiae.

Central bank lawyer Neuhaus went first. He managed just a few lines before Judge Pooler started to poke. She didn't like the decrees.

"Didn't the decrees," Pooler asked in a friendly voice, "change the character of the property?"[30]

Neuhaus responded that regardless of ownership, repaying the IMF is a "classical" central bank activity, and thus the funds were immune.

Judge Pooler persisted. "If it's a classical central bank function what does it need a decree for?"[31]

Neuhaus countered that decree was just a form of payment instruction from one part of the government to another.

Stepping in, Judge Cabranes prompted Neuhaus to reiterate his strongest argument by asking him to explain how the immunity for a central bank was different from that of its parent government. Neuhaus answered the question but also used the opportunity to point out that the $105 million in New York was never intended to be used to repay the IMF.

At this point it looked like an open-and-shut case.

Judge Cabranes then threw a curveball at Neuhaus in the form of a hypothetical: "Assume for the argument that the decree did indicate that the funds of the Banco Central at the Federal Reserve Bank of New York were intended to be used to repay the IMF. Assume that, *arguendo*. How would that affect your position?"[32]

"The funds would still not be attachable," Neuhaus responded, "because the Republic is still a stranger to the account here at the Fed."[33] That is, as a distinct legal entity, the central bank was not liable for the republic's debts.

Adding a new dimension to the debate, Judge Cabranes next asked whether the immunity of the central bank assets would be compromised if all the bank's money was in fact completely controlled by the Argentine government and thus actually the republic's.

Neuhaus responded, "I think you can get there through an alter ego argument."[34]

That's the answer Judge Cabranes seemed to be fishing for. His question was akin to asking if the nice, well-behaved Dr. Jekyll (the central bank) was really the same person as Mr. Hyde (the Republic of Argentina). If that were the case, the two could be considered the same legal entity—alter egos—and that would make the central bank's assets attachable for the payment of the republic's debts.

In response, Neuhaus gave two reasons why the Central Bank of Argentina should win the argument against attachment even if an alter ego relationship was found. His first was procedural. Elliott's NML and Dart's EM could have but failed to assert the alter ego theory, so it was too late to bring it up. His second reason was to reiterate the argument he made to Judge Pooler: repaying the IMF was not a commercial activity because it was a classical central bank activity performed only by governments, so the attachment would fail under §1610 of the FSIA.

When Neuhaus finished, Serrin Turner, the U.S. government's lawyer, stepped up to the podium to support Argentina's position. In a stiff bureaucratic monotone Turner said,

> The United States does not routinely enter into litigation brought under the Foreign Sovereign Immunities Act, but we have done so here [because NML and EM's interpretation of the statute] is misguided and can do considerable harm to U.S. interests. Plaintiff's interpretation of 1610 would undermine the ability of the IMF to perform its vital role in the global economy;

and their interpretation of 1611 would undermine security for the reserves
and deposits in this country with potentially serious repercussions for the
U.S. economy's [role in the] international system.[35]

Judge Cabranes asked, "Is it your position" that if payments to the IMF
are ruled not a commercial activity under §1610, "that that would end the
inquiry?"

"Absolutely," replied Turner.[36]

Blackman, the republic's lawyer, opened his argument with a jab, saying that Elliott "never loaned a penny to Argentina. It bought debt in the
secondary market at a steep discount knowing that Argentina was in financial difficulties."[37] One of Blackman's central points was that the cases
were in court not because Argentina was a deadbeat but instead because
Elliott and Dart were trying to game the court system to make excess
profits. As such, Blackman argued, the court should strictly interpret the
law, which was designed to make it hard to collect from sovereigns and
foreign central banks, saying that the plaintiffs "have to take the bitter
with the sweet and they have to play by the rules, and the rules here are
rules of the Foreign Sovereign Immunities Act. And, as my colleagues
have pointed out, those rules under both §1610 and §1611 don't permit the
attachment of this account."[38]

Judge Cabranes's Alter Ego

Judge Cabranes's suggestion that the Central Bank of Argentina could be
the alter ego of the republic had a rapid and indelible effect on the litigation. Alter ego theory turns the normal assessment of sovereign liability
on its head. The assets of state-owned entities are not generally available
to repay a state's debts. If a state-owned enterprise, such as an airline, is
set up as an independent legal entity, for example, and is not under the
government's day-to-day control, the law treats it as an unrelated party. If
that is the case, the government's creditors can't look to that enterprise for
repayment of the government's debts following a default. If, however, the

government doesn't keep a state-owned entity at arm's length, alter ego theory comes into play.

In 1983, the Supreme Court addressed this issue in *First National City Bank v. Banco Para El Comercio Exterior de Cuba (Bancec)*. In this ruling, the court said that sovereign corporate entities were entitled to a presumption of independent status. "Freely ignoring the separate status of government instrumentalities would result in substantial uncertainty over whether an instrumentality's assets would be diverted to satisfy a claim against the sovereign, and might thereby cause third parties to hesitate before extending credit to a government instrumentality without the government's guarantee." The court added a caveat, however: "Where a corporate entity is so extensively controlled by its owner that a relationship of principal and agent is created," one may be held liable for the actions of the other. The court also specified that the legal wall separating a country from its corporate entities could be broken down when not doing so "would work fraud or injustice."[39]

Bancec thus sets out the two items NML and EM would have had to prove in order to win an alter ego claim against the Central Bank of Argentina: a principal-agent relationship and a fraud or injustice. To make that claim, however, they would have to first solve a procedural problem. The courts generally require parties to lay out all their arguments in writing before hearings are held or forever hold their peace, and in this case the firms had failed to bring an alter ego claim in a timely fashion. Mitigating NML and EM's procedural failure was Judge Cabranes's interest in the topic; his comments in court suggested that the circuit court might entertain a fresh claim. Within a month, Elliott's NML and Dart's EM filed a new joint complaint against the Central Bank of Argentina, seeking a ruling from Judge Griesa that it was the alter ego of the Republic of Argentina and asking for a new set of attachment orders on the $105 million at the New York Fed.[40] This new complaint was filed before the Second Circuit had ruled on their appeal, which had just been heard. The idea was that these new orders would replace the firms' existing attachment orders, which would disappear if the Second Circuit ruled against NML and EM on their pending appeal, which seemed likely. The question was whether Griesa would allow this new effort to attach the same asset to proceed.

Judge Griesa Asks Where the Cases Are Going

On November 3, 2006, Judge Griesa held a telephone hearing with the lawyers for Argentina, the Central Bank of Argentina, NML, and EM to discuss the plaintiffs' newly filed alter ego complaint against the central bank. It was a technical conversation focused on whether, at least temporarily, Elliott and Dart should be allowed to overlay a second attachment on the $105 million at the New York Fed to keep the assets frozen in case the appeals court ruled against them. The interesting part of the hearing came after the technical discussion was over, when Griesa asked the parties on the call where all the cases were going.[41]

What was on Judge Griesa's mind was whether the holdout cases were worth the effort the plaintiffs were making. The case against the central bank was failing, so why try again especially when everyone knew that efforts to attach the assets of foreign sovereigns typically fail? Always mindful of the efficient use of the resources of the federal court system, Griesa must also have been wondering how much more of his time would be spent overseeing fruitless legal activity. Would it be worth years of effort if it all led nowhere?

At the end of the telephone hearing, Judge Griesa announced that he was scheduling a hearing in his chambers for all the parties in all the lawsuits to come together to discuss the direction of the litigation as a whole. He said, "I think we've got to get serious about figuring out what is going to happen to these lawsuits. There are lots of them. And my chambers are occupied and have been for some years with a lot of activity processing these motions, and I want to know for what purpose."[42]

Judge Griesa had another issue on his mind too, which he also brought up. As he had begun to demonstrate in the central bank hearing earlier in the year, he was increasingly frustrated at his lack of power to compel Argentina to show some flexibility toward the holdouts, and he was frustrated with Argentina's use of the FSIA as a shield to avoid honoring his judgments. Griesa complained,

> We talk about this hundred million dollars and Mr. Neuhaus was articulating all kinds of reasons why the attachment can't be pursued. But I will tell you that one of the things I am going to consider in connection with any procedure before me is the fact that these plaintiffs have judgments pursuant to the provisions of the bonds, and it seems to me that the federal court system had ought to give some consideration to a way to enforce those judgments. That's very difficult and it may end up there is no way. But as a federal judge on these cases I don't like to think that.[43]

The important word here was "ought." Judge Griesa was making a statement of his judicial philosophy: creditors should be paid, even creditors that strategically held out of sovereign debt deals and used the courts as leverage to negotiate a better payout for themselves than the creditors who had accepted the official offering. The contrast between Griesa's attitude toward Elliott in this case and Judge Sweet's attitude toward Elliott in the Peru case couldn't have been starker: Griesa indicated that the court ought to help the holdouts, while Sweet, at a similar juncture, quoted Simone Weil waxing poetically about the duality of bankruptcy. In this case, Elliott was lucky to have drawn Griesa, even if it took the judge a few years to come around to the plaintiffs' way of seeing things.

Jonathan Blackman and Robert Cohen Respond

At the end of the November 3 conference call, Argentina's lawyer Jonathan Blackman gave an impromptu answer to Judge Griesa's question about where all the cases were going:

> We all wish that there had never been this financial crisis. We all wish that the bonds could have been paid according to their original tenor.
>
> I think, as I told your Honor the first time we saw you on these cases quite a few years ago, that it was impossible. And what the Republic had

to do was to engage in a voluntary debt restructuring. And as the Court pointed out, a large number, 76% of the creditors[,] accepted that and the others didn't, and they had every legal right not to accept it. Disclosure for those bonds also said very clearly, and I've read it many times, that these are bonds issued by a foreign state. It's protected by the Foreign Sovereign Immunities Act, and that recovery on a judgment may be extremely difficult or impossible, and the creditors that are on this call in particular are very sophisticated people who make a business in investing in sovereign debt, so they know the risks as well as the rewards in terms of high interest rates and the ability to conduct litigation against a sovereign which if it were in the private sector would obviously have sought protection of the bankruptcy laws, and we wouldn't have had any of the litigation that we've had over the last four years.

Were it my call, your Honor, were I the president of the Republic, we would certainly be trying to satisfy these creditors. But the Court has to realize, and I think you do, we can't simply pay them, because we paid 76 percent of our creditors a considerable discount, and we can't just turn around and say, we are going to pay the holdouts 100 cents. It just can't happen.[44]

Judge Griesa responded testily, "I've never heard a word about settlement on any basis."[45]

Blackman then brought up the problem of the RUFO price-match guarantee in Argentina's deal, the one that would require the country to top up the amount paid to deal participants if they paid more to holdouts. He also blamed the lack of a deal on the plaintiffs:

The difficulty is, you have to treat people the same, and it would be a very difficult thing. Indeed, it would be legally impossible under the terms of the exchange offer to offer to pay these creditors more than the amount that was paid to the creditors who accepted the exchange offer. I personally would be delighted . . . to hear what they want. I've never had a demand from any of the plaintiffs other than 100 cents on the dollar which they know the Republic could not do other than through their litigating and attempting to enforce a judgment. I've never heard a demand from them.

So while I understand the Court's frustration and again, I appreciate enormously the patience and the dedication that you've brought to this, your Honor. We've never heard what the plaintiffs even want.[46]

Judge Griesa responded, "I've said what I wanted to say and, Mr. Blackman, you have responded. I appreciate that. And we are going to have a meeting. And if these lawsuits all end up with judgments on the record which yield zero cents, then that has been an unfortunate expenditure of legal and judicial effort."[47]

Elliott's lawyer, Robert Cohen, responded to Judge Griesa's question about where the cases were going during the follow-up hearing on November 9:

Elliott Associates is a fund run by Paul Singer that has been in business for 30 years, and a small part of its portfolio for years has been invested in Sovereign debt. Some of it performs. In fact, most of the debt of Argentina that NML bought, it bought before default. But sometimes default happens.

For the last dozen years or so, I have represented NML or other Elliott affiliates in efforts to collect Sovereign debt. We have never failed to collect on the Sovereign debt. It's a long, hard battle. It's a battle that involves cooperation from the court in which the action is brought. It involves cooperation from courts overseas. It involves sometimes waiting for a change in administration in the country that's issued the debt so that attitudes change. Sometimes it involves the requirement of that country to come back into the capital market in the U.S. And because the creditors are there and will interfere, they find it better to settle than to continue to resist.

It's a long, hard fight. These judgments last for 20 years. And some of the creditors in this room are prepared to fight that battle. We will look for assets wherever we can find them. . . .

What we would ask, your Honor, is to be receptive to us when we come to you with ideas. We don't have any preconceived notion that we're entitled to attachment over anything, but we would like you to continue to listen to us when we come to you with ideas.[48]

Judge Griesa understood. Recapitulating, at the end of the hearing, he said, "You are engaged in these lawsuits with the idea that even though it's difficult, you do have an objective of recovery. Maybe I should have realized that without calling you all in, but I really didn't. And I was, frankly, mystified as to what people had in mind because thus far there hasn't been recovery. That doesn't mean I would terminate the cases or anything, but I was just wondering."[49]

Judge Cabranes's Famous Footnote Numbers 2 and 17

Civil litigation is a hurry-up-and-wait process, one that typically takes years. Plaintiffs file complaints when they want to sue, but then they often have to wait a long time before a hearing is held in the district court. Once a hearing is called, the pace of activity is frantic: motions, briefs, and declarations are filed with the court, and all the parties prepare for the hearing. But then the process slows down again, with the parties more often than not waiting months for the court to rule. Appeals processes, however, are much slower. It typically takes six months to a year to get a circuit court hearing date, and then the parties frequently wait another three to six months after the hearing for the ruling.

In this case the parties didn't have to wait quite that long to hear the Second Circuit's answer on the matter of the attachment of the $105 million at the New York Fed. The answer came on January 5, 2007, about four months after the hearing, and the ruling was no surprise. The funds were immune to attachment. Judge Cabranes took some shine off of Argentina's victory, however, by weaving some sharp messages into his opinion's footnotes.

In footnote 2, which is just over one thousand words long, Judge Cabranes recounted the history of Argentina's defaults on foreign creditors, including instances in 1827, 1890, 1956, and 1982 and then again in 2001. About the 1980s debt crisis, he cited a source who wrote that "Argentina emerged as the single most resistant debtor in international finance." On behalf of the court Cabranes also wrote, "We note that Argentina has made many contributions to the law of foreign insolvency through its numerous defaults on its sovereign obligations, as well as through what we might term a diplomacy of default."[50]

Footnote 2 was just a warm-up, however. In footnote 17 Judge Cabranes suggested that an alter ego theory might prevail, and he ended with a quote from the plaintiff's brief in which NML's and EM's lawyers called Argentina's shifting of reserves to the BIS a "shell game."

Judge Griesa read the footnotes. A year later in a hearing about whether he should allow NML and EM to belatedly pursue an alter ego claim against the Central Bank of Argentina, he said, "The Court of Appeals opinion almost reads like an invitation to raise this. . . . It seems to me they quite seriously talked about this subject as if it were something that could be explored. And then there's that footnote about the possible fraud because of the movement of funds. That's quite a serious footnote. I mean they don't play around with that kind of thing."[51]

Judge Griesa was right. Judges, particularly circuit court judges, don't add extra words to published legal opinions just for the fun of it. Savvy readers of court opinions understand that everything a judge writes has meaning, and what Judge Cabranes had written seemed to contain two specific messages to Griesa: don't trust Argentina's intentions, and feel free to send the case back up to us on an alter ego claim. What's more, Cabranes, a Spanish speaker and a keen observer of Latin American politics, put down a marker by suggesting that Argentina was playing politics in court. It was an early indictment, and Cabranes's footnotes 2 and 17 would be remembered. The immediate effect, however, was that Griesa allowed Elliott and Dart to pursue their alter ego claim against the Central Bank of Argentina and kept the $105 million frozen in place at the New York Fed while they did so.[52]

6

All Plaintiffs Big and Small

(June 2005–December 2009)

Elliott Associates was the big name in the litigation, front and center in the press. Having prevailed so spectacularly over Peru in 2000, Elliott was the one everyone was watching after 2005 when the Argentina litigation heated up. Even today, many experts speak of the Argentina bond cases as if it were just Elliott versus Argentina. The truth, however, is that Elliott was not the dominant plaintiff in the early years of the litigation, just one of many. Hundreds of cases were filed on behalf of tens of thousands of plaintiffs, and the litigation was about dozens of different matters, not just Elliott's attachments and pari passu as the press and academics would have you think. Understanding the full scope of the litigation is crucial not just because it's fascinating but also because it's essential for understanding why Judge Thomas P. Griesa ultimately ruled the way he did on pari passu: the promise of bringing an end to the mess of cases clogging his courtroom was hard to resist.

In numbers, small cases dominated the docket. Between 2002 and 2010, holders of relatively small legal claims (worth less than $2 million on average) brought 66% of the 181 cases filed in the Southern District against Argentina (out of 272 eventually filed through April 2016), while investors holding very large claims (worth more than $50 million) brought only 34%.[1] Sadly for Judge Griesa, judicial complexity scales with the number of lawsuits, not with the size of the claims, so a lot of his time was spent on these smaller cases.

The biggest number of small-plaintiff cases, about fifty of them, came from a single source: a partnership between Argentine lawyer Patricia

Rosito Vago and Dreier LLP's Marc Dreier. Vago's involvement started at home; she and her husband owned defaulted bonds. While they pondered their choices, Vago's phone started ringing with clients who wanted help with their bonds. Sensing a business opportunity, Vago reached out to Marc Dreier—the counsel of record on the first Argentina case—to propose a partnership. Vago would find and organize the plaintiffs, while Dreier LLP would do the litigating. They would split the fees down the middle.[2]

Vago and Dreier set up an assembly line: Vago rounded up groups of investors in Argentina, Italy, and elsewhere, and Dreier lodged a suit every time a critical mass of plaintiffs came together. At its peak in 2005, the Dreier-Vago factory churned out twelve complaints in just ten months on March 3, 17, and 22; April 19; May 2 and 6; June 28; July 5 and 21; September 23; October 12; and December 19.[3]

The average number of plaintiffs in the Dreier-Vago cases was 15, although the team filed some cases on behalf of a single plaintiff, and their two largest cases were on behalf of 74 and 109 plaintiffs, respectively.[4] In all, Dreier and Vago represented about 800 plaintiffs of seventeen nationalities who owned, collectively, about $400 million of defaulted bonds.

The Dreier-Vago cases were a nightmare for the court to administer. The granting of judgments was a particularly arduous process. Each claim made by each plaintiff had to be calculated separately, and if a single plaintiff owned five different defaulted bonds, the judgment on each one had to be calculated separately. Making this task even more cumbersome, there were more than a hundred different defaulted bonds, each with their own coupon rate and payment dates, meaning that their cash flows had to be separately modeled. It took the court about two years just to grant the first of the many judgments in the Dreier-Vago cases.

For the investors who worked with them, the Dreier-Vago partnership offered a way to play the litigation game at an affordable price. No single small plaintiff could have afforded to bring a stand-alone suit. By spreading the cost of litigation over many virtually identical cases, however, Dreier and Vago could bring the average expense per client down. For an up-front fee of about 1% of holdings and a back-end fee of about 10% of any recovery, the Dreier-Vago factory would add you to the assembly line.[5] This was a good deal for their small-plaintiff clients, but it was a risky bet for Dreier and Vago, albeit one with potentially high returns. Their upside was that they could make $40 million if their clients all recovered 100 cents on the dollar, but if there was no deal, they would lose millions of dollars' worth of time to servicing the cases.

Already working on behalf of small plaintiffs were Guillermo Gleizer, who had a solo practice, and Mark Kalish and David Gelfarb from Moss & Kalish, as detailed in chapter 2. A new entrant serving small clients was Andrea Boggio, a professor at Bryant University in Rhode Island who brought suits for several clients including one for Andrarex, Ltd., an Italian company, in 2007.[6]

The lawyers for the small plaintiffs displayed different styles, skills, and strategies in the courtroom. The lawyers for Dreier LLP and Moss & Kalish were conventional and persistent litigators, bringing new motions and litigating the points. In contrast, Professor Boggio played a passive game, copying motions made by other plaintiffs and letting them do the arguing. Gleizer was a surprise generator, several times digging up hard-to-find information on Argentina's assets.

There were also twenty-three class-action lawsuits. All but eight of them failed to lead to a settlement, however, and those that did settle represented a tiny percentage of Argentina's outstanding defaulted debt. Tiny though they were, these cases were painful for Judge Griesa to adjudicate because class-action procedures are poorly designed to facilitate sovereign debt cases. It is virtually impossible to define the scope of the class in a sovereign bond case, the very basic first step. Unlike in a product liability case in which "all people harmed by a consumer product" is a well-defined class, the scope of the class in a sovereign bond suit is unstable because bonds trade. On day one of a lawsuit there might be ten thousand holders of a defaulted bond, all of which have suffered equal harm and are considered members of the class unless they later opt out. On day two, however, two thousand of the original ten thousand class members might sell their bonds. The new owners would not be class members because they were not holders on the day the suit was filed, so the size of the class would drop to eight thousand. Unstable class sizes weren't the only problem in the Argentina class-action cases, but they were the big one. Altogether, the class-action plaintiffs were involved in twenty-four hearings in the district court and seven appeals,[7] all to settle just 0.3% of Argentina's defaulted debt.[8] They are worth remembering if only because they soaked up a lot of judicial resources and were particularly aggravating to Griesa and the Second Circuit Court of Appeals.[9]

The Small-Plaintiff Attachment Efforts

The small plaintiffs didn't just bring a disproportionate number of suits; they also brought multiple attachment and discovery actions against Argentina, all of which added to the court's load. Every attachment effort generated reams of paperwork, necessitated multiple hearings, and required Judge Griesa to make a painstaking review of the particular facts and circumstances. Moreover, the small-plaintiff litigation was chaotic in nature, the various plaintiffs not coordinating with each other, so barely a day would go by without Griesa being presented with another suit, another motion, another hearing to prepare for, another opinion to write, or another judgment to hand down. Much of this work was mundane, repetitive, and ultimately fruitless. Here are a few examples.

On February 12, 2004, for example, Gleizer filed a motion to attach the assets of Argentina's postal system, Correo Argentino, including bank accounts held at BNP Paribas and Lehman Brothers. Gleizer targeted Correo Argentino because it was under the control of the Argentine government through its court system as a consequence of a failed privatization. On March 12 Judge Griesa rejected the motion because there was insufficient evidence that the Republic of Argentina had an interest in the accounts.[10]

On March 1, 2007, lawyers for Old Castle and Lightwater, two of the plaintiffs mentioned in chapter 2, also made a go at Correo Argentino's assets. They sought a turnover of the money being sent to Correo Argentino from UPS, FedEx, and DHL to pay for completing the domestic legs of international package deliveries. Judge Griesa rejected the motion on the grounds that the activity of Correo is "exclusively in Argentina as far as the record shows, and there is no evidence of commercial activity in the United States sufficient to justify an attachment," as §1610 of the FSIA would require.[11]

On March 27, 2007, two of Guillermo Gleizer's clients, Michelle Colella and Denise Dussault, obtained a temporary attachment order from Judge William Alsup in the U.S. District Court for the Northern District of California against the Argentine presidential airplane, Tango-1.[12] Judge Alsup soon dismissed the attachment for two reasons. First, the plane wasn't being used for a commercial activity as required under §1610 of the FSIA, and, second, the plane was an asset of the Argentine military, which made it immune from attachment under §1611.[13] In this action, however, Gleizer displayed his talent for digging up compromising information on the Argentine government. He informed the court when making his filing that Tango-1 was on its way to the United States for engine service and that "the pilots will be carrying a significant amount of cash with which to purchase fuel."[14]

On April 18, 2008, Gleizer, as joint cocounsel for several class-action cases, sought a temporary restraining order on billions of U.S. dollar–denominated global bonds held in Argentina's local clearing system. These bonds were serving as collateral backing bonds Argentina had issued to domestic investors in late 2001 as part of a predefault domestic debt restructuring. Several plaintiffs obtained temporary restraints, although Judge Griesa ultimately ruled that the property was held in Argentina, not the United States, and was therefore not attachable under §1610. Griesa's rationale was that New York law says that the situs of a security—an intangible object with no definitive physical location—is the location of the custodian of the ultimate owner.[15] In this case, an Argentine trust was the ultimate owner, and a Buenos Aires–based entity was the trust's custodian, making the situs of the security Argentina and the property not attachable.

In March 2009, Moss & Kalish sought to attach assets of government-owned Aerolíneas Argentinas on the basis that it was an alter ego of the Republic of Argentina. Judge Griesa denied the motion for lack of evidence that such a relationship existed. In July 2009 some of the class-action plaintiffs also tried to attach Aerolíneas's assets, but they were shot down for the same reason.[16]

The Small Plaintiffs Seek Discovery

The small plaintiffs didn't just seek to attach Argentina's assets; they sought discovery too. "Discovery" refers to the right of a party in a lawsuit to seek pertinent information from its opponent and third parties. Usually, one party sends a demand to another party asking for a laundry list of information. Then, the receiving party turns over little, if any, information, and the matter ends up in front of a judge. In court, the sending party makes a motion to compel the delivery of the information, while the receiving party makes a motion to deny it. This is conventional stuff in civil litigation, but when sovereigns are involved it becomes complicated. Take the following exchange between Old Castle and Lightwater's counsel Mark Kalish and Judge Griesa on December 19, 2006.

During the hearing, Mark Kalish complained about Argentina's poor response to his client's January 2005 discovery requests and asked Judge Griesa to sign an order to compel compliance:

> All we've managed to do after addressing this matter once before the Court and in three separate conferences with counsel, all we've managed to do is to get from counsel in response governance documents for 12 of the some 25 companies with respect to which we requested information. That doesn't even begin, your Honor, to address the scope of the interrogatories and quite simply the Republic has taken the position that they are not going to answer any other interrogatories.[17]

Judge Griesa was unsympathetic in his response. "I'm really not willing to allow discovery where I think it is impossible at the end of the line to find any assets that can be executed from. I think the law in the United States is that the courts have to be quite careful about not allowing discovery against foreign sovereigns. . . . And so that's my obligation."[18]

Judge Griesa's attitude toward discovery against Argentina would change over time, materially. After 2010 he let Elliott pursue worldwide discovery to uncover Argentina's global "financial circulatory system," as expansive a discovery allowance ever given in a sovereign debt case.[19] By then, however, Griesa was in a much different mood, and a much more famous lawyer was arguing the point on behalf of a much more significant claimant.

Task Force Argentina at the ICSID

Italy's TFA took a different approach in prosecuting its litigation on behalf of its members, about 195,000 small Italian investors. The organization did file three suits in New York,[20] but instead of seeking judgments, attachments, and discovery like the others, TFA stayed its cases while pursuing binding arbitration at the ICSID in Washington, D.C. The brainchild of Washington-based lawyers at White & Case, this idea came to the fore in mid-February 2005 when the battle for the hearts and minds of Italian mom-and-pop investors was at its most intense. As discussed in chapter 3, TFA used the ICSID idea as the basis for offering to underwrite the cost of litigation against Argentina for the Italian retail investors who opted to hold out. This promotion, in turn, convinced a large number of small investors in Italy to hold out.

The inspiration for White & Case's idea was the Lock Law, the statute enacted by the Argentine Congress in February 2005 to scare small investors into the transaction by saying that holdouts would never get paid. The law firm likened the law to expropriation, which put the ICSID forum into play. White & Case also asserted that seeking arbitration at the ICSID was a better approach than suing in New York. In a memo published by GCAB on February 15, 2005, White & Case partner Owen Pell wrote, "In our experience, nations pay their ICSID awards."[21] He added that it was easier to attach sovereign assets abroad with an ICSID award in hand than with a judgment from a U.S. court. These arguments were innovative on two counts: nobody had ever brought a sovereign debt claim to the ICSID, and no one had ever combined tens of thousands of claimants into one action. The downside was that the ICSID moves slowly. It wasn't obvious that Italian mom-and-pop investors, mostly retirees, were well situated to wait for an arbitration process that might take more than five years to play out.

Nonetheless, TFA successfully attracted a very large number of Italian retail investors into its ICSID arbitration process. TFA filed its claim on September 14, 2006,[22] and by February 2007 it had signed up 195,000 investors.[23] It was a massive undertaking, which required TFA to collect several pieces of information from each investor and entailed significant risks to its organizers because investors could drop out at any time. Yet TFA kept its action together, and as of September 2009 only 15,000 investors out of the original 195,000 had dropped out.[24] This high retention rate was at least partly due to TFA's excellent communications program, which included an informative, well-designed website and regular press releases.

TFA was slow in getting results for its members, however, even by the standards of an ICSID case. Processing the paperwork of so many plaintiffs was an extremely complicated process, health issues arose with one of the arbitrators, and Argentina took various actions to slow down the proceedings even further. By the end of 2009, some three years after TFA filed its initial arbitration claim, the ICSID panel had yet to hold even its first week of hearings to determine whether it would accept jurisdiction over the sovereign debt cases. This situation was frustrating for the many Italian retirees who had taken TFA's advice to hold out of the transaction.

Outside of TFA's arbitration effort, a small percentage of Italian holdout investors chose to sue their banks rather than Argentina. They hired small law firms to represent them in suits brought against the banks in local Italian courts, often winning judgments and full legal expense reimbursement. Supporting them was businessman Egidio Rolich, who set up an organization called Associazione Risparmiatori Tangobond, which promoted the idea that the Italian banks should cover investors' losses.[25] He ran a website and claims to have organized a network of 250 lawyers to bring cases against the banks. As of February 15, 2011, Rolich claimed—on a now defunct website—that 23,000 Italian investors had settled with their banks for a total sum of €690 million.[26] Asked about these claims, TFA's Nicola Stock noted that his understanding from working with the Italian banks on the Argentina issue for many years was that there were several thousand lawsuits and maybe several tens of millions of dollars of such claims settled both in and out of court.[27] This difference suggests the need for an academic study of the Italian litigation triggered by Argentina's default.

The Large Holdouts

While the small plaintiffs engaged in almost frantic activity in the early years of the litigation, the large plaintiffs picked their spots. Between 2005 and 2010, the most significant attachment efforts were made by Elliott working alongside Dart, although they were not the only ones litigating in this period. In the background, Elliott and its FRAN plaintiff partners were quietly making progress in their litigation against Argentina over the value of these securities, while some large sophisticated plaintiffs filed new lawsuits, having bought defaulted bonds leftover from the wreckage of Argentina's 2005 transaction.

The most significant new arrival was Mark Brodsky, the head of Aurelius Capital. Brodsky was an Elliott alumnus who left in February 2005 to form his own firm.[28] Like Elliott, Aurelius employed a large team of top-flight lawyers, and its 2007 arrival in the litigation added the potential for drama. Because creditor attachment works on a first-come, first-served basis, having two experienced plaintiffs in the game meant that they might end up competing to attach one juicy asset, if one appeared.

Alongside Aurelius from beginning to end was a plaintiff named Blue Angel Capital I, a Delaware corporation backed by Davidson Kempner Capital Management, a New York–based hedge fund.[29] Because Aurelius took the lead on both firms' actions, this book often refers to the pair as "Aurelius" for simplicity. The two firms filed twelve suits against Argentina between 2007 and 2010 with regard to total holdings of about $475 million in Argentine bonds.[30]

Another substantial litigant was CVI, the firm that tried but failed to attach the $1 billion of Brady bond collateral held at the New York Fed during the course of the 2005 exchange offer, as detailed at the end of chapter 3. The consequence of this failure was that the New York Fed released most of the $1 billion of collateral it held to Argentina's agents in 2005 when the country settled its transaction. Collateral worth $250 million remained at the New York Fed, however, because the holders of about one-quarter of Argentina's Brady bonds had not accepted the country's offer. In May 2005, CVI appealed Judge Griesa's ruling to the Second Circuit to get its hands on what was left and won.[31] CVI couldn't take possession of the collateral because it was already pledged to holders of Argentina's Brady bonds, but the firm did obtain something of value, namely, blocking power. If Argentina canceled any of these bonds going forward—as they would in any exchange offer—the Fed would be obliged by the attachment order to deliver the collateral to CVI, destroying any savings Argentina would have hoped to make from such a transaction. Argentina was thus blocked from completing any more settlements with its Brady bond holders as long as CVI's attachment was in place. CVI followed up this successful attachment with efforts to seize a number of other related or analogous accounts. Along the way, it obtained judgments worth $52 million and $104 million with respect to holdings of U.S. dollar–denominated bonds and €54 million with respect to holdings of euro-denominated bonds.[32]

CVI was very active in court, a party to thirteen stand-alone hearings and five appeals. The relationship between CVI and Judge Griesa was poor, however, with the firm's lawyers never recovering from a procedural faux pas made in their initial appeal. Griesa repeatedly ruled against CVI, including four times when his rulings were reversed or vacated on appeal.[33] It seems that CVI's lawyers had angered the judge in their May 2005 appeal by seeking to attach two different Argentine accounts with the circuit court, while the firm had only sought to attach one of those accounts in Griesa's court. Griesa thought that the district court should rule on all matters before they were brought up on appeal, so CVI's move here was insulting. While it is speculative to suggest that this procedural error affected Griesa's subsequent rulings, that he was mad about it is a matter of court record. At a hearing two years later when Aurelius's lawyers brought up one aspect of the opinion the circuit court rendered in CVI's appeal, Griesa called CVI's move "an affront."[34] Griesa did voice many technical concerns about CVI's various motions, so it's hard to discern the balance of reasons behind his decisions. The one thing that is for sure, however, is that the CVI cases had a rhythm and tone that differed from the rest of the litigation.

Two other funds that sought recovery through litigation were Teachers Insurance and Annuity Association and College Retirement Equities Fund (TIAA-CREF)[35] and the Boston-based fund manager GMO.[36] Unlike Argentina's other large creditors, TIAA-CREF and GMO are mainstream money managers, not hedge funds. As its name suggests, TIAA-CREF invests money for educators, and the firm has over $1 trillion of assets under management on behalf of five million individual clients and fifteen thousand institutions.[37] GMO is famous for its outspoken cofounder and chief investment officer, Jeremy Grantham, as well as for its family of mutual funds, although the firm also manages other types of accounts.[38] Both TIAA-CREF and GMO had been members of the ABC, GCAB, or both, so it's fair to assume that they held out and sued because they were severely disappointed with both the terms of Argentina's 2005 offer and Argentina's refusal to negotiate with GCAB. In 2007 TIAA-CREF obtained a judgment of $105 million,[39] and GMO obtained three judgments totaling $326 million.[40] Like other holdouts, they would have trouble collecting, although they were relatively passive in their attempts to do so, only joining one major attachment action as we shall see shortly.

The final group of big plaintiffs were members of the FRAN plaintiffs group: Elliott, Bracebridge, and Montreux Partners. As mentioned in chapter 3, these three firms lodged suits against Argentina with respect to their holdings of these bonds immediately after the country announced the results of its transaction. But they didn't stop there. All three funds continued to build their positions, scooping up the small number of FRANs remaining in the market over the next five years. In all, Elliott lodged five separate stand-alone suits with respect to its holdings of $132 million of FRANs.[41] Bracebridge brought two actions, one joint suit in

2005 on behalf of the FFI Fund Ltd., which owned $69.275 million of FRANs, and the 100% Yale-controlled FYI Ltd., which owned $46.1 million,[42] and a second suit in 2010 on behalf of the Olifant Fund, which owned $5 million.[43] Montreux Partners L.P. brought its first suit in 2005 to which it added suits in later years on behalf of Los Angeles Capital, Cordoba Capital, and Wilton Capital. For simplicity, this book refers to these four entities as "Montreux" and "the Montreux group," since they did everything together and were managed collectively by Michael Straus and Eric Hermann. The Montreux group owned $42.363 million of FRANs in aggregate.[44]

Collectively, the FRAN plaintiffs came to own about $300 million of FRANs in total, on which they obtained judgments in 2009 totaling an incredible $3 billion, or ten times their face value.[45] Using round numbers, their holdings were worth about 1,000% of face amount because their contracts obligated Argentina to pay them par value (100% of the face amount) plus 812% of par (eight years of interest at the FRANs' final reset rate of 101.5% per annum) and 100% of par (interest on interest).[46] Needless to say, Argentina appealed, arguing that a 101.5% interest rate was unconscionable and should be reduced by the court using its equitable powers. This appeal was heard on February 2, 2010.[47]

Elliott's Other Early Attachments

Elliott was selective in its attachment efforts, generally focusing its resources on attaching assets where it was likely to win. For example, as discussed in chapter 5, Elliott and Dart attempted to attach the Central Bank of Argentina's reserves in December 2005 in response to the two presidential decrees that appeared to blow their immunity. In its first effort to attach Argentine assets, however, Elliott acted with no evident justification.[48] On February 4, 2004, the firm obtained temporary attachment orders on nineteen Argentine diplomatic properties in the Washington, D.C., area, including two military warehouses, the house of the Argentine ambassador to the United States, and the residence of the Argentine ambassador to the Organization of American States.[49] When Argentina's lawyers brought this out-of-state legal action to his attention, Judge Griesa was flabbergasted, as everyone—even nonlawyers—are well aware that diplomatic properties are immune under the Vienna Convention. Griesa said,

> I really cannot—I just find that unbelievable that such a thing could occur. . . . Certainly, some inquiry, rudimentary inquiry would tell you whether it is the home of the ambassador or not. . . . It is impossible for me to believe that you could not find out what these things were used for. . . . And what you have done is, in my view, is to create a wholly unnecessary need for litigation in two jurisdictions because you didn't find out the facts. I think you should withdraw those—I don't think there should be litigation. I think you should withdraw those attachments.[50]

In response, Elliott released the D.C. attachments except for one condominium unit that housed a branch of PNC Bank and from which Argentina collected potentially attachable rent, perhaps a few thousand dollars a month.[51] The Washington attachments were a big misstep, with the CVI cases suggesting the cost of getting on the wrong side of Judge Griesa. Elliott did, however, subsequently raise its game, as we saw in the central bank attachment litigation in 2005 and 2006 in which Elliott's (and Dart's) efforts were better founded and in which the firms' lawyers succeeded in drawing the judge's ire against Argentina.

Elliott's first headline action following the central bank hearing at the Second Circuit took place on May 22, 2007, when Elliott and Dart obtained an attachment on nine million government-owned shares of the Argentine mortgage bank Banco Hipotecario.[52] Finding these shares took some digging. In their quest to find assets owned by the government of Argentina, Elliott's and Dart's researchers discovered that the country controlled thirteen fiduciary funds, which might own assets abroad. The May 22, 2007, attachment was targeted at finding any assets owned by these funds at nine different financial institutions: American Express Bank, the New York branch of Banco de la Nación Argentina (BNA), the Bank of New York, Citibank N.A., Credit Suisse, Deutsche Bank, JPMorgan

Chase, U.S. Bank Trust N.A., and the New York Fed. Elliott and Dart struck gold at U.S. Bank Trust, which held all the shares for an account in the name of BH Options Trust on behalf of one of the thirteen targeted funds. These shares were worth between $23 million and $80 million[53] —their value was hard to pin down due to their illiquidity and volatility. In 2009 Judge Griesa confirmed the attachment,[54] and in 2010 the Second Circuit affirmed his ruling.[55] This was Elliott's and Dart's only really big score—until their successes with pari passu after 2010—although they continued to try to find and seize Argentine assets over the ensuing years.

Elliott and Dart Seek to Attach BNA: September 2008

Elliott and Dart's next attachment effort came late in the afternoon of Friday, September 12, 2008, just three days before Lehman Brothers went bust.[56] The target was the New York branch of government-owned Banco de la Nación Argentina, Argentina's largest bank, which had eighteen thousand employees and branches all over the world. The hearing at which the attachment was sought is notable because it was one of the few cases in which the full transcript of a plaintiff-only ex parte hearing was unsealed and made available in the docket. As such, it offers a unique opportunity to be a fly on the wall during an attachment.

The hearing held in the Robing Room at the Southern District court started at 5:00 p.m. and lasted about twenty minutes.[57] Judge Griesa presided. Robert Cohen and Dennis Hranitzky stood in for Elliott's NML Capital, Ltd., while Suzanne Grosso and Paul Lee represented Dart's EM Ltd.

"What do you have today?" Judge Griesa asked.[58]

Cohen responded:

We have today, your Honor, a proposed attachment and restraining order. We have been working on this for quite some time. We have located between $70 and $100 million on deposit in banks in New York being used clearly for commercial purposes that are available for attachment. That may sound too good to be true, given what we have heard for the last few years.

There's a little back story I need to tell. That is, the assets belong to Banco de la Nacion, Argentina, BNA. BNA is a creature of statute created in Argentina, wholly owned by the government of Argentina. It operates ostensibly as a commercial bank but it actually operates as an arm of the government. It performs acts for the government, including the collection of taxes to disbursements of taxes. It operates fiduciary funds in the name of the government that are off balance sheet operations for the government. Its president is appointed by the president of Argentina, who has been replaced nine times in the last 13 years. It is an instrumentality of Argentina that carries out the political will of the government that happens to be in power.

And I know your Honor has indulged us in the past in considering press reports. . . . It's reported in Argentina that the government has finished setting up the financial engineering that will allow Banco Nacion to finance infrastructure projects. The board of directors for the central bank may approve today the rules that will allow Nacion to execute operations at this time.

Although Nacion's charter forbids the bank to finance public sector projects, in this case the bank would not be violating this prohibition, at least formally, because the deposits are going to a trust, not directly to the state. The trick is that the government will be able to apply this . . . 10 billion pesos to projects without its appearing as an expenditure because funds of the official bank not treasury funds are involved. This is typical of the way they use that.[59]

Judge Griesa interrupted, "What are you reading from?"[60]

Cohen responded, "This is from an article in *Ambito Financiaro* which is an Argentine financial press. This is just the latest of maybe 20 examples that we have in our papers of the way in which the government of Argentina has used BNA to carry out the policies of the country. And use it, in effect, as its own piggy bank."[61]

Cohen went on to explain the technical structure of the proposed order. Elliott and Dart's idea was to obtain a lien on the reserves that BNA held under New York State regulations. In a creative twist, however, they designed the proposed orders to seek a second lien on the bank's reserves to avoid disrupting the day-to-day operations of the bank.

"Now, if I sign this this afternoon, what happens?" Judge Griesa asked.[62]

Cohen explained:

We will serve—and we also ask your Honor for permission to serve the attachments by Federal Express because we don't know for sure in which institutions this pledge is on deposit. It can be at any bank in the State of New York. We have an exhaustive list. Believe it or not, it is 3,000 banks. We are prepared to send Fed Exes this weekend to 3,000 banks.[63]

"Which will arrive when?" Judge Griesa asked.[64]

"Monday morning, we're told by 10:30 am for most banks. There are a few banks upstate that it will arrive later in the day," Dennis Hranitzky explained. Robert Cohen added, "We will serve BNA when it opens in the morning. We will [be] meeting with the banking department [of the State of New York], at 9:30 Monday morning we have an appointment to tell them what's going on. If they have any concerns, they can voice them. We have approached this in a very conservative manner. If we're wrong no one will be harmed, but if we are right we have something to look to."[65]

Judge Griesa signed the orders.

The subsequent hearings to confirm the attachment involved two-way arguments with Argentina's counsel and did not go in Elliott and Dart's favor. A confirmation of their attachments relied on the court finding that BNA was an alter ego of the republic, but Judge Griesa found the evidence for such an assertion lacking. Still, Elliott and Dart won a consolation prize because one of their three thousand Fed Exes hit a nugget of gold: $3.2 million at HSBC that was being held on behalf of Agencia Nacional de Promoción Científica y Tecnológica, an Argentine government agency. Since the agency was a part of the government itself and not an arms-length company, its money, though intended for the purchase of an electron microscope to be used for scientific research, was attachable. The nuance was that the act of purchasing a microscope was something anyone in the market could do—it was a commercial activity—which meant that the $3.2 million was attachable under §1610 of the FSIA. Griesa confirmed the attachment at a later hearing,[66] and the Second Circuit affirmed his opinion.[67] Elliott and Dart received a court order to take possession of the funds on November 26, 2012.[68] While much smaller in value than their capture of Argentina's Banco Hipotecario shares, it was a notable score.

A Race to the Courthouse: October–November 2008

While scholars often talk about attachment in sovereign debt litigation as being a "race to the courthouse," it's hard to find real-life examples. The mundane reality of the Argentina litigation was that only the firms that did painstaking research were able to bring attachment efforts to fruition. Elliott and Dart were alone in going for the $105 million at the New York Fed in 2005. CVI was alone in attaching the Brady bond collateral at the New York Fed as discussed above, although some small plaintiffs lobbed on copycat "me-too" attachments much later on. Elliott and Dart were alone in seeking to attach the Banco Hipotecario shares. There were no races to the courthouse, at least not until late October 2008.

President Cristina Fernández de Kirchner, who succeeded her husband in December 2007, waved the starter flag on October 21, 2008, by announcing the nationalization of Argentina's private pension fund managers. These funds managed assets on behalf of Argentina's social security agency in a hybrid system first put in place in the 1990s. Under this arrangement, some funds were managed directly by the government, and the rest were outsourced to private managers. For years, politicians criticized this system for the funds' high fees and indistinguishable performance. Still, the government takeover was a shock. The trigger was the Lehman collapse, which threatened Argentina's access to funding. Commandeering the private pension fund assets would give the government control over the big part of the republic's debt that the funds held, thereby ensuring that the country would have stable finances during the global financial crisis, which was deepening by the day.[69]

Argentine markets took it badly, however, with the Buenos Aires Stock Exchange plunging 14% upon news of the takeover.[70] The immediate concern was that by taking over the private pension fund assets, the government would come to own a big portion, even a majority, of the shares of many Argentine companies. Since there was no telling how the government would act as the dominant shareholder, many investors sold their shares. But to holdout creditors in New York, the chaos in Buenos Aires was an opportunity. They quickly realized that the soon-to-be-nationalized private pension fund managers likely held hundreds of millions of dollars of stocks and bonds in New York and that these assets were about to become attachable. They were about to become government property, they were located in New York, and they were being used for a commercial purpose: investment. A race to the courthouse was on.

Here are the times of the runners:

Aurelius and Blue Angel obtained attachments on October 29, 2008, on what ultimately amounted to $250 million of Argentine private pension fund assets.[71]

Elliott and Dart clocked in second, their orders signed at 11:30 a.m. on October 31, 2008.[72]

Professor Boggio was third, obtaining orders for Andrarex on November 3, 2008, after seeing Aurelius and Blue Angel's attachments when stopping by the records room at the Southern District court on a visit to New York.[73]

GMO was fourth, with orders signed at 11:30 a.m. on November 5.[74]

CVI and the many cases brought by Dreier LLP were tied for fifth on November 6.[75]

Moss & Kalish clients Lightwater and Old Castle placed sixth on November 12.[76]

The laggard, TIAA-CREF, finished last place on January 7, 2009, at 1:15 p.m.[77]

While it is fascinating to measure the response time of various investors to Argentina's private pension fund nationalization, the million-dollar question was whether the late arrivers would get a dime. Attachment is a first-come, first-served process, and because Aurelius and Blue Angel were first—and they had combined judgments totaling hundreds of millions of dollars—the likelihood was that all the captured assets, if collected, would go toward satisfying Aurelius's and Blue Angel's judgments. Nothing would be left over for anyone else. That's how debt settlements work in the absence of access to bankruptcy; there is no equitable distribution of recovered property. The first mover—the smart money—wins at the expense of everyone else.

Priority Fight!

While Aurelius won the footrace, Elliott ended up first in line to collect on the $250 million of Argentine private pension fund assets frozen in New York, to the consternation of everyone involved, including Judge Griesa. How this happened was the subject of an acrimonious hearing held on April 6, 2009, featuring a three-way fight among lawyers for Aurelius, Elliott, and GMO. Aurelius's position was that it had gotten there first, while GMO argued that the plaintiffs should share the collateral since they were all equally deserving creditors. And Elliott asserted that there had been two footraces and that it had won the second one, the one that mattered.

At the time the attachments were granted to the different plaintiffs in late October and early November 2008, Argentina's social security assets in New York were still the legal property of the private pension managers. They were therefore not attachable under the law, so according to Elliott's lawyers, the initial set of attachments granted by the court were not valid. The only valid attachments, they said, were a second set the plaintiffs had served on Argentina after the nationalization was completed in December 2008. The various plaintiffs obtained these second attachment orders from the court in late November after a series of hearings on the situation. Among this second set of orders, Elliott and Dart were the first to serve their papers on Argentina, so they were first in line at least according to their logic.

How Elliott and Dart delivered their second attachment orders showed just how superior they were at playing the litigation game. The two firms inserted a clever feature into their second orders, which Judge Griesa signed in late November 2008. The clause allowed them to be served on Argentina by either the U.S. Marshals Service or by the firms' counsel. In contrast, the other plaintiffs' orders allowed delivery only by the marshals. The rest was history: Elliott's and Dart's lawyers served the new orders on Argentina on December 9, 2008,[78] immediately after the nationalization went into effect, while the U.S. Marshals Service served the rest of the plaintiffs' orders after Griesa released his December 11 opinion confirming the validity of the new set of attachments. Elliott and Dart got there first by at least two whole days.[79]

Elliott and Dart's victory was a cause of great frustration for the court. During the April 6 hearing, Judge Griesa appeared both agitated and defensive about what had happened. In particular, he wasn't happy that he'd signed a bunch of papers without understanding the commercial implications:

> When I signed the order for Aurelius, I did not intend to do anything, as far as I was concerned, to deal with priority. When I signed the order or orders for NML, I did not intend to do anything about priority. When I wrote my December 11 decision, I had something at the end saying that there is nothing in here that is intended to affect priority. . . . It is of some importance to me that I was not intending to do anything about priority. And, of course, all of a sudden, we have this issue.[80]

Aurelius's counsel, Tyler Robinson, asserted that priority should be fixed based on the time stamps that were given by the U.S. Marshals Service when plaintiffs submitted their first orders for delivery. He said, "There's a window, Judge, that the marshal service has in the courthouse where you go and deliver your writ, or your attachment order. It gets stamped. You get a receipt that shows you when it was delivered."[81] He complained that chaos would result if any other approach were allowed: "You are going to have Mr. Cohen hiding behind a tree on 500 Pearl Street, and Mr.

Robinson crouched behind a car on the Worth Street entrance waiting for deputies to come out to get in a foot race about priority."[82]

It was a frustrating situation, and doing what he so often did when frustrated, Judge Griesa vented:

> I want to tell you, and I want to say this to everybody, that there are a lot of judgments here. There are some claims that have not yet been reduced to judgments. New cases keep coming in. And, obviously, some of the cases have been around a long time, and some of these judgments have been around a long time. I know this isn't a bankruptcy Court, it is not a receivership where I distribute assets on some notion of mine about fairness. But, still, it is not altogether satisfactory to me to have a group of plaintiffs who are really equally deserving. They have all suffered these defaults. Maybe they don't come in as fast as some people, but you have got equally deserving plaintiffs. . . . Is it really right to have it go to any one plaintiff or group [of] plaintiffs when you have got a whole lot of people who are equally deserving, and it's really rather fortuitous that somebody gets the jump?[83]

After Aurelius's lawyer tried but failed to interject a new point, Judge Griesa blasted, "I tell you what. You all may persuade me of this. I may never sign an ex parte order again. . . . I may never sign one until I have had a town meeting."[84]

It was an extraordinary moment that laid bare just how unfair existing attachment law is to most creditors; it's a winner-takes-all system under which only the smartest money wins.

Discovery and Contempt

If the April 6, 2009, hearing on priority was acrimonious, a hearing held later that month was downright poisonous. The topic was the breaking news that Argentina's social security agency had taken some potentially nonimmune, attachable assets out of the United States just before they could be discovered by the plaintiffs. The initiating event was a March

2009 order by Judge Griesa for the agency to turn over information on its assets by early May.

An emergency meeting that commenced at 4:40 p.m. on April 24 began with Aurelius's lawyer waving an article from Argentina's *La Nación* in Judge Griesa's face.[85] The article reported that Argentina's social security system had just taken more than $200 million of assets out of the United States, despite Griesa's standing orders not to do so. The assets were Argentine securities backed by shares of U.S. companies. Argentina sold the structured instruments to an Argentine fund manager, who then liquidated the underlying U.S. instruments.[86] Griesa was furious, and on May 29, 2009, he found Argentina in contempt of court for the maneuver.[87] Even so, he did not levy a financial penalty, as the plaintiffs suggested he should, because he felt that he didn't have the power to do so under the law. He was probably also sure that Argentina wouldn't pay any financial penalty, so levying one would just create yet one more dispute that he would have to resolve.

Let That Tanker Go: August 2009

Two months later on August 7, 2009, Elliott launched a solo effort to grab a tanker full of liquified natural gas that was in the middle of the Atlantic Ocean on its way from Egypt to Argentina. The firm's lawyers filed an attachment motion and an alter ego lawsuit against Energía Argentina S.A., better known as ENARSA, the Argentine state-owned company that was purchasing the gas.

In a pair of hearings held on August 7 and August 11, Elliott explained that it wanted to attach the value of the cargo worth $20 million, even though the ship was in the middle of the ocean and not in the United States, as required under §1610 of the FSIA.[88] To this end, the firm moved to attach ENARSA's "contract rights," which it deemed to be located in New York, not the ship itself. Elliott's idea, as explained in court, was to take ENARSA's position in the contract and fail to make the final $5 million payment due under the contract, thereby creating a default.[89] As a result, the cargo would not be delivered, which in turn would allow the firm to ask for the return of the $15 million that ENARSA had already paid to Morgan Stanley.

It was a clever ploy, but Judge Griesa was unimpressed and said he wouldn't take an action in support of the deliberate breach of a performing contract between two parties. He was also reluctant to cut off the supply of an essential commodity, having heard testimony from Morgan Stanley that the consequence of an attachment might be a cutoff of power in the middle of a cold winter in Argentina. Instead, he gave Elliott an ultimatum: step into ENARSA's shoes and make the final $5 million payment on the contract and step into its shoes as buyer of the cargo of liquified natural gas or get nothing. Its bluff called, Elliott said no, and Griesa denied the attachment.[90]

Creditors Lose on Pension Assets, and Dreier LLP Collapses

For the plaintiffs, the decade of the aughts ended on a down note. On October 15, 2009, the Second Circuit Court of Appeals, strictly reading the law and precedent, reversed Judge Griesa's ruling in favor of the attachment of the $250 million of pension assets found in New York. Argentina had cleverly drafted its nationalization law to order the immediate return of the private pension fund assets as soon as the law took effect. The instant the government took control of the assets, they were deemed, under law, to be on their way back to Argentina. Creditors were shocked. They had thought that the circuit court would affirm Griesa's ruling because it would take some time for Argentina to return the assets to Argentina after the nationalization, that is, the assets would be "used for a commercial activity" in New York for at least a few hours. The judges, however, ruled against the plaintiffs, narrowly reading the §1610 commercial activity exception because the law and judicial precedents required them to do so. But the court took no pleasure in handing down this ruling. Senior judge J. Clifford Wallace wrote, "We understand the frustration of the plaintiffs who are attempting to recover on judgments they have secured.

Nevertheless, we must respect the Act's strict limitations on attaching and executing upon assets of a foreign state."[91]

Meanwhile, the Dreier-Vago clients were suffering a different kind of misery. In early December 2008, Marc Dreier was caught selling bogus promissory notes to hedge funds—including Elliott Associates—to prop up his failing law firm.[92] As a result, all the Dreier-Vago plaintiffs needed to find a new lawyer, while some also had to dislodge their bonds from the bankruptcy estate of the firm. Most of them stayed with the litigation, with many signing new representation agreements with Patricia Vago and Michael Spencer from Milberg LLP; others signed with Duane Morris, where Anthony Costantini led the effort.

While perhaps it had been an exciting choice to hold out and sue, excitement turned to disappointment as the legal wisdom handed down over the years proved true: it is easy to sue but hard to collect from a sovereign in default. Five years with no payments and no victories in court left most creditors in desperate shape as the end of the decade approached. As a result, when Argentina reopened its restructuring offer in 2010 on largely the same terms it had offered in 2005, most holdouts capitulated.

The flipside of creditor misery at the end of the aughts was happiness in Argentina. Its economy was hitting on all cylinders, having bounced strongly from its 2002 depression lows. The cheapening of the exchange rate made the country more competitive, and soybean prices were steadily rising, buoyed by strong demand from China. On debt, the 2005 transaction left a clear runway to grow, with Argentina having reduced the stock of its foreign bonds substantially through the transaction, and the country wasn't paying a penny to the holdouts. When the country needed to raise dollars it could legally insulate itself by raising the money in domestic bond offers, the proceeds of which were received locally, not in New York, so they couldn't be attached by the holdouts; only later would the new bonds be sold to offshore investors. This two-step process added cost, but it was a simple way to cut out the risk of attachment. In the second half of the aughts Argentina was on a best-case trajectory, as shown in figure 6.1, with the country enjoying steady growth and rapidly increasing foreign

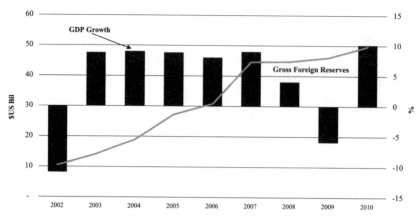

Figure 6.1. Argentina foreign reserves versus real annual GDP growth
(2002–2010)

Source: World Bank, "GDP Growth (Annual %)," The World Bank Group,
accessed Sept. 15, 2022, https://data.worldbank.org/indicator/NY.GDP.MKTP
.KD.ZG; and World Bank, "Total Reserves Minus Gold (Current US$)," The
World Bank Group, accessed Sept. 15, 2022, https://data.worldbank.org/indicato
r/FI.RES.XGLD.CD.

reserves except in 2009 when the country, like the rest of the world, was
hit by the shock of the global credit crisis.

The bald unvarnished truth was that the litigation in New York was
generating ugly headlines but was not harming the country. While it was
costing the country millions of dollars of legal expenses a year, that was a
small price to pay if the alternative was to pay the $19.6 billion of holdout
creditors in full plus their claims for past due interest and other accruals.
Argentina's economic success didn't go unnoticed in New York, however.
Plaintiffs made sure to tell Judge Griesa how well the country was doing
to stoke his anger at Argentina for not helping him deal with the holdouts, and it worked. At a hearing on April 30, 2008, he said,

> One of the most interesting things I got out of all of the papers about the
> 100 million filed by Sullivan & Cromwell was a very bold statement about
> how well Argentina is now doing. They are running a surplus. They can
> borrow money so cheaply they don't have to go through all of the things,

the shenanigans that the plaintiffs say they go through to get money out of the Central Bank. They've got surpluses, and they can borrow so cheaply. If they can do it, why don't they just pay their just debts?[93]

As the decade drew to a close, Argentina's holdout debt situation was in flux. In Argentina's favor, its economy was strong, and most of its holdout investors were eager to drop out of the fight. On the other hand, Judge Griesa was increasingly irritable, and there was no hint that the large sophisticated plaintiffs would give up anytime soon. These were tectonic forces that presaged big changes, and 2010 proved to be a pivotal year.

7

Turning Point

(2010)

The audience of bondholders at the January 31, 2008, *LatinFinance* conference in Miami groaned when a last-minute addition to the agenda,
Marcelo Etchebarne, a young, Harvard-trained lawyer from Argentina,
reached his main point. He said that the holdouts from Argentina's exchange offer should agree to a reopening on the same terms as before
because it would be in everyone's interest.[1] Argentina would resolve its
long-festering holdout problem, while bondholders would double their
money. The math was simple: the new bonds plus the GDP warrants that
would be offered in the reopening transaction would be worth fifty cents
on the dollar, while the defaulted bonds were now trading at twenty-five
cents on the dollar.

It was a fine financial idea but not what the audience had come to
hear that day. The title of the conference was "The Road Ahead: An Examination of Argentina's Economic and Political Future," and the preliminary agenda had a distinctly procreditor, anti-Kirchner slant.[2] While
the first panel featured a balanced spectrum of speakers and topics, the
second panel, the one Etchebarne spoke on, was "U.S. Policy and the
Protection of Foreign Investment," and it was decidedly less neutral. Its
discussion prompts included the following questions:

"How can the Foreign Sovereign Immunities Act be changed to strengthen
   creditor rights?"
"Should the U.S. intervene in court on the side of U.S. investors?"
"Should the U.S. exclude sovereigns in default on court judgments in G7
   countries from selling their bonds in the United States?"

"Did Argentina set a bad precedent by signaling to other emerging markets sovereigns that it is easy and costless to default?"

After a coffee break the third panel focused on the "Chávez Effect," with
prompts including "How harmful will it be for forthcoming foreign investment, if Argentina's new President continues to align the country
with Chávez's movement and economic favors?" This anti-Argentina,
anti-Kirchner orientation wasn't surprising given the prominence of
speakers from American Task Force Argentina (ATFA) on the agenda.[3]
AFTA was a high-power lobbying group whose website listed Elliott Associates and FRAN plaintiff partners Bracebridge and Montreux as members.[4] Its mission was to lobby for the full repayment of the holdouts from
Argentina's 2005 debt restructuring. As was disclosed in a mandatory
filing with Congress by one of its lobbyists, ATFA was formed to engage
Congress, the State Department, the U.S. Treasury, and the Inter-American Development Bank with the goal of getting Argentina to pay the $3
billion owed to the organization's sponsors.[5]

Notwithstanding the slant of the agenda, Etchebarne put his procom-
promise idea on the table. He was young and had the habit of speaking
his mind. In his speech he argued that "the holdout debt situation is not
binary. It doesn't have to be: Argentina paying nothing, or creditors winning full payment in foreign courts. There is a middle way," which was
to reopen the 2005 offer on pretty much the same terms. Etchebarne's
middle way would allow Argentina to claim victory and avoid breaching
the Lock Law, while creditors would score a big profit versus the market
price, with the new package worth around fifty cents on the dollar, the
value many holdouts had wanted in the first place. The audience wasn't
happy, but Etchebarne made it through his presentation. Stepping off the
podium, he felt like he could have made a mistake speaking up like he did
in favor of a compromise at such an event.

As Etchebarne was exiting the building, however, an audience member ran to catch up with him. "Wait," the young fund manager said, "we
need to talk."

The fund manager was an employee of Connecticut-based Gramercy

Funds Management LLC, a hedge fund specializing in emerging markets debt.[6] He said that Etchebarne needed to talk to his boss, Robert Koenigsberger, who was already working on the idea of reopening the 2005 offer on similar terms. Maybe they could work together.

Putting the Reopening Deal Team Together

When they met, Marcelo Etchebarne and Robert Koenigsberger hit it off. They shared a general belief that a reopening of the 2005 offer would be a win-win for the market and for Argentina, and they realized that they needed each other. Gramercy had large holdings of bonds to anchor a transaction, while Etchebarne had access to the government in Buenos Aires, so they agreed to work together for a few months to try to get the deal done.

They quickly realized that closing the deal would be hard to pull off without a major investment bank standing in the middle to handle the exchange of cash and bonds. A bank could also help increase the size of the deal to maybe $5 billion, which would make it more appealing to Argentina. To this end, after failing to make progress with another bank, Etchebarne and Koenigsberger asked Barclays Capital investment banker Gustavo Ferraro and his colleague Carlos Mauleon to join the team. Ferraro was a good fit because he was Argentine, he had worked with the Argentine Ministry of Economy on the 2005 deal, and Barclays knew all the players in the market, which meant that they were well positioned to convince other funds who still held the defaulted bonds to join the transaction. The legal arrangement was that Koenigsberger would hire Barclays and Etchebarne to help his firm execute the deal, with Etchebarne providing transaction advice through Arcadia Advisors, a boutique advisory firm based in London and Buenos Aires set up by his half brother Emilio Ocampo, a former Salomon Brothers banker.[7]

Argentina Sidetracked by Agricultural Taxes

Gramercy's Koenigsberger, Etchebarne, and Barclays' Ferraro set off with high hopes of quickly closing a historic multibillion-dollar deal with Argentina, maybe within a month or two; they quickly hit a wall, however.

On paper, early 2008 was a good time to approach the government with a new idea. Cristina Fernández de Kirchner had just been sworn in as her husband's successor on December 10, 2007, and she had tapped Martín Lousteau, a young market-oriented economist, to serve as her minister of economy. The word was that her new administration would be more moderate than her husband's, and in a cable the U.S. embassy in Buenos Aires described Lousteau as "young, bright, open-minded, and not tied to Argentina's protectionist industries."[8] Lousteau's appointment was good news for the team seeking to pitch the reopening deal to the government. It was rumored that the new president was open to doing something about the holdout creditor problem, whereas her husband's administration had been a brick wall on that topic.

Lousteau did not last long, however, since his first policy initiative was a spectacular failure. His idea was a solid one: a modification of the formula for export taxes on soy, wheat, and other agricultural products so they would float with commodity prices. Under the new formula, the government would take a larger cut of farmers' profits when prices were high and a smaller cut when prices were low, which in theory would be more efficient for both parties. Lousteau launched the reform initiative without prior consultation with the agricultural sector, however, and farmers attacked the proposal, seeing it as yet another scheme for the city dwellers to stick it to them. Of particular concern was an immediate step-up of tax rates under the new scheme, a consequence of high prevailing prices on agricultural goods. Protests broke out all over the country.[9]

Despite the backlash, the government of Fernández de Kirchner pressed on with the reform. In the press, she vilified the critics and said that the farmers were earning enough profits. Her approach sparked a multimonth nationwide conflict that featured tense stand-offs on highways around the country, with Kirchner-aligned truckers pitted against antitax farmers who were blocking the roads.

The climax of the 2008 battle came when President Fernández de Kirchner put the agricultural bill up for a vote in the Argentine Congress. It passed in the lower chamber but failed in a high-drama Senate imbroglio in which the tie-breaking vote was in the hands of Vice President Julio Cobos, who hailed from the agricultural province of Mendoza. After an emotional forty-minute speech early on the morning of July 17, 2008, Cobos cast his vote with his province, not his president, and the agricultural reform was dead.[10] It was a stunning political defeat for the new president.

Heads rolled in the aftermath, with Minister Lousteau and long-time cabinet chief Alberto Fernández let go. It was a frustrating turn of events for the Gramercy-Barclays-Arcadia team. With the government missing in action, six months had passed, and they had achieved no traction. In fact, they hadn't even landed a single meeting to discuss the proposal. There was soon cause for renewed optimism, however, when President Fernández de Kirchner appointed Sergio Massa, the popular thirty-six-year-old mayor of the Buenos Aires suburb of Tigre, as Alberto Fernández's replacement.[11] Cabinet Chief Massa was a media darling and a known pragmatist. Massa was someone they could work with if they could get a meeting.

Stop, Start, Stop Again

As soon as Cabinet Chief Massa took office, Etchebarne reached out for a meeting to talk about the reopening of the 2005 offer. Scheduling a meeting with the new cabinet chief was almost as hard as getting a meeting with the president, however. In Argentina, the cabinet chief takes the lead in policy matters, with the president hovering above the fray. As a result, everyone in the country wanted a meeting with Massa in his first month in office.

Etchebarne rang Massa's secretary and asked for a spot on his calendar. She put him off, telling him to call back the next week. Etchebarne couldn't wait any longer, however; his credibility was on the line. While Koenigsberger was patient, sooner or later he and the other investors who had lined up to take the deal would have to show Barclays and Arcadia the door if the two firms couldn't deliver the government side of the trade. Barclays and Arcadia's mandate had already been extended to August 31, and it was unclear if Gramercy and the other investors would renew it again without proof that the team was getting traction in Buenos Aires.

Etchebarne decided it was time to play hardball. He convinced the team that the next step was for Barclays and Arcadia to send a formal written proposal for a reopening of the 2005 exchange offer directly to President Fernández de Kirchner. Such a letter, Etchebarne knew, would be stamped and registered on arrival, and the government would have to take action. It was a desperate measure, the procedural equivalent of throwing a hand grenade, because such a stamped letter might become public later if reporters knew to look for it. The problem was not in sending a letter per se but rather in sending one about the holdout issue, a politically delicate topic to say the least. The letter was dated August 12, 2008, but it was filed and stamped three days later because the original copy was signed by Barclays in New York and had to be sent by courier to Buenos Aires.[12] The proposal included a target of exchanging $10 billion, or about half of the $19.6 billion in holdout bonds, combined with a new money financing of up to $2.5 billion dollars.

As hoped, Massa's office called almost immediately, and Etchebarne was given an appointment. The new cabinet chief was annoyed at the tactic Etchebarne had used to get a meeting but saw the logic of the Gramercy-Barclays-Arcadia proposal and said he would bring it to the president. A few days later, Massa called Etchebarne and told him "I talked to the President and she likes it."[13]

With presidential support, things started moving quickly. The next step was for the deal team to meet with Massa and with Secretary of Finance Hernán Lorenzino in Buenos Aires. Given the high profile of the transaction, Barclays sent four senior bankers to join Etchebarne at the meetings in Buenos Aires: Gustavo Ferraro from fixed income; Carlos Mauleon, the managing director for investment banking in Latin America; Robert Helbling, the chair of Barclays in Argentina; and Barclays chairman Hans-Joerg Rudloff, who flew in from London to demonstrate that the bank was putting its reputation behind the successful completion of the transaction, the sort of thing governments like to see before undertaking a potentially risky, politically sensitive transaction.

The bankers said that reopening the 2005 transaction would be a quick and simple procedure because Gramercy and other investors were lined up to do the deal. All they needed was a green light and a few days to execute. The legal and operational mechanics would be minimal because it would be done as a private offer, with Argentina exchanging bonds directly with the participants and with only Barclays standing in the middle, obviating the need for the complicated settlement mechanics of the 2005 deal.

The bankers immediately hit a snag, however. The government—and the government's lawyers in New York—believed that the deal should be done as a public offer, not a private offer, so that all the holdouts could be invited to join. Why clean up just one-quarter of the problem when you might be able to clean it all up and put an end to the litigation? It was a sensible position to take, but it was terrible news to the Gramercy-Barclays-Arcadia group, which was seeking a quick, simple transaction. And there was more bad news. Argentina wanted to add Citi and Deutsche Bank to the deal, which would make the process more cumbersome and reduce the advisers' fees, because now they would have to be shared.

Still, the Gramercy-Barclays-Arcadia team had years of experience and could deal with new partners and delay. The complications might add three to six months to the transaction timeline, which was a wall they could easily climb. Then they hit a much bigger obstacle. The global contagion that followed in the wake of the Lehman Brothers collapse caused such dislocation in the price of Argentina's bonds that the deal no longer made sense. Now they would have to wait for the market to recover. But the deal was not dead. Argentina wanted to do the deal, and the Ministry of Economy team got going on the preparations.

The Great Capitulation: The 2010 Reopening of Argentina's Offer

Argentina's 2010 reopening of its 2005 offer made it into the market on April 30, 2010, and settled on September 27.[14] There is not much to say about it other than that it happened, that it was a great success, and that it did not trigger any big political battles or media fights. It was a technical offer that attracted those who were tired of waiting and those who had given up on litigating.

The transaction succeeded thanks to the strong participation of institutional funds anchored by Gramercy, combined with a massive take-up by Italian retail investors who were tired of waiting for a payout. This time TFA lodged no objection, although it said it would continue to pursue litigation on behalf of Italian investors still intent on suing. Of the $19.6 billion in outstanding holdout bonds, $12.4 billion were tendered into the exchange, leaving just $6.8 billion remaining.[15] With these additions, Argentina achieved an aggregate participation rate in its two transactions of about 92%, an unprecedented result for a transaction with such a deep haircut.[16] Uruguay, by contrast, achieved a similar participation rate on its foreign bonds in its 2003 transaction in which investors suffered no haircut at all, just a five-year average extension of maturity.

The success of the reopening left Argentina facing far fewer holdouts. Two-thirds of TFA's members dropped out, leaving just sixty thousand Italian investors working with the group.[17] TIAA-CREF, the most highly regarded U.S. institutional investor to have joined the hedge funds in holding out, submitted all its bonds into the 2010 reopening and dropped its lawsuit against Argentina.[18] Other U.S. institutional holdouts also took the deal in whole or in part.[19]

While a headline success for the country, Argentina's 2010 reopening was also a boon for the remaining holdouts. The remaining holdout debt, just $6.8 billion, was small compared to the country's foreign reserves, now $50 billion, making it clear to all observers that the country could pay if it chose to. This simple comparison of holdout debt to foreign reserves mattered a lot, because the plaintiffs could now credibly argue in court that the lawsuits were still ongoing only because Argentina was unwilling to pay the holdouts, not because it was unable to pay, the country's defense up to that point. Judge Griesa took note of the shifted context when he made subsequent decisions.

Efforts to Disrupt Argentina's 2010 Reopening

While Elliott surely had no intention of taking Argentina's 2010 offer, the firm had a keen eye on the transaction as it was developing. In the fall of 2009 Elliott sent subpoenas to Barclays, Citi, and Deutsche Bank for information on the deal, although Judge Griesa denied its motion to compel a response.[20] Other investors tried to block the transaction. During 2010, class-action plaintiffs filed several motions to disrupt or block the exchange offer. Griesa denied these motions, undoubtedly eager to facilitate the settlement of a large portion of Argentina's remaining defaulted debt.[21]

Judge Griesa failed, however, to facilitate additional settlements with Argentina's Brady bond holders. The problem was CVI's second lien attachment of the collateral backing Argentina's Brady bonds, as discussed in chapter 6. Notwithstanding the attachment, Griesa ruled in 2010 that Argentina's Brady bonds could be included in the reopening transaction, but the Second Circuit Court of Appeals reversed his decision, saying Argentina couldn't access the collateral with CVI's attachment in place.[22] This ruling blocked the holders of Argentina's $1 billion of remaining Brady bonds from participating in the country's 2010 reopening.

Elliott Steps Up the Attack

Argentina's 2010 reopening did not distract Elliott from using the power of the courts to compel Argentina to settle with it on favorable terms. During 2010 the firm kept up the pressure, making motions and sending lawyers to argue at hearings about attachments, discovery, and the value of its FRANs.

While less of a focus in the early years of the litigation, discovery became a major tool from 2010 on. In one initiative Elliott sought unprecedented worldwide discovery from the international banks that made day-to-day payments for Argentina, demanding that the banks disclose all the details of all the payments they made from all of their U.S. and non-U.S. branches and subsidiaries. Unprecedented though this discovery effort was, Elliott and Aurelius later enjoyed a victory at the Supreme Court on their right to obtain this information from international banks doing transactions for countries in default. This win was particularly noteworthy, since the plaintiffs were unlikely to be able to use such information to successfully attach Argentina's assets. The law limits attachments to assets used for a commercial activity in the United States. The court was nonetheless unwilling to block offshore discovery because the text of the FSIA provided no jurisdictional limit on the scope of discovery. The justices concluded that it was the responsibility of Congress, not the judiciary, to assign such limits and left it to the district court judge handling the cases to determine the appropriate scope of discovery in any particular case.[23] Another Elliott discovery initiative was less successful and not particularly well regarded. In October 2010, Elliott served subpoenas on the general manager and the directors of the BIS—including the heads of the French and Swiss central banks—when they were in the United States to attend the World Bank–IMF Annual Meetings in 2010.[24] The courts in New York and Washington quashed these subpoenas but only after all the targeted officials hired lawyers and submitted papers to the court. While learning about Argentina's offshore banking payments might be of value when seeking attachments from a foreign court, this particular effort was of no obvious economic value, since the chance of ever recovering assets from the BIS was nil given its bulletproof immunity under Swiss law.

Elliott and its FRAN plaintiff partners also saw important progress during 2010. On September 23 the Second Circuit affirmed the $3 billion in judgments that Judge Griesa had granted to the FRAN plaintiffs in 2009. The circuit court confirmed that the plaintiffs were owed the contract amount, that is, ten times the face amount of the bonds that they held,[25] although one ancillary part of the calculation was referred to a New York State court for review. This was a huge victory, a legal ruling that few other investors thought would be possible back in 2004 and 2005 when Elliott and the other plaintiff members started litigating these bonds.

While there were important developments related to discovery and the FRANs during 2010, the most dramatic legal event of the year was the explosive opinion Judge Griesa handed down on April 7 in the long-running

Central Bank of Argentina case.[26] Entering the year, the $105 million in foreign reserves were still frozen, as they had been since December 30, 2005. But the case had gone quiet for several years as Griesa pondered how to rule. Between 2007 and 2009 he had held numerous hearings on technical issues and had requested more information from the parties, but new events on the ground in Buenos Aires gave him the impetus to rule.[27] In December 2009 Argentine president Cristina Fernández de Kirchner ordered central bank president Martín Redrado to lend the government $6.6 billion. When he said no—to avoid creating inflation, as such lending tends to do—he was pressured to resign and was replaced by a Kirchner loyalist, who quickly lent the government the money the president had asked for.[28] This chain of events helped convince Griesa that the Central Bank of Argentina was under the day-to-day control of the republic, which allowed him, in turn, to rule that the Central Bank of Argentina was the alter ego of the republic, making the $105 million attachable as originally suggested by Judge Cabranes in 2006.

Judge Griesa's 2010 opinion in the central bank case was later overruled because the Second Circuit thought that the special immunity of central banks under §1611 of the FSIA still blocked the attachment, but his April 2010 opinion is an important document because what he wrote says much about his state of mind going into the pari passu litigation that followed. In his April 7, 2010, opinion Griesa wrote that Argentina's central bank was "the servant of the Republic"[29] and that Argentina was doing "everything in its power" to avoid enforcement on the judgments.[30] He also dismissed the arguments the Federal Reserve Bank of New York had made in an amicus brief. While the Fed supported Argentina's position that the FSIA forbade the attachment of the central bank assets, Griesa said overriding considerations should govern:

> The court has seriously considered the Federal Reserve's position. . . . However, there are other important institutions. One of these is the court system. What is going on between the Republic of Argentina and the federal court system is an exercise of sheer willful defiance of the obligations of the

Republic to honor the judgments of a federal court. Of course, the immunities provided for in the FSIA must be given effect by the court. But the basic, overriding obligation of the Republic is to honor and to pay judgments lawfully entered against it by the federal courts, to the extent that it is able to do so. The Republic's prominently declared position is to refuse this course, and the Republic has thus enmeshed the court in years of wasteful litigation with no end in sight."[31]

Judge Griesa accusing Argentina of "sheer willful defiance" and blaming the litigation mess on Argentina was a strong signal that it was time for Elliott to finally roll out its long-awaited pari passu attack. The filing came on October 20, 2010, just weeks after two other pending pieces of business were resolved. In September 2010 Argentina's second exchange offer closed, giving the country the capacity to pay the remaining holdouts, and the Second Circuit affirmed Griesa's ruling that the FRAN plaintiffs' extraordinary contracts had to be paid in full.[32] Thus, almost exactly ten years later it was Peru 2000 all over again: Elliott was in court seeking an injunction against a developing country's payments on its foreign bonds to force repayment of its holdout debt.

Yet Elliott was facing anything but a sure win. Judge Griesa was indeed hopping mad, and Argentina had the money to pay the holdouts in full, but the bald truth of the matter was that Griesa, up to that date, had consistently ruled against any effort by holdout creditors to interfere with creditors that had settled. Also, as evidenced from Elliott's failed 2009 effort to interfere with Argentina's gas delivery contract, Griesa wasn't necessarily going to give Elliott everything that it wanted. Asking Griesa for a pari passu blockade on payments to holders of $30 billion of performing debt was no small ask. Moreover, Elliott's pari passu theory was a long shot. Scholars derided Elliott's "equal payments" theory, and Griesa himself had said that the Belgian court had used an "odd interpretation."[33] Scholars also made a strong public policy argument that injunctions against payments to bondholders would be damaging to financial markets.[34] However, some scholars pointed out that Elliott could win in court on pari passu not because of its equal payments theory but instead because Argentina's Lock Law, by itself, could breach the clause.[35] As a result, the upcoming battle between Argentina and Elliott on pari passu generated excitement. The trial didn't disappoint.

8

Equal Treatment

(October 2010–May 2014)

After 2010, the fate of Argentina's finances hinged on the meaning of an obscure Latin term. While the English translation of pari passu is "with an equal step,"[1] nobody was 100% sure what that meant under New York law, since its meaning had never been litigated in the state. When Elliott Associates filed papers accusing Argentina of breaching its pari passu clause in October 2010, it became Judge Thomas P. Griesa's job to decide the matter. The debate in his courtroom would be about whether the clause required Argentina to pay its foreign bondholders equally or whether it obliged the country to rank its foreign bonds equally. On this difference would turn Argentina's finances as well as the global practice of sovereign debt restructuring. On the one hand, ruling for the equal payment interpretation would serve to justify the imposition of an injunction, because making any payment to exchange bondholders without an equal payment to holdout creditors would breach the covenant. On the other hand, an injunction would not be an obvious remedy for a breach under the equal ranking interpretation. Lawyers and policy makers around the world watched developments with bated breath. They expected that an Elliott victory would undermine future sovereign debt restructurings, because once a U.S. court showed that it was willing to issue such an injunction, many more investors would be tempted to play the holdout game.

With billions of dollars at stake and the future of sovereign debt restructuring hanging in the balance, the lawyers on both sides were itching for the fight, so much so that they started to throw punches before the issue made it into the courtroom. In the fall 2010 edition of Duke Law

School's *Law and Contemporary Problems*, Argentina's lawyer Jonathan Blackman wrote that Elliott's equal payments interpretation was facing a "conclusive defeat" after reviewing rulings made in a handful of cases touching on the matter over the prior decade.[2] Elliott's lawyer Robert Cohen countered Blackman's analysis in "Sometimes a Cigar Is Just a Cigar: The Simple Story of *Pari Passu*," published in the *Hofstra Law Review*, in which he argued for an equal payments interpretation of the clause and provided an alternative interpretation of two of the post-Peru pari passu cases Blackman cited in his paper, namely, a 2004 ruling in the Belgian case *Republic of Nicaragua v. LNC Investments LLC* and a 2002 ruling in the Central District of California case *Red Mountain Finance, Inc. v. Democratic Republic of Congo*.[3]

The battle commenced on October 20, 2010, when Elliott filed papers asserting that Argentina had breached its pari passu clause and asking Judge Griesa to impose an injunction on the country to remedy the infraction. Argentina filed its response on December 10, 2010,[4] and Elliott filed a reply memo on January 14, 2011.[5] This rapid-fire exchange notwithstanding, Griesa took his time reviewing the material, only convening a hearing eleven months after Elliott had filed its initial motion.

When the hearing finally took place on September 28, 2011, it was a very unusual one. While Judge Griesa had given both sides ample time to make their arguments in previous hearings, in this session he cut off lawyers on both sides. The tone he used that day suggests that he was angry at Argentina and impatient to rule against it. It was a fascinating hearing. A consequence of Griesa's interruptions, however, is that the transcript is a jumble of half-made arguments, which in turn means that it is necessary to look to the legal memos Elliott and Argentina posted to follow the arguments made by both sides.

NML's Memorandum of Law

In the opening paragraph of its October 20, 2010, brief, Elliott's NML Capital, Ltd. laid out its four central reasons for imposing an injunction against Argentina: the country's breach of its pari passu clause by not making equal payments to holdout creditors, its highhanded treatment of its creditors, its disrespect for the authority of the court, and the Lock Law, which breached the country's pari passu clause when interpreted as an equal ranking obligation. NML wrote:

> NML Capital, Ltd., respectfully moves for partial summary judgment on its claim that the Republic of Argentina has breached its contractual obligation under the bonds at issue in these cases and, in particular, its obligation to treat NML equally with other external creditors. NML also requests an injunction requiring Argentina to pay NML ratably if and when it makes payments to other external creditors, including bondholders who participated in Argentina's 2005 and 2010 "exchanges."
>
> For most of the past decade, NML has litigated over its right to receive payment on billions of dollars of defaulted Argentine bonds. Although NML has won a mountain of favorable judgments, Argentina has steadfastly refused to honor those judgments. Instead of respecting the authority of this Court, Argentina has gone to extraordinary measures to evade repayment, enacting laws that proclaim that it will *never* repay NML or satisfy its U.S. judgments because NML refused to submit to Argentina's coercive "exchange offers," which would have forced NML to accept pennies on the dollar in return for releasing its multi-billion–dollar claims. Those creditors who did acquiesce to these take-it-or-leave-it demands now receive payments from Argentina, while NML—despite this Court's judgments—receives nothing.
>
> Argentina's refusal to pay NML while paying other creditors not only breaches Argentina's payment obligations under the bonds, but also independently violates a provision of the bond documents that requires all creditors who demand payment to be treated equally. . . . By creating a class of creditors who are guaranteed payment while formally condemning NML to a lower rank that is barred from receiving any payment at all, Argentina has breached this Equal Treatment Provision. In the wake of Argentina's exchange offers

and its infamous law not only barring payment under non-tendered bonds, but also barring payment of the judgments of this Court, Argentina's payment obligations to NML simply cannot be said to "rank at least equally" to those of the performing bonds issued under the exchange offers. NML thus seeks partial summary judgment . . . for Argentina's breach of contract.

NML requests that this Court specifically enforce the Equal Treatment Provision by requiring Argentina to pay NML ratably if and when it makes payments on other external indebtedness, including payments to the bondholders who participated in exchange offers.[6]

Included in Elliott's papers was an expert witness brief written by Harvard professor Hal S. Scott. His curriculum vitae, which was also incorporated into the brief, noted the numerous books and articles he had written and his many high-profile roles in the legal community.[7] Scott had served as reporter for the committee responsible for updating the Uniform Commercial Code, an expert witness for the U.S. government in various cases, and former president of the International Academy of Consumer and Commercial Law and was a former governor of the American Stock Exchange. He was also the current director of the Committee on Capital Markets Regulation. In other words, he was well qualified to weigh in on the pari passu dispute.

Professor Scott used his brief to compare the wording of Argentina's pari passu clause to that used by fifteen other governments. Differences in wording, he argued, proved that Argentina's pari passu clause promised investors equal payment. Specifically, Argentina used the words "payment obligations," terminology some other countries didn't use.[8]

Here is the text of Argentina's clause as it appears in the country's 1994 Fiscal Agency Agreement,[9] with the words that Professor Scott emphasized in his brief highlighted in bold and all caps (emphasis added):

1. The Securities will constitute . . . direct, unconditional, unsecured and unsubordinated obligations of the Republic and shall at all times rank *pari passu* and without any preference among themselves; and

2. THE PAYMENT OBLIGATIONS of the Republic under the Se-

Anne Krueger, acting managing director of the International Monetary Fund, answers questions at a news conference in Washington, D.C., on April 22, 2004 (Photo credit: MANNIE GARCIA/Getty Images)

John B. Taylor, U.S. undersecretary of treasury for international affairs, speaks in South Korea on May 16, 2004 (Photo credit: SEOKYONG LEE/ Bloomberg via Getty Images)

Economy Minister Roberto Lavagna speaks in Buenos Aires on December 22, 2004 (Photo credit: ALI BURAFI/AFP via Getty Images)

Finance Secretary Guillermo Nielson arrives at the International Monetary Fund on November 13, 2002, in Washington, D.C. (Photo credit: JOYCE NALTCHAYAN/AFP via Getty Images)

U.S. president George W. Bush welcomes Argentine president Néstor Kirchner in the Oval Office at the White House on July 23, 2003 (Photo credit: MANNY CENETA/AFP via Getty Images)

President Cristina Fernández de Kirchner with her husband and outgoing president Néstor Kirchner during her inauguration ceremony at the Congress building in Buenos Aires, on December 10, 2007 (Photo credit: JUAN MABROMATA/AFP via Getty Images)

The frigate ARA *Libertad* as it approaches the port of Manila on July 8, 2008 (Photo credit: JAY DIRECTO/AFP via Getty Images)

Paul Singer of Elliott Investment Management speaks at the World Economic Forum Annual Meeting 2011 in Davos, Switzerland, on January 27, 2011 (Photo credit: TOMOHIRO OHSUMI/Bloomberg via Getty Images)

Attorney Robert A. Cohen arrives at the U.S. federal courthouse in New York on August 8, 2014 (Photo credit: STAN HONDA/AFP via Getty Images)

Mark Sobel, acting assistant secretary of the treasury for international affairs, speaks during a Senate subcommittee hearing on September 30, 2009 (Photo credit: ANDREW HARRER/Bloomberg via Getty Images)

Attorneys David Boies (left) and Theodore Olson (right) discuss the issue of marriage equality at the LBJ Presidential Library on April 8, 2014 (Photo credit: Robert Daemmrich Photography Inc/Corbis via Getty Images)

Poster depicting Judge Thomas P. Griesa as a vulture in Buenos Aires on August 12, 2014 (Photo credit: MARCOS BRINDICCI/REUTERS)

Attorneys Carmine Boccuzzi (right) and Jonathan Blackman (left) arrive at the U.S. federal courthouse in New York on July 22, 2014 (Photo credit: DON EMMERT/AFP via Getty Images)

Special Master Daniel Pollack arrives at the U.S. federal courthouse in New York on August 8, 2014 (Photo credit: STAN HONDA/AFP via Getty Images)

Finance Secretary Luis Caputo at a news conference in Buenos Aires on February 29, 2016 (Photo credit: DIEGO LEVY/Bloomberg via Getty Images)

curities shall at all times rank at least equally with all its other present
and future unsecured and unsubordinated External Indebtedness.

In Professor Scott's reading, the first of these two sentences promised investors that they would enjoy "equal ranking," while the second promised "equal payment."

To hammer home its analysis, Elliott Associates defined the second sentence of Argentina's pari passu clause as the "Equal Treatment Provision." This was a clever choice of terminology, because it shifted the language used in court toward the concept of equal treatment and away from the words "equal ranking" actually used in both legs of the republic's clause. This rhetorical sleight of hand proved its power over time: the term "equal treatment provision" was used frequently in court even though it appears nowhere in Argentina's bonds.

Argentina's Memorandum of Law

Argentina's memorandum of law, which its lawyers delivered to the court in December 2010, argued forcefully for an "equal ranking" interpretation of the country's pari passu clause. The country's lead-off argument was procedural, however, with Argentina making the case that Elliott had presented its pari passu motion too late in the process for it to be granted under the common-law doctrine of laches. Making reference to the preliminary hearing on pari passu held on January 15, 2004, Argentina argued as follows:

> Nearly seven years ago, the Republic sought a declaratory judgment
> specifically to protect the anticipated restructuring of its unmanage-
> able indebtedness from an attack by holdout creditors, in particular
> NML, based on a spurious and unprecedented reading of the "pari
> passu" clause previously invented by NML's corporate parent. NML at
> that time *prevented* the resolution of the issue, arguing both in 2004
> and at the time of the Republic's Exchange Offer in 2005, that it was
> premature to decide the question because there was supposedly no
> evidence that it would pursue a "pari passu" claim then or in the

future. After that time, the Republic and holders of interest in over
91% of its defaulted debt (over $74.5 billion) went forward with the
largest sovereign restructuring in history through two Exchange Offers in 2005 and 2010, and the Republic has made regular interest
payments totaling billions of dollars on the new performing bonds
since June 2005.

Now, almost seven years after NML disavowed an intent to pursue
its pari passu theory, and over five years after the successful completion of the Republic's first Exchange Offer (which NML sought
to block, although on different grounds), NML moves for summary
judgment and injunctive relief under the same incorrect interpretation of the pari passu clause, based on alleged violations of the clause
that supposedly began in 2005, when the Republic entered into its
first Exchange Offer and began making payments on the new debt
issued on that Offer. This unjustified *five year* delay, and the serious
harm to the Republic and its bondholders arising from that delay,
bar NML's claim for injunctive relief under the doctrine of laches.[10]

To the merits of Elliott's argument, Argentina responded that its pari
passu clause imposed an equal ranking obligation—not an equal payment obligation—and that scholars, the market, and the U.S. government
agreed. The country's lawyers also asserted that Argentina's Lock Law did
not breach this clause:

> Were the Court, despite this extraordinary and prejudicial delay, to
> reach the "merits" of NML's motions, the plain language of the con-
> tract clause and the overwhelming weight of custom and scholarly
> authority establish that the Republic has not violated the pari passu
> clause. NML claims that the pari passu clause prevents a debtor from
> paying any debt to any of its creditors, unless it simultaneously pays
> all of its other creditors, and asserts that this proposition means that
> the Republic cannot service its new restructured debt . . . or anyone
> else to whom it owes money unless it also pays NML the full amount
> on its non-restructured debt. No U.S. court has ever accepted this
> radical and unprecedented interpretation, which this Court noted to
> be "very odd" when the issue was raised over six years ago. To the

contrary, caselaw, the overwhelming weight of academic commentary and statements by the United States Government, the Federal Reserve Board of New York and the New York Clearing House Association have repeated again and again that the clause does not require a debtor to pay all creditors or pay none. The clause simply forbids, at most, legal ranking among indebtedness, something that has not occurred here, notwithstanding NML's incorrect invocation of the so-called Argentine Lock Law, legislation in effect *since* 2005 that in no way created any legal ranking precluded by the pari passu clause.[11]

Argentina's lawyers delivered numerous scholarly papers and amicus briefs supporting its position, including briefs from the U.S. government and the New York Clearing House Association, the organization whose brief helped convince the Second Circuit Court of Appeals to rule in the banks' favor in the Allied Bank case in 1985. Argentina's expert witness, New York University professor Stephen Choi, pulled all these materials together into a consolidated thesis to parry the arguments Professor Scott from Harvard had made on behalf of NML. Like Scott, Professor Choi boasted impressive credentials. His curriculum vitae included a degree from Harvard Law School, where he graduated first in his class and served as supervising editor of the *Harvard Law Review*; a PhD in economics from Harvard; a stint as a professor at Berkeley; and authorship of a leading casebook on securities laws and more than fifty law journal articles.[12]

Professor Choi offered a market-based explanation of why pari passu clauses—including Argentina's—imposed an obligation to maintain equal ranking among debt instruments, not to make equal payments among creditors:

> By using the Pari Passu clause to obtain a disproportionately higher payment than the other creditors, holdout creditors threaten the welfare of the entire group of creditors. Once a sovereign is in financial distress, an equal payment interpretation of the Pari Passu clause would encourage holdouts and thereby lead to fewer, value-increasing restructurings. It is therefore unlikely that creditors as a group would have negotiated for a Pari Passu clause that takes the equal payment interpretation advanced by NML.

For the reasons above, the United States government, the Federal Reserve Bank of New York, the New York Clearing House Association all rejected the equal payment interpretation of "rank at least equally."[13]

Professor Choi also argued that "the equal payments interpretation of the Pari Passu clause goes against longstanding expectation and customary usage in the sovereign debt market."[14] That is, equal ranking was what creditors bargained for when they bought the bonds. This was an intentions argument, which stood in stark contrast to Professor Scott's exclusive focus on the wording of Argentina's clause.

Here is a repeat of Argentina's clause with emphasis added to the word "rank," as Professor Choi interpreted it:

1. The Securities will constitute . . . direct, unconditional, unsecured and unsubordinated obligations of the Republic and shall at all times RANK *pari passu* without any preference among themselves; and

2. The payment obligations of the Republic under the Securities shall at all times RANK at least equally with all its other present and future unsecured and unsubordinated External Indebtedness.

With Professor Choi's reading, there is a reason for the existence of the two parts of the clause. In the first part Argentina promised to rank the new bonds equally against each other, while in the second part it promised to rank the new bonds equally to all other external debt of the country. In contrast, Elliott's brief focused mostly on the second part, which it relabeled the "Equal Treatment Provision." Interpreting how the two parts worked together should have been an essential aspect of the litigation, yet it was never discussed in Judge Griesa's courtroom because he rolled into court on September 28, 2011, ready to rule.

The September 28, 2011, Hearing

The hearing on the interpretation of Argentina's pari passu clause commenced at 11:30 a.m. on September 28, 2011.

Former solicitor general Theodore Olson, Elliott's counsel, led off by saying that "the Argentina bonds purchased by NML contain a straightforward, unambiguous commitment that Argentina's payment obligations, payment obligations under the bonds, would at all times rank at least equally with all present and future bonds."

Then, he paused to let his carefully crafted opening words sink in.

"All right, go ahead," said Judge Griesa.

However, when Olson started to get into the meat of his argument, Judge Griesa said, "Can I just interrupt you?"

Judge Griesa said, "I hate to cut off very fine arguments by very fine lawyers, but I have to tell you that I have studied the matter—I say to both sides—and it's hard for me to believe that there is not a violation of the pari passu clause accomplished by the congressional legislation in '05 and '10, simply saying that the Republic will not honor these judgments. . . . I have to say, I don't think it is a terribly hard question. I regret not hearing more of your argument."

Turning to Argentina's table, Judge Griesa addressed attorney Carmine Boccuzzi of Cleary Gottlieb, saying,

> and Mr. Boccuzzi . . . I think the hard question is what to do. But to me, there's simply no doubt at all that what the Republic has done is to violate the pari passu clause no matter what interpretation. It can't be interpreted to allow the Argentine government to simply declare that these judgments will not be paid, and that's what they have done. So if you could go ahead to what I really think is a difficult question, and that is, what to do about the breach.

Tacking on another stinker, Judge Griesa added, "And also I see no merit in the laches argument at all," which killed Argentina's lead-off argument that Elliott had asserted its pari passu claim too late in the game.

That off his chest, Judge Griesa returned the floor to Olson, who used his remaining time to make his most powerful point: the injunction was "a way out for all of this litigation . . . because Argentina, which has the money to pay these bills, will then pay them."[15]

Judge Griesa: Now, Will You Pay? Argentina: No.

When Carmine Boccuzzi started into his argument, Judge Griesa afforded him equal treatment; that is, he interrupted Boccuzzi after a few minutes, just as he had interrupted Theodore Olson when he had tried to make his case.

Judge Griesa broke in, "What is the Republic going to do to satisfy those debt obligations?"

Boccuzzi started to argue the problems with the injunction, but Griesa interrupted him again.

"What is the Republic going to do to satisfy these debt obligations?" Griesa repeated.

Boccuzzi said, "I think in a matter of time things get worked out. I don't know."

"And what will be done to work them out?" Griesa persisted.

Boccuzzi said, "Your honor, I'm not aware of anything right now. But I know, for example—"

"Well, it's your client. Your client is the Republic, is it not?" interrupted Griesa.

"It is, your honor," Boccuzzi answered.

"And your client owes these debts, does it not?" Griesa said.

"It does, your honor," Boccuzzi agreed.

"Yes, it does. What is the Republic—you must know what your client intends to do about these debts," Griesa said.

Boccuzzi responded, "I know it wants to resolve them. I know there's nothing in the immediate future," and he pointed out that about 92% of the debt had been successfully restructured in 2005 and 2010.

"But that, for the people who wanted to take 30 cents on the dollar . . . that was their privilege, but it is also the privilege of the people who want to have their judgments honored, to have those judgments honored. Those judgments exist," Griesa retorted.

When Boccuzzi finished, Judge Griesa turned to Theodore Olson and asked how Elliott's proposed injunction would be implemented. Olson spoke to the question.

In his closing, Judge Griesa gave Elliott some good news and some bad news. The good news was that he saw a clear violation of the pari passu clause. The bad news was this: "Now, I am not at this moment prepared to go so far as to grant a motion about the relief. I am denying it at this time with leave to pursue the matter very promptly with a further hearing or briefing or whatever is appropriate." This ruling must have been a grave disappointment to the Elliott team, who now faced the possibility of winning on the pari passu clause interpretation but losing on its motion for an injunction. If that was Elliott's immediate thought, what Griesa said next must have been cold comfort:

> It seems to me that what should be considered is requiring the Republic to provide information about contracts that it is making anywhere in the world. . . . As part of that there should be discovery as to the assets of the Republic because the Republic still denies it has the money to pay off these bonds. I don't think that's true, but there should be discovery. . . . So it seems to me that as part of really showing the Republic that it cannot eternally get by with evading these judgments, it's going to have to provide information to this Court, on a very comprehensive basis, about its activities.

More discovery was hardly the remedy that the Elliott team had in mind.

Yet that was not the only surprise Judge Griesa had at the end of the hearing. He said he wouldn't write a lengthy, formal opinion on pari passu as he had in the central bank case the year before. Instead, he would leave it to the parties to propose a form of order to memorialize what he'd said at the hearing:

> I've got to interrupt you because I have to go to another meeting. What I am doing—and I am saving myself some time these days and I am not going to write a formal opinion, so I will count on a rather full order to be submitted, but I am granting the motion for partial summary judgment to the extent of finding that the pari passu clause has been violated by the enactments of the Argentine Congress, which in effect declared that the Republic would

not pay the bond indebtedness, including any judgments, would not pay or settle.[16]

This was a gift to the plaintiffs, whose draft order he'd inevitably sign. It provided Elliott's lawyers an opportunity for them to push the ball far beyond what Judge Griesa had said at the hearing that day.

The December 2011 Order

Judge Griesa's December 7, 2011, order in the pari passu matter was expansive, going far beyond the ruling the judge had made from the bench on September 28, 2011. In September, Griesa had only said that the Lock Law violated Argentina's pari passu clause. In his December order, one undoubtedly based on a draft presented by plaintiffs' counsel, he ruled that paying deal participants while not paying the holdouts was also a violation. He wrote:

> It is DECLARED, ADJUDGED, and DECREED that the Republic
> is required under Paragraph 1(c) of the [1994 Fiscal Agency Agreement] at all times to rank its payment obligations pursuant to NML's Bonds at least equally with all the Republic's other present and future unsecured and unsubordinated External Indebtedness.
>
> It is DECLARED, ADJUDGED, and DECREED that the Republic's payment obligations on the bonds include its payment obligations to bondholders who have brought actions to recover on their defaulted bonds, and on judgments entered pursuant to judicial action brought by bondholders.
>
> It is DECLARED, ADJUDGED, and DECREED that the Republic violates Paragraph 1(c) of the [1994 Fiscal Agency Agreement] . . . by failing to pay the obligations currently due under NML's Bonds while at the same time making payments currently due to holders of other unsecured and unsubordinated External Indebtedness or by legislative enactment.
>
> It is DECLARED, ADJUDGED, and DECREED that the Republic lowered the rank of NML's bonds . . . when it made payments

currently due under the Exchange Bonds, while persisting in its refusal to satisfy its payment obligations currently due under
NML's bonds.

It is DECLARED, ADJUDGED, and DECREED that the Republic lowered the rank of NML's bonds . . . when it enacted [the Lock
Law].[17]

Remarkably, this important ruling, which supported the equal payments
interpretation of Argentina's pari passu clause that, in turn, made it much
more likely that a payment blockade would be imposed, attracted little
comment in the press and didn't move the market. Payments to holders
of $30 billion of performing bonds that Argentina had issued in its 2005
and 2010 offers were now at risk, but the market was asleep at the wheel.

February 23, 2012: Theodore Olson Quickly Hits a Wall

The follow-up hearing to discuss what to do about Argentina's breach of
its pari passu clause commenced at 11:15 a.m. on February 23, 2012. The
question of the day was whether it was legal for Judge Griesa to impose
the injunction Elliott Associates had proposed.

Elliott's counsel, Theodore Olson, argued first, which is usually an advantage. That day, however, it meant he was first in line to be pummeled.

Not long into Olson's argument Judge Griesa interrupted: "Now look,
this would indeed be a mechanism for enforcement but it also presents a
very serious problem. So let me ask you this. Is there any legal authority,
is there any legal basis for me to use the pari passu clause to interfere with
the payment to the exchangers?"

Dodging, Olson responded, "What I submit your Honor is doing with
this order is making specific performance ordering Argentina to comply
and telling Argentina and its agents, subordinates and intermediaries do
not do anything to violate or assist." The injunction would be effective, he
was arguing, because Argentina's agents would not facilitate payments to
Argentina's exchange bondholders in violation of a court order, which he
suggested would be "aiding and abetting" a crime.

Judge Griesa shot back. "The banks wouldn't be aiding and abetting. The banks only pay the exchange offer people. That's what they do."

"Now," the judge continued, "if I entered this order, this would impose an obligation on the banks and it might impose an impediment upon the banks with respect to the exchange offer people which does not exist now. . . . This would obviously present an impediment, a condition. Is there any legal basis for doing that?"

Olson reiterated that the order would prevent the banks from driving the "get-away car" if Argentina tried to make an illegal payment: "You may not assist in violating the court's order. You may not assist Argentina in implementing activities which directly violate the orders of this court."

Judge Griesa countered that ordering the injunction was "a huge difference from . . . simply ordering the Republic to comply with the pari passu clause. . . . Now, maybe I missed something, but I don't see a legal authority for me saying to the Republic, you cannot pay the exchange offer people unless you pay NML."

Stymied, Olson switched to arguing that Judge Griesa had already, in effect, made the ruling he was asking for, the order he signed on December 7 almost dictating the injunction remedy:

Your Honor, if I might interrupt. You ordered that on December 7. Paragraph 2 on page 4 of the order that you issued on December 7, "it is DECLARED ADJUDGED and DECREED that the Republic is required at all times to rank its payment obligations" and so on and so forth. You specifically ordered on December 7 that Argentina must rank those payment obligations equally. You ordered them if they were going to make payments to make the payments equally. That was on December 7.

"Wait a minute," interrupted Judge Griesa, "you are looking at what paragraph of the order?"

"I am looking at page 4, paragraph 2, where it says 'it is DECLARED, ADJUDGED and DECREED,'" answered Olson.

"Just a second," said Judge Griesa.

The court waited while Judge Griesa reread the order he had signed two months before.

Having gathered his thoughts, Judge Griesa explained:

> Now, that does not necessarily mean that as a condition of the exchange offer people getting paid, the Republic must pay an amount.
>
> I say this once more. I accept the idea, I think it's embodied in my December order, that the Republic has two obligations; one, to pay the exchange offers because they have agreed to do that, and they have a second obligation under the pari passu clause to make an appropriate payment to NML. Two obligations. But that, as a matter of grammar, as a matter of my understanding, does not necessarily mean that as a condition of paying the exchange offers they must pay an amount.
>
> Another way to put it is, I don't understand the pari passu clause or my order to mean that the Republic is forbidden to pay the exchange offers unless they pay NML.

Olson stood to speak.

"Just one second!" Judge Griesa barked.

"To me," Judge Griesa continued, "just as a matter of grammar, it's a difference of saying someone can have two obligations" and saying that "the fulfillment of the second is a condition for them fulfilling the first. Do you see what I am driving at?" Judge Griesa asked.

Olson was stuck: Judge Griesa did not want to block payments to the exchange bondholders, even conditionally. He didn't want to put performing contracts at risk via a court order that blocked payments to nondefaulted bonds.

Adjusting his approach, Olson said, "I see what you are saying, your Honor. But it seems to me. . . . If you pay one and don't pay the other, you are violating the requirement that they be treated equally. That means that the payment of one is conditioned on the payment of the other equally, so it has to be done concurrently, or the equivalent of concurrently, or the provision is violated. All we have done is implemented the order that you issued on December 7."

"I really don't agree with that," Judge Griesa retorted. "The rights of the exchangers were not conditional on NML getting paid under the pari passu clause."

Olson's response was that the exchange bondholders were not innocent third parties. He said that the 2005 exchange offer participants not only knew about the Lock Law but also asked for it to be put in place. Furthermore, he pointed out, Argentina's 2005 prospectus specifically warned participants that a court order could potentially block payments. In other words, the possibility of a blockade was an investment risk they specifically undertook.

Shifting gears, Judge Griesa threw out a hypothetical, asking what if the defendant was not Argentina but an asset-rich domestic corporation: "If you had a normal law-abiding, asset-holding [debtor] . . . you wouldn't have to interfere with the rights of the first people. Do you see what I mean?"

"Yes, your honor," Olson answered.

"So," Judge Griesa continued, "the reason I go through all the cogitation I am going through is and the reason for the provisions in your proposed order is the suspicion that the Republic may not want to honor its obligations under the pari passu clause and that the Republic may not abide by a court order and may not have any assets against which a court order could be recovered, something we have gone through for 10 years. So we have as we all know the most abnormal situation you can imagine as far as complying with legal obligations."

Yet Judge Griesa continued to have doubts about disrupting payments to the exchange bondholders:

I don't think you are going to give up your position, but I have to say, and maybe I am wrong, but I have to say that the exchange offers are not new to me and I have in one way or another dealt with them to the extent it has come up before me as being something that the Republic had a right to do, the exchange offers had a right to exchange and get new obligations, and I have felt that it was not any province of mine at all to interfere with those exchange offers or rights acquired under them.

I know again you are sticking very well to your argument, but I have to tell you I am sticking to my position. I think I cannot interfere with the rights of the exchange offers by putting conditions on them or impediments on them.

Olson stood to speak.

"Wait a minute!" Judge Griesa snapped at Olson for the second time that day. "If I felt there was legal ground to do so, then it would have to be something frankly with all due respect to you, it would have to be something beyond what you are now saying. If I felt there was a legal ground for doing so that would be something. I just don't think there is."

Facing this resistance, Olson brought the conversation back to Judge Griesa's "honorable debtor" scenario.

Olson said, "In the hypothetical you gave of an honorable debtor, you would order that two payments be made equally?"

"I would," confirmed Judge Griesa.

"And they would be paid equally," Olson said, "because the honorable debtor would not want to be in contempt of your court's orders."

That hit home. Judge Griesa now said,

The thing is the order that you propose would be no problem if you had an honorable debtor in the form of the Republic, it would be no problem at all. . . . It would be no problem at all, because the Republic would pay and they would pay both.

The thing is I guess I have such a mindset after 10 years of history that I am assuming something that maybe I ought not to assume. I think that's your point. I ought not to assume in making a ruling that the Republic will disobey the order of the court.

"Exactly, your Honor," Olson responded.[18]

February 23, 2012: Argentina's Argument

After a short recess, Carmine Boccuzzi stood to argue for Argentina:

> Good afternoon. Your Honor, you asked Mr. Olson several times whether
> there was legal authority to support an order that would interfere with
> payments to the exchange offer-takers. In a word, no, there is no legal au-
> thority. There is also no legal authority for this conditioning that Mr. Olson
> is seeking to impose. That is the point your honor raised when you said why
> is the obligation to pay the exchange offer-takers conditioned on NML also
> being paid. There is no legal authority that would link those two together.
> There is nothing in the pari passu clause that does that.

Boccuzzi then went on to explain that the proposed injunction was viewed
as legally wrong by a large number of important parties, including the
U.S. government, the Federal Reserve Bank of New York, the New York
Clearing House Association, and the Bank of England.

Boccuzzi then dove into an important legal technicality: To impose
the injunction, Judge Griesa needed to make two challenging findings
under the rules of equity jurisprudence. First, to meet the standard established by judicial precedent, he had to find that Elliott would suffer "irreparable injury" if the ruling were not made and that no adequate remedy
was available under statute or judicial precedent. Second, he also had to
find that the proposed injunction was "equitable" in light of the totality of
circumstances, including its effect on third parties. Boccuzzi homed in
on the effect on third parties:

> When you look at the equities, what they are trying to do is interfere with
> those payments to the bondholders. Those bondholders are in the position
> of receiving payments on performing debt because they took the exchange
> offer, an exchange offer that your honor protected from disruption back in
> 2005. I don't think your honor was condoning or allowing an inequitable act
> at that point; it certainly was not, and the Second Circuit affirmed as specif-
> ically noted that the restructuring is obviously of critical importance to the
> economic health of the nation.

Now it was Boccuzzi's turn to use Judge Griesa's own cases against him: "In 2008, in the [CVI] case, the Second Circuit specifically said, instructed, on remand, the district court should take care to craft attachment orders so as to avoid interrupting Argentina's regular payments to bondholders."

"So," Boccuzzi concluded, "there is no authority. To the contrary, the authority is to the opposite. There is no authority to allow them from interfering or putting payment to them as the price to paying other bondholders."

Judge Griesa responded with evident frustration:

> That's all well and good. The thing is the Republic has been in here for years saying "no." Now, you have done [a] pretty good job of it. But the "nos" are always to prevent the plaintiffs from recovering. . . . .
>
> But the reason that such paragraphs would even be suggested is because of the problems your client is raising. It isn't that the plaintiffs want to do something bizarre; they just want to get their judgments paid. And what the Republic has forced is a series that goes on year after year of attempts in obviously very strained ways and generally unsuccessful ways to get some assets of the Republic so these people can get justly paid.
>
> Now, if there was any belief that the Republic would honestly pay its obligations, there wouldn't be any need for these kinds of paragraphs. If there is merit to the pari passu argument, then there could be a court order against Argentina not in any way conditioned on anything about the exchange offer. But nobody really has any hope that the Republic will honestly honor its obligations without some unusual mechanisms. That's why this is being done. . . .
>
> The plaintiffs come in with difficult proposals, one after the other. Why? It isn't because they are interested in difficult legal problems. It's because your client defended by your firm persists in defying the court and . . . in refusing deliberately to honor its obligations. I don't see any sign of Cleary Gottlieb helping to lead us out of this. I don't see any sign of the Republic helping to lead us out of this at all.

Judge Griesa admitted, "There are lots of problems with this pari passu argument at this point, lots of problems. But there is a way that the plaintiffs are seeking after all these years to finally get some leverage so that they might have hope of getting paid."

Frustrated, Judge Griesa said, "It would be so nice to hear from Cleary Gottlieb something constructive and affirmative about how to get out of this mess. I never hear such a thing. Do you have anything to offer? Probably not."

Boccuzzi's response was that the country had suffered a great financial crisis. Judge Griesa retorted that Argentina now had ample resources to repay its creditors, its foreign reserves having grown to more than $50 billion with the economy's recovery. Boccuzzi then shifted the conversation back to the language in Argentina's pari passu clause, arguing yet again that it did not imply an equal payment obligation. He then repeated his earlier points that Elliott couldn't prove irreparable harm and that the proposed injunction would lead to an "inequitable" result. Doubling down on technicalities, Boccuzzi concluded that the essence of Elliott's proposed injunction was, in effect, a turnover order, a court order for Argentina to use its offshore money to repay onshore obligations, which, he said, was not allowed under the FSIA.

"Is there no remedy?" Judge Griesa asked.

This essential question hung in the air. Was there really no way to put an end to the mess of cases clogging Judge Griesa's courtroom?

Now Judge Griesa vented at Boccuzzi:

> Basically, you are saying there is no remedy. This language was put in there. It would be very interesting for future investors to know that a major law firm representing the Republic of Argentina has now stated that a very important clause has no remedy. . . . It would be nice, I assume, for people who want to get financing with the Republic to know that here is a very important clause and their law firm is basically saying there is no effective remedy.[19]

February 23, 2012: Judge Griesa Grasps at Laches

Judge Griesa was in a bind. He didn't want to move forward (impose the injunction) and he didn't want to move backward (do nothing). But all the arguments had been made, and all eyes were on him; it was time to decide.

Or was it? Maybe Judge Griesa could sidestep the issue altogether. He could dismiss Elliott's pari passu claim because it was brought too late, Argentina's laches argument.

Judge Griesa turned to Olson and said, "Isn't it a little late to be asserting the pari passu clause?"

Olson hit back hard:

> You specifically dealt with that in September. You specifically held the issue open and said that you didn't want to get to it when it was brought up earlier. You specifically addressed the laches issue. We made the point that we brought this well within the period of the statute of limitations. There were full and complete justifications for what these bondholders did when they brought this case. Every effort has been made to enforce the legal obligations of Argentina, and as you have pointed out as the Court of Appeals has pointed out, Argentina disregards those legal obligations and the judgments. . . .
>
> All we are talking about today is enforcing a provision that was written by Argentina and its lawyers put in the bonds to get people to buy those bonds. . . .
>
> The amount we are talking about is two-thirds of the amount in December it paid to the exchange bondholders. So I submit to you that what's going to happen if you sign this order is that Argentina is going to pay the exchange bondholders because it cannot afford not to. . . . It will pay those bonds. But what it will also do is comply with your court's order and when it does so, it will pay the NML bondholders and the other people here today, because it is obliged finally to do so in a way that it can no longer weasel out of.
>
> It will comply with these obligations. It will bring an end to this litigation.[20]

With nowhere to turn, Judge Griesa ruled to impose the injunction.

February 23, 2012: Judge Griesa Makes the Ruling

Speaking philosophically, Judge Griesa made his historic ruling:

The facts of life are this, that there is the pari passu clause in the documents. We do not have a normal situation. We don't have a situation where you have an honest debtor with assets available that can be subjected to the normal processes of the court. We don't have it. We have litigation that goes on and on.

What the plaintiffs here are trying to do is to see if there is yet another device which might get them their just payments and end the litigation. It has a lot of problems, but Mr. Olson and his colleagues, they know their problems. They are not poor law students. But they are trying to do something which is intended to overcome the lawlessness of the Republic.

I am going to sign the order. It's not the first time that a court has signed an order that may have problems. But to me the bigger overriding problem is the lawlessness of the Republic. When I say lawlessness I mean the deliberate, continued failure to honor the most clear-cut obligations in the debt instruments, the most clear-cut assurances in the debt instruments. Those have been turned into a dead letter by the Republic. Well, they are not a dead letter in this courtroom.

I fully recognize that there are problems with the order that the plaintiffs present and I am sure this will go very quickly to the Court of Appeals and there are problems on appeal. . . . But I believe that there is enough reasonable rational legal basis for the order to make it a wise thing to sign that order.

The pari passu clause exists; it is not meaningless. It has been violated flagrantly by the Republic in ways that I spelled out in my December 7 order. It's a clause that should be enforced, it should have meaning, and there should be a remedy. . . .

There is a reasonable basis for everything that is proposed. Whether it will ultimately be sustained on appeal, that's not my business. But there is a reasonable basis for everything that is proposed in that order, particularly under the circumstances that exist.

It seems to me that after all these years of difficult litigation and the obduracy of the Republic, it seems to me that there is something highly salutary in attempting to fashion a remedy which is effective here. That is really what is done instead of saying there is a clause and it's there but we can't do anything with it.

I want to say a word about timing. The effort under the pari passu clause comes late. But it is absolutely true and this court knows the facts and history painfully well, it is true that the plaintiffs have tried in many ways to enforce their rights. They are now attempting to make use of a very important provision in the contract or in their bond arrangements. They are trying to make use of that. They are entitled to do so.

The rights of the exchange bondholders need not be interfered with at all if the Republic will honor its legal obligations. That's all the Republic has to do. The Republic owes the money that is requested, has owed it for years, and the Republic really can't in any good conscience say that the court and Mr. Olson and his clients are jeopardizing the rights of the exchangers. This court is not doing such a thing. Mr. Olson and his clients are not doing any such thing.

What the problem is is the failure of the Republic to do what it is legally obligated to do and all that has to be done is to comply with the Republic's obligations. That's all that has to be done.

He concluded by parroting Olson's point that Argentina would pay the holdouts to avoid a blockade on payments to the exchange bondholders. Judge Griesa said, "It's very simple and very basic and very uncomplicated. And this litigation will be over with."[21]

But of course it wasn't.

February 23, 2012: The Order

After the hearing Judge Griesa signed Elliott's proposed order, requiring Argentina to pay the firm if it made any payments to its exchange bondholders. He ruled that Elliott would suffer "irreparable harm" in the absence of the injunction and that "the equities and public interest strongly support issuance of equitable relief to prevent the Republic from further violating" its pari passu clause. He also wrote that "the public interest of enforcing contracts and upholding the rule of law will be served by the issuance of this Order, particularly here, where creditors of the Republic have no recourse to bankruptcy regimes to protect their interests and must rely upon courts to enforce contractual promises."[22]

Judge Griesa's February 23, 2012, order included provisions prohibiting Argentina from trying to evade the injunction. This was included because Elliott had convinced Griesa that Argentina might try to amend its bonds so it could pay its bondholders offshore, out of the reach of the court. It was a perceptive addition, because Argentina later tried to do exactly that.

Judge Griesa also agreed to stay the imposition of the injunction pending an expected appeal of his ruling by Argentina.

Creditors Wake Up but Do Nothing

Judge Griesa's February 23, 2012, order finally woke the market from its deep slumber. EMTA held a seminar devoted to the topic for its members on April 18, 2012,[23] for example, while Georgetown's Anna Gelpern posted commentary on the case to the *Credit Slips* blog.[24] Most observers and market participants were sanguine about how it would turn out, however, assuming that the Second Circuit would shoot down Griesa's ruling or that Argentina would cave and pay the holdouts if it lost on appeal. The possibility that Argentina might default on $30 billion of performing bonds just to avoid paying Elliott seemed remote. So, the exchange bondholders sat on their hands, expecting the problem to go away. None of them filed motions with the court to head off the ruling, at least not until it was too late.

It Wasn't Just Elliott versus Argentina

Even today, most commentators speak of the pari passu litigation as if it were a grand battle between Elliott Associates and Argentina. This is a common framing. For example, in July 2012, Felix Salmon wrote a piece with the title "Why Argentina's Likely to Beat Elliott Associates," which doesn't mention that other investors were involved in the pari passu case.[25] Others joined the litigation, including Aurelius and Bracebridge, but did so after a delay, so it didn't elicit much press comment.

The very first group of plaintiffs to join Elliott's pari passu litigation, however, was invited to join near the beginning and for strategic purposes: a group of Argentine retail investors who had bought their bonds at par. Organized by Patricia Vago and represented by Milberg's Michael Spencer, these plaintiffs were known as the "Varela plaintiffs." Even though they owned just $367,000 in bonds,[26] they were the only plaintiffs to join Elliott ahead of the September 28, 2011, hearing. Inviting these retail plaintiffs to join early was a transparent attempt to put a human face on the overall plaintiff group and to head off the predictable argument from Argentina that it would be inequitable to impose an injunction just to hand a huge profit to some hedge funds that had bought bonds at pennies on the dollar.[27] Inviting in mom-and-pop investors who had bought their bonds at par was a shrewd move.

The second plaintiffs to join Elliott's action were Elliott alum Mark Brodsky's Aurelius Capital and its litigating partner Blue Angel, both of which lodged motions for summary judgment and injunctive relief on October 26, 2011.[28]

The third was Bracebridge's Olifant Fund, which joined on January 26, 2012.[29] Like Bracebridge's FFI Fund and FYI Ltd., its Olifant Fund only owned FRANs.

The list of plaintiffs joining the pari passu litigation at this stage was exclusive. There were many holdouts waiting in the wings—none of whom had been paid a penny since 2001—but the numbers were limited, one can assume, to keep the litigation manageable.[30] Yet there was also a particular legal consideration holding other plaintiffs back (which we get to in chapter 10), one that also explains why Elliott cohorts Dart and Montreux didn't join at this stage.[31]

Still, the addition of the Varela plaintiffs, Aurelius, Blue Angel, and Bracebridge rounded out Elliott's side. Unlike in its 1990s litigation against Peru, this time the firm was not standing alone in court, which improved its chance of victory. Elliott now had a human shield against the accusation that the firm was just gaming the courts to make superprofits at the expense of everyone else.

Argentina's Waterloo at the Second Circuit

The Second Circuit's review of Judge Griesa's pari passu ruling was intense. In a yearlong process, the appeals court wrote two full-length opinions and held two lengthy hearings. One could say that such an intense review was necessary because Griesa's ruling was unprecedented and of great consequence to global financial markets and also because the judge had been unusually emotional in making his ruling. The truth is, however, that the Second Circuit was just doing its job, parsing through a new and complicated situation. They were, after all, a three-judge panel reviewing the work of a one-judge trial court, themselves possibly subject to review by the nine-judge U.S. Supreme Court. These were the normal workings of a system designed to weed out human error, facilitate healthy change, and protect the integrity of the law.

The first hearing was held on July 23, 2012, and went on for an hour and a half.[32] The court released its opinion three months later on October 26, 2012,[33] affirming Judge Griesa's decision that Argentina had breached its pari passu clause. The court discarded the arguments made by Argentina, New York University professor Choi, and the New York Clearing House Association that the pari passu clause obligated "equal ranking," not "equal payment," and wrote, "We are unpersuaded that the clause has this well settled meaning." Instead, the court opined that Argentina's clause obligated both, saying that the first part of Argentina's clause "prohibits Argentina as bond *issuer* from formally subordinating the bonds by issuing superior debt" and that its second part "prohibits Argentina as bond *payor*, from paying on other bonds without paying on the [Fiscal Agency Agreement] Bonds." This, the court said, "makes good sense in the context of sovereign debt: When sovereigns default they do not enter bankruptcy proceedings where the legal rank of debt determines the order in which creditors will be paid. . . . In this context, the Equal Treatment Provision prevents Argentina as payor from discriminating against the [Fiscal Agency Agreement] Bonds in favor of other unsubordinated, foreign bonds." The court concluded, "The record amply supports a finding that Argentina has effectively ranked its payment obligations to the plaintiffs below those of the exchange bondholders."

The court also found that Judge Griesa did not abuse his discretion by imposing the injunction, which was allowed under the law. To the specifics of the injunction, the court concluded that Griesa had "considerable latitude in fashioning the relief." To the concern raised by Argentina that ruling for Elliott would wreck future sovereign debt restructurings, the court said, "It is highly unlikely that in the future sovereigns will find themselves in Argentina's predicament," because starting in 2003, virtually all sovereign debt issuers except Jamaica had included CACs in their bond documentation. Finally, the court dismissed—on technical grounds—Argentina's laches argument that Elliott had brought its pari passu motion too late.

With the release of this opinion, the court remanded the case to Judge Griesa to clarify two matters: the effect of the injunction on financial intermediaries and how the injunction would work financially. The court was uncertain whether Griesa's injunction would require Argentina to pay Elliott everything it was owed up front or over time.

The Exchange Bondholders Join the Fight

The Second Circuit's October 26, 2012, ruling on pari passu finally shook the market into action. The price of Argentine dollar bonds dropped more than ten points upon the news,[34] and holders of the exchange bonds were soon hiring lawyers to try to head off the injunction that threatened the payments due on their holdings. The first challenge came from the Exchange Bondholder Group, a group of four funds brought together by Gramercy's Robert Koenigsberger.[35] Other challenges came from David Martínez's Fintech Advisory, Inc.,[36] owners of euro-denominated bonds documented under English law,[37] and a group of holders of GDP warrants.[38]

Policy makers and financial institutions also jumped into the fray. Briefs and motions flowed into the court on Argentina's behalf from the Bank of New York (the bond trustee and paying agent),[39] former IMF first

deputy managing director Anne Krueger,[40] Euroclear (a European clearing system),[41] the U.S. government,[42] and The Clearing House (the rebranded New York Clearing House Association).[43] Elliott also had friends
of the court briefs from powerful people and institutions, including the
Washington Legal Foundation[44] and Kenneth Dam, George W. Bush's former U.S. deputy treasury secretary.[45]

The Endgame at the Second Circuit

A few days after the Second Circuit released its ruling, Judge Griesa
scheduled a hearing to discuss next steps. At a November 9, 2012, hearing, he asked a group of parties that now included the new challengers to
address the issues the Second Circuit had raised.[46] Ahead of the hearing,
the Exchange Bondholder Group argued in a brief that the injunction
should be refashioned to require pro rata payments to all creditors instead
of requiring Argentina to pay the holdouts in full if it made any payment
to exchange bondholders.[47] Yet Griesa didn't budge. Without having given
the lawyers for the exchange bondholders time in court to argue for their
proposed alternative payment formulation, on Wednesday, November 21,
2012, the day before Thanksgiving, he signed slightly amended orders
under which Argentina would have to pay Elliott's full legal claim if it
made any payment to the exchange bondholders.[48] This triggered a frantic
effort over the holiday weekend to put in motion paperwork to stay the
ruling pending appeal, as Argentina had upcoming payments on December 2, 15, and 31.[49] On November 26, Griesa wrote a new order clarifying
that the injunction would first apply to the upcoming payment due on
December 15.[50] On November 27, Argentina filed an emergency motion
with the Second Circuit, and on November 28, the Second Circuit stayed
the injunction pending further review.[51]

    The Second Circuit held a second hearing on the topic of pari passu
on February 27, 2013.[52] For the world of sovereign debt, this hearing was a
cross between the O. J. Simpson trial and Woodstock. Like the O. J. Simpson trial, it had a global audience and gripping performances by legal su-
perstars. Like Woodstock, the crowd was overflowing: so many investors,

lawyers, government officials, academics, and reporters showed up for the hearing that the court had to set up screens in other rooms and even in the elevator lobby to accommodate everyone.

On March 1, 2013, a few days after the hearing, in a highly unusual if not totally unprecedented move, the Second Circuit Court of Appeals released a letter asking Argentina to propose an alternative payment plan,[53] opening up the possibility that the court might accept a less onerous pro rata payment formula such as the one the Exchange Bondholder Group had proposed in November. This was a clear invitation for Argentina to propose a face-saving compromise. But Argentina stood its ground, and on March 29, 2013, it responded to the court that the only payment plan it would accept would be for the holdouts to sign on to another reopening of its 2005 exchange offer.[54]

In the face of this unyielding response, the Second Circuit didn't mince words in its second opinion, which was released on August 23, 2013:

> Recognizing the unusual nature of this litigation and the importance
> to Argentina of the issues presented, following oral argument, we
> invited Argentina to propose to the appellees an alternative pay-
> ment formula and schedule for outstanding bonds to which it was
> prepared to commit. Instead, the proposal submitted by Argentina
> ignored the outstanding bonds and proposed an entirely new set of
> substitute bonds. In sum, no productive proposals have been forth-
> coming.[55]

Using the same angry tone, the court criticized trash talk from top Argentine officials, noting that President Fernández de Kirchner had recently said that the court was "unaware" of its own laws and that the country would not pay one dollar to the holdouts. The court also called out Argentina's economy minister for saying that "Argentina isn't going to change its position of not paying vulture funds. . . . We will continue to follow that policy despite any ruling that could come out of any jurisdiction, in this case New York." Putting a label on what it thought of the country's behavior, the court called Argentina a "uniquely recalcitrant debtor" and topped it off by citing Judge Cabranes's 2007 footnote, the one in which he accused Argentina of engaging in a "diplomacy of default."

As assertive as the court's second opinion reads on the topic of Argentina's behavior, it is equally defensive on the logic it applied in its first opinion, specifically addressing criticism of the court's October 2012 ruling.

In response to criticism of the court's equal payments reading of Argentina's pari passu clause, the court wrote,

> Our decision here does not control the interpretation of all *pari passu* clauses or the obligations of other sovereign debtors under *pari passu* clauses in other debt instruments. As we explicitly stated in our last opinion, we have not held that a sovereign debtor breaches its *pari passu* clause every time it pays one creditor and not another, or even every time it enacts a law disparately affecting a creditors' rights. We simply affirm the district court's conclusion that Argentina's extraordinary behavior was a violation of the particular *pari passu* clause found in the [Fiscal Agency Agreement].

To criticism of its argument that the use of CACs would neutralize the damage its ruling would do to future sovereign debt restructurings, the court responded, "Argentina and *amici* respond that, even with CACs, enough bondholders may nevertheless be motivated to refuse restructurings and hold out for full payment—or that holdouts could buy up enough of a single series to defeat restructuring of that series. But a restructuring failure on one series would still allow restructuring of the remainder of a sovereign's debt."

Capping off its point on CACs, the court wrote, "Ultimately, though, our role is not to craft a resolution that will solve all the problems that might arise in hypothetical future litigation involving other bonds and other nations." This was the bottom line. The court was tossing the public policy problem it was creating back to policy makers, saying in effect that if your CACs aren't solving your holdout problem, go ahead and find a way to fix them; it is not our problem.

Yet the Second Circuit stayed imposition of the injunction pending Argentina's expected appeal of its ruling to the Supreme Court.

Flashback: Highlights from the Second Circuit's 2012 and 2013 Hearings

While we have already reviewed the rulings handed down by the Second Circuit on the topic of pari passu, we back up now to review some highlights of the two hearing they held before making these rulings. Held on July 23, 2012, and February 27, 2013, these hearings were unmatched in passion and are of such importance in the history of sovereign debt that it would be remiss not to pause to give a taste, even though scholars would want to take the couple of hours needed to listen to the recordings all the way through.

The main speakers in both hearings were Theodore Olson for Elliott and Jonathan Blackman for Argentina, both of whom made their arguments with great passion and energy. New to the podium in the first hearing was U.S. attorney John Clopper, who spoke in favor of Argentina on behalf of the U.S. government. In the second hearing, superlawyer David Boies appeared for the first time as counsel for the Exchange Bondholder Group. Boies's addition contributed personal drama to the affair because he was now arguing against Theodore Olson, against whom he had argued in the famous *Bush v. Gore* Supreme Court case of 2000. Making matters even more interesting, at the time of the hearing, Olson and Boies were working side by side on a marriage equality case that would soon be heard by the Supreme Court.

The first notable moment was when Clopper took heavy flak in the first hearing from Judge Reena Raggi, who nailed him for not having a position on the Lock Law. This wasn't Clopper's fault, because the U.S. amicus brief specifically avoided the topic, but when questioned about whether the Lock Law caused a breach of the clause, Clopper gave the unsatisfactory answer that he had no authority to speak to the issue, triggering a quick smack from Judge Raggi for "arguing 75% of the facts in this case, or 50%, and not helping us with what the totality of circumstances are."[56]

The second notable moment in the first hearing came when Judge Raggi and Judge Pooler simultaneously corrected Argentina's Jonathan Blackman after he took a swing at Elliott for being a hedge fund that had purchased its bonds at a deep discount. The judges shot back in unison "some of them are individuals," and that was true, for Elliott had invited the Varela plaintiffs into the initial pari passu cases, the case in front of the circuit court that day.[57]

At the same hearing, Judge Pooler asked Blackman why anyone would lend money to Argentina given its history of defaulting. Positioning it as an informal aside, she asked, "Why would anyone who can read ever lend money to Argentina?"[58] Blackman replied that investors had bought Argentine bonds because of their huge 12% coupons and explained that the country had defaulted only because it was suffering from a terrible economic crisis in 2001:

> Argentina didn't default whimsically. There was a financial crisis in Argentina that was worse than the Great Depression. I mean at the end of 2001 there was rioting in the streets. There were four presidents in the space of several weeks. The economy was so in the tank that kids were passing out in school from hunger. And I remember the first time I went down to Buenos Aires. It was like you read about Weimar, Germany. There were middle class people in the street selling their possessions on street corners.[59]

The February 2013 hearing is notable because it is the first circuit court hearing at which a lawyer for the exchange bondholders appeared. At the hearing, David Boies pounded on the unfairness of the injunction to the exchange bondholders:

> I understand the Court's frustration here. All right. You've got Argentina and it hasn't paid its bonds, and there doesn't seem to be any way to get them to pay those bonds, and what the Court is trying to find is—they're trying to find, how can we fashion an order that somehow makes them pay?

And what I'm saying is that there are certain ways you can do it. There are certain ways that the congress has said you can't do it.

But what the law—I suggest and the Constitution is quite clear, is that you can't say to us we're going to hold you hostage. We're going to say that you don't have a right to accept your lawfully negotiated contractual payments. Remember, Your Honor, these were bond holders that started off with the same kind of bonds. They exchanged them . . . and both sides have agreed in the District Court that we have an unconditional right to that payment. We have an unconditional right to that payment. . . . That unconditional right for us to be paid cannot be broken, cannot be blocked, cannot be prevented, even for a good purpose, and particularly done in a case in which we're not even a party. . . .

When you're using the powers of equity, what you're trying to do is do that in a way that is fair and reasonable, and I suggest to you that it's not fair and reasonable to try to fashion an order, particularly a coercive order on third parties, the purpose of which is to give one group of people, the holdout bond holders, much greater return on what they paid than the exchange bond holders.[60]

While the judges gave David Boies ample time to make his case against the injunction on behalf of his clients, whose voices had not yet been heard, the most visceral—and memorable—moment of the hearing occurred when Judge Raggi asked Jonathan Blackman if Argentina would be willing to propose an alternative payment formula or if it would refuse to obey any terms other than what the country had proposed. Blackman responded that Argentina was "firm on that issue."

Judge Raggi's responded, "So the answer is yes, that you will not obey anything other than what you have just proposed?"

Blackman said, "We would not voluntarily obey such an order, but I'd like to explain—"

Judge Raggi said, "What does that mean, voluntarily obey? I mean, we would issue an order, and I just want to be sure you're telling us it wouldn't be obeyed."

Blackman said, "I'm telling you it wouldn't be voluntarily obeyed."[61]

This wasn't a happy place for Jonathan Blackman, especially with the whole world watching. His answer was an honest one, even if it might have been better phrased: Argentina's policy was that all creditors from the 2001 default would get the same deal, and it was on that basis that it planned to make or not make payments on its various bonds should the ruling go into effect. Ultimately, the country was true to the words spoken by its lawyer in court that day.

9

Argentina's Economic Stumbles and Elliott's Worldwide War

(October 2010–June 2014)

Pari passu was not the only thing going on in the Argentina bond cases after 2010. Other fights were taking place in U.S. federal courts outside of New York and in courts in Europe and in Africa as well as in the court of public opinion. Other wheels were also turning. Important political developments were taking place in Argentina, its economy was starting to deteriorate, and its relationship with the Obama administration was heading downhill. The U.S. government was increasingly turning the screws on the country for a series of bad policy choices unrelated to the pari passu litigation, the one area where the U.S. government was still supporting the country. At the same time, the U.S. Treasury was dealing with another problem: how to protect future sovereign debt restructurings from holdouts in the wake of Argentina's pari passu loss in New York and Greece's troubled 2012 sovereign bond restructuring.

This context matters. In sovereign debt, a multitude of factors are deeply interconnected: legal aspects, political events and alignments, and economic developments. In this case, economic and political events shifted Argentina's and Elliott Associates' willingness to settle. Legal developments had economic and political ramifications that also influenced the parties' willingness to settle, sometimes positively, sometimes negatively. This chapter fills in the broader picture, taking in the world outside the New York courts mostly after 2010. The following is a necessary pause before the most dramatic events in the pari passu saga, which came in 2014.

The Death of Former President Néstor Kirchner

On October 27, 2010, just seven days after Elliott launched its pari passu
attack, Argentina experienced its most consequential political event in
almost a decade: Former president Néstor Kirchner died of a heart attack.[1]
While he had been in and out of the hospital over the years with various ailments, his death was a shock. Politically, his loss was momentous
because the unbreakable partnership of Cristina and Néstor Kirchner
had dominated Argentine political life since May 2003. Now she was the
grieving widow, and she was on her own in making policy.

Less than a year after Néstor Kirchner's death, on October 23, 2011,
Cristina Fernández de Kirchner won a second term in a landslide victory.[2]
Not only did she win 54% of the vote, versus 17% for the first runner-up,
but her Front for Victory also picked up seats in the Chamber of Deputies
and the Senate, which assured her total dominance of policy through the
midterm elections in 2013.[3] As a result, as the pari passu battle in New
York rolled toward its grand climax, President Fernández de Kirchner was
firmly at her country's helm. Behind her stood a population with fond
memories of her husband. At rallies, Kirchner supporters would chant
"Néstor no se murió, Néstor no se murió. Néstor vive en el Pueblo, la puta
madre que lo parió" (Néstor did not die, Néstor did not die. The [expletive]
still lives among his People).

Capture of the Frigate ARA *Libertad*

On October 2, 2012, just three weeks before the Second Circuit Court
of Appeals stung Argentina by affirming Judge Thomas P. Griesa's pari
passu ruling, Elliott grabbed headlines around the world by attaching
Argentina's naval vessel, ARA *Libertad*, when it stopped in Ghana for a
goodwill visit.

The *Libertad* is a beautiful 340-foot-tall, three-masted ship operated
by the Argentine navy.[4] It is used for goodwill visits to countries around
the world. Its voyages are also used as training missions for members

of the Argentine navy as well as for guest sailors from friendly nations. The *Libertad*, a ship of state with tremendous grace and beauty, is an important symbol of national pride. To Argentines, the *Libertad* is a sort of floating Statue of Liberty, which made its attachment a highly symbolic and political act rather than just a legal and commercial one.

The *Libertad* commenced its fateful tour in June 2012. Its itinerary included stops in thirteen countries, including several in West Africa. At the end of September 2012 as the ship neared the coast of Ghana, there were 326 people on board,[5] including officers, enlisted men, trainees, and invitees from the navies of Bolivia, Brazil, Chile, Paraguay, Peru, South Africa, Suriname, Uruguay, and Venezuela.[6]

The ship arrived at the Ghanaian port of Tema on October 1, 2012. That evening, a formal welcoming ceremony was held aboard the ship. Governmental authorities, representatives of the Ghanaian Armed Forces, and members of the diplomatic corps were all invited.[7]

At 8:00 the following evening,[8] events took a turn for the worse when a court official arrived with an order signed by Ghanaian High Court judge Richard Adjei-Frimpong arresting the ship on behalf of Elliott and demanding the turnover of the crew and passenger manifest, international certificates, safety documents, training and drill records, fuel and waste disposal records, security records and certificates, and the ship's flag locker.[9]

The Argentine officers who met the official refused to accept the papers.

In the days that followed, Argentine and Ghanaian officials worked furiously to find a quick diplomatic end to the situation. There was no simple solution, however, because the Ghanaian executive branch did not have the power to revoke a judicial branch order. Despite protests of immunity from Argentina, the judge confirmed his order on October 11, and the parties dug in for the long haul.

On October 24, Argentina flew 281 people from the *Libertad* out of Ghana on a charter, including most of the vessel's crew and all the trainees and officers from foreign states. Forty-four crew members remained on the ship.[10] On October 29, Argentina notified Ghana that it was seeking international arbitration pursuant to the United Nations Convention for the Law of the Sea.[11] This action started a two-week waiting period after which Argentina could ask for a hearing to address the matter at the International Tribunal for the Law of the Sea (ITLOS) in Hamburg, Germany.

Meanwhile, back at the port things were heating up. Tema port officials were distressed that the *Libertad* was parked in berth 11, the port's most lucrative berth; the lost revenue amounted to $160,000 a day.[12] Port officials obtained a court order that would allow them to move the ship to berth 6, which was less centrally located. Early in the morning of November 7 the port authorities tried to board the ship, first cutting off the power and water. Guns drawn, the Argentines repelled "the invasion," much to the excitement of the press back home in Buenos Aires.[13] After diplomatic complaints, power and water were restored, and the port authorities gave up on their mission to move the ship.

On November 14, Argentina submitted its complaint to the ITLOS asking "that Ghana unconditionally enables the Argentine warship Frigate ARA *Libertad* to leave the Tema port and the jurisdictional waters of Ghana and to be resupplied to that end."[14]

The hearing took place at the ITLOS courthouse in Hamburg on November 29 and 30.[15] On December 15, the tribunal unanimously ordered Ghana to immediately refuel and release the ship.[16] The *Libertad* departed Ghana on December 19, 2012, and arrived at the Argentine port of La Plata on January 9, 2013.[17]

It took almost a year to clean up the diplomatic and legal mess. At issue was the $10 million in legal and port costs accrued during the standoff. The dispute now made its way to the Permanent Court of Arbitration in The Hague, an organization set up in 1898 that is used to resolve border disputes and other country-to-country frictions. Argentina and Ghana were due to face off at the Permanent Court of Arbitration in October 2014.[18] The arbitration process was cut short, however, when on June 20, 2013, the Supreme Court of Ghana ruled that the arrest of the *Libertad* had been illegal under Ghanaian and international law.[19]

The Mother of All Homecomings

President Cristina Fernández de Kirchner pulled out all the stops for the return of the *Libertad* to the port of La Plata in January 2013.[20] The choreography was pure genius. President Fernández de Kirchner, her entire cabinet, and the captain stood on a stage in front of the ship; above them, the entire crew of the ship stood on the deck, the officers in full uniform and sailors in their finest whites. In the streets below, thousands of flag-waving Argentines cheered the president and the crew. The entire event was shown live on TV on every channel.

At this epic event President Fernández de Kirchner spoke to the nation:

> Gentlemen and Ladies, officers and non-commissioned officers of our Fragata *Libertad,* welcome to the homeland. . . .
>
> Today more than ever—"Patria sí! Colonia no!" [Homeland yes! Colony no!]—represents a particular moment, when Argentina is once again suffering the attacks from the vulture funds. . . . Because—when lots, or maybe not lots, but powerful, and with high media repercussions—asked that we surrender, asked that we pay to those vulture funds what they don't have right to, we showed respect to a historical legacy, left by a man almost ten years ago, when he told us from the Legislative Palace that he was not going to leave his principles at the door of the Government House. Those convictions that in this occasion were supported by International Law, by ratified treaties and by the whole global legal order which stated that we were right, but nevertheless there are always discordant voices. . . .[21]

The crowd chanted, "Néstor no se murió, Néstor no se murió. Néstor vive en el Pueblo, la puta madre que lo parió."

President Fernández de Kirchner continued:

> A figure for memory and for pain: between 1991 and 2001, we paid six times in interest only the amount we gained in the privatizations. And today, Argentina since 2005, with the first restructuring, the one that Néstor

started . . . and that I continued in 2010, has contemplated and given the opportunity to restructure their debt to 93% of the country's creditors. And since 2005, we have been honoring that same debt with our own work and effort, without asking a single peso from anyone. . . .

The other day, when it happened, because it seems like a long time ago, I was just telling Captain Salonio how long was it? To him, and to the crew, it must have seemed a lot: Seventy days alone aboard there and surrounded. I want to tell you that they were accompanied by all Argentines in good faith, who also recognize the worthy defense they made of our flagship vessel, we did not expect anything else from you guys. In those seventy days some centennial newspaper said that we had to honor the debts and pay the vulture funds. And I say why don't they start paying themselves all the money they owe the Argentine state in taxes. . . .

What are the vultures? They are the birds who fly over the dead to eat the dead meat. What do they do? They fly over the countries in default, when they fall they buy their bonds at 10% and then they get payment for 100%. . . . That is why it is necessary to understand that this fight that the Argentines are fighting, is not something that concerns only our country, but also to a big extent, the future of a new order that is needed in the world. Even now, with the current rules, we can see how many are realizing that it is necessary to take a firm and serious position in the face of these global social predators in defense of the people's welfare and the survival of the States.[22]

It was a powerful moment, one that can still be readily accessed on YouTube.

Argentina's Economic Stumbles

The outrage in Argentina over the events in Ghana was well timed for President Fernández de Kirchner's domestic purposes. She needed all the help she could get because the economy was tanking: growth was down, the Argentine peso was under pressure, inflation was up, and foreign credit was out of reach. Figure 9.1 shows the country's steadily deteriorating

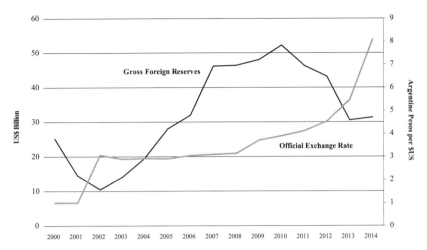

Figure 9.1. Argentina foreign reserves versus exchange rate (2000–2014)

Source: World Bank, "Total Reserves Including Gold (Current US$)," The World Bank Group, accessed Sept. 15, 2022, https://data.worldbank.org/indicator/FI.RES .XGLD.CD; and World Bank, "Official Exchange Rate (LCU per US$, Period Average)," The World Bank Group, accessed Sept. 15, 2022, https://data.worldbank .org/indicator/PA.NUS.FCRF.

foreign reserves and exchange rate from 2010 through 2014, although the real conditions were worse than suggested by the official numbers. Argentine pesos traded in an unofficial market at a deep discount to the reported official exchange rate, and reported gross international reserves were boosted by a $10.3 billion three-year currency swap with the People's Bank of China.[23] Figure 9.2 displays Argentina's real GDP growth and overall government fiscal balance from 2005 through 2015, which showed a general reversion toward historical norms after 2010.

Argentina's economic woes came from many sources.

In finance, Argentina was cut out of the international bond market because of the holdout litigation. At the same time, the country was (mostly) cut off from bilateral and other official financing because of an ongoing default to Paris Club lenders and because its continuing unwillingness to pay the foreign owners of utilities the ICSID arbitration awards they had won in compensation for the deep damages they suffered when

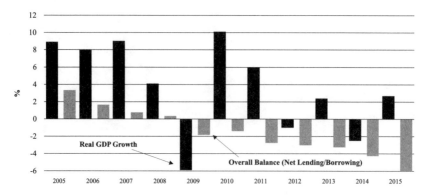

Figure 9.2. Argentina real annual GDP growth (year-on-year) and overall fiscal balance (2005–2015)

Source: IMF Datamapper, "General Government Net Lending/Borrowing (% of GDP)," IMF, accessed Dec. 2, 2022, https://www.imf.org/external/datamapper /GGXONLB_G01_GDP_PT@FM/ARG?year=2022; and IMF Datamapper, "Real GDP Growth (Annual % Change)," IMF, accessed Dec. 2, 2022, https://www.imf .org/external/datamapper/NGDP_RPCH@WEO/ARG?year=2022.

Argentina froze utility tariffs in January 2002. Refusing to pay these awards also put the country at odds with the international community, since honoring investment treaty obligations and commitments to arbitrate disputes underpins global economic development.

Meanwhile, Argentina's fiscal deficit was mushrooming. An expansion of pension entitlements, a boost in public employment, and the continued practice of subsidizing energy costs (which by 2016 was costing the country 4% of GDP, according to the IMF)[24] drove this increase. As figure 9.2 shows, Argentina's budget balance turned sharply negative after 2010, which didn't bode well for the country's future financial stability.

Adding to Argentina's woes, loose fiscal policy led to loose monetary policy, including direct loans to the government from the Central Bank of Argentina, which drove inflation higher.[25]

Finally, lack of confidence in the government hit investment markets. In a widely reviled move, the Fernández de Kirchner government replaced the head of the country's statistical agency in early 2007, after which it began systematically underreporting inflation, creating equity market doubt.[26] Investor confidence fell further when the government subsequently went on a nationalization spree that culminated in the contentious 2012 taking of shares of YPF (Argentina's national oil company) owned by Spain's Repsol.[27]

As a result, when the pari passu litigation came to a head in 2014, Argentina was under pressure to regain normal access to international finance to help it deal with economic stresses at home, which provided an incentive to settle its various international disputes. Ultimately, though, the country chose to start settling its outstanding international utility and corporate claims rather than its holdout creditor claims, which it continued to fight with all its energy.

Argentina's creditors certainly appreciated the potential benefits of pressure on the country to regain normal access to the international debt capital market, but in the bigger scheme of things Argentina's economic woes were a double-edged sword. Yes, the country had a growing incentive to settle, but if Argentina ran out of foreign reserves before it paid the plaintiffs, the country would go back into default on all of its bonds, leaving everyone back at square one and the holdouts with nothing but legal expenses to show for their decade of effort. Tensions were rising, to be sure, but on all sides at once.

Argentina Fights with Its Neighbors and Cozies Up to Iran

Argentina's problems in its international relations in the wake of its 2001 default were not limited to those related to its defaulted bonds and foreign-owned utilities. From 2005 through 2014, Argentina battled its neighbors, Washington, and the world at the same time. In South America, Argentina engaged in a bitter fight with Chile over a gas supply contract while simultaneously clashing with Uruguay over pollution expected from a newly built paper mill.[28] Meanwhile in Washington, D.C., policy makers had issues with Argentine government policy, including officials' unwillingness to cooperate with the biannual economic reviews mandated under Article IV of the IMF's charter; the country's misreporting of economic numbers, including inflation; and the nonpayment of ICSID awards noted above. And then Argentina cozied up to Iran.

In January 2013, Argentina shocked observers at home and abroad by suddenly announcing a rapprochement with Iran. Relations between the two countries had been frosty for more than twenty years because Iran had never owned up to its responsibility for the July 1994 bombing of the Jewish community center Asociación Mutual Israelita Argentina in Buenos Aires, which killed eighty-five people and injured about three hundred. It is a murky story because the Menem government in the 1990s fumbled the investigation. After his election in 2003, Néstor Kirchner, who had promised to make human rights the hallmark of his administration, put aggressive prosecutor Alberto Nisman on the case. Nisman pushed hard and in 2007 obtained Interpol arrest warrants for nine former Iranian officials.[29] However, some twenty years after the bombing and now looking for trade and money, President Cristina Fernández de Kirchner signed an agreement with Iran to set up a joint commission to investigate the matter.[30] The reaction was swift. Critics lambasted this initiative as "bizarre," an "about-face," and "at odds with Argentina's own history of holding human rights violators accountable."[31] From this point on Nisman became a thorn in Fernández de Kirchner's side, persisting in attacks on the Iran deal until his untimely death in 2015, which we discuss in the next chapter.

The United States Starts Getting Tough with Argentina

Argentina was a problem for the Obama administration and not just because of its rapprochement with Iran. The United States wanted Argentina to win in court against Elliott because a holdout victory would have hurt the prospects for future sovereign debt restructurings. Over time, however, the Obama administration found it increasingly hard to support the country given its policies, and so the United States started reducing economic support with the aim of forcing a change. In September 2011, the Obama administration announced in Congress that it would withhold support for most new loans to Argentina from the World Bank and the

Inter-American Development Bank.[32] In March 2012, the United States suspended trade benefits for Argentina under the Generalized System of Preferences.[33] And in February 2013 while the pari passu battle at the Second Circuit was reaching its climax, the United States supported a motion at the IMF Executive Board to censure Argentina for misreporting inflation.[34]

While interested in heading off a court-ordered blockade of Argentina's finances, the United States was hamstrung in its ability to help in court. The U.S. briefs that argued against the imposition of a pari passu injunction also noted the U.S. government's strong reservations about Argentina's behavior: "The United States has several concerns regarding Argentina's failure to honor its international obligations. We encourage Argentina to continue to work with the International Monetary Fund ('IMF') and to participate in IMF surveillance as required under its Articles of Agreement, to improve its statistical reporting, clear its arrears to the United States and other Paris Club members, and honor final awards of arbitration panels convened under the auspices of the International Centre for Settlement of Investment Disputes ('ICSID')".[35]

Also quite damaging, the U.S. briefs didn't speak to whether the Lock Law constituted a breach of the pari passu clause, which didn't go down well at the Second Circuit. This qualified support for Argentina had a cost. While U.S. courts often defer to the executive in matters touching on foreign policy, the U.S. government was giving the Second Circuit an option to ignore its brief by bringing up these reservations and by not speaking to the Lock Law, one of the most important issues at hand.

After Argentina lost in the Second Circuit, the Obama administration refused to write an amicus brief on behalf of the country's appeal to the U.S. Supreme Court. Not only that, but the United States—embarrassingly for the IMF—blocked the IMF from delivering an amicus brief that it had already prepared and had announced that it was about to send.[36] The lack of these briefs was damaging. They potentially could have helped convince the Supreme Court to hear the case, potentially because amicus briefs from the U.S. government and other highly respected parties might be thought of as tiebreakers, not determinative, as to whether the Supreme Court will hear a particular case. And in this instance it could be argued that the Supreme Court had no reason at all to hear Argentina's appeal. After all, it had to do with the interpretation of a New York law contract and the fashioning of a unique equitable remedy to end a particularly thorny commercial dispute, not standard fare in the U.S. Supreme Court's docket. On the other hand, the lack of a U.S. amicus brief was an invitation to decline the appeal.

The U.S. Treasury Fills the Gaping Hole Left by Argentina and Greece

For Mark Sobel, the U.S. treasury deputy assistant secretary for international monetary and financial policy, 2012 was déjà vu. There was a gaping hole in the international framework for restructuring sovereign debt—the same one Anne Krueger spoke of in her famous November 2001 speech—but now it had grown much bigger. Not only had Elliott won on pari passu at the Second Circuit, promising by itself a significant increase in holdout activity, but Greece's 2012 debt restructuring also had shown that the CACs adopted by the market in 2003 were too weak to stop holdouts from prospering.

How powerful a CAC is in deterring holdouts has everything to do with its voting rules, which in turn determine how many bonds a holdout investor needs to buy to block its activation. Under the 2003 voting rules promoted by the U.S. Treasury, holding out was cheap and easy, as Greece's 2012 debt restructuring proved. The relevant part of the transaction was the country's efforts to restructure €20 billion of English law bonds that Greece had issued in thirty-five separate series. The crux of the problem was that the average size of these bond issues was about €570 million, which meant that holdout investors had to purchase only about €142.5 million of a bond series (25% of €570 million) to block its CACs from doing their job. This was chump change for most hedge funds, especially since they could have probably purchased €142.5 million of Greek bonds, which were trading near fifty cents on the dollar, for about €71 million. As a result, hedge funds were able to block the CACs from working on seventeen of Greece's thirty-five English law bonds, a total disaster compared to Greece's domestic debt restructuring, which was 100% successful.[37]

CACs had a problem, and U.S. Treasury's Sobel knew how to fix it: change the voting rules so that investors would have to buy far more bonds to block bonds' CACs from working. Sobel's solution was simple: aggregated voting.[38] Under an aggregated voting rule, Greece would have had to carry out only one vote for its thirty-five series of bonds, a much easier and much less error-prone proposition than carrying out the thirty-five separate votes that it did. An aggregated voting rule would also magnify the costs and risks of holding out. Pooling the debtor's entire debt stock together for one vote meant that holdouts would have to buy 25.1% of a much bigger amount of debt to block a vote. Under this scenario, holding out of Greece's transaction would have required that investors purchase 25.1% of €20 billion, or more than €5 billion of bonds, which would have cost €2.5 billion, far more than the €71 million that it took to hold out of the country's 2012 transaction, something few if any funds would have had the capacity to do individually. Aggregated voting was a game changer, but first Sobel had to convince the market to adopt it.

Sobel dusted off the playbook that U.S. Treasury undersecretary for international affairs John Taylor and his deputy Randal Quarles had used to convince the market to accept CACs in 2003, a playbook Sobel knew because he'd been part of the team that wrote it. Sobel convened a working group of leading sovereign debt issuers and investors to build a consensus in favor of reforms. The group included Alejandro Díaz de León from Mexico, Azucena Arbeleche from Uruguay, and a handpicked group of investors, bankers, and lawyers known for their cooperative attitude toward sovereign debt restructuring. The working group had two essential tasks. First, design new pari passu clauses to make it 100% clear that they meant "equal ranking," not "equal payments," to solve the problems observed in Argentina.[39] Second, design new voting options for CACs to reduce the power of holdouts in order to solve the problems observed in Greece. The working group held its first meeting in April 2013 on the fringe of the World Bank–IMF spring meeting in Washington. They quickly agreed on new language to kill Elliott's "equal payments" interpretation of the pari passu clause, but it took several meetings over a number of months to reach a consensus on exactly how to strengthen CACs. There were many options, and the creditors in the room didn't want to give away too much of their bargaining power, which could come back to bite them the next time a country came to restructure its debt.

Ultimately, Sobel's working group reached a consensus on adding two new voting options to sovereign bonds. The first was the aggregated voting method described above, subject to a 75% majority, paired with an antiabuse feature requiring all countries using aggregated voting to offer all bondholders the exact same deal. This feature would prevent a country such as Greece from making a significantly worse offer to holders of just two out of thirty-five series of bonds because it knew it had the votes it needed to activate the CACs from the holders of the other thirty-three. A second new voting option permitted sovereigns to make different offers to different bond series but at the cost of reinstating series-by-series voting. Under this second option, two conditions had to be met. First, each bond series must achieve a 50% participation rate, and second, two-thirds of all holders of all the eligible bonds must accept the offer. This second option would facilitate deals structured like Uruguay's 2003 transaction, in which the country offered holders of its various bonds equal maturity extensions, not exactly the same bonds (e.g., Uruguay offered holders of old two-year bonds new seven-year bonds and holders of old ten-year bonds new fifteen-year bonds).[40]

The next step for Sobel was to introduce the proposed new clauses to the wider market. At this point the U.S. Treasury opted to play a quiet behind-the-scenes role, passing leadership over to the International Capital Markets Association (ICMA), a London-based organization whose members include six hundred financial institutions. ICMA focused on two separate aspects of the project: finalizing the drafting of the new clauses and carrying out a consultation with its members. With the first, Deborah Zandstra, a lawyer with Clifford Chance in London, led a working group of Wall Street lawyers in drafting the new clauses. In the second, ICMA posted to its website a consultative paper on the issues and options in December 2013.[41] This process culminated with the posting of new standard pari passu language and CACs on ICMA's website in August 2014,[42] which was good timing because fresh developments in the Argentina cases provided bondholders with a convincing reason to accept these powerful new clauses with no complaint.

Elliott's Legal Attacks outside New York

While the U.S. government was focused on plugging the gap in CACs, Elliott was ramping up pressure on Argentina in courts all over the United States and around the world. Although there is relatively little public data about Elliott's foreign actions because courts in non-common-law countries provide less disclosure than do those in the United States,[43] the firm's actions in U.S. states other than New York are well documented in federal court records.

For example, Elliott made three distinct attempts to attach assets related to Argentina's space program. In New York the firm sought to attach a satellite guidance system at Honeywell,[44] while in California it attempted to attach an Argentine satellite at Spaceport Systems International[45] and an Argentine satellite launch slot with SpaceX.[46] These three efforts were unsuccessful.

Elliott's discovery efforts were particularly intense in the energy and chemical sectors. These attempts started in 2008 when the firm sought discovery in the Southern District of Texas from Excelerate Energy LLC, a shipper of natural gas to Argentina's ENARSA.[47] Elliott ramped up discovery in this sector in 2012 after Argentina nationalized Repsol's share of YPF. That year, Elliott sought discovery from Apache Oil Corporation, ExxonMobil Corporation, and EOG Resources, Inc., in the Northern District of Texas;[48] from ConocoPhillips in the Southern and Western Districts of Texas;[49] from Petrobras S.A. and Petrobras America, Inc. in the Southern District of New York and the Northern District of Texas;[50] and from Chevron Corporation in the Northern District of California, the denial of which it appealed to the Ninth Circuit.[51] In 2013, Elliott sought discovery from Dow Chemical in the Eastern District of Michigan.[52]

After 2010, Elliott and Aurelius were both very active in pursuing worldwide discovery from Argentina's international banks, including Bank of America. Judge Griesa allowed them to pursue this information, the Second Circuit affirmed his ruling, and the U.S. Supreme Court ruled for the plaintiffs on appeal. The Supreme Court released its opinion on this matter in June 2014, together with its decision not to hear Argentina's appeal on pari passu.[53]

In addition to these fairly conventional efforts to obtain information from the defendant, Elliott lodged a significantly less conventional attack in an attempt to uncover information on the BIS, where Argentina had moved its foreign reserves, as discussed in chapter 5. Elliott's lawyers went so far as to serve subpoenas on the general manager and two directors of the BIS while they were in the United States for the 2010 World Bank–IMF Annual Meetings. BIS general manager Jaime Caruana was served papers in New York when preparing to speak at a conference organized by the *Financial Times*.[54] In Washington, Banque de France governor Christian Noyer and Swiss National Bank governor Philipp Hildebrand were also served.[55] The courts, predictably, quashed these subpoenas, but these officials still had to hire lawyers and file statements. Given the impenetrable immunity that Swiss law affords the BIS, there was never any likelihood of a successful attachment of the Argentine assets housed at the BIS, which made this particular effort look wasteful and aggressive.

In 2013 Elliott's discovery efforts took on a new twist, as the firm began seeking information from Argentina's lawyers, Cleary Gottlieb, in New York. Elliott's specific concern at the time was that Cleary Gottlieb was encouraging Argentina to default, helping Argentina figure out how to evade the court's pari passu injunction, or both. This concern was valid, as Argentina did eventually try to evade the injunction, but discovery against opposing counsel in a lawsuit is not good form, nor is it particularly effective in light of attorney-client privilege. Elliott's angle was to ask the court to waive Argentina's and Cleary Gottlieb's privilege, claiming that the law firm was not responding adequately to permitted information requests. These efforts brought an angry response from Cleary Gottlieb's

Carmine Boccuzzi, who at one hearing told Judge Griesa that Elliott "just wants litigation about litigation . . . discovery about discovery."[56]

Elliott's Political Attacks on Argentina

Elliott's worldwide debt war extended well beyond conventional methods such as attachment and discovery and even included a political influence campaign against Argentina with a scope and character rarely seen in the history of sovereign finance. The organ for these attacks was ATFA, which started operating in late 2006. Its budget over the years, as uncovered through its federal tax filings, exceeded $36 million, and its activities included lobbying in Washington, New York State, and abroad.[57]

As noted in chapter 7, ATFA was operated by a trio of former Clinton administration officials: former assistant attorney general Robert Raben, former ambassador Nancy Soderberg, and former undersecretary of commerce Robert J. Shapiro.[58] Assisting the trio were Timothy Matthew McKenna, who served as the secretary, and Justin Peterson, who in later years served in that role. The organization was set up as a 501(c)(4) corporation in the Commonwealth of Virginia on January 11, 2007. As such, grants to the organization were deductible business expenses for its grantors. The organization ran the www.atfa.org website, and its operatives appeared in the media, published op-eds, spoke at conferences, lobbied the government, and hired other high-powered Washington insiders to assist ATFA in carrying out its mission.

Details on ATFA's spending can be found in the Form 990s the organization filed with the Internal Revenue Service as its tax-exempt status required. The group funneled $27 million to Washington insiders in 2013, 2014, and 2015, when the pari passu issue was hottest.[59] The biggest chunk, about $17 million, went to the Washington lobbying firm DCI Group LLC, which is currently managed by Justin Peterson. Other beneficiaries were Robert Raben's Raben Group, Robert Shapiro's Sonecon, Washington lobbyist Douglas B. Davenport, and the law firm Covington & Burling.

Exactly how all this money was spent is a mystery, but where it came from is not, because ATFA listed its members on its website in a roster that included Elliott, Elliott's FRAN plaintiff partners Bracebridge and Montreux (as well as Eric Hermann's FH International), GMO, and, at least initially, Hans Humes's Greylock Capital.[60] All of ATFA's initial members were investment firms that had cases before the federal courts.

ATFA's membership evolved in an unusual direction over time, however. In 2009 ATFA's ranks shot up to almost fifty members, but none of the new additions was an investment firm. Instead, the roster suddenly included a hodgepodge of organizations representing ranchers, farmers, minority groups, educators, and taxpayers. Among ATFA's new members were the Indiana Farmers Union, the Kansas Cattleman's Association, the Association of New Jersey County College Faculties, Montana Women Involved in Farm Economics, the National Black Chamber of Commerce, and the National Taxpayer Union.[61] This unusual growth in membership invited adverse coverage in the *Wall Street Journal*. In its 2012 piece "Argentine Lobby Mystifies Members," the newspaper quoted the heads of two listed organizations who denied affiliation. The leader of an agricultural group said, "We don't have anything to do with Argentina's debt," and the spokesperson for the Colorado-based association of university professors said, "This is absolutely foreign to me."[62] Yet the newspaper did find a bona fide member: a spokesman for the U.S. Cattleman's Association said, "We're grateful the task force is getting the word out about Argentina's bad acts—and how it affects everything from teachers to businessmen in rural America." The impression left by the *Wall Street Journal* article was that ATFA was astroturfing, or dressing up its lobbying campaign to look like a grassroots effort. Interestingly, in 2015 the *New York Times* called out the DCI Group for astroturfing for hedge funds that were lobbying against PROMESA, the law enacted to facilitate the restructuring of Puerto Rico's debt.[63]

ATFA's lobbying effort focused on a tight set of talking points designed to undermine Argentina's position in the United States, Europe, and elsewhere. ATFA claimed that Argentina's 2005 debt restructuring was a harsh deal that achieved a below-par success rate because it was unfair and was not appropriately negotiated; Argentina's 2005 restructuring was very costly to U.S. investors and U.S. taxpayers; Argentina was a lawbreaker for not paying court-ordered judgments and for "evading" its creditors by moving its foreign reserves offshore; the United States should terminate Argentina's participation in the General System of Preferences; the United States should stop supporting new loans to Argentina from the World Bank and the Inter-American Development Bank; the United States should stop submitting amicus briefs in favor of Argentina; and the U.S. Congress should pass a law to exclude Argentina from the U.S. debt capital markets, the so-called Judgment Evading Foreign States Accountability Act. ATFA also proposed in 2010 that New York State pass a law that would tax Argentine bond payments flowing through New York.

A report released by ATFA in 2006 is a telling example of how the group operated. "Discredited—The Impact of Argentina's Sovereign Debt Default and Debt Restructuring on U.S. Taxpayers and Investors" used a kitchen sink approach to claim that Argentina's default led to $84 billion in direct costs and $74 billion in indirect costs to investors and U.S. taxpayers.[64] To arrive at these numbers, authors Robert Shapiro and former World Bank, Standard and Poor's, and Scudder Investments employee Nam Pham added together the cost of devaluation; losses on bonds, currencies, and equities; and lost taxes on potential gains—even though the money in dispute at the time was just the $19.6 billion of holdout bonds.

A second noteworthy report is "Sovereign Debt Default: Cry for the United States, Not Argentina," a piece Harvard professor Hal S. Scott wrote for the Washington Legal Foundation in 2006. While no mention is made of its funding source, this forty-three page analysis was written by the same professor who later filed a brief for Elliott in the pari passu litigation and was featured on ATFA's website for years.[65] The report formalized into academic language the worldview espoused by Elliott. It began:

> This Working Paper argues that the United States policy of siding
> with sovereign defaulters against U.S. creditors is fundamentally
> misguided. The root of the sovereign debt problem is that sovereigns

overborrow, borrowing in excess of their institutional capacity to efficiently employ the borrowed capital. Overborrowing results from the
fact that sovereigns face few consequences as a result of default. Often they are bailed out by International Monetary Fund (IMF) loans,
with the consent of the United States. The default does not impede
their access to future credit because creditors have short memories.
The only effective remedy against sovereign overborrowing is to
allow creditors to enforce their contract rights effectively against
sovereigns in default. Any well functioning debt market depends on
strong creditor rights.[66]

In this report, Professor Scott also lauds Elliott's victory over Peru in the
Belgian court in 2000, saying the ruling appeared to introduce some
"creditor discipline" into the system and calling it a "high watermark of
creditor rights."[67]

The character and intensity of ATFA's lobbying efforts can also be
seen in the transcript of a hearing held in Albany on April 23, 2010, at the
New York State Assembly.[68] This source is unique because it provides a
record of the pathos employed by ATFA in making its case and displays
the great lengths the group went to in organizing opposition to Argentina.
This three-hour hearing of the New York State Senate Standing Com-
mittee on Banking was attended by Senators Brian X. Foley, Jeffrey D.
Klein, and Liz Krueger. The speakers were Dr. Robert Shapiro and Robert
Raben (from ATFA), Carolyn Lamm (from White and Case, Task Force
Argentina's lawyer), Dr. Claudio Loser (a senior fellow at Inter-American
Dialogue, a Washington-based think tank), James M. Roberts (the Heri-
tage Foundation), Mark Botsford (a private citizen), Dr. Thomas Halper
(chair of Baruch College's Political Science Department), Dr. Richard
Rahn (chairman of the Institute for Global Economic Growth), Dennis
Hranitzky (Dechert), Robert Cohen (Dechert), Alexander Yanos (Fresh-
fields), Arturo Porzecanski (American University in Washington, D.C.),
and John Missing (Debevoise & Plimpton).

During the hearing, ATFA's Shapiro called Argentina's 2005 exchange offer "the single most lawless exercise in the financial markets" and asserted that New York, as the financial center of the world, needed to take a stand against "countries which systematically violate the norms of international lending." Extending the argument, Mark Botsford, the private citizen, said that Argentina should not be able to continue "riding roughshod over the rights of Americans"; warned that "if this is allowed to continue, it will not be long before other countries will follow in her footsteps"; and concluded that the Federal Reserve Bank of New York should be worried about "this new superhighway of default, leading to the door of New York State." ATFA's operatives clearly pulled out all the stops for this event. Their effort must have been costly, it being neither cheap nor easy to organize so many people, coordinate their messages, and get them to show up on time.

Yet ATFA did more than lobby U.S. politicians. For one, it operated internationally. Its tax records show that it made payments to an operative in Brazil,[69] while Stefan Engelsberger—the German debt activist from Inzell—has confirmed that ATFA hired him to help the firm lobby the European Union.[70] For another, ATFA targeted legal processes. High on ATFA's agenda was stopping the U.S. government from intervening in court on behalf of sovereign debt defaulters. ATFA's singular victory in this regard was helping convince the United States (and thereby the IMF) not to send an amicus brief to the U.S. Supreme Court in 2013.[71] ATFA also likely played a role in helping get the mom-and-pop Varela plaintiffs to Washington and New York, where they participated in lobbying sessions. While including the Varela plaintiffs may have been good politics in Washington, the cost for the Varela plaintiffs themselves was high. They were criticized at home in Argentina for suing their country and were subjected to tax audits and negative press.[72]

Elliott Goes Directly for Cristina Fernández de Kirchner

ATFA tactics grew even more aggressive in July 2014 as the pari passu standoff reached its crescendo. As part of its shift, ATFA rebranded its online

effort, taking www.atfa.org down and replacing it with www.factcheck
Argentina.org.[73] Its focus? Alleged corruption by President Fernández de
Kirchner and her "cronies."

Featured prominently on the website was a page with the title "Follow
the Money," which listed twenty-eight individuals and organizations that
ATFA suspected of corruption.[74] Clicking on any of them brought readers
to a corresponding "Money Trail Player Card." The top portion of the
card featured FactcheckArgentina's logo, the middle section presented a
photograph of the targeted individual or business, and the bottom section
gave the name of the person or organization in bright red, along with
a "Rat Score" of three to five rats. Target número uno—with a five-rat
score—was Argentine businessman Lázaro Báez, whom the ATFA website accused of funneling money to the Kirchners, including through various hotel deals.[75]

In a set of actions that subsequently received international attention,
Elliott Associates launched a concerted effort to go after Báez in Nevada
in 2014. Elliott's NML sought discovery against 123 allegedly Báez-owned
companies and an outfit known as MF Corporate Services, which had
played a role in incorporating all 123. Elliott hit pay dirt on September 11,
2014, during a court-ordered deposition of MF Corporate Services employee Patricia Amunategui.[76] She disclosed that her office was setting
up hundreds of shell companies every year for the Panamanian law firm
Mossack Fonseca, whose involvement was hidden. Under pressure from
Elliott and an investigative reporter from Argentina, her deposition was
unsealed in early 2015. The released information was embarrassing to
both Argentina and Mossack Fonseca.[77] Perhaps it was no coincidence
that a massive data leak hit Mossack Fonseca the following year, a leak
commonly known as the Panama Papers scandal.[78] While there is no specific evidence to link this scandal (which brought down Mossack Fonseca)
to Elliott's discovery activities in Nevada, it wouldn't be surprising if outrage over the unsealed testimony motivated the leaker to act. In any case,
Elliott was the first to expose the law firm's dubious business practices.

Elliott's Nevada discovery effort was not the first time the firm sought
to use disclosure of wrongdoing to help it collect on a debt claim. Elliott

used a similar tactic against Congo-Brazzaville in the early 2000s in a case litigated in the UK courts. Elliott—it is said with the assistance of private investigators[79]—uncovered massive corruption by Congo-Brazzaville's leaders, which it used to try to force a settlement. The details appear in a *Sunday Times* article from June 15, 2008, titled "'Vultures' Expose Corruption."[80] This kind of press, which showed the firm uncovering corruption, gave Elliott a talking point it could use to deflect criticism of the firm's role in proposing the pari passu injunction that Judge Griesa imposed, which led to a default on tens of billions of dollars of performing bonds.[81]

Under Pressure, Argentina Shifts

All this pressure was taking a toll on Argentina. Its economic deterioration, the lack of credit in Washington, and the nonstop attacks in courts all around the world meant that Argentina wasn't in a good place as its pari passu litigation was reaching a climax. As a result, the country started shifting course. In late 2013 and early 2014, Argentina cut rapid-fire settlements with its largest arbitration claim holders and with the Spanish oil company Repsol (whose shares of YPF it had taken), giving the parties new bonds, which they then sold into the market.[82] And on May 29, 2014, Argentina announced a settlement with its Paris Club lenders.[83] These settlements were intended to "isolate the holdouts," but as chapter 10 will show, it was too little, too late.

10

It All Falls Apart

(June 2014–November 2015)

The U.S. Supreme Court handed down its pending rulings on the morning of June 16, 2014, and the score was Elliott Associates, 2, and Argentina, 0. The Supreme Court decided not to hear Argentina's appeal of the pari passu injunction,[1] and the court ruled in favor of Elliott on the topic of worldwide discovery.[2] Judge Thomas P. Griesa's February 2012 pari passu injunction now became effective.

Argentina was in a box—a tight one—because its next payments on its exchange bonds were due fourteen days later, on June 30. The question then became, What would Argentina do? Would it capitulate and pay Elliott and the exchange bondholders? Would it pay neither Elliott nor the exchange bondholders? Or would Argentina try to find a way to evade the order?

Fernández de Kirchner and Kicillof Vow to
Evade the Injunction

Argentine president Cristina Fernández de Kirchner's answer, given on national TV later that day, was that Argentina was going to try to evade the order. Her speech started with a deep dive into history. She blamed the country's debt on the military dictatorship of the 1970s, on the IMF, on the banks, and on Presidents Carlos Menem and Fernando de la Rúa. Next, Fernández de Kirchner applauded her husband's success in renegotiating the debt in 2005 and her own success in reopening the offer in 2010. Turning to Elliott, she said that hardworking Argentines were suffering while the hedge fund was out to make a 1,600% profit. Apropos whether to pay up or fight, she said, "Now there are some who say: why not pay this $1.5 billion and finish everything already?" This, she explained, was "absurd" and "impossible," because the total cost of paying all the holdouts, not just Elliott, would be about $15 billion, about half of the country's now-diminished foreign reserves. She also pointed out that the RUFO price-match guarantee clause in the exchange bonds was still in effect, which meant that if the holdouts were offered a better deal, the increase in value over the country's 2005 offer would have to be paid to the 92% of bondholders that had already settled, which would be prohibitively expensive. It was a contractual fact that the price-match guarantee would be in effect until the end of 2014. Paying the holdouts, she said, would make Argentina "fall over like a house of cards." So, she continued, "I have instructed the Economy Ministry and all the technical agencies of the national state to make available all the instruments and all the strategies necessary for all those who have trusted in Argentina, to receive their money, to receive the dollars which we have committed to pay." She closed by saying that "I think it is the duty of all who have the responsibility of government to take care of our obligations and among our obligations there is, among other things, paying our creditors, but also not to allow ourselves to be extorted by those who speculated and profited from misery and even want to harm the 92% of creditors who did trust in Argentina."[3]

The next day, Economy Minister Axel Kicillof announced that he would bring to the Argentine Congress a law to exchange the 2005 and 2010 bonds into new bonds that would be paid in Argentina where Judge Griesa couldn't block the payments. Kicillof said, "They shall not pass, they are not going to turn our restructurings upside down."[4]

Back in Judge Griesa's Courtroom

Judge Griesa was unruffled by Argentina's post–Supreme Court statements. At a hearing held on 2:00 p.m. on Wednesday, June 18, 2014, he listened patiently as creditors' attorneys complained bitterly about what

Fernández de Kirchner and Kicillof had been saying in Buenos Aires that week. After the attorneys finished, Griesa turned to Carmine Boccuzzi and asked him what the "intention of the Republic" was.[5]

This time Boccuzzi did not disappoint. He announced that Argentina was now willing to negotiate in good faith with the holdouts and that the government would be coming to New York the following week to start the process. That's what Judge Griesa wanted to hear or maybe expected to hear, having brought his wife into court to watch the proceedings that day, presumably to witness the moment Argentina finally started cooperating with the court.

Enter Special Master Daniel Pollack

By now, Judge Griesa understood that getting to a settlement wasn't going to be quick and easy. It was going to require a messy, multiparty, emotionally charged commercial negotiation, one that he was ill-equipped as a judge to sort out. He knew just the person to help him resolve the Argentine conundrum: Daniel Pollack, a partner at McCarter & English. Pollack was a friend of many years—his and Griesa's families often shared Thanksgiving dinner together[6]—and Griesa thought that Pollack had the unique skill set needed to bring the messy Argentina cases to a close.[7]

The son of a famous Southern District judge, the silver-haired and dapper seventy-year-old Daniel Pollack was combative and commanding in conversation, a negotiator through and through. In the early 1970s in one of his first cases, he defeated Goldman Sachs, which had sold his client some Penn Central commercial paper just weeks before the railroad defaulted. Later in his career, Pollack argued two cases before the Supreme Court. He also went toe to toe with then New York attorney general Eliot Spitzer, who had accused one of his clients of malfeasance.[8] People who knew Pollack, who passed away in October 2019, say he was a good person to have at your side in a high-stress, high-dollar employment or marital dispute. His former colleagues say he was a brilliant reader of people—and of juries—but that he usually worked on his own. Yet Pollack knew nothing about sovereign debt or the Argentine litigation, Judge

Griesa having been cautious not to mention the ongoing cases when they had met as friends over the years.

Judge Griesa called Pollack on Saturday, June 21, 2014, to ask him to serve as special master, a kind of mediator whom judges can call in at their discretion under the Federal Rules of Civil Procedures.[9] Pollack told Griesa that he'd think about it and get back to him and then spent the afternoon poking around on the internet to get up to speed on the cases.[10] When he got back to Griesa, Pollack told him that he'd take the job but only if he was granted extraordinary powers over the parties. Griesa agreed, and the order appointing Daniel A. Pollack as special master on the Argentina bond cases was posted to the docket on Monday, June 23, 2014. According to the order, Pollack was engaged to deal only with the lead plaintiffs, had full flexibility in how he worked with the parties, had no obligation to produce reports, would have open access to the judge, and could hire support as needed.[11] The order stated that all the parties were to give Pollack their full cooperation. With this, Pollack was ready to mediate. It was a game-changing moment in the judicial dynamics, with the now eighty-three-year-old judge relying on his friend Pollack in much of what follows, and, as one lawyer later reported to the author, he saw Pollack exiting the judge's chambers before every hearing from then on.

The Scope of the Injunction in Dispute

One would think that in June 2014, more than two years after Judge Griesa signed the order, that he—and the horde of lawyers in his courtroom—would know how the pari passu injunction was supposed to work. But that would be wrong. Of course, at a ten-thousand-foot level, they all understood that Argentina couldn't pay the exchange bondholders unless it paid Elliott and its coplaintiffs in full. Where they disagreed was over the scope of the injunction, namely, to which Argentine bonds it would apply. The exchange bondholders argued that the injunction covered only the exchange bonds issued under New York law, while the holdout bondholders argued that the injunction also covered bonds issued under English, Japanese, and Argentine law. One source of the confusion was that the legal arguments made in court up to that date had only discussed blocking the payments on the New York law bonds whose payments passed through the state, giving the impression that the injunction would apply only to those bonds. The language of the injunction, however, could be read to imply that all the exchange bonds were covered.

The issue of the scope of the injunction came to a head in a hearing held on June 27, 2014, just three days before Argentina's next payments on any of its bonds were due. Karen Wagner from Davis Polk (counsel for Citibank, the paying agent on the Argentine law bonds) pushed hard to exclude the Argentine law bonds from the scope of the injunction. Aurelius's counsel countered that these bonds were exchange bonds and were thus covered by the injunction. Judge Griesa responded, "I simply disagree with everything you're now saying. I will grant Ms. Wagner's motion."[12]

The Bank of New York (BONY), the paying agent for most of Argentina's bonds, had another problem to bring to Judge Griesa's attention that day. In an overt breach of the injunction, Argentina had just paid $500 million into BONY's account in Buenos Aires under the supposition that the bank would use the money to pay Argentina's various exchange bondholders. The firm asked Griesa what to do with the money. He answered that this payment was "improper" and "a violation of court orders" and that the money paid to BONY "should simply be returned to the Republic," although he later instructed BONY to hold on to the money pending further developments.[13]

Still, Judge Griesa was in a chipper mood. That's because he knew that Argentina's bonds, like most sovereign bonds, provided the country with a thirty-day grace period to make payments. And that meant that his friend, master negotiator Daniel Pollack, had time to get the two sides to reach an agreement before the unthinkable—a fresh default—happened. At least, that was the plan.

The July 7 Meeting

On July 3, 2014, Special Master Daniel Pollack announced that the negotiations were about to begin. He said in a press release that a senior team from Argentina would meet with him in New York on July 7.[14] The Argentine negotiating team would include two senior officials from the Ministry of Economy and one from the Argentine Treasury. Minister of Economy Axel Kicillof was not on the list, which was a disappointment to Special Master Pollack, who wanted the decision-makers in the room. When surfing the internet on the evening of Sunday, July 6, however, Pollack learned that Kicillof would be joining after all. Seeing the good news, Pollack called Argentina's lawyers at Cleary Gottlieb to confirm, but they said they knew nothing about it. Calling back a few minutes later, Cleary Gottlieb confirmed that Kicillof would indeed be coming to New York, although they had some bad news too: the Minister of Economy was only willing to meet with Pollack one-on-one and not with the hedge funds.[15]

Pollack wasn't happy. He ran negotiations according to strict rules that he had honed over the years. As he told the parties on both sides, he wanted meetings to be civilized ("no throwing brickbats"), he wanted meetings to be confidential ("no notes, no quotes"), and he wanted the principals to sit face-to-face ("I don't do alone"). Kicillof insisted, however: If you want me, no hedge funds, at least not at the first meeting. Pollack relented. He figured it was better to meet with Kicillof one-on-one than to not meet with him at all.

Pollack's first impression of Kicillof was that he was short and that he looked a bit like Fidel Castro. Pollack's second impression was one of annoyance at Kicillof for having shown up in his office for a mano a mano with an entourage of twenty.

Kicillof asked to begin by presenting Argentina's position and proceeded to walk through a lengthy PowerPoint presentation. When Kicillof finished, Pollack laid down the law, his law, the law that would apply to the negotiations. Pollack said, "Axel, my name is Dan. No formalities." Then, Pollack got straight to the heart of matters.

There are several things that occur to me:

#1. You contend that these people made an outsized profit. May I point out if there is no secondary market there is no primary market. You can't expect people to buy your bonds and just hold them. Also, these people you call vultures buy and sell bonds. That's not illegal, and that's not immoral.

#2. You call them vultures. I don't want you to do that in my office. We are here to do a deal.

#3. You told me you have a small child and a wife. At some point when she needs medical treatment and the kids need school, you will need money. Now, let's say you bought your house for $100,000 and then sold it one year later for $200,000 to raise cash. That is not illegal or immoral.

According to Pollack, Kicillof set two conditions on his end. First, the injunction must be stayed through the end of the year to let the RUFO price-match guarantee expire so that Argentina didn't have to top up the exchange bond holders, the 92% who had accepted one of the country's two offers, and second, Argentina wanted a negotiated solution with all the holdouts, not just Elliott Associates, as it would be of little use to settle with one firm and still be stuck in endless litigation with the rest. If the country was going to pay billions of dollars, it wanted a complete and clean solution.

About the proposed delay of the injunction, Pollack said, "I can't do it. Go ask the judge."

Later that week there was a second meeting, this time with the hedge funds, sort of. The Argentine delegation refused to sit in the same room as the hedge funds, so they were set up in two different rooms, with Pollack shuttling between them; Kicillof did not attend.[16]

It was a start.

Shadowboxing, July 2014

In July 2014, Elliott Associates had a problem: the possibility that Argentina would default on the exchange bondholders instead of paying everyone on July 30. If Argentina caved, Elliott would be a hero in the sovereign debt market for forcing the country to finally pay its holdout creditors what they were owed. But if the country defaulted, the firm would be a zero for having asked for the injunction.

Facing the threat head-on, Elliott portfolio manager Jay Newman published an opinion piece in the *Financial Times* on July 7 to stake out the moral high ground:

For more than 12 years we have tried to convince Argentina to put
its 2001 default behind it by negotiating in good faith with the remaining holders of its defaulted debt. I have travelled to Buenos
Aires to try to initiate a dialogue. But our requests for talks have been
ignored.

Mr. Kicillof is in New York again this week to meet a mediator appointed by the US District Court overseeing this case, and again he
has made no plans to meet us. Argentina says it will not even begin
to negotiate with creditors unless the court suspends indefinitely
a ruling that prevents the country from paying any of its creditors
without also paying the holders of defaulted bonds. The court has
said that such requests should be a matter for negotiation. Our firm
could be persuaded to give Argentina more time if its government
took concrete and serious steps toward meeting its legal obligations.
But the silence from Argentina is deafening. It does not appear serious about reaching a timely resolution of its debts.[17]

After reviewing the history of Argentina's relationship with its creditors,
Newman said that Elliott and the other creditors would be willing to receive bonds as part of a settlement and that the firm would agree to a
deal that was affordable for Argentina. But he closed with a dig: "Defiant
speeches have not helped the country move on from the 2001 default. A
single honest discussion could relegate it to the past."

The *Financial Times* published Economy Minister Kicillof's response
two days later on July 9:

Sir, I am writing to set the record straight regarding Jay Newman's
opinion piece.

Elliott Management Corporation's NML Capital purchased Argentine bonds in 2008 and immediately sued Argentina. These bonds,
defaulted in 2001, were bought with the sole purpose of obtaining a
favorable judgment to make an exorbitant profit.

Mr. Newman wants to portray Argentina as a country that does not
negotiate. This is outright false. Following lengthy negotiations, Argentina offered two debt exchanges, in 2005 and 2010, which were
voluntarily accepted by 92.4 per cent of the country's bondholders.

The vulture funds never negotiated. They never lent money to Argentina. NML purchased bonds at a value close to $50 million.

U.S. District Judge Thomas Griesa's order would allow NML to cash more than $800 [million], securing it a 1,600 per cent yield in only six years. If instead of litigating NML had accepted the debt exchanges offered by Argentina, it would have tripled or even quadrupled, its investment.

Argentina has made clear its willingness and capacity to negotiate since 2003. After an unjust ruling by US courts, earlier this week I met Daniel Pollack, the special master appointed by Judge Griesa, proving our willingness to move forward in a dialogue to ensure fair, equitable and legal conditions, taking into account the interests of 100 per cent of bondholders.

Argentina has requested the reinstatement of the stay order. The vulture funds oppose the petition, showing their true colors—they do not want to negotiate; they either get their claim in full or try to force Argentina into default. But this will not happen: Argentina will defend its successful debt restructuring process by paying its bondholders. . . .

The vulture funds never wanted to abide by the terms accepted by the overwhelming majority of creditors. They seek to extort a sovereign country. They want privileged conditions and they will stop at nothing: they will interrupt a flow of payments to Argentina's exchange bondholders denying these bondholders property that is rightfully theirs; they will speculate with the future of 40 [million] Argentines; they will cause irreparable damage to the international financial system rendering all future debt restructurings impossible.

This is why the international community is standing with Argentina's position in this case.

Vulture funds do not negotiate; that is why they are vultures.[18]

TFA's Nicola Stock also joined the fray, offering a letter on behalf of small Italian bondholders on July 17 in which he said Kicillof "totally ignores that his predecessors never (I repeat, never) negotiated those offers with the creditors, even though, at the time, the Argentine officials were literally overwhelmed with negotiation requests from all over the world."[19]

It was a short but powerful exchange of words that captured the differing worldviews and historical perspectives of the key players, with the creditors saying that Argentina was and had always been inflexible and unwilling to negotiate and with Argentina retorting that it had worked with 92% of its creditors and that the hedge funds were abusing the system to make superprofits.

Meet Continuously!

Emotions still high, the second week of July 2014 was a washout. Despite his best efforts, Special Master Daniel Pollack could not convince the two sides to meet in the same room even though the clock was ticking. To get things moving, Judge Griesa ordered the parties to his courtroom on July 22 to discuss the situation.

The official topics for this hearing were a series of motions involving the scope of the injunction and Argentina's injunction-violating $500 million payment to BONY. Judge Griesa's primary focus that day, however, was on the thirty-day grace period that was about to expire. After listening to all the issues put on the table by all the different parties, Griesa said, "I want to turn now to something that is really of the greatest possible importance, and that is that if sensible steps are not taken, there could well be a default by the Republic as of the end of July."[20]

Pointing to Pollack, Judge Griesa said, "I have appointed a special master, Daniel Pollack, to work with the parties to the litigation about an attempt to settle. Mr. Pollack is here. Could Mr. Pollack stand up." Then, after reviewing the history of the cases, Griesa announced that he had signed an order requiring the parties to meet with Pollack "continuously" until they reached an agreement.

Argentina's lawyer Jonathan Blackman shot up to speak.

Blackman said it was simply not possible for a country to meet continuously. What was needed, he said, was to stay the injunction through January 2015 to allow the RUFO price-match guarantee to expire and to give the country enough time to develop a comprehensive solution with all its holdout creditors. Blackman explained to Judge Griesa that he had worked with governments for years and that what the judge was now asking for was completely unrealistic. Working with a government, Blackman said, is not like dealing with a private person or a corporation; there are processes to go through that take time:

> The Court's order contemplates things that I remember, I'm sure the Court does, from earlier days when labor/management negotiations would go on around the clock, and so on, and there would be a federal mediator. I have visions of reading the newspapers from the '50s and '60s.
>
> States don't operate like that. With all respect, your Honor, a minister cannot be expected to sit in New York in Mr. Pollack's office continuously. He has to hear. He has to report. He has to consult at the literally highest level of the state, its president. These are not only economic decisions, they are political decisions, they are policy decisions.
>
> Very importantly, and this is the next constraint, there are constitutional and legal decisions. Argentina can't just sign a contract. It has laws that need to be addressed. It has constitutional obligations incumbent on its officials, including . . . criminal penalties and the like.[21]

Blackman ended his comments by reiterating his request for a stay of the injunction through the end of the year and warned that the ordered pressure-cooker, stay-up-all-night approach would backfire.

Judge Griesa was unmoved. At the end of the hearing he pointed again to the special master, who asked all the parties to come promptly to his office at 10:00 the following morning, evidently following a game plan that he and Griesa had agreed to in advance of the hearing. It was the logical step to take to force an end to the standoff, with no real negotiations having taken place in the month that had passed since the Supreme Court's June announcement. Subsequent events, however, would prove that Judge Griesa would have been wise to heed Blackman's warning—then or a little later that month after some progress had been made—because sovereigns, when rushed and backed into a corner, often make the wrong move. A former South American government official once said in a conversation that a cornered country is like a cornered cat, more likely to scratch you and run through your legs than to jump into your arms.

A Face-to-Face Meeting on July 29, 2014

While Judge Griesa's "meet continuously" order added much-needed urgency to the negotiations, the follow-up meeting was a washout. The sides remained far apart—quite literally—because the Argentines still refused to sit in the same room as the hedge funds. As a result, Default Day (D-day) minus seven was wasted.[22] And so too were the next six days.

Finally, with one day to go to D-day, on July 29, 2014, there was a breakthrough, the first face-to-face meeting between officials from Argentina and representatives of the largest holdout creditors: Elliott, Dart, Aurelius, Blue Angel, Montreux, and Bracebridge. In a late-night press release, the special master announced, "A delegation from the Republic of Argentina, led by the Minister of the Economy, Axel Kicillof, and the principals of the large bondholders met tonight for several hours in my office and in my presence. These were the first face-to-face talks between the parties. There was a frank exchange of views and concerns." Nonetheless, he reported, "The issues that divide the parties remain unresolved. Whether and when the parties will meet tomorrow (July 30) remains to be determined overnight."[23]

Pollack later disclosed that one stumbling block was the hedge funds' request that Argentina put a couple hundred million dollars into escrow as a condition for approving the country's request for a stay of the injunction through the end of the year, a request that not surprisingly was unacceptable to the Argentine authorities. While the posting of earnest money is a widely accepted practice in commercial disputes between private parties, it makes no sense in a sovereign context, where the political cost to the government's leaders would be fatal if they lost the earnest money but didn't settle the dispute; in some countries government officials have been jailed for less.

D-Day

While face-to-face negotiations stagnated, a deal was in the works behind the scenes. Privately owned banks in Argentina were working on a way to maneuver around the RUFO price-match guarantee.[24] The banks would buy Elliott's bonds and hold them until January 2015, the month after the RUFO's expiration, when Argentina would pay for the defaulted bonds by giving the banks new bonds that they could then sell into the market. Elliott offered the Argentine banks an attractive discount, some say 35% on their legal claim value. There was a fly in the ointment, however: The banks couldn't agree to the deal on their own; they needed approval from the government. They needed to borrow the purchase price from the Central Bank of Argentina, and they also needed assurances from the government that it would buy Elliott's bonds from them in January 2015 at no loss. Those conditions put the deal back into Minister Kicillof and President Fernández de Kirchner's court. The government would be lending private banks hundreds of millions of dollars to fund the purchase, which might in turn trigger the RUFO price-match guarantee. The essential commercial relationship was transparent: the government, not the private banks, would be the end purchaser of the bonds. It was a tantalizing proposal, to be sure, but there were operational and legal complexities, and time was short.

It was in this context that Argentina and the creditors reconvened under the watchful eye of Daniel Pollack on the morning of July 30, 2014. The session was unproductive, possibly because the parties were hoping that the private bank buyout offer would go through.

After lunch, Economy Minister Kicillof decamped to the building's atrium to talk to President Fernández de Kirchner on the phone. Their conversation lasted for several hours, according to Special Master Pollack.

Around 5:30 in the afternoon of D-day, Minister Kicillof found Special Master Pollack to tell him the outcome of his conversation with the president: no deal.[25]

Kicillof then left the building and gave a press conference at Argentina's

New York consulate, criticizing Judge Griesa's decisions. The country was not going into default, he explained, because it was in compliance with its contracts, having deposited the required money for the payment with its paying agent. According to Kicillof, the default was Griesa's fault, since he was blocking the payment.[26]

Taking a cue from the country's leaders, the local press heralded the nonpayment on the country's bonds not as a default but instead as a "GrieFault."[27] It was in this way that Judge Thomas P. Griesa of the U.S. District Court for the Southern District of New York became a much-vilified national enemy of the people of Argentina. Judge Griesa himself was now part of the conflict, public enemy number two in Argentina, derided in political speeches and portrayed in unflattering caricatures pasted on walls all over Buenos Aires. Elliott, of course, was still public enemy number one.

Bitterness

Argentina defaulting on everyone was not the way it was supposed to work out. Back in 2012, Judge Griesa had told a room full of lawyers that imposing the injunction would be "simple" and "uncomplicated," and Theodore Olson had said in court that Argentina would pay if the injunction were imposed. More recently, Daniel Pollack had been meant to pull off a brilliant settlement before a default occurred. Now, Griesa's hopes and dreams lay in a pile of rubble, crushed by the bitterness and distrust that divided the parties. At this rate, the cases might never come to an end, at least during his lifetime. Nonetheless, he had to keep trying. He called a hearing for August 1, 2014, to discuss the way forward.

The mood at the August 1 hearing was somber. Judge Griesa kicked off this first postdefault proceeding with a complaint about Argentina's "we didn't default" narrative. He called it "misleading" and asked Argentina to cease making such claims.[28] He also encouraged the parties, notwithstanding the horrendous situation, to keep working toward finding a solution.

Jonathan Blackman spoke next, reiterating Argentina's view that the

RUFO made it impossible for the country to settle before January 2015. Then under direction from Argentina, Blackman sheepishly asked Judge Griesa to fire Special Master Pollack. Argentina, he said, had lost trust in Pollack for terming the country's missed bond payment of July 30 a "default" in the press release the special master had sent out that evening.[29] According to Blackman, this language risked triggering credit default swaps (a type of credit insurance), which would formalize Argentina's July 30 nonpayment as a default event in the market's eyes.

Defending Pollack, Elliott's lawyer, Robert Cohen, pointed out that it was only because of the special master's skillful intervention that the parties had met face-to-face for the first time.

Closing the session, Judge Griesa confirmed that Special Master Pollack was still on the job, and the judge asked the parties to cool down and stick to the facts.

Yet on August 8, a scant one week later, they were all back in court, and Judge Griesa was furious. On August 7, Argentina had placed full-page spreads in the *Washington Post*, the *Wall Street Journal*, and the *New York Times* that said, under the heading "Legal Notice," that no event of default had arisen under Argentina's bond contracts and that the district court had made "erroneous and improper interpretations."[30]

Judge Griesa started off the hearing with a ten-minute diatribe accusing Argentina of making "false and misleading" statements.[31]

With the spotlight on Argentina, Jonathan Blackman spoke first. Defending his reputation at the bar, Blackman explained to Judge Griesa that the press statements were not "prepared by my firm, by me, by anyone associated with us, and we knew nothing about them until I read them, probably the same time your Honor did, in the *New York Times* yesterday."[32]

Making a 180-degree spin, Blackman then accused Elliott of spreading false and misleading information:

> I have to bring to the court's attention the fact that this week, every day this week, an organization called American Task Force Argentina, which was created by [Elliott] Associates, which is the owner of the plaintiff NML and funded by it, has put out on its web site false and misleading statements

about me and about my law firm. It has put out statements saying that we are responsible for Argentina's default; that I personally have told the president of Argentina to default.[33]

Blackman showed the judge material from the website that, among other things, depicted Blackman's face on the body of a vulture. [34] He called the material "false," "misleading," "reprehensible," and "outrageous" and said,

The people who prepared that . . . have acted in a way that is malicious and evil, a way that no one—no human being—should act toward another human being. There have been high tempers in this case, and obviously, the court knows, a great deal of animosity between clients. But to attack a lawyer and his law firm in that fashion personally, day after day, so that my family has to read this sort of stuff, just goes beyond any bounds of human decency. It is just absolutely wrong and improper.[35]

Judge Griesa thanked Blackman for his statement, saying, "I am very glad that you made clear that you and your firm did not play a role in drafting this so-called notice. This is a fact that is highly important. On the other points you have made, I deeply regret any personal attacks or disparagement upon you."[36]

Judge Griesa ended the hearing by urging the parties to move forward and behave professionally. "So let us stick to the resolution of the issues before the court. Let us avoid any further false and misleading press releases or statements by the Republic, and let us continue with the process of settling this case. That is what will assist real human beings. Thank you."[37]

Yet the pain and misery continued.

Argentina started advancing legislation to replace BONY as the paying agent on its bonds, which would allow the country to evade the injunction. For this effort, Judge Griesa found Argentina in contempt of court on October 3.[38]

Litigation also continued over the scope of the injunction, namely,

whether it applied to Argentina's domestic law bonds paid in Buenos Aires, not in New York.[39] Although Judge Griesa had initially ruled on June
27 that these bonds were exempt from the injunction, he reversed his
position in July 2014, saying that the issue had to be tried. There was one
simplification, however: The creditors clarified in July that they would
allow Argentina to continue paying its Argentine law peso-denominated
bonds paid in Buenos Aires and that they were only challenging payments to be made on the country's U.S. dollar–denominated Argentine
law bonds.[40]

A Judge's Lament

Judge Griesa was deeply bothered—perhaps even distraught and de-
pressed—that not only were his cases not settled but also that Argentina
was now in fresh default on tens of billions of dollars of bonds in connection with his ruling. During a September 29, 2014, hearing he told the
parties gathered in his courtroom what was on his mind, which was that
none of this had to have happened. All that was needed was for Argentina
to have been more flexible about dealing with its holdout creditors:

> When the Republic made the exchange offers in 2005 and 2010 most people
> accepted. So, you have a lot of exchange bonds and interest due on those
> bonds.
>
> Now, it wasn't compulsory. Everybody did not accept. And so what you
> were left with is a situation where a lot of people have new bonds and they
> have certain assurances that accompany those new bonds and so forth.
>
> Then you have the people who did not accept. The problem that has
> existed for a long time is this. It seems to me that if the Republic had been
> responsible, the Republic would have recognized that there was a problem
> here, and there was a problem: How to deal with the people who did [not]
> exchange. Not easy.
>
> But the problem was exacerbated because what should have been done
> is that the Republic goes to representatives of those people . . . and tries
> to start working something out. Problems have existed harder than that.

And instead of doing that, the Republic, in all kinds of rhetoric and so forth simply said: We're not going to recognize. We're not going to pay. We're not going to deal with that. That's what has created the problem; to take a very important and substantial amount of debt and try to say it doesn't exist and we won't pay it and we call it vultures and all of that.

Why didn't the Republic say we have something to work out? Why didn't they do that instead of doing everything opposite to that that they could think of? That's the thing that is bothersome.[41]

2014's Silver Lining: Collective Action Clauses Get a Power Boost

For all the misery in the New York court in the fall of 2014, things were looking up in the world of sovereign debt restructuring. They were looking up, in fact, because of all the misery in Judge Griesa's courtroom. Argentina's default and recent events in Greece were proof positive that sovereign bonds needed clearer pari passu clauses and more powerful CACs to deter holdouts and put an end to messy sovereign debt litigation. Indeed, the timing worked out almost perfectly because the ICMA working group—which had taken the baton from the U.S. Treasury working group—was poised to launch its initiative to reform sovereign bond contracts at precisely the moment Argentina defaulted.

The market quickly adopted the new clauses, responding positively to a carefully choreographed rollout.

On July 30, Argentina defaulted on its exchange bonds.

On August 29, ICMA announced the publication of the new model pari passu and CAC contract terms on its website.[42]

On September 2, the *Financial Times* ran an article on the new CACs with the title "Sovereign Debt Plan Takes on Holdouts." Its lead-off paragraph said it all: "Got a 'vulture' problem? Bond market heavyweights, backed by Washington, have come up with a plan they say should avoid a repeat of the sovereign debt meltdown between Argentina and its holdout creditors."[43]

On September 21, the Group of Twenty (G20) finance ministers and central bank governors announced, "We look forward to upcoming discussion around the International Capital Markets Association's proposal on possible means to reinforce collective action clauses in sovereign bonds, given the challenges litigation poses to the predictable and orderly resolution of sovereign debt restructuring processes."[44]

On October 6, the IMF Executive Board announced its support for the new CACs and pari passu clauses.[45] The IMF also released "Strengthening the Contractual Framework to Address Collective Action Problems in Sovereign Debt Restructuring," a forty-seven-page staff report that provided technical analysis and historical context.[46]

On October 10, the IIF held a panel on the topic while investors and officials were in Washington for the World Bank–IMF Annual Meetings. The meeting room was jam-packed with investors and policy makers, and the mood was positive.[47]

On October 14, Kazakhstan issued $2.5 billion in new ten- and thirty-year bonds with the new clauses.[48]

On November 16, the G20 released a statement welcoming recent progress with sovereign bond contracts.[49]

And on November 25, Mexico, the world's bellwether sovereign debt issuer, blasted out a $2 billion ten-year bond with the new CACs and pari passu language.[50] As expected, the entire market followed suit: since October 2014, nearly every single sovereign bond issued around the world has included the new clauses.[51]

This shift in practice was a great victory for policy makers and for the market, that is, for everyone but prospective holdouts.

2015: Annus Horribilis

If 2014 was bad for everyone party to the Argentina bond litigation, 2015 was worse. New Year's Eve came and went. Argentina's RUFO price-match guarantee expired. But Argentina was nowhere to be seen; no offer was made, and no substantial discussions were being held. Why? Politics. It was a presidential election year in Argentina, with Néstor Kirchner's former vice president Daniel Scioli running for the party in power because

Cristina Fernández de Kirchner couldn't serve three times in a row. The disincentive for negotiating in 2015 was that opposition candidate Mauricio Macri had said that he would settle with the holdouts if he won,[52] which apparently led the party in power to think that it would be better to wait until after the election to take up the issue again. After all, it would only be a twelve-month delay to a process that had been under way for fourteen years.

With negotiations stalled, Elliott Associates was in a bad place. The firm wasn't being paid, and if Fernández de Kirchner's party won the election it might never get paid. So, the firm continued to do what it did best: it litigated hard, and it lobbied hard. In 2015 ATFA spent $13.38 million lobbying against Argentina, its highest amount on record.[53] Some, including Cristina Fernández de Kirchner, have claimed that Elliott used its money to try to sway the election toward Macri, who had said that he'd settle with the holdouts.[54]

In addition to lobbying harder than ever, Elliott opened a new front in its war against Argentina and anybody that did business with the country. In 2015, Elliott started going after international banks that helped Argentina raise money offshore. Since 2005, the country's financing strategy had been to issue U.S. dollar bonds under Argentine law in a local auction process to local affiliates of international banks, who would then sell the newly issued bonds to international investors, including institutional investors located in the United States. Now that the injunction was effective, Elliott made its first move to try to block Argentina from accessing international capital via this mechanism. When rumors of such deals surfaced in February and April 2015, Elliott killed them by seeking discovery from the underwriters.[55] This, in turn, brought three new parties into the ever-expanding litigation: Deutsche Bank, JPMorgan Chase, and BBVA. Soon Deutsche Bank was accusing Elliott of "harassment" in the financial press, calling its discovery efforts "a long-running fishing expedition."[56] Before this point, most international banks had avoided the litigation.

Meanwhile, the courtroom battle over the scope of the injunction continued. In March 2015, Judge Griesa ruled that the injunction applied to the U.S. dollar–denominated bonds Argentina had issued under

Argentine law in its 2005 and 2010 offers. This ruling left Citibank, the local paying agent under these bonds, in a no-win situation: If it made the payment on Argentina's local-law U.S. dollar bonds, it would be in breach of the court's order; if it didn't, it would be in breach of Argentine law for not fulfilling its contractual obligations to the government. Stuck with no alternative, on March 18, 2015, Citibank informed Griesa that it would sell its local Argentine custody business to step out of the middle of the dispute.[57]

Elliott also aggressively pursued discovery on Argentina's law firm, Cleary Gottlieb. In late 2015, Elliott asked the court to waive Argentina's attorney-client privilege on the basis of claims that Cleary Gottlieb had responded inadequately to information requests.[58]

The FRAN Plaintiff's $3 Billion Merger Doctrine Problem and Copycat Cases Are Filed

Beneath the surface during 2014 and 2015 and for some years before was an issue that few were following and even fewer understood: the possibility that a New York State legal rule, called the "merger doctrine," would make it impossible for Elliott and its FRAN plaintiff partners to obtain a pari passu injunction with respect to the $3 billion in judgments on their FRAN holdings. If the pari passu injunction didn't work with FRANs, Argentina could potentially save a lot of money by paying all its outstanding claims in full except for the $3 billion it owed on these securities. After the non-FRAN claims were paid off, litigation on all other bonds would cease. Argentina could then refuse to pay the FRANs, standing on their extraordinary ten-times-par payout and banking on the courts not doing much to help the three remaining holdouts enforce these legally correct but commercially egregious bond claims. No doubt aware of this possible scenario, the lead plaintiffs worked to make sure that the merger doctrine didn't prevent them from obtaining pari passu injunctions on their FRANs and their other postjudgment claims.

The New York State merger doctrine implies that a plaintiff's entire legal claim is merged into a money judgment when one is granted. The original bond disappears, and only the money judgment remains. The $3 billion question was whether a bond's pari passu covenants survived the granting of a money judgment. The law was unclear on the point, so Judge Griesa could potentially rule that the holdouts couldn't get pari passu injunctions on their FRANs and other postjudgment claims. To head off this possibility, the hedge funds lobbied the New York State Legislature to change the law to specify that bond covenants survive the granting of money judgments.

The lobbying took place in 2011, with Milberg's Michael Spencer later testifying that "in February 2011, I spoke with Mr. Cohen about joining a contingent of hedge fund representatives for a planned meeting with state legislators in Albany about 'anti-merger legislation,' a bill to clarify state law on the merger doctrine in order to foreclose one possible objection to Equal Treatment motions in post–money-judgment cases."[59] This lobbying effort failed, but the plaintiffs still won the issue because in June 2015 Judge Griesa granted the plaintiffs injunctions on their FRANs and other postjudgment claims.[60] It was a technical ruling but one worth billions to the FRAN plaintiffs.

This specific concern about the merger doctrine helps explain why so few plaintiffs were included in the early pari passu cases, a pattern of activity first noted in chapter 8. The superficial and no doubt still important reason must have been to limit the numbers because it would be simpler to run the test case with just a handful of parties. But the bigger concern must have been that if all the plaintiffs sought pari passu injunctions with respect to all of their pre- and postjudgment cases in the first go, Judge Griesa might allow only the injunctions on the prejudgment bonds to keep things simple or to limit the impact on the market. Delaying seeking injunctions with respect to the lead plaintiffs' $3 billion in postjudgment FRAN claims also cleverly sidestepped a predictable argument in court from Argentina and exchange bondholders that it would be inequitable to grant an injunction that would block payments to holders of tens of billions of dollars of performing bonds to help the FRAN holders achieve a ten-times-par recovery.

Whatever the rationale, the plaintiffs decided to bring their prejudgment cases first and their postjudgment cases later. For this strategy to work, however, all the many plaintiffs had to fall in line. If even one tiny plaintiff asked for an injunction on a postjudgment claim and lost, the court would apply the same ruling to all the others. The lead plaintiffs' cases were only as strong as their weakest link, so the lead plaintiffs undoubtedly worked hard to convince all the other plaintiffs to hold off from bringing any pari passu claims until the lead plaintiffs gave the all clear. Their strategy worked, although one plaintiff jumped the gun by a few weeks. Mark Kalish at Moss & Kalish filed his copycat motion with respect to Old Castle's and Lightwater's postjudgment bonds on June 5, 2014, eleven days before the Supreme Court came back with its answer on Argentina's appeal.[61] Kalish states that not unexpectedly, he received a call from Elliott's Jay Newman, who told him he was risking the whole thing and offered to purchase his clients' bonds. Kalish's clients refused to sell because the price Elliott suggested was much less than what they expected to be paid after the injunctions went into effect.[62]

New Entrants and the Funny Math of Court Claims

If the merger doctrine was a major strategic concern of Elliott and the other long-litigating plaintiffs, it was not the primary concern of a dozen or so hedge fund plaintiffs who joined the action after 2011.[63] None of these plaintiffs had asked the court for a final money judgment, so the merger doctrine was of no concern to them because all their bond covenants remained intact. Why they didn't ask for a final money judgment, however, is of interest and also helps uncover an intriguing element of Elliott's, Aurelius's, and Blue Angel's strategies: the funny math of court claims under which it pays not to ask for a final money judgment. Bond claims with final money judgments grow much more slowly in value (e.g., 1% a year) than bond claims without final money judgments (e.g., 10% a year). The difference derives from the treatment of court claims under state and federal law. Here's the math: Before a federal judge grants a judgment, New York law applies, and bond claims accrue interest at their contractual interest rate plus interest-on-interest. After a federal judge grants a final money judgment, however, federal law takes over, and the applicable claim accrues at the prevailing yield of a one-year U.S. Treasury bill,[64] typically a much lower level. For the Argentina bond claims then being litigated, not obtaining a judgment meant that investors could see their bond claims grow at more than 10% a year because of the high coupon of the bonds, while getting a money judgment meant growth of only about 1% a year, the then-prevailing one-year Treasury rate.

Whether investors had chosen to ask for a final money judgment therefore had a profound effect on the size of their legal claims when the lawsuits were finally settled in 2016. Those who had obtained a judgment back in 2003 had claims that had grown to about 1.5 times par value, while those who held off asking for a final money judgment had claims that had grown to about 3.5 times par.[65] Such was the value of accruing claims at the higher rate.

Macri Wins

Closing out 2015 was Argentina's national election, with President Fernández de Kirchner's party fielding Daniel Scioli, a Peronist stalwart and former vice president to Néstor Kirchner, against Mauricio Macri, a businessman who headed a coalition called Cambiemos, which means "let's change."

It was going to be tough for Macri to beat Scioli, with the Kirchners having had a tight hold on the country since 2003. The economy was struggling, however, and more and more people were frustrated with the nonstop crises of the Fernández de Kirchner government. Helping tip the scales toward Macri was the suspicious death in January 2015 of special prosecutor Alberto Nisman, who was found shot, alone in the bathroom of his apartment, killed by a bullet to his right temple the night before he was due to air a claim in the Argentine Congress that President Fernández de Kirchner was trying to cover up Iran's involvement in the 1994 attack on the Jewish center Asociación Mutual Israelita Argentina.[66] Thousands poured into the streets holding signs that said "Yo Soy Nisman," the Argentinization of the "Je Suis Charlie" signs held up in France in the aftermath of the *Charlie Hebdo* massacre that had occurred just a few weeks earlier in Paris.

On November 22, 2015, Mauricio Macri edged out Scioli to win the presidency.[67] It was a dream come true for the holdouts, since Macri was saying that he would settle with them; their payday was coming soon, or at least that's how they must have seen it. Little did they know, however, that as they celebrated the results of the election there was an obstacle standing between them and their money: Luis Caputo, a former Wall Street bond trader whom President-elect Macri would soon tap to serve as Argentina's secretary of finance. Caputo, it turns out, was dead-set against the holdouts getting all the money they were demanding, especially on their 10-times-their-money FRAN claims and their 3.5-times-their-par-value prejudgment bond claims.

A new battle was about to begin, but this time the hedge funds—who had been controlling the process for quite a few years—didn't know what was about to hit them.

11

The Settlement

(December 2015–April 2016)

"We're the victims here," Argentine finance secretary Luis Caputo asserted when he first met Special Master Daniel Pollack in December 2015. "Macri is not Kirchner, and he's willing to negotiate in good faith to get this deal done—and quickly."[1] Caputo tried to relate to the special master that the hedge funds were asking for too much and would drag their feet because their claims were accruing value at such a high rate, but he quickly realized that he was facing a wall of skepticism given all that had happened up to that point.

Finance Secretary Caputo also understood that support of the U.S. government would be important, so he traveled to Washington, D.C., to make the same pitch to Deputy Assistant Secretary for the Western Hemisphere Michael Kaplan and others at the U.S. Treasury. Besides general political support, one specific objective was to reopen access to multilateral funding, which was sorely needed in the country.

Caputo talked to the special master and the Treasury numerous times in January and the following month. While Caputo's initial entreaties were certainly welcome, he could tell that his counterparts were wary. When he first met Pollack, for example, he sensed that the special master was biased against Argentina and that he thought that Argentines were a bunch of crooks. To counter Pollack's impression, Caputo pleaded, "We are not here to waste your time. We will be tough, but we will negotiate in good faith to cut a deal." But the finance secretary's suspicions were on point: Special Master Pollack told the author that when he first saw

Caputo he thought he looked like Kicillof, not a positive association given all that happened in 2014.[2]

Caputo realized that before attempting to advance any negotiations, he would need to gain the special master's trust. An important part of winning his support for Argentina's position was to explain in detail the math of the situation. In January 2016, Caputo showed the special master and U.S. government officials his calculations explaining that the plaintiffs were asking for 10 times par on their FRANs and 3.5 times par on other bonds. Seeing their reactions, Caputo quickly realized that they hadn't seen these calculations before.

Caputo's efforts bore fruit, because over time the special master and the U.S. Treasury came to understand why Caputo was arguing that it wasn't equitable for Elliott Associates and the other lead plaintiffs to be using the courts not to recover par but instead to win extraordinary returns. But their minds weren't moved overnight. Caputo made a strong start with these first conversations, but he had his work cut out for him, because the trust deficit was large and the plaintiffs he would soon face were anticipating being repaid in full as their court orders specified.

The First Battle: January 13, 2016

The first negotiating session with President Mauricio Macri's team took place on January 13, 2016, in the Midtown Manhattan offices of Special Master Pollack's firm, McCarter & English. Finance Secretary Luis Caputo attended the meeting with Eugenio Bruno, a Ministry of Economy lawyer. Representing the holdouts were Elliott's co-CEO Jonathan Pollock, Elliott portfolio manager Jay Newman, Kenneth Johns for Dart, Michael Straus for the Montreux group, Michael Brodsky for Aurelius, and Nancy Zimmerman for Bracebridge.[3] Special Master Pollack sat in the middle playing referee.

The meeting was an hour and a half long, and the topic of the day was process. The creditors wanted full control of the process, and they handed over a lengthy draft nondisclosure agreement that would limit when Argentina could launch an offer and what it could say in public during the negotiations. Argentina countered that all that was needed was a short two-page agreement promising to keep discussions confidential until the country launched a settlement offer to all creditors, maybe in ten days. Pollack sided with Argentina—he liked short and simple—so a compromise was reached along those lines.[4]

The parties agreed to reconvene to discuss commercial terms on February 1, 2016. Privately, Pollack pressed Caputo not to put a deal on the table without previewing it with him first, in writing. Caputo agreed.

Going Public in Davos

The following week, Argentina launched a press campaign to win international policy makers and financial markets to its side. It was Davos week, and all the world's leaders were congregating in Switzerland for the annual meeting of the World Economic Forum. President Macri and Economy Minister Alfonso Prat-Gay used the event to introduce the narrative that Argentina had changed its ways. They pushed this message in private one-on-one sessions with world leaders and heralded it out on the street. Macri told a press gaggle, "We want to reach a settlement, find a fair agreement," and he said that he wanted a deal "this year, early this year."[5] The financial press lapped it up.

On January, 22, 2016, Chris Giles, Gillian Tett, Elaine Moore, and Benedict Mander of the *Financial Times* reported that Argentina was now willing to pay creditors one hundred cents on the dollar on the holdout bonds plus a premium for a portion of past-due interest. The article quoted Minister Prat-Gay as saying that "I want to honor the debt and let's talk about the interest bill."[6] Putting a number to it, he said that Argentina was willing to pay a 20% premium to creditors for past-due interest for a total payment of $120 per $100 face amount of bonds. The holdouts must have choked when they read the story. The 1.2-times-par-value settlement Prat-Gay suggested was far below the 3.5 times par value they were seeking on their prejudgment bonds and the 10 times par they were seeking on their FRANs.

In addition to good press, Argentina scored an important victory

that week with the U.S. government: Treasury Secretary Jacob Lew announced after meeting with Minister Prat-Gay in Davos that the United
States would no longer vote against loans to Argentina at the boards of
the World Bank and the Inter-American Development Bank.[7] The political
winds were shifting in Argentina's favor.

Caputo and Bausili: 24/7

After Davos, Secretary of Finance Caputo's team worked nonstop. For
the next three months Caputo and Undersecretary of Finance Santiago
Bausili—also a former banker—led the negotiations in New York, while
the team at the Ministry of Economy worked day and night dealing with
the myriad legal and financial technicalities associated with settling
with the holdouts.

On Wednesday, January 27, 2016, Caputo and Bausili had a long and
painful meeting with Cleary Gottlieb in New York to discuss Argentina's
plan to replace the firm. A key element of the government's strategy was
to convince Judge Griesa to lift the injunction on the basis that the government's approach had changed, and it seemed incongruous to have the old
lawyers tell the new story.[8] Argentina wanted to put a fresh face in front of
the judge, and the next day, Caputo and Bausili interviewed candidates to
replace the firm, eventually hiring Cravath, Swaine, & Moore to represent
the country in court in the upcoming hearings. Cleary Gottlieb was still
in the picture, however, there being no way to replace a law firm in the
middle of such complex litigation.

After a long day of meetings with various law firms, at 5:00 p.m. on
Thursday, January 28, Caputo and Bausili met with nine of the "new entrant" hedge funds, the ones that had bought bonds and joined the pari
passu litigation during 2014 and 2015. The funds told Argentina that they
wanted a quick deal, not years of litigation.[9]

On Friday, January 29, Argentina announced that its central bank
had obtained a US$5 billion one-year secured loan, which demonstrated
that the international banking community was standing with Macri.[10]
That evening, Caputo had dinner at Special Master Pollack's apartment

to talk before the big negotiation slated to begin the following Monday morning. At dinner Caputo showed Pollack a draft of the proposal Argentina was planning to present to creditors. Pollack responded that it was "not enough, you need to do better."[11]

On Saturday, January 30, Caputo and Bausili met with TFA chair Nicola Stock to discuss settling with the sixty thousand Italian retail investors still represented by the creditor rights organization. This was a critical meeting for Argentina, because if the country could cut a relatively low-cost deal with TFA over the weekend, the Ministry of Economy team could put it in the face of the hedge funds on Monday morning. For Stock it was a meeting long overdue, as he had been chasing successive governments for over ten years to deal with the Italian retail investor problem, all to no avail. Hopeful of making progress with the new government, Stock had sent a letter of congratulation to Macri shortly after he won the election.[12]

TFA: Argentina's Soft Target

On the morning of January 30, 2016, Finance Secretary Luis Caputo and Undersecretary Santiago Bausili sat across from Nicola Stock and TFA's lawyers for the first time. Introductions were made, views were exchanged, and the two sides agreed it was high time to cut a deal.

With the meeting looking like a success, Stock said, "We've had a good meeting. Let's meet again tomorrow to discuss terms."

"No," Caputo responded. "Let's do it now."[13]

So, then and there Argentina and TFA hammered out a deal to pay Italian retail investors 100% of the face amount of their bonds plus 50% more to cover a portion of the interest that had gone unpaid since the default. That was the deal: full repayment and a good-looking premium.

This was a win-win solution. Stock would be a hero back home in Italy for delivering a juicy-looking 150% of par for his clients who hadn't been paid a penny in fifteen years, and the amount would be paid in cash. And Caputo would have a 1.5 times par value settlement benchmark to use as leverage in negotiations with the hedge funds, who would be asking for 3.5 times par on similar bonds. Partly driving this deal was the reality that neither side knew how the ongoing arbitration at the ICSID would turn out. The arbitration panel was due to grant an award, but its value was uncertain and could have been as low as the value Argentina offered investors in 2005 and 2010 or as high as the 3.5 times par that the smart money investors were asking for. This uncertainty fed both sides' interest in settling, and a deal cut at 1.5 times par value was somewhere near the middle.

Argentina signed its settlement agreement with TFA the next day, Sunday, January 31, 2016, a momentous occasion since this was its first settlement with any of the holdouts following more than a decade of litigation. In numbers, Argentina agreed to pay $1.35 billion in cash against the approximately $900 million in bonds the TFA claimants still owned, about 10% of the holdout debt then outstanding.[14]

Hard Faces

On February 1, 2016, Argentina and the large holdouts reconvened in McCarter & English's twenty-seventh-floor conference room. Finance Secretary Caputo and Undersecretary Bausili sat across the table from the same creditors whom Argentina had met two weeks before: Pollock, Newman, Straus, Johns, Brodsky, and Zimmerman. The negotiations went on for two hours, including breakouts. It was not an easy conversation.[15]

Secretary Caputo led off by making an impassioned plea to the creditors to put an end to all the fighting. He said that the country wanted to move forward, and he made what he felt was a fair offer.[16] It was a two-part offer: a base offer of 1.5 times par to all holdouts and a pari passu offer equal to 70% of the full accreted value of the creditors' high interest claim to only the plaintiffs who had obtained an injunction from the court. This distinction was a relevant one because not all plaintiffs had filed motions to obtain pari passu injunctions. And there was one more nuance: Although many small plaintiffs' counsels had filed for a pari passu injunction, most had also obtained judgments many years before, so they ended up taking the 1.5 times par standard option because 70% of their accreted postjudgment claims would have amounted to less than 1.5 times par.[17] As a result and with only a few exceptions, the pari passu offer was only a viable option for the investors sitting across the room from Argentina and the new entrant hedge funds who had never filed for a judgment.

Under the terms Caputo outlined, in round numbers the FRAN plaintiffs would get 7.0 times par versus the 10.0 times par legal value of their holdings, and the holders of prejudgment global bonds would get 2.5 times par versus the 3.5 times par legal value of their holdings. This offer was a sea change from what Argentina had been offering for over a decade, but Caputo's proposed 30% discount on the creditors' bona fide legal claims would cost the funds more than $1 billion dollars, no small discount to ask from the plaintiffs after a decade of bitter litigation and when they held the injunction in their hands.

The creditors went to a breakout room to talk among themselves. When they came back, the news was bad: NML explained that Argentina's offer was too low. What's more, to continue negotiating, the creditors wanted Argentina to sign a new nondisclosure agreement.[18] This turn of events disappointed both Argentina and Special Master Pollack, who were hopeful that the creditors would accept or at least respond positively to Caputo's offer.

The United Front of Creditors Crumbles

If Argentina's mood was gloomy as the negotiation session broke on February 1, 2016, it soon shifted to excitement. That is because after the group meeting ended, Michael Straus and Kenneth Dart's representatives separately agreed to have one-on-one conversations with Argentina's negotiating team. Pollack reported that Dart's representative pulled him aside after the meeting and said they didn't need a non-disclosure agreement; they wanted their money.[19] The united front of holdouts was crumbling.

That afternoon Dart's representative returned to McCarter & English's offices to meet with Pollack and Caputo for a relatively easy settlement. Since Dart had obtained a judgment on his bonds in October 2003, his claim was worth only 1.42 times par at its fully accreted value. Argentina

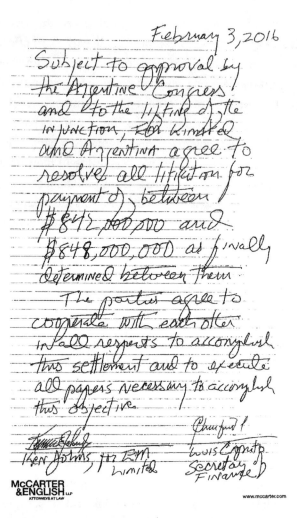

Figure 11.1 Settlement Agreement with Dart's EM Ltd.

Source: ¶872-2, Exhibit B, *NML Capital, Ltd. v. Republic of Argentina*, No. 08 Civ. 6978 (S.D.N.Y. Feb. 17, 2016).

agreed to pay Dart's claim in full, about $848 million versus his holdings of $595 million in bonds.[20] Dart's settlement agreement with Argentina, which was signed two days later, was a simple one. It was two sentences long and handwritten by Daniel Pollack on a McCarter & English notepad, as shown in figure 11.1.

On February 3, Finance Secretary Luis Caputo met with Montreux's Michael Straus and Eric Hermann. Straus told Caputo that Montreux was willing to discuss a mutually acceptable resolution. After some negotiation, Montreux agreed to accept a cash payment of 72.5% of their legal claim value, subject to a step-up to 75% if the country subsequently paid more to Elliott and the others. Argentina agreed to pay Montreux $298.7 million against its four entities' holdings of $42.4 million of FRANs, subject to a step-up to $308.6 million if Argentina paid more to the others.[21] The investors made a multihundred-million-dollar profit, while Argentina enjoyed a $103 million discount from the funds' full legal claim, an important compromise for both sides to reach after so many years of litigation.

One noteworthy aspect of Argentina's settlements with Dart and Montreux was that the country agreed to pay the plaintiffs in cash. Many had assumed that Argentina would pay the firms in new bonds, which is how Argentina had settled its ICSID and Repsol claims in 2013 and 2014. However, Caputo's bond trader instincts told him that the country would get a better deal by paying the holdouts in cash and issuing new bonds into the market to fund the settlement. He anticipated that if the country paid the holdouts in bonds, they would demand that they be issued at a discount to market value even though he was sure that Argentine bond prices would rise in value upon the announcement of the settlements. Caputo made an astute call, because Argentina later funded the deal at a far better price than would have been available had the holdouts received new bonds instead of cash in exchange for their claims.[22]

Paul Singer Gets Involved

The situation coming to a head, Elliott Associates head Paul Singer moved to get involved for the first time. On February 2, 2016, the CEO wrote an email to Special Master Pollack, saying, "Dan, in light of the events of this week, I think it is time that you and I to have a face-to-face meeting. I would like to go to your office. What do you think about tomorrow at 8:30 am?"[23]

They met at 4:00 p.m. the following day because Pollack and Argentina were busy closing their deals with Dart and Montreux. Pollack was pleased that Singer had reached out. Pollack knew that the ultimate decision-makers had to be involved for a deal to be cut, and this meeting opened up the necessary channel of communication to Elliott's head, even if Singer wouldn't be expected to attend day-to-day negotiating sessions. From there on out, Pollack kept in close contact with Singer. The special master later said the two exchanged 175 emails, talked on the phone dozens of times, and met three times in the weeks following Singer's February 2 email.[24]

Tempers Flare on February 4

The next face-to-face negotiation session was held on February 4, 2016. The mood was sour, with Elliott, Aurelius, Blue Angel, and Bracebridge undoubtedly angry that Argentina had picked off Dart and Montreux, although there is no public record of these funds' reaction to the two funds that broke ranks.

The February 4 meeting started with the remaining hedge funds, now joined by Michael Spencer from Milberg,[25] putting a counteroffer on the table that was much higher than what Finance Secretary Caputo had proposed. The Wall Street–wise Caputo thought his offer was quite fair and was furious at their aggressive response. He stood up and announced that he was going back to Buenos Aires because the negotiations were going nowhere. He then headed to JFK Airport to catch the evening flight home. It was all over in less than twenty minutes.[26]

Don't Get on the Plane!

Caputo's phone rang nonstop as he sat in the departures area ready to board his flight. The president's cabinet chief called, telling him not to come back home without a deal. The finance team, in contrast, thought that a show of breaking off the negotiations would be more effective. Helping Caputo decide, Pollack called right before he boarded the plane and told him that Paul Singer had reached out and asked to have a call first thing in the morning.[27] Caputo stayed in Manhattan to go another round with the holdouts, although he had to improvise his wardrobe, having decided to stay after it was too late for him to get his bags off the plane.

Pollack Bashes Some Heads

Special Master Daniel Pollack knew that if a deal was going to get done, he had to bash some heads. So, on the morning of February 5 he had two back-to-back phone calls: one with Argentine president Mauricio Macri and one with Elliott's Paul Singer.

The call with President Macri lasted six minutes, and Caputo joined Pollack at his apartment to make the call.

Pollack asked Macri if Argentina could pay more to get the deal done.

President Macri said, "No. We've gone as far as we can."

"Are you willing to make a settlement offer to the entire market knowing that Elliott and the others won't come in and will keep suing you?" Pollack asked.

"Yes," said President Macri, "we're willing to live with that risk."[28]

The next call was with Singer, but there is no public record of what was said.

Argentina Unleashes La Propuesta

Momentum in its favor, Argentina unleashed what it hoped to be a knock-out blow against Elliott, Bracebridge, and Aurelius later the same day, February 5. The country published a limited-time offer to all its remaining holdout creditors based on the terms already agreed with TFA, Dart, and Montreux. The country would pay 1.5 times par to all creditors, as agreed with TFA; the full amount of judgments worth less than 1.5 times par as agreed with Dart; and 70% of accreted value for claims held by creditors who had the benefit of a pari passu injunction, as agreed with Montreux, plus a 2.5% premium for investors who took the offer by February 19.[29]

Argentina expected most creditors to take this offer. Its officials also knew, however, that it would be hard to convince the big four holdouts to agree to these terms without significant pressure from the court. Argentina's purpose in launching the offer and announcing that it was already reaching settlements with important creditors was to convince Judge Griesa to lift the injunction. After all, the country was now negotiating in good faith with its holdout creditors. Since the injunction provided the only leverage the plaintiffs ever had with which to force Argentina to pay them anything, taking it away would devastate their bargaining position, which, of course, was the point. Argentina's motion to lift the injunction came quickly, just a few days after the publication of its February 5 offer, which became known as La Propuesta (The Proposal).

It took Judge Griesa over a week to rule on Argentina's motion, as he needed to allow the various plaintiffs time to deliver briefs in response to Argentina's motion, and then he needed time to read them and decide how to rule.[30] Special Master Pollack immediately threw his weight behind La Propuesta, however. On February 5, the day Argentina released its offer, Pollack issued a press release in which he called La Propuesta a "historic breakthrough" and praised Argentina for showing "courage and flexibility in stepping up to and dealing with this long-festering problem."[31] The special master's statement was a game changer because it substantially raised the odds that his friend Griesa would lift the injunction.

La Propuesta Changes Everything

The good news started flowing for Argentina from the moment its Propuesta hit computer screens around the world.

On the afternoon the terms were released, VR Global Partners, one of the late entrant hedge funds that bought bonds and sued after 2010, called Santiago Bausili to tell him "we're in."[32]

On February 7, U.S. treasury secretary Jacob Lew complimented Argentina in a press release on its "good faith efforts to resolve this long-standing dispute."[33]

On February 8, influential Bloomberg columnist Matt Levine spun out a detailed analysis of the stupendous profits Elliott was set to make on its FRANs.[34] It is funny how that story popped up at just the right time after eight years without any press coverage of these unusual bonds that came to be worth ten times their face value; Argentina was evidently managing the media as actively as it was managing its relationship with the U.S. Treasury, probably realizing that gaining widespread public sympathy for its position would be a factor in winning the terms that it wanted to achieve.

On February 16, the Brecher class-action plaintiffs signed a settlement agreement with Argentina.[35]

On February 17, two more hedge funds—Clarex and Fiscella—settled.[36]

On February 18, Moss & Kalish clients Old Castle and Lightwater came in.[37]

On February 19, Capital Ventures International and two new-entrant hedge funds signed settlement agreements with Argentina.[38]

And as the clincher, on February 19, Judge Griesa released an "indicative ruling" in favor of lifting the injunction, although with two caveats: the Argentine Congress would have to repeal the Lock Law, and Argentina would need to pay the investors who had signed settlement agreements with it by the end of February.[39]

Judge Griesa's action put Elliott, Bracebridge, Aurelius, and Blue Angel in a corner. Once the injunction was lifted they would have little chance of recovering even a fraction of what they were owed. They were not going to go down without a fight, however. And the next battle took place at the Second Circuit Court of Appeals.

Back at the Second Circuit

As of February 2016, Judge Griesa didn't have jurisdiction over the pari passu cases, which is why he filed an indicative ruling to lift the injunction rather than an actual ruling on February 19. Control over the cases rested with the Second Circuit because Argentina had appealed Griesa's June 2015 ruling to grant pari passu injunctions to postjudgment claims, including the FRANs. To return jurisdiction to Griesa, which would allow him to convert his indicative ruling to a final one, Argentina dropped its appeal of his 2015 ruling. This in turn led to a hearing at the Second Circuit on February 24 to discuss granting an order to dismiss Argentina's appeal.

Matthew McGill, Olson's partner at Gibson Dunn, spoke for Elliott, Aurelius, and Bracebridge, whose funds owned 65% of the outstanding holdout claims in aggregate.[40] He argued that the Second Circuit should block Judge Griesa from quickly lifting the injunction.

McGill said, "Let me paint the picture of what the indicative ruling does and permits. On Monday, that's February 29th, . . . Argentina's public tender offer closes. And on Tuesday, Argentina can fulfill the conditions set forth in the order. The injunctions are automatically lifted. There is no hearing. . . . [I]t is a springing vacatur of the injunction."

In response, Judge Peter W. Hall said, "This District Judge has been on this case forever. . . . You're asking us to weigh in and see if we can help you get a better settlement."

McGill said, "No, no, I'm not. All I'm asking for is for a little time for the settlements that Argentina claims that they want to take place. My point, my core point is that this February 29th deadline is needless and counterproductive."

Judge Raggi now weighed in: "Why should this Court use a delay in either granting a dismissal motion or deciding the appeal? Why should it delay either of those in order . . . to give you time on something that's really a District Court matter?"

McGill explained that the district court was not listening to his client's concern about how the settlement worked, and there was a risk that Argentina would use the opportunity to harm the remaining creditors:

Here's the problem. . . . If Argentina satisfies the conditions on Tuesday and the injunctions are automatically lifted on Tuesday, on that same day, Argentina can change the payment mechanisms that have been in place for years, that the injunction prohibits them from changing, and thereby render the restoration of effective injunctive relief impossible. . . .

My clients, the 65%, we have had . . . an agreement on economic terms with Argentina since Thursday. We're this close to a deal, this close. We've been discussing payment mechanics, ancillary provisions. And I should mention that our deal . . . on economic terms is closer to their public tender offer than 100%. We are this close.

Unfortunately, we've had some hiccups in negotiating these mechanics. You know, the first payment mechanic . . . that was suggested by the Special Master . . . it involved . . . the use of paper checks coming through FedEx.

That was not going to work. So, we're trying to find payment mechanics that work. This is a $5 billion transaction, and we're being told that we have to sign it up on a page and a half agreement by Monday. If we have just a little time, we can finish the deal. The economic terms are agreed.[41]

After a recess, the judges of the Second Circuit dismissed Argentina's appeal and returned jurisdiction over the cases to Judge Griesa. They also stayed the lifting of the injunction for two weeks and ordered Griesa to hold a hearing on the topic with all the relevant parties before doing so.[42]

This was a good outcome, but Special Master Pollack was outraged that Matthew McGill had publicly disclosed the status of the confidential negotiations between Argentina and the big holdouts to make his case. So, at 2:15 that afternoon Pollack shot off a press release:

A lawyer for certain "holdout" Bondholders made a statement in court this morning to the effect that Argentina and NML had reached an Agreement in Principle on economic terms. That statement violated the confidentiality of the discussions between the parties, which is an inviolable principle of all negotiations through me as Special Master. If and when there is a signed Agreement in Principle reached between those or any other parties, I will announce it as Special Master.[43]

Pollack was doubtlessly angry because there were still big money issues to resolve in the negotiations, such as who would bear the responsibility for tens of millions of dollars of legal expenses and any discount that would apply to the settlement of offshore claims. The deal was not done yet, and saying otherwise to win a ruling in court was not the way he did business.

Pollack Pulls Rank

At this point Argentina had the remaining holdouts in a corner, but there were still some big issues to deal with. Progress was slow, and tempers flared. It became increasingly likely that no deal would be reached when the Propuesta expired on February 29, which would put the Argentina/holdout relationship back into a legal no-man's-land.

Wednesday, February 24, passed without a deal.

Thursday, February 25, passed without a deal. At some point during that day, Luis Caputo wrote in an email, "DAN, NO DEAL. THIS IS A JOKE," in response to a list of conditions demanded by Elliott.[44]

With the February 29 deadline looming, Special Master Pollack knew that another day could not pass without a deal being cut. On the morning of Friday, February 26, he typed out a court order on his home computer and went to Judge Griesa's apartment to have it signed. At 10:30 a.m. Pollack served the court order on Elliott Associates via email. The order commanded CEO Paul Singer to come to Pollack's office at McCarter & English at 1:00 p.m., just two and a half hours later.

At 11:00 a.m., Pollack got a call from Jonathan Pollock, Singer's co-CEO.

"Is Paul coming?" Special Master Pollack asked.

"It's an offer we can't refuse," Elliott's Pollock answered.

At eight minutes to 1:00 p.m., Pollack got an email from Elliott: "We are on our way but are stuck in traffic."

"Don't worry you have eight minutes," the Special Master responded.

Elliott made it to Pollack's office at the stroke of the hour.

That's how the final negotiations began.[45]

No Deal/Deal

Argentine secretary of finance Caputo and Elliott CEO Paul Singer faced off for the first and only time on the afternoon of Friday, February 26. The battle positions were as follows: Singer and his co-CEO Jonathan Pollock sat with Special Master Pollack in McCarter & English's offices, while Caputo was on speakerphone from Buenos Aires.

The final issue concerned assets that Elliott had captured in the course of the litigation through attachments. Elliott had already agreed that these assets would either be returned to Argentina or credited against the pending settlement amount. But Argentina wanted these assets returned and for Elliott to provide as part of the agreement a schedule of all the pending attachments to be released. On a prior phone call that afternoon, Caputo had told Pollack that without agreement on attachments, there would be no deal.[46]

Before getting Caputo on the line, Pollack explained to the Elliott team that Argentina wanted Elliott to give the captured assets back. It was a matter of national pride.

Singer would not agree to the demand.

Pollack said, "You are getting over $1.5 billion and you are horsing around about a few million? I think you ought to know how strongly Argentina feels."

To break the impasse, Pollack got Caputo on the speakerphone.

According to Pollack, Singer said that Elliott wouldn't agree to the change.

"I am sick and tired of this bullshit! If you don't give back this money there will be no deal!" Caputo exploded.

"Get this guy under control!" yelled Singer, according to Pollack.

But Caputo had hung up the phone, and it was just the Elliott team and Pollack.

Special Master Pollack now faced the critical moment of his assignment. It was time for him to intervene, whereas up to this point he had only been nudging things along.

Pollack said to Singer, "If you don't take this deal you will be in a spaceship circling the moon and not landing."

"Griesa won't lift the injunction without me," Singer shot back, according to Pollack.

"Trust me, he will lift the injunction," Pollack retorted.

"Okay," said Singer, finally capitulating, according to Pollack.
"Good," said Pollack.[47]

And with that, the terms were agreed.[48]

Pollack's Victory Lap

On Monday, February 29, Special Master Daniel Pollack told the world
that the deal was done. In a press release he wrote, "It gives me greatest
pleasure to announce that the 15-year pitched battle between the Republic
of Argentina and Elliott Management, led by Paul E. Singer, is now well
on its way to being resolved. The parties last night signed an Agreement
in Principle after three months of intense, around-the-clock negotiations
under my supervision."[49]

Pollack also honored President Macri and Finance Secretary Caputo,
calling their course correction "nothing short of heroic," and gave a shout-
out to Argentine economy minister Prat-Gay, Cabinet Chief Marcos Peña,
Deputy Cabinet Chief Mario Quintana, and Undersecretary Bausili. As
to the holdouts, Pollack called Paul Singer "a tough but fair negotiator"
and acknowledged the role of Jonathan Pollock, Singer's second-in-
command. As for the rest, Pollack commended "all of the senior principals" of the hedge funds for their "vast talent." He reflected, "No party
to a settlement gets everything it seeks. A settlement is, by definition, a
compromise and, fortunately, both sides to this epic dispute finally saw
the need to compromise, and have done so."

Under the agreement, Argentina would pay the big holdouts 75% of
their claim value, amounting to $4.418 billion against their legal claims of
$5.891 billion. Argentina also agreed to pay an additional $235 million to
cover the plaintiffs' legal fees and to settle various non–New York claims.
The beneficiaries and cosigners of this settlement agreement were Elliott's NML Capital, Ltd., various funds managed by Aurelius, Davidson
Kempner Capital Management's Blue Angel Capital I LLC, and the three
funds managed by Bracebridge, the Olifant Fund, the FFI Fund Ltd., and
FYI Ltd.[50]

Later that day, fifty reporters showed up to attend a press conference Special Master Pollack called to announce this historic settlement.[51]

Back in Court with Judge Griesa

While Argentina now had settlement agreements with a large percentage of the holdouts in hand, including the most important holdouts, there was still work to do to bring the cases to an end. Most notably, Judge Griesa had to hold a hearing with all the various affected parties because the Second Circuit had ordered him to do so when it returned jurisdiction to the district court. The hearing was held on March 1, and a veritable cast of thousands was invited to speak. The list included Robert Cohen and Theodore Olson for NML; Edward Friedman for Aurelius and Blue Angel; Michael Mukasey for Dart; Michael Shuster for the Montreux group; Michael Paskin from Cravath for Argentina; Christopher Clark for the euro bondholders; Michael Spencer for the Milberg plaintiffs; Anthony Costantini for the Duane Morris plaintiffs; Jennifer Scullion for the class-action plaintiffs; Eric Schaffer for the Bank of New York, the bond trustee; and a few other lawyers representing small investors and late-entrant hedge funds. While in some sense the hearing was a formality because Griesa had already announced that he intended to lift the injunction, it nonetheless gave all the parties a chance to voice any concerns they might have.

Judge Griesa at the start off the hearing said, "Good afternoon. Please be seated. Today's hearing is to give those who favor my indicative ruling and those who oppose my indicative ruling the opportunity to be heard."[52]

In the lead-off position was former U.S. attorney general and former chief judge of the Southern District of New York Michael Mukasey of Debevoise & Plimpton,[53] who argued for Kenneth Dart. Mukasey recounted the history of the cases and cited the many recent events. He said that Argentina had changed its ways and that it was essential for Judge Griesa to lift the injunction to avoid harming those who had already settled. Mukasey said, "At this point, I think it's fair to say it's the injunction itself, not Argentina, that stands in the way of resolving this dispute."[54]

Next up was Michael Shuster for the Montreux plaintiffs, who voiced extraordinary support for the settlement and, in a rare move for the representative of a onetime dedicated holdout, admitted that Argentina was a poor country:

> Your Honor, my clients favor the indicative ruling and support Argentina's motion now that the ruling be made permanent. The indicative ruling was correctly decided. My plaintiffs were an early settler. My plaintiffs settled early because it was obvious to them that Argentina had changed dramatically its approach to this dispute, that it was very serious about settling and resolving this and putting the case behind it, and because it made an offer that was fair and reasonable. . . .
>
> From our perspective, the equities here have shifted dramatically. We are highly sensible of the fact that on the other side of this dispute is a sovereign state, a sovereign state whose public finances have been handcuffed by virtue of the injunctions . . . but its conduct has changed. Argentina fought an election over this issue. President Macri was elected in part over this issue. This is a matter of central concern to the national life of a sovereign state—and not a wealthy state, a state which needs to be able to now gain access to the capital markets so that it can raise capital not only to settle this litigation but so that it can benefit its people who are by no means wealthy.[55]

The next speakers were Michael Paskin for Argentina and Christopher Clark for the euro bondholders. Both asked Judge Griesa to lift the injunction.

Elliott's lawyer Theodore Olson asked Judge Griesa to delay lifting the injunction for a month in order to give the remaining 15% of holdouts a chance to sign settlement agreements. Edward Friedman for Aurelius and Blue Angel, Michael Spencer and Anthony Costantini for their small bondholder clients, and a few others echoed Olson's call for more time.

Jennifer Scullion, counsel for the Seijas class-action cases, aired a lengthy list of complaints against the country, calling Argentina's Propuesta a "take-it-or-leave-it" offer and demanding that her tiny pool of clients be allowed to negotiate its own terms.

After all the plaintiffs against lifting the injunction were done speaking, lawyers in support of lifting it offered a rebuttal. Dart and Montreux's lawyers rebutted the need for a delay, while Christopher Clark for the euro bondholders attacked Scullion and others small plaintiffs' argument that Argentina's settlement process was unfair:

> Your Honor heard from a number of small parties here who are asking your Honor to give more time so that they can individually negotiate with Argentina. There are thousands of claimants, your Honor. There is one Special Master. He's [worked] tirelessly. But the idea that a claimant with $10,000 worth of bonds is going to sit down individually with the Republic of Argentina and the Special Master to work out a tailored deal for the $10,000 worth of bonds while my clients wait for their $3.1 billion in interest that hasn't been paid for years is, I think, the definition of inequity.
>
> Your Honor, it's been a fair process. It's been a transformative process. The Special Master has brought a settlement to the table that all parties could have adopted, should have adopted, and can still maybe adopt. We should no longer be held hostage by small parties who want a better deal than everyone else got.[56]

Clark thus captured the essential problem of sovereign debt litigation without bankruptcy or CACs: At what point should the courts stop going to bat for holdouts trying to get a better deal: When 76% of claims are settled? When 92% are settled? When 99% are settled? When 99.9% are settled? At what point should the objective of restoring a normal market override the rights of individual plaintiffs to seek to get paid in full?

Judge Griesa Rules to Lift the Injunction, but the Hedge Funds Appeal

Judge Griesa granted the conditional lifting of the pari passu injunction on March 2, 2016.[57] In theory, all that needed to happen now was for Argentina to repeal the Lock Law and pay the holdouts that had signed settlement agreements, although Griesa stayed the ruling pending possible appeal.

In a surprise move, the next day Elliott, Bracebridge (including its Yale-owned FYI Ltd.), Aurelius, and Blue Angel appealed Judge Griesa's decision to lift the injunction, even though they had all signed settlement agreements with Argentina.[58] The war was on again. As unsporting as it was, one might guess that their idea was to hold Argentina's feet to the fire until they were paid.

Argentina kept pushing forward.

On March 4, Argentina reached a settlement with ten small investors for a total of $6.7 million.[59]

On March 9, the country reached a settlement with Boston-based GMO, BNP Bank, and some other holdouts that together owned more than $190 million in defaulted bonds.[60]

On March 18, a settlement was reached with 115 retail investor plaintiffs.[61]

On March 23, the U.S. government submitted an amicus brief to the appeals court in favor of the lifting of the injunction.[62]

On March 31, the Argentine Congress lifted the Lock Law.[63]

On April 10, Argentina settled with late entrants Fore Research, Honero Fund, and Stone Harbor, as well as with thirty-one individual investors for a total of $253 million.[64]

On April 12, Judge Griesa ruled against a handful of late-entrant hedge funds that were seeking to force Argentina to pay settlements on time-barred claims, that is, claims for which the owners had failed to file a lawsuit within the applicable six-year statute of limitations.[65] Argentina reached an agreement with Yellow Crane for a total of $255 million on the same day.[66]

Argentina's remaining problem at this stage was the still-pending appeal. The country was in a bind because the Second Circuit had agreed to hear the hedge funds' appeal on April 13, which was unfeasibly close to Argentina's April 14 deadline for paying Elliott and the other large plaintiffs. If Argentina didn't pay the large funds by April 14, they could withdraw from their February 29 settlement agreements. As such, Argentina was desperate to persuade the Second Circuit to affirm Judge Griesa's ruling before April 14, which would ensure that the funds would stick with their agreements even if payments were somewhat delayed. In that context, Economy Minister Prat-Gay wrote a letter to the Second Circuit on April 11 begging the court to make its ruling the same day as the hearing.[67] It was an unorthodox move, but it worked, and the court affirmed Griesa's ruling at the close of the hearing.[68] Griesa's injunction was now conditionally lifted, and the hedge funds didn't drop out of the agreement even though it took Argentina a week past April 14 to raise the money to pay them.

On April 22, 2016, Argentina issued $16.5 billion in new global bonds, with the funds used to pay the holdouts and to make up missed payments to exchange bondholders.[69] In association with the payments, settling plaintiffs filed papers with the court terminating their lawsuits and releasing any outstanding attachments.

The litigation was over, at least most of it.[70] There were still a handful of stragglers and complainers to contend with.

Stragglers, Complainers, and the Death of Pari Passu

Not every holdout accepted Argentina's Propuesta. A handful of small investors complained that they hadn't gotten a chance to negotiate with the country. Some even tried—but failed—to attach a part of the proceeds of the deal that was put into a trust to fund future settlements. Among the stragglers were the eight Seijas class-action cases that took two additional years to settle because of special procedural requirements followed by a fee dispute among the various law firms that had represented these plaintiffs.

The most significant investor to reject Argentina's Propuesta was Willi Brand, a Luxembourg-based mutual fund manager who had been involved with the cases from the very beginning. However, after the 2005 deal closed—without his participation—Brand kept buying more defaulted Argentine bonds, some at a very deep discount. The face value of his holdings in 2016 was just under $100 million, and he was represented by Michael Spencer of Milberg, whom he had hired after Dreier LLP went bust.[71]

Brand complained to Spencer about the terms of the Propuesta.

Brand wasn't happy that he was being offered only $162.5 million[72]—a little over 1.5 times the par value of his holdings—when he wanted to get a recovery multiplier much closer to what the big plaintiffs were getting. He dumped Spencer and hired a different law firm to help him attach assets as a way of forcing Argentina to pay more.[73] In April 2017 Brand tried to attach two Argentine helicopter engines that were in the United States for repair, but the judge in Ohio, where the case was heard, rejected the attachment based on the FSIA exemption for military property.[74] On May 31, 2017, after a conversation with Special Master Pollack and Santiago Bausili, Brand signed on to the Propuesta's terms.[75] At their meeting Pollack encouraged Brand to take the settlement, because if he didn't "you will fly around the moon and never land on it," essentially the same line he had used on Elliott CEO Paul Singer the year before.[76]

Some plaintiffs, including White Hawthorne, asked the court to impose new pari passu injunctions on Argentina for not paying their claims. On December 22, 2016, Judge Griesa ruled against these holdouts. He said that Argentina was no longer in breach of its pari passu clause because the country had repealed its Lock Law and changed its course of conduct.[77] With that, it was acceptable once again for Argentina to not pay holdouts while paying exchange bond holders in full. Argentina's pari passu saga was finally over. So too was policy makers' panic over the potential market implications of the cases. This ruling meant that potential future holdouts could no longer bank on the courts automatically handing down pari passu injunctions if a country selectively paid some creditors and not others. To be sure, Elliott won an important precedent, but Argentina had been so uncooperative for so long and imposing the injunction ended up being so disruptive and led to such an unequal settlement that the courts should be wary of making a similar ruling anytime soon. As the Second Circuit said, Argentina had been "a uniquely recalcitrant debtor."

Epilogue

While Argentina's pari passu saga was over by the end of 2016, its debt troubles weren't. For one, starting in January 2019, the country faced a new wave of lawsuits—including from Aurelius—over selective non-payment of its GDP warrants. The issue was that in 2014 the country applied a new methodology to calculate its inflation and GDP growth. This change, in turn, reduced the payments on its GDP warrants to less than what some bondholders thought they were owed.[1] This litigation is ongoing.[2]

More significantly, since 2016 Argentina has defaulted on and restructured its debt once again. While President Mauricio Macri's administration got off to a strong start, its plan to get the country's economy back on track faltered in late 2017. In June 2018 the country obtained about $50 billion from the IMF in a program that quickly went off track.[3]

With Argentina's economy yet again in crisis, Macri lost the 2019 presidential election to Alberto Fernández, Néstor Kirchner's former cabinet chief.[4] Fernández ran with Cristina Fernández de Kirchner as his running mate. COVID-19 hit shortly thereafter, putting further pressure on the economy. Argentina defaulted again in May 2020 and completed the restructuring of almost 100% of its bonds within three months. This quick and clean result was possible because virtually all of Argentina's bonds included CACs that provided for aggregated voting, protecting the transaction from disruption by holdouts.[5]

At the time of this writing, Argentina is still experiencing deep financial difficulties, although its on-again, off-again relationship with the IMF has recently switched back on.[6] Unfortunately, Argentina remains on the short list of countries that investors fear will default in the near term.[7] In other words, for Argentina, the story ends much where it began:

the country in crisis. Yet the world of sovereign debt is forever changed, the market having adopted powerful holdout-killing clauses in bond contracts in the wake of Argentina's travails.

Conclusion

Argentina's 2005 debt restructuring will long be remembered as the lengthiest, messiest sovereign debt restructuring in history. And it begs the question of who or what was to blame. Was it Argentina's fault? Was it the fault of the hedge funds? Was it the lack of a sovereign bankruptcy law? And what did we learn from it anyway? This concluding chapter approaches these questions in the hope of distilling some lessons learned so that what happened to Argentina and its creditors may never happen again. Let's first take a moment to review, however.

Recapitulation

This was a story in three acts: Argentina's disputed 2005 debt restructuring, the litigation through October 2010, and the litigation over Elliott Associates' pari passu claim through the 2016 settlement.

Chapters 1 through 3 covered the period from Argentina's 2001 default on its debt through the completion of its 2005 restructuring. The distinguishing feature of this transaction was the country's decision to go it alone in the wake of a breakdown of its relationship with the IMF. Argentina's transaction came under fierce attack from GCAB, and the country resorted to unusual gambits to achieve an adequate success rate. This approach was largely successful, but the rub was that the country was left with a $19.6 billion contingent liability to manage: the legal claims brought by the holdout creditors.

Chapters 4 through 7 told the story of how Argentina managed this liability from 2005 through 2010. The country didn't pay any of its holdout creditors—as it promised it wouldn't—and came under broad-based attack in the courts. Hundreds of cases were filed against Argentina, and many attachments were attempted, although only a few were marginally successful. This set the stage for two-thirds of the holdouts to accept Argentina's reopening of its deal in 2010.

Chapters 8 through 10 were about the pari passu attack led by Elliott. These chapters featured an angry Judge Thomas P. Griesa throwing the book at Argentina and imposing an extraordinary injunction against the country for showing no willingness to settle with its holdout creditors. The Second Circuit Court of Appeals affirmed Judge Griesa's ruling, the appeals court itself angered when it gave Argentina the option to propose a compromise, but the country refused to budge. The U.S. Supreme Court took a pass, with the U.S. government not even filing a brief to encourage the high court to hear the case.

Chapter 11 was about the surprisingly good deal the government of Mauricio Macri was able to negotiate with support of the court. Macri's team, led by Luis Caputo, quickly turned the tables on Elliott and the other sophisticated hedge funds, focusing Special Master Daniel Pollack, the U.S. government, and the financial press on how the hedge funds were positioned to make superprofits—not par—from the situation. Before the hedge funds knew what hit them, Judge Griesa indicated that he would lift the injunction, and Elliott and the other remaining large holdouts were forced to settle for around 75% of their legal claim value. It was an astounding end to the messy saga.

In the background of all this drama, we also witnessed the first use of CACs in U.S. dollar sovereign bonds in 2003 and their later enhancement in the wake of Argentina's injunction-triggered 2014 default.

That in a nutshell is what happened. But what useful lessons can we draw from these events?

The Sturm and Drang of Argentina's 2005 Debt Restructuring and Its Cleanup

The first item to address is what we have learned about sovereign debt restructuring from Argentina's 2005 deal.

While still much criticized, the basic financial structure of Argentina's

2005 offer made sense: Argentina sought a pro forma level of debt that it could safely pay, and the GDP warrants were an effective mechanism for sharing any upside with creditors. Indeed, the warrants paid out when Argentina's economy rebounded, just as the country had promised they would even though the deal's critics called them worthless at the time. The deal was also supported by six international and local banks that did their own analysis of the country's capacity to pay. It was a hard deal, but it was not a thoughtless or an arbitrary one.

The deal's biggest problems were political and institutional. Argentina's president chose the minimum payment to creditors among the options he was shown. U.S. creditor activists were determined to use Argentina's deal to institute a new way in sovereign debt restructuring, one in which countries were obliged to prenegotiate with them before offering deals to the market. Then, the Italians, Germans, and Japanese appear to have tried to use their board seats at the IMF to help their countries' retail bondholders obtain a better deal. These pressures—which are not all that unusual in the context of a sovereign debt restructuring—were never adequately managed, and Argentina's IMF deal fell by the wayside. Without explicit IMF support, Argentina's 2005 debt restructuring achieved a suboptimal 76% success rate.

One important reason these competing political and institutional pressures were not adequately managed was the U.S. Treasury's insistence that the IMF abide by a precedent-breaking laissez-faire approach to sovereign debt restructuring. In theory, the Treasury's idea was a great one. Commercial disputes should be resolved without government interference. This hands-off approach failed, however, when applied to Argentina's debt restructuring. Why? Possibly because the theory was applied inconsistently, possibly because the theory was not applicable to the subject matter, or possibly both.

Viewed through a Shultzian policy lens, the truly startling thing about the Washington drama surrounding Argentina's 2005 transaction is that the exact dynamic George Shultz warned about played out. He had warned that the willingness of high administration officials to become involved in a dispute would result in their exploitation by one side or the other, and that's exactly what happened. There is no question that the creditor activists associated with GCAB tried to use the IMF's internal good faith negotiations policy as leverage to force Argentina to pay much more than it was willing to pay. That this was happening was discussed in the pages of the *Financial Times*, with one creditor activist even bragging that "the official sector is so f***ing on our side, it's unreal." Yet it is hard to pin the blame entirely on poor execution, as Shultz's nonintervention philosophy was poorly suited for the task at hand. The United States simply could not stand above the fray and let the market work its magic when it was deeply involved: in court, through diplomatic channels, and as an indirect lender to Argentina (as a shareholder of the IMF, the World Bank, and the Inter-American Development Bank). Remarkably, the United States backed away from its laissez-faire approach in late 2005, and the IMF recently softened the good faith negotiations rule that proved so problematic during Argentina's transaction.[1]

On a purely technical level, Argentina's deal was unusual in many ways, including the price-match guarantee, the Lock Law, the powerful GDP warrant, and the lack of an exit consent. Argentina's lapse of its relationship with the IMF was behind some of these irregularities. To close its deal while under attack from creditor activists and without moral support from IMF staff and management, Argentina relied on several features that embedded the threat that nonparticipants wouldn't get paid. These innovative features helped scare investors into the deal but came with a cost: the Lock Law infuriated Judge Griesa and arguably created a continuing breach of the pari passu clause, and the price match guarantee made it hard for Argentina to settle in July 2014 when it had an opportunity to head off a fresh default. The complexity of the deal also had a cost: in retrospect, Argentina put too much potential upside into its complicated GDP warrants, instruments the market undervalued at the time of the deal.

Immediate posttransaction commentary from independent experts has aged well. Brad Setser at the Council on Foreign Relations said that Argentina should have paid a bit more to reduce its contingent liability from the holdout bonds. Nouriel Roubini said that Argentina should immediately reopen the offer on the same terms to give "hapless retail creditors," particularly in Italy, a second chance to come in. In retrospect, either paying somewhat more or reopening the deal more quickly would likely have made the country's holdout problem less costly to manage.

To be sure, President Cristina Fernández de Kirchner's reopening of the deal in 2010 was a critically important operation that substantially reduced the size of the country's contingent liability from the holdout bonds; many billions of dollars were saved. Argentina, however, took a generally lax approach to dealing with its holdout problem, waiting so long to reopen the offer that the legal value of the plaintiffs' court claims compounded to extraordinary levels. The country's strategy appears to have been to remove assets from the United States and to rely on the protections afforded under the FSIA to shield its assets from attachment. Argentina was very successful in employing this strategy in the early years, with creditors winning little of importance until 2012. From 2012 on, however, the country's legal strategy for dealing with the detritus of its 2005 and 2010 exchange offers fell short. What should have been a great victory at the end of 2010—having restructured 92% of its defaulted debt on historically attractive terms—became a nightmare when the country couldn't find a smooth way to manage the last 8%.

Yet the Macri government found a brilliant face-saving way to finally resolve the mess, albeit only after Argentina went through its second bond default since the turn of the century. The math of the 2016 settlement is fascinating, Argentina obtaining a 25% discount on the full value of the plaintiffs' most important claims. However, the savings were greater than suggested by this single number. By choosing to pay the plaintiffs with money raised from issuing new bonds into the market, the country obtained much more savings than it would have achieved had it simply issued new bonds to the plaintiffs at a discount. Moreover, getting the deal done so quickly put an end to the expensive claims accruals and jump-started the economy, which was needed after so many years of isolation.

Macri's government achieved this success because it changed the narrative. It convinced the court that it was willing to negotiate in good faith and proved it by quickly reaching bona fide negotiated settlements with TFA, Dart, and Montreux. Then, by immediately launching the Propuesta, Luis Caputo and Santiago Bausili spurred the court to quickly lift the injunction, leaving Elliott and the other large holdouts with little room to maneuver. It was a master class in negotiating.

Sovereign Debt Law: The Affliction and the Cure

As a story about sovereign debt law, this book follows a broad narrative arc that runs from 1976 to 2014. The enactment of the FSIA in 1976 planted the seeds for the trouble that followed by giving individual creditors the right to sue and seek enforcement in U.S. courts. Disruption from holdout creditors was sure to follow; it was just a question of when and who. Elliott was the first to make a business of it, as we've seen in these pages. But as we've also seen, winning was not always easy. The big banks encouraged Peru to fight Elliott in court, and Elliott suffered a tremendously embarrassing defeat upon Peru's champerty allegation in the district court. Participants in Argentina's 2005 deal were wary of holdouts too, asking Argentina to add the price-match guarantee to the deal. The market learned, however, that such stopgap measures were not enough; a permanent solution was needed. In the wake of Elliott's pari passu injunction, in 2014 the market adopted superpowerful CACs in sovereign bonds to make sure that holdouts never disrupted a sovereign debt restructuring again. With the adoption of these clauses, the gaping hole opened by the enactment of the FSIA of 1976 was finally closed.

The Argentina bond cases themselves set many precedents. The cases tested the limits of the law from what assets can and can't be attached to the scope of discovery. The pari passu injunction—which put payments to third parties at risk to compel the payment of judgments—was unprecedented and will surely be talked about by legal scholars for years to come. It is harder to gauge how much of an afterlife Griesa's pari passu ruling will have. What Argentina was found guilty of was being uncooperative, of being a "uniquely recalcitrant debtor" in the words of the Second Circuit Court of Appeals. The legal and contractual analysis was a secondary consideration. My conjecture is that it won't have a long-term impact because the powerful CACs adopted by the market in 2014 make it so hard to hold out that a comparable case is unlikely to arise any time soon.

Argentina: Default Nation?

People often ask why Argentina has such a lengthy history of defaulting since its independence from Spain. Why nine defaults?[2] It is an interesting question, but I find that this default statistic is used in a noxious way: as a personal attack on the people of Argentina. Who really cares if Argentina defaulted in 1827 and 1890? On that timescale, plenty of developed countries and U.S. states have defaulted on their debt. And in the 1930s when Argentina didn't default, the United States effectively did by removing the gold payment clause from tens of billions of dollars of bonds by legislative fiat ahead of an anticipated devaluation of the dollar.[3]

Yet recent history—from 1989 through today—shows that Argentina does have a problem. Most of its peers, including Brazil and Mexico, have not defaulted since they reformed their economies and finances in the context of their Brady plans, while Argentina has defaulted three more times. Argentina is an outlier. Moreover, Argentina had a golden opportunity to cement its financial future after the conclusion of its successful 2005 debt restructuring, but it didn't follow through.

How Argentina can finally graduate from its miserable boom-bust-default economic cycle is the question of the day. The conditions in the country are so bad right now that people are searching for answers. As an outsider and as a writer about debt, it is not my place to tell the country how to realign its domestic social contract to achieve a fairer, healthier trajectory for its economic growth. What I can say would apply anywhere: to retain financial stability, a country needs a policy framework and a medium-term plan that places limits on the pace of debt growth and money printing, and any such plan needs to be followed consistently.

Elliott and the American Task Force Argentina

This book has not primarily been about Elliott Associates or Elliott Capital Management, as the firm is now known. The book has been about Argentina, Judge Griesa, and sovereign debt law and contracts. Elliott's prominence in the story, however, requires comment. My view is that the firm is a legally savvy investor, smarter than most. About the cases at hand, I think that the firm won in court because Elliott prosecuted its cases efficiently, effectively, and with great energy. It is a toss-up, however, as to whether the firm beat Argentina or whether the country defeated itself by being so uncooperative with Judge Griesa and the Second Circuit Court of Appeals.

ATFA is another matter. Its efforts on behalf of the plaintiffs were really quite extraordinary. The more than $36 million that ATFA spent over the years dwarfs all but the biggest plaintiffs' claims. This eye-popping number begs for an answer. Why spend so much? What was the goal of the effort? Why was this effort necessary if the plaintiffs were so sure that their legal theories were right?

I found one possible answer in *Redeeming the Dream*, a fascinating book by David Boies and Theodore Olson describing their work on the marriage equality cases.[4] In these cases, they set up an umbrella lobbying organization called the American Foundation for Equal Rights at the beginning of the process. One might conclude from this parallel that the plaintiffs set up ATFA because they too expected that their cases would go all the way to the Supreme Court and that some cheerleading would be needed along the way. However, if you look closely at the work ATFA sponsored or promoted, or both, much of it focused on one legal aspect of the cases. At conferences, in scholarly works, and in press releases, ATFA repeatedly complained that the U.S. government was getting involved in sovereign debt lawsuits on behalf of the debtors in default. It is clear from these materials that one of ATFA's top priorities was to lobby the U.S. government and the IMF to not submit amicus briefs for Argentina, an effort that was ultimately successful in stopping the delivery of such briefs to the Supreme Court, as discussed in chapter 9.

Yet it is hard to tell if ATFA's lobbying made any difference in the outcome, given Argentina's lack of responsiveness to the court and the ineffectiveness of the heavily qualified amicus brief the United States filed with the Second Circuit on pari passu. Determinative or not, ATFA's activities are striking when viewed in context: while the plaintiffs' lawyers were in court decrying Argentina for not obeying the "rule of law," the plaintiffs' lobbyists were pushing elected officials to change the rules to their advantage. As for ATFA's anticorruption activities, the organization shut down a few weeks after its hedge fund sponsors received their multibillion-dollar payouts in 2016, its mission of helping creditors collect on their judgments complete.[5]

That said, I didn't come across a single shred of evidence that any of the big plaintiffs or their lobbyists did anything illegal. It would have been foolhardy for them to break any rules with billions of dollars at stake in the cases.

Parting Words

Argentina's 2005 bond restructuring is one that hasn't gotten a fair shake. It wasn't the most lawless exercise in history, as some critics have labeled it. It was a troubled transaction, but the trouble was multifaceted, and the crisis was so deep that it was always going to be messy.

The main lesson we learned from the deal itself was that the United States needs to participate actively in international financial crisis resolution and that financially stressed countries need to work cooperatively with the IMF, particularly in advance of presenting debt restructuring proposals to the market. We learned from Argentina's experience that selling a deal without IMF support and relying on innovative devices to threaten investors into the deal is a bad idea.

The lesson we learned from the litigation is the need for CACs or some other mechanism to aggregate creditors when a restructuring is required. Without such a mechanism, holdout creditors will thrive, and the smart money will profit at the expense of everyone else. All debt issuers and all debt buyers should always insist on the use of these clauses. My guess is that one hundred years from now the powerful CACs adopted by the market in 2014 will still be a standard feature in sovereign bond contracts and that the world will not have forgotten how the Argentina bond litigation cemented the case for using the clauses.

Acknowledgments

This book would not have been possible without the support of friends, family, interview subjects, research assistants, experts in the field, and Georgetown University Press. While taking full responsibility for the end product, I would like to thank everyone who helped make this work possible.

The many people I interviewed, some of whom prefer to remain anonymous, participated in open and frank discussions of the topics and events discussed in this book: Paul Blustein, Andrea Boggio, H. Willi Brand, Joel Chernov, Juan J. Cruces, Marcelo Delmar, George Estes, Gustavo Ferraro, Martín Guzmán, Sean Hagan, David Haskel, Hans Humes, Matías Isasa, Anne Krueger, Desmond Lachman, Horacio Liendo, Karin Lissakers, Meg Lundsager, Leonardo Madcur, Daniel Marx, Carlos Mauleon, Jeremiah Pam, Anoop Singh, Michael Spencer, Hector Torres, and Hans-Joerg Rudloff. Special thanks go to the interview subjects who each sat for several interviews and agreed to have their comments cited in the endnotes, including Santiago Bausili, Luis Caputo, Stefan Engelsberger, Marcelo Etchebarne, Mark Kalish, Roberto Lavagna, Guillermo Nielsen, Mark Sobel, Nicola Stock, Patricia Rosito Vago, and Vladimir Werning. I only wish that I had the opportunity to thank Special Master Daniel Pollack, who described to me the play-by-play of the 2016 settlement in fabulous detail, but he passed away before the completion of this work; instead, I would like to extend my gratitude to his wife and family, who are rightly proud of the critical role he played in bringing an end to the fifteen years of fighting described in this book.

I also offer my deepest gratitude to the numerous experts without whose help I could not have constructed a work of this complexity and scope: Attorney Lee Buchheit; University of North Carolina School of Law professor Mark Weidemaier; former State Department lawyer Mark

B. Feldman (who helped draft the Foreign Sovereign Immunities Act in 1976); Sherman & Sterling's Antonia Stolper and Reade Ryan; and Eurasia Group's Robert Kahn. I am also grateful to fund manager Ben Heller and Charlie Blitzer of Blitzer Consulting (and formerly of the International Monetary Fund's International Capital Markets Department) for many helpful discussions about the bondholder perspective. I received helpful comments on the manuscript from Ed Bartholomew, Elena Duggar, Aitor Erce, Marc Flandreau, Clay Gillette, Freyr Hermannsson, Mitesh Kaphle, Carey Lathrop, Rhoda and Dwight Makoff, Théo Maret, Layna Mosley, Carlos Steneri, Emiliano Trigo, Annamaria Viterbo, Vladimir Werning, and Miranda Xafa. I am also thankful to have had the opportunity to check selected facts with professionals from Elliott Investment Management and several other funds.

At a research and production level, I would like to express my infinite thanks for the friendship and support of my inside team: Jane Isay (publishing guru), Amy Resnick (story development adviser and editor), my wife Eileen Makoff (style editor and biggest supporter), Hilary Claggett (acquisitions editor at Georgetown University Press), Celeste Makoff (general research), Martín Reydó (Argentina research), Pierre Clément Mingozzi (Italy research), Brittany Stange (legal research), Ram Balasubramanian (data science), Charles Glasser (First Amendment law advisory), Jeffrey Makoff (general advice, manuscript review, and fact-checking supervisor), Carla Russo (Argentina fact checking), Willem Lee (proofing), and Julie Hodgins (graphics editor). Special thanks also go to Tom Hofer and Steve Nuchols for contributing cover art ideas and to the Georgetown University Press team who developed the final design.

Appendix A

Featured Characters

Government of Argentina

Administrations of Eduardo Duhalde and Néstor Kirchner

Eduardo Duhalde	President Jan. 2002–May 2003
Néstor Kirchner	President May 2003–Dec. 2007
Cristina Fernández de Kirchner	Wife of President Kirchner
Jorge Remes Lenicov	Minister of economy Jan. 2002–Apr. 2002
Roberto Lavagna	Minister of economy Apr. 2002–Nov. 2005
Guillermo Nielsen	Finance secretary

Administration of Cristina Fernández de Kirchner

Cristina Fernández de Kirchner	President Dec. 2007–Dec. 2015
Axel Kicillof	Minister of economy Nov. 2013–Dec. 2015

Administration of Mauricio Macri

Mauricio Macri	President Dec. 2015–Dec. 2019
Alfonso Prat-Gay	Minister of economy
Luis Caputo	Finance secretary
Santiago Bausili	Finance undersecretary

United States Government

Administration of George W. Bush

George W. Bush	President Jan. 2001–Jan. 2009
Paul O'Neill	U.S. treasury secretary Jan. 2001–Dec. 2002

John Snow   U.S. treasury secretary Feb. 2003–June 2006
John Taylor   Undersecretary for international affairs
Randal Quarles   Assistant secretary for international affairs

Administration of Barack Obama

Barack Obama   President Jan. 2009–Jan. 2017
Jacob Lew   U.S. Treasury secretary
Mark Sobel   Deputy assistant secretary for international monetary
                       and financial policy

Judges and Lawyers

Judges of the Southern District of New York and the Court of Appeals for the Second Circuit

Thomas P. Griesa   Southern District of New York
José A. Cabranes   Second Circuit Court of Appeals
Rosemary S. Pooler   Second Circuit Court of Appeals
Reena A. Raggi   Second Circuit Court of Appeals
Robert W. Sweet   Southern District of New York (Peru case)

Special Master Appointed by Judge Thomas P. Griesa

Daniel A. Pollack   Lawyer at McCarter & English

Counsel for the Republic of Argentina and the Central Bank of Argentina

Jonathan Blackman   Lawyer at Cleary Gottlieb
Carmine Boccuzzi   Lawyer at Cleary Gottlieb
Joseph Neuhaus   Lawyer at Sullivan & Cromwell

Counsel for Elliott's NML Capital, Ltd.

Robert Cohen   Lawyer at Dechert
Dennis Hranitzky   Lawyer at Dechert
Matthew McGill   Lawyer at Gibson Dunn
Theodore Olson   Lawyer at Gibson Dunn, former U.S. solicitor general

Counsel for Other Plaintiffs

Andrea Boggio	Professor at Bryant University (Andrarex)
Anthony Costantini	Lawyer at Duane Morris (for small plaintiffs and late-entrant hedge funds)
Marc Dreier	Head of Dreier LLP (for small plaintiffs)
Edward Friedman	Lawyer at Friedman, Kaplan (for Aurelius and Blue Angel)
Guillermo Gleizer	Lawyer (for Macrotecnic and other plaintiffs)
Mark Kalish	Lawyer at Moss & Kalish (for Old Castle and Lightwater)
David Rivkin	Lawyer at Debevoise & Plimpton (for Kenneth Dart)
Jennifer Scullion	Lawyer at Proskauer Rose (for class action plaintiffs)
Michael Spencer	Lawyer at Milberg (for small plaintiffs)
Patricia Rosito Vago	An Argentine lawyer (works with Dreier LLP and Milberg)

International Monetary Fund

Horst Köhler	Managing director 2000–2004
Anne Krueger	First deputy managing director 2001–2006

Creditor Industry Organization Representatives

Michael Chamberlin	Executive director of the Emerging Markets Traders Association
Charles Dallara	Managing director of the Institute of International Finance

Creditor Rights Activists and Critics of Argentina's 2005 Bond Restructuring

Stefan Engelsberger	Head of Interessengemeinschaft Argentinien e.V
Hans Humes	Cochair of the Global Committee of Argentina Bondholders member of the Argentina Bondholders Committee
Adam Lerrick	Chairman of the Argentine Bond Restructuring Agency PLC negotiating team company
Abigail McKenna	Chairman of the Emerging Markets Creditors Association and member of the Argentina Bondholders Committee

Nicola Stock   President of Task Force Argentina and cochair of the
                        Global Committee of Argentina Bondholders

Investors

Elliott Associates

Paul Elliott Singer   Head of Elliott Associates (now known as Elliott In-
                        vestment Management)
Jay Newman   Portfolio manager at Elliott Associates

Other Large Holdout Investors

Blue Angel Capital I   An investment vehicle affiliated with Davidson Kemp-
                        ner Capital Management
Mark Brodsky   Head of Aurelius Capital Management
Capital Ventures   An investment vehicle affiliated with Susquehanna
  International   Advisors Group, Inc.
Kenneth Dart   Wealthy investor, Cayman Islands–based
Eric Hermann   Affiliated with Montreux group entities
Michael Straus   Affiliated with Montreux group entities and worked as a
                        lawyer for Elliott in the Peru case
Nancy Zimmerman   Head of Bracebridge Capital

Key Actors in Argentina's 2010 Reopening of Its
2005 Exchange Offer

Marcelo Etchebarne   An Argentine lawyer affiliated with Arcadia Advisors
Gustavo Ferraro   Barclays Capital
Robert Koenigsberger   Gramercy Capital, an anchor investor
Hernán Lorenzino   Finance secretary, Republic of Argentina

Appendix B

Timeline of Events

2001

November 26	IMF first deputy managing director Anne Krueger announces the SDRM initiative.
December 6	The IMF refuses to disperse expected payment to Argentina.
December 23	Argentina announces a debt moratorium.

2002

January 1	Eduardo Duhalde appointed president of Argentina.
April 27	Roberto Lavagna sworn in as minister of economy.
September 4	The IMF amends its "good faith negotiations" rule to require countries in default to negotiate with creditor committees.
November 15	Argentina defaults on the World Bank to gain leverage over the IMF on lending conditions.

2003

January 24	The IMF approves a transitional program for Argentina; Argentina indicates that it is seeking a 70% haircut from international creditors.
May 25	Néstor Kirchner sworn in as the president of Argentina.
July 23	President George W. Bush meets with Kirchner at the White House.
September 10	The IMF announces a new program for Argentina.
September 22	Argentina announces indicative terms of its restructuring deal in Dubai.
December 4	Guillermo Nielsen speaks at EMTA's annual meeting.
Mid-December	IMF management takes Argentina's first review off the agenda for the December board meeting.

2004

January 15	Preliminary hearing on pari passu.
January 28	The IMF Executive Board approves Argentina's first review.
February 4	Elliott Associates attempts to attach Argentine diplomatic properties in the Washington, D.C., area.
March 22	Argentina passes its second review and recognizes GCAB as one of many creditor counterparts.
June 1	Argentina announces improved terms of its offer in Buenos Aires.
August 4	GCAB announces the completion of a global roadshow criticizing Argentina's offer.
August 12	The *Financial Times* reports that Argentina is lapsing its program with the IMF until after the debt restructuring is completed.

2005

January 12	Argentina launches its offer.
February 9	Argentina enacts the Lock Law.
February 25	Argentina announces that more than 75% of its creditors agreed to accept its offer.
March 29	Judge Thomas P. Griesa rules against Elliott and other creditors seeking to disrupt the closing of the transaction.
May 13	The Court of Appeals for the Second Circuit affirms Judge Griesa's March 29 decision.
June 2	The transaction closes with about $19.6 billion of holdout bonds left outstanding.
November 4	Anti-U.S. protests take place while President Bush attends the Summit of Americas in Mar del Plata, Argentina.
November 28	President Kirchner fires Minister of Economy Roberto Lavagna.
December 15	Argentina announces that it will repay the IMF in full.
December 30	Elliott and Dart obtain a temporary attachment on $105 million of Central Bank of Argentina reserves held at the Federal Reserve Bank of New York.

2006

January 12	Judge Griesa denies Elliott and Dart's attachment of the $105 million at the Federal Reserve Bank of New York.
August 29	The Second Circuit hears Elliott and Dart's appeal of Judge Griesa's ruling to deny attachment of the $105 million.
September 14	TFA launches an action against Argentina at the ICSID in Washington, D.C.
September 28	Elliott and Dart launch an alter ego action against the Central Bank of Argentina.

2007

January 5	The Second Circuit affirms Judge Griesa's denial of Elliott and Dart's attachment of $105 million at the New York Fed; the $105 million remains frozen pending the outcome of the alter ego litigation.
March 1	Moss & Kalish seeks to attach assets of Correo Argentino for its clients.
March 27	Guillermo Gleizer seeks to attach Tango-1 in California for two clients.
April 2, 3	Aurelius and Blue Angel file their first lawsuits against Argentina.
May 22	Elliott and Dart attach Argentina's shares in Banco Hipotecario held in New York.
December 10	Cristina Fernández de Kirchner sworn in as president of Argentina.

2008

April 18	Guillermo Gleizer leads an effort to attach Argentine global bonds held by Caja de Valores in Buenos Aires in trust for certain domestic bondholders.
September 12	Elliott and Dart seek to attach shares of Banco de la Nación Argentina but end up attaching $2.3 million of cash held at the bank for Agencia Nacional de Promoción Científica y Tecnológica.
September 15	Lehman Brothers files for bankruptcy.

October 21	Kirchner announces the takeover of private pension managers.
December 2	Attorney Marc Dreier is arrested.
December 11	Judge Griesa rules to allow attachment of Argentina's private pension assets.

2009

May 18	Judge Griesa rules that the holders of floating rate accrual notes (FRANs) are due contractual interest at a rate of more than 100% per annum.
May 29	Judge Griesa holds Argentina in contempt of court for its pension system's action to strip assets from the United States in advance of a mandated discovery deadline.
August 7	Elliott attempts to attach a tanker carrying liquefied natural gas on its way from Egypt to Argentina.
October 15	The Second Circuit reverses Judge Griesa's decision to allow the attachment of Argentina's private pension assets.

2010

January 29	Martín Redrado resigns as head of the Central Bank of Argentina under pressure from President Fernández Kirchner to loan money to the government.
April 7	Judge Griesa rules that the Central Bank of Argentina is the alter ego of the Republic and allows attachment of $105 million.
April 30	Argentina reopens its 2005 offer.
September 23	The Second Circuit affirms Judge Griesa's ruling on the contractual interest rate due to the holders of floating rate accrual notes, and two technical matters are referred to New York State.
September 27	Argentina's 2010 Reopening is completed; only $6.8 billion of holdouts remain outstanding.
October 20	Elliott launches its pari passu attack.

2011

February 7	Elliott seeks to attach an Argentine satellite guidance system at Honeywell International, Inc.
April 25	Elliott seeks to attach an Argentine satellite at Spaceport Systems International.
August 4	The retail investors known as the Varela plaintiffs join the pari passu litigation.
September 28	Judge Griesa rules from the bench that the Lock Law caused a breach of Argentina's pari passu clause.
October 26	Aurelius and Blue Angel join the pari passu litigation.
December 7	Judge Griesa signs an order finding Argentina in breach of its pari passu clause.

2012

January 26	Bracebridge's Olifant Fund joins the pari passu litigation.
February 23	Judge Griesa imposes the pari passu injunction on Argentina.
October 2	Elliott attaches the frigate ARA *Libertad* in Ghana.
October 26	The Second Circuit affirms Judge Griesa's ruling that Argentina has violated its pari passu clause, but asks for clarifications on the mechanics of the injunction.
November 21	Judge Griesa publishes an amended injunction order. Shortly thereafter he rules that the injunction will apply to a payment due by Argentina on December 15, 2012.
November 28	The Second Circuit stays the injunction pending further review.
December 15	The International Tribunal for the Law of the Sea orders the release of ARA *Libertad*.

2013

March 1	The Second Circuit asks Argentina to present an alternative payment formula.
March 29	Argentina responds that the creditors could take the same terms accepted by investors in the 2005 and 2010 offers.
August 23	The Second Circuit affirms Judge Griesa's pari passu injunction and calls Argentina a "uniquely recalcitrant debtor."

| October 14 | Argentina settles outstanding disputes with five ICSID claimants including four foreign utility companies. |

2014

March 25	Elliott seeks to attach an Argentine launch slot contract with SpaceX.
April 21	The U.S. Supreme Court hears Argentina's appeal on world-wide discovery.
May 29	Argentina announces a settlement agreement with its Paris Club lenders.
June 16	The U.S. Supreme Court announces that it will not hear the pari passu case and that Argentina lost on worldwide discovery.
June 30	The first payment date on Argentine bonds following the effective date of the injunction; a thirty-day grace period commences.
July 22	Judge Griesa asks Argentina and creditors to "meet continuously" with the aim of reaching a settlement before the expiration of the grace period.
July 30	The thirty-day grace period expires, and Argentina goes into default.
August 29	ICMA announces new standard pari passu and collective action clauses.
October 3	Judge Griesa finds Argentina in contempt for trying to evade his order by taking steps to replace its paying agent, the Bank of New York, with a local bank that would pay investors despite the injunction.
October 14	Kazakhstan issues bonds with the ICMA 2014 collective action clause.
November 25	Mexico issues a bond with the ICMA 2014 collective action clause.

2015

| January 18 | Argentine prosecutor Alberto Nisman is found dead; protests follow. |
| February 9 | Elliott subpoenas JPMorgan Chase and Deutsche Bank about a pending bond deal for Argentina. |

| April 22 | Elliott goes to court about a pending Deutsche Bank and BBVA bond deal for Argentina. |
| November 22 | Mauricio Macri is elected president of Argentina. |

2016

January 13	Preliminary meeting between the largest holdout investors and Argentina.
January 31	Argentina signs a settlement agreement with TFA.
February 1	First negotiating session with the largest holdout investors.
February 3	Dart and the Montreux group separately settle with Argentina.
February 4	Second negotiating session with remaining large holdout investors.
February 5	Argentina launches its offer to settle with all plaintiffs (the Propuesta).
February 19	Judge Griesa "indicatively" lifts the injunction.
February 29	Special Master Daniel Pollack announces a settlement agreement between Argentina and Elliott, Bracebridge, Aurelius, and Blue Angel.
March 2	Judge Griesa rules to lift the injunction, subject to Argentina lifting the Lock Law and paying investors who signed settlement agreements.
March 3	Elliott, Bracebridge, Aurelius, and others appeal Judge Griesa's decision to lift the injunction.
April 13	The Second Circuit affirms Judge Griesa's decision to lift the injunction.
April 22	Argentina completes a $16.5 billion bond deal and pays settling plaintiffs.
December 22	Judge Griesa refuses to impose a pari passu injunction in the White Hawthorne case.

Glossary

American Task Force Argentina (ATFA) A U.S.-based organization set up to lobby against Argentina

Argentina Bondholders Committee (ABC) A U.S.-based creditors rights organization

Argentine Bond Restructuring Agency PLC (ABRA) A company set up in Ireland by Adam Lerrick and partners to facilitate retail bondholder participation in Argentina's transaction

authority A judicial decision or other legal material used to support a legal argument or ruling

Banco de la Nación Argentina (BNA) A commercial bank owned by the Republic of Argentina

Bank for International Settlements (BIS) A bank for central banks located in Basel, Switzerland

Bank of New York (BONY) A U.S.-headquartered commercial bank (now BNY Mellon)

bond A debt instrument traded in the market, most often with a fixed coupon and maturity date and, in this story, typically documented under the law of the state of New York

Capital Ventures International (CVI) An investment vehicle affiliated with Susquehanna Advisors Group, Inc.

clearing system An electronic custodial system that tracks the ownership of bonds and other securities held in custody by banks, brokerages, and other financial institutions

collective action clause (CAC) A feature of a sovereign bond that allows a supermajority of its owners to force 100% of its owners into a debt restructuring offer

debt sustainability analysis (DSA)   A comprehensive methodology developed by the IMF to evaluate the ability of a country to repay its debt under a wide range of scenarios; an analytical tool used to determine the haircut required from creditors in a sovereign debt restructuring

discovery   Compulsory disclosure, at a party's request, of information that relates to ongoing litigation

Emerging Markets Creditors Association (EMCA)   An association of emerging markets debt investors later merged with EMTA

Emerging Markets Traders Association (EMTA)   A New York–based association of investment banks, brokerage firms, and investment funds

EM Ltd.   An investment vehicle associated with Kenneth Dart

Energía Argentina S.A. (ENARSA)   An Argentine state-owned energy company

enforcement (of debt claims)   Procedures to collect on court judgments, including orders to restrain, attach, or garnish a debtor's assets

equity jurisprudence   An area of law that relies on principles of fairness rather than statute; originating in English chancery law, a common current-day application is the imposition of an injunction, whose terms are fashioned by the court to remedy an injustice that cannot otherwise be remedied under the law

exchange offer   A form of debt restructuring in which a debt issuer invites owners of bonds to offer their old defaulted bonds to the borrower in exchange for new performing bonds

fiscal policy   The use of government spending and taxation to influence the economy

floating-rate accrual notes (FRANs)   Debt instruments issued by the Republic of Argentina whose contractual interest rate varied in relation to the yield of other outstanding Argentine bonds

Foreign Sovereign Immunities Act (FSIA)   The U.S. federal law that governs lawsuits against foreign countries with respect to commercial disputes

Global Committee of Argentina Bondholders (GCAB)   A group comprising U.S.-based ABC, Italy-based TFA, and Germany-based ABRA, plus nominal members from Switzerland and Japan

gross domestic product (GDP) A number that represents the total value of all final goods and services produced within a country during a specified period of time, such as one year

Group of Seven (G7) An informal group of the world's leading economies: the United States, Canada, France, Germany, Italy, Japan, and the United Kingdom

Group of Ten (G10) The G7 + Belgium, the Netherlands, Sweden, and Switzerland

Group of Twenty (G20) G10 + Argentina, Australia, Brazil, China, India, Indonesia, the Republic of Korea, Mexico, Russia, Saudi Arabia, South Africa, Turkey, and the European Union

haircut The reduction in value or principal amount of debt subject to a debt restructuring

Institute of International Finance (IIF) Washington-based lobbying group for banks and financial institutions

International Capital Markets Association (ICMA) A London-based association of bond underwriters and investors

International Centre for Settlement of Investment Disputes (ICSID) A Washington-based institution that facilitates the arbitration of international investment disputes

International Monetary Fund (IMF) An international institution based in Washington, D.C., that lends to countries suffering financial crises

International Tribunal for the Law of the Sea (ITLOS) An independent judicial body established by the Third United Nations Convention on the Law of the Sea to adjudicate disputes arising out of the interpretation and application of the convention

monetary policy Governmental policies that deal with a country's interest rate, money supply, exchange rate, and foreign reserves

NML Capital, Ltd. An investment vehicle affiliated with Elliott Associates

primary surplus A government's net cash flow before debt service: revenues less nondebt expenses; when specified over a time horizon, a primary surplus provides a boundary on cash flow available for debt service

Rights Upon Future Offers (RUFO)   A price-match guarantee offered to participants in Argentina's 2005 transaction that was effective through December 31, 2014

sovereign debt restructuring mechanism (SDRM)   A proposed quasi-legal organ to be set up under the auspices of the IMF to facilitate the restructuring of sovereign debt

structural reforms   A broad term covering governmental policies affecting economic growth, fiscal sustainability, and financial sector stability

Task Force Argentina (TFA)   An Italian creditors' rights organization

Teachers Insurance and Annuity Association and College Retirement Equities Fund (TIAA-CREF)   A leading U.S. asset manager and insurance company originally founded to manage retirement savings for teachers

Note on Sources

This work is based primarily on public records. Citations are provided in the format specified in the twenty-first edition of *The Bluebook: A Uniform System of Citation* compiled by the editors of the *Columbia Law Review*, the *Harvard Law Review*, the *University of Pennsylvania Law Review*, and the *Yale Law Journal*. The most frequently cited sources are materials available at the International Monetary Fund's (IMF) website (www.imf.org), the IMF's digital archives (https://archivescatalog.imf.org/search/simple), official press statements of the U.S. Department of the Treasury (https://home.treasury.gov/news/press-releases), statements of the Global Committee of Argentina Bondholders (www.gcab.org as viewed on archive.org/web/), web postings of the American Task Force Argentina (www.atfa.org as viewed on archive.org/web/), the *New York Times*, the *Financial Times*, the *Wall Street Journal*, the *Washington Post*, *La Nación*, court documents obtained from Public Access to Court Electronic Records (www.pacer.uscourts.gov), transcripts purchased from the Southern District court reporters, and court documents obtained from the clerks' offices at the U.S. District Court for the Southern District of New York, and the United States Court of Appeals for the Second Circuit. The author also carried out over 125 interviews with participants regarding the events described in the book.

Endnotes are numbered by their appearance within chapters and appear at the back of the book. Where in-court dialog is cited, the endnote numbers are placed either at the end of a quotation or at the end of a sequence of quotations, which applies when all of the dialogue in the sequence can be sourced to a continuous block of text in a transcript.

Notes

Foreword

1. As portrayed in the television and movie franchise Star Trek, the Kobayashi Maru scenario was a training exercise for cadets at the Starfleet Academy in the twenty-third century. It was deliberately designed to be a completely no-win scenario.

2. This was made clear at a hearing held on September 28, 2011. At that hearing, Argentina's lawyer reported to Judge Griesa that holders of 92% of the defaulted bonds had accepted Argentina's debt restructuring offer. Judge Griesa responded, "But that, for the people who wanted to take 30 cents on the dollar [the present value of Argentina's restructuring offer] . . . that was their privilege, but it is also the privilege of the holdouts to have their judgments honored." See chapter 8.

Introduction

1. World Bank, *Country Assistance Strategy for the Argentine Republic 2006–2008: Annex B Sovereign Debt Restructuring and Debt Profile*, Report No. 34015-AR, at 84 (May 4, 2006). (Debt restructured by Argentina in 2005 was $81.835 billion eligible debt plus $20.731 interest arrears for a total of $102.566 billion.)

2. Anne Krueger, First Deputy Managing Director, IMF, *A New Approach to Sovereign Debt Restructuring*, Address given at the National Economists Club Annual Members' Dinner at the American Enterprise Institute, Washington, D.C. (Nov. 26, 2001), https://www.imf.org/en/News/Articles/2015/09/28/04/53/sp112601.

3. Anne Krueger, *A New Approach to Sovereign Debt Restructuring*, IMF, at 23 (April 2002), 35, https://www.imf.org/external/pubs/ft/exrp/sdrm/eng/sdrm.pdf. ("*Activation of a stay on creditor action* would require a request by the sovereign debtor and IMF endorsement" and describing "establishing a new judicial organ" at the IMF to carry out the SDRM function.)

4. *Id.* at 6 ("During the 1980s debt crisis, collective action problems were limited by the relatively small number of large creditors, the relatively homogeneity of commercial bank creditors, the contractual provisions of syndicated loans, and, on occasion, moral suasion applied by supervisory authorities.") and *supra* note 2.

5. *Supra* note 2.

1. Argentina Defaults and Then Fights with the IMF

1. Anthony Faiola, *Argentina, Near Default, Seeks IMF Help*, Was. Post (Dec. 7, 2001), https://www.washingtonpost.com/archive/business/2001/12/07/argentina -near-default-seeks-imf-help/00186c77-4476-4b74-abf4-12a934bf03de/. For details on prior funding agreement, see IMF, *IMF Augments Argentina Stand-By Credit to $21.57 Billion, and Completes Fourth Review*, Press Release 01/37 (Sept. 7, 2001), https://www.imf.org/en/News/Articles/2015/09/14/01/49/pr0137/.

2. Felipe González, *Preface* to Eduardo A. Duhalde, Argentina Aflame, at xv (English First Edition e-Libro, 2009). ("they all should go").

3. IMF, *The IMF and Argentina 1991–2001*, Evaluation Report (2004), at 98–100.

4. Michelle Wallin and Pamela Druckerman, *Argentina's President de la Rúa Resigns, Unable to Quell Deepening Finance Crisis*, Wall St. J. (Dec. 21, 2001), https:// www.wsj.com/articles/SB1008839567321991160.

5. Thomas Catan, *Argentina Defaults on Debt but Keeps Dollar Peg*, Financial Times (Dec. 23, 2001), (mimeo).

6. Anthony Faiola and Steven Pearlstein, *Argentina to Suspend Debt Payment*, Was. Post (Dec. 24, 2001), https://www.washingtonpost.com/archive/politics/2001 /12/24/argentina-to-suspend-debt-payment/aba7a36a-0d38-49db-a666-459d1 52de33f/.

7. Nicole Hill, *Backstory: Lives Recycled in Argentina*, Christian Science Monitor (Jan. 25, 2006), https://www.csmonitor.com/2006/0125/p20s01-woam.html.

8. For different theories of the origins of Argentina's 2001 default, see IMF, *The IMF and Argentina 1991–2001*, Evaluation Report (2004); and Romi Bandura and Anne Le Brun, *NBER Project on Exchange Rate Crises in Emerging Market Countries: Argentina*, NBER (July 17, 2002), https://www2.nber.org/crisis/argentina_report .html.

9. See *supra* no. 4 for the IMF's Independent Evaluation Office's analysis of the failure of Argentina's program of the 1990s.

10. IMF, Transcript of a press conference on the interim World Economic Outlook, Dec. 18, 2001, https://www.imf.org/en/News/Articles/2015/09/28/04/54 /tr011218.

11. *The Meltzer Comm'n: The Future of the IMF and World Bank: Hearing before the Comm. on Foreign Relations United States Senate*, 106th Cong. 657 (2000) (statement of Jerome I. Levinson) at 31, 32.

12. Todd S. Purdum and David E. Sanger, *Forum in New York: The Meeting; 2 Top Officials Offer Stern Talk on U.S. Policy*, N.Y. Times (Feb. 2, 2002), https://www .nytimes.com/2002/02/02/world/forum-in-new-york-the-meeting-2-top-officials -offer-stern-talk-on-us-policy.html.

13. *Remarks by National Security Advisor Condoleezza Rice on Terrorism and*

Foreign Policy, George W. Bush White House (Apr. 29, 2002), https://georgewbush -whitehouse.archives.gov/news/releases/2002/04/20020429-9.html. ("It is not an unwillingness to have international assistance go to Argentina. It is an understanding that the conditions have to be right so those resources actually make a difference. And some of the things that Argentina needs to do will improve confidence in Argentina just by doing them.")

14. Martin Edwin Andersen, *Argentina Crying over 'Hired Guns,'* Insight on the News (June 10, 2002) (mimeo). (Secretary of State Colin Powell warning that economic reform was necessary and that Argentina "must also address the underlying political and institutional flaws that encourage excess public-sector borrowing, corruption, politicized judicial systems and a lack of transparency in government activities.")

15. Alan Beattie, *IMF Insists on Reforms before Loan*, Financial Times (Apr. 21, 2002), (mimeo).

16. Jane Bussey and Gregg Fields, *Huge Default Has Far Reach*, Miami Herald (Dec. 25, 2001), at 2C (mimeo).

17. *Supra* note 1, IMF press release.

18. John B. Taylor, *Chapter 3: Avoiding Global Financial Contagion*, in Global Financial Warriors: The Untold Story of International Finance in the Post 9/11 World, 70–97 (2007).

19. *"Thoughts on the Global Economy": Remarks by Kenneth W. Dam Deputy U.S. Treasury Secretary Delivered to the World Affairs Council of Washington, D.C.*, U.S. Treasury Dept. (Jan. 25, 2002), https://home.treasury.gov/news/press-releases/po948.

20. Eduardo Duhalde, Argentina Aflame, 55–67 (English 1st ed. e-Libro, 2009). (Appointment on Jan. 1, 2002.)

21. *Supra* note 3 at 100.

22. IMF, Argentina: 2005 *Article IV Consultation—Staff Report,* IMF Country Report No. 05/236, at 10 (July 2005), https://www.imf.org/external/pubs/ft/scr /2005/cro5236.pdf.

23. Paul Blustein, *Argentina's Plan Stirs Worries Elsewhere; IMF, U.S. See Danger in Bid to Ease Pain*, Was. Post (Jan. 9, 2002) (mimeo).

24. Kevin G. Hall, *Argentina Turns from Open Market*, Miami Herald (Jan. 5, 2002), at 13A (mimeo).

25. Thomas Catan, *Argentina Unveils Sweeping New Economic Plan*, Financial Times (Feb. 4, 2002) (mimeo) (addressing fiscal policy, exchange rate policy, and bank restructuring aspects of the government's program); and *supra* note 3 at 100. This timeline details the dates that capital controls were introduced, the dates of devaluations and changes in exchange rate policy, and the announcement of the restructuring of bank balance sheets; it does not, however, detail the date freezing of utility tariffs, which also occurred in January 2002.

Notes to Pages 13–16

26. Eduardo Amadeo, *La Salida del Abismo Memoria Política de la Negociación entre Duhalde y el FMI*, 78 (Grupo Editorial Planeta 2003) (meeting with Köhler).

27. Larry Rohter, *2 Blows to Argentine President: Economy Minister Quits and Senate Balks at Crisis Bill*, N.Y. Times (Apr. 24, 2002), https://www.nytimes.com/2002/04/24/world/2-blows-argentine-president-economy-minister-quits-senate-balks-crisis-bill.html.

28. Interviews with Roberto Lavagna (May 10, 2017, Dec. 5, 2017, and May 22, 2018), Buenos Aires, Argentina, and via telephone (Oct. 1, 2020) (hereinafter Lavagna interview).

29. Anthony Faiola, *Key Economic Aides in Argentina Quit as Plan Stalls*, Was. Post (Apr. 24, 2002), https://www.washingtonpost.com/archive/politics/2002/04/24/key-economic-aides-in-argentina-quit-as-plan-stalls/d92454a1-9e19-4f56-b04b-709711c29a42/.

30. William Echikson, *Lavagna Promises Hard Measures to Restore Argentina's Economy*, Wall St. J. (Apr. 25, 2002), https://www.wsj.com/articles/SB1019772142663035080 (Lavagna warns that foreign investors and creditors "will have to suffer as much as the general public."); Lavagna interview.

31. Roberto Lavagna, Construyendo la oportunidad, at 462 (1st Ed. Buenos Aires, Sudamericana, 2015). (Lavagna quits in response to issuance of a "festival of bonds.")

32. Roberto Lavagna, *El Desafío de la Voluntad: Trece Meses Cruciales en la Historia Argentina*, 24 (Editorial Sudamericana SA 2011). (Arrival at airport.)

33. *Id.* at 26 (meeting with President Duhalde).

34. Larry Rohter, *Argentina Partly Opens Banks and Names an Economy Minister*, N.Y. Times (Apr. 27, 2002), https://www.nytimes.com/2002/04/27/world/argentina-partly-opens-banks-and-names-an-economy-minister.html; Lavagna, *El Desafío de la Voluntad*, at 27 (swearing in on Apr. 27).

35. Lavagna, *El Desafío de la Voluntad*, at 34–36 (meeting with political leaders).

36. *Id.* at 37 (announcement of program); and Larry Rohter, *Back in Business, Argentina Calms Down and the Peso Perks Up*, N.Y. Times (Apr. 30, 2002), https://www.nytimes.com/2002/04/30/world/back-in-business-argentina-calms-down-and-the-peso-perks-up.html.

37. Lavagna, *El Desafío de la Voluntad*, at 38 (helping from the outside).

38. Lavagna, *El Desafío de la Voluntad*, at 39 (hiring Nielsen).

39. Interview with Guillermo Nielsen (various dates 2017–2022, Buenos Aires and New York) on Nielsen's background and hiring of team members (hereinafter Nielsen interview).

40. *Id.*

41. Lavagna, *El Desafío de la Voluntad*, at 50 (meeting with Archbishop Bergoglio).

42. Austen Ivereigh, The Great Reformer. Francis and the Making of a Radical Pope, 269 (2014) (Argentina Dialogue).

43. Jorge Bergoglio, La Patria Es Un Don, La Nación Una Tarea: Refundar con Esperanza Nuestros Vínculos Sociales, at 57–67 (Editorial Claretiana 2013). (Text of sermon.)

44. Luke 19:1–10.

45. Paul Blustein, *IMF Crisis Plan Torpedoed; Treasury Official Rejects Proposal a Day after It Is Advanced*, Was. Post (Apr. 3, 2002) (mimeo).

46. For general information on the U.S. Treasury Department's activities, see Randal Quarles, *Herding Cats: Collective-Action Clauses in Sovereign Debt—The Genesis of the Project to Change Market Practice in 2001 through 2003*, Law and Contemporary Problems, 73, No. 4, 29, 29–38 (Fall 2010) (discussing background to U.S. Treasury approach to reform). For the legal structure of CACs, see Group of Ten (G10), *Report of the G-10 Working Group on Contractual Clauses* (Sept. 26, 2002), https://www.bis.org/publ/gten08.htm.

47. Roberto Lavagna, *Trust Argentina*, Financial Times (May 2, 2002) (mimeo).

48. *Duhalde Asegura a Aznar que Argentina Cumplirá en Breve las Demandas del FMI*, El Pais (May 18, 2002), https://elpais.com/internacional/2002/05/19/actuali dad/1021759201_850215.html; and Lavagna, *El Desafío de la Voluntad*, at 71 (meeting with Prime Minister Aznar).

49. Amadeo, 128 ("face of a dog").

50. Lavagna, *El Desafío de la Voluntad*, at 72–73 (dinner with Krueger and Singh).

51. Lavagna, *El Desafío de la Voluntad*, at 73–75 (meeting with Köhler); and Lavagna interview.

52. IMF, *IMF Managing Director Meets Argentine Economy Minister, Board Extends Argentina's Repayment of SRF*, News Brief 02/43 (May 21, 2002), https://www .imf.org/en/News/Articles/2015/09/29/18/03/nb0243.

53. Group of Seven (G7), *Statement of G7 Finance Ministers* (June 15, 2002), https://tspace.library.utoronto.ca/bitstream/1807/317/2/fm061502.htm.

54. For Argentina's perspective on the country's negotiations with the IMF during 2002, see generally Amadeo and Lavagna, *El Desafío de la Voluntad*.

55. For the IMF staff's perspective on its negotiations with Argentina during 2002, see generally IMF, *Argentina—Banking System—Developments, Reforms, and Vulnerabilities*, EBS/02/214 Supp. 1 (Dec. 23, 2002); IMF, *Argentina-Selected Issues*, SM/02/385 (Dec. 23, 2002); and IMF, *Argentina: 2002 Article IV Consultation—Staff Report*, IMF Country Report No. 03/226 (July 2003).

56. Lavagna, *El Desafío de la Voluntad*, at 105 (meeting with O'Neill); and Lavagna interview.

57. IMF, *IMF's Köhler Welcomes Progress in Talks with Argentina*, News Brief 02/56 (June 28, 2002), https://www.imf.org/en/News/Articles/2015/09/29/18/03 /nb0256.

58. IMF, *IMF Managing Director Horst Köhler Announces Advisory Group on*

Argentina, News Brief 02/61 (July 10, 2002), https://www.imf.org/en/News/Articles /2015/09/29/18/03/nb0261.

59. IMF, *IMF Managing Director Köhler Welcomes Independent Advisors' Report on Argentina*, News Brief 02/80 (July 29, 2002), https://www.imf.org/en/News /Articles/2015/09/29/18/03/nb0280.

60. IMF, *Total Reserves Excluding Gold for Argentina [TRESEGARM052N]*, FRED, Federal Reserve Bank of St. Louis, https://fred.stlouisfed.org/series/TRESEG ARM052N (Sept. 7, 2022).

61. Pablo Morosi, *El Piquete que Cambió la Argentina*, La Nación (June 26, 2003), https://www.lanacion.com.ar/politica/el-piquete-que-cambio-la-argentina -nid506674/; *Adelantan las Elecciones Presidenciales*, La Nación (July 3, 2003), https://www.lanacion.com.ar/politica/adelantan-las-elecciones-presidenciales -nid410646/.

62. Paul Blustein, *Logic of Bailout Prevails Again*, Was. Post (Aug. 9, 2002), https://www.washingtonpost.com/archive/business/2002/08/09/logic-of-bailout -prevails-again/e412a1b9-b705-48d1-9165-906bbe7b4ea7/. ("Brazil is getting a $30 billion loan from the International Monetary Fund.")

63. Paul Blustein, *U.S. to Lend Uruguay $1.5 Billion*, Was. Post (Aug. 4, 2002), https://www.washingtonpost.com/archive/politics/2002/08/04/us-to-lend-uru guay-15-billion/1956c6f8-c12f-499e-b093-c22d7fd47683/.

64. John B. Taylor, U.S. Treasury Undersec'y Intl. Affairs, The U.S. Commit-ment to Uruguay and Latin America, Remarks at Embassy of Uruguay upon Receipt of the Medal of the Oriental Republic of Uruguay Washington, D.C. (Feb. 14, 2005), https://home.treasury.gov/news/press-releases/js2250 (discussing U.S. Treasury loan to Uruguay).

65. U.S. Dep't. of the Treasury, *Treasury Secretary O'Neill to Discuss Trip to South American Nations*, Media Advisory (July 31, 2002), https://home.treasury.gov/news /press-releases/po3308.

66. U.S. Dep't. of the Treasury, *Statement of United States Treasury Secretary Paul O'Neill after Meeting Minister of Economy Roberto Lavagna* (Aug. 7, 2002), https://home.treasury.gov/news/press-releases/po3335.

67. Larry Rohter with Edmund L. Andrews, *I.M.F. Agrees to Loan of $30 Bil-lion for Brazil*, N.Y. Times (Aug. 8, 2002), https://www.nytimes.com/2002/08/08 /business/imf-agrees-to-loan-of-30-billion-for-brazil.html (discussing O'Neill's trip to Buenos Aires and the Brazil loan); and Thomas Catan, *Argentina Looks on as Brazil Given Aid*, Financial Times (Aug. 9, 2002) (mimeo). (Father Christmas comment).

68. IMF, *IMF Extends Argentina's SRF Repayment by One Year*, Press Release 02/39 (Sept. 5, 2002), https://www.imf.org/en/News/Articles/2015/09/14/01/49 /pro239.

69. IMF, *Argentina: 2002 Article IV Consultation—Staff Report,* Country Report No. 03/226 (July 2003), https://www.imf.org/external/pubs/ft/scr/2003/cr03226.pdf (discussing state-owned banks, at 22, and the utility sector, at 24).

70. *Id.* at 53. ("August 15: Congress approves a bill extending for 90 days [through mid-November 2002] the provision that suspends certain kinds of creditor-initiated nonbankruptcy law enforcement actions.")

71. *Id.* at 53. ("August 22: The Supreme Court declares unconstitutional the 13 percent salary cut for federal government workers and pensioners, implemented from July 2001"; "September 5: The federal administrative dispute chamber, an appellate court, rules that the decrees establishing the [capital controls] and [pesification] were unconstitutional. The ruling applies to only one case, but opens the door to further similar rulings"; and "September 13: The Federal Court of Appeals declared the [capital controls], [pesification], . . . unconstitutional; the decision allows depositors to claim their deposits in court immediately.")

72. Alan Beattie, *IMF to Roll Over Argentine Debt,* Financial Times (Sept. 6, 2002) (mimeo).

73. IMF, Transcript of an IMF briefing on Latin America, Sept. 23, 2002, at 5, https://www.imf.org/en/News/Articles/2015/09/28/04/54/tr020923 (Krueger and Köhler quotes).

74. Larry Rohter, *Argentina Says It Will Skip Int'l Loan Payment,* N.Y. Times (Sept. 25, 2002), https://www.nytimes.com/2002/09/25/business/argentina-says-it-will-skip-international-loan-payment.html (Lavagna quote and declining reserves rationale for threat).

75. IMF, *Transcript of a Press Conference by IMF Managing Director Horst Köhler prior to the 2002 IMF–World Bank Annual Meetings,* Sept. 26, 2002, https://www.imf.org/en/News/Articles/2015/09/28/04/54/tr020926.

76. Lee C. Buchheit, *Of Creditors, Preferred and Otherwise,* Intl. Fin. L. Rev. 12–13 (June 1991).

77. Thomas Catan, *Buenos Aires Hits Back at IMF Criticism,* Financial Times (Sept. 24, 2002) (mimeo). (Discussing tensions between Argentina and the IMF and Argentina's lack of trust in IMF advice.)

78. IMF, *Transcript of a Press Briefing by Thomas C. Dawson, Director, External Relations Department,* Oct. 10, 2002, https://www.imf.org/en/News/Articles/2015/09/28/04/54/tr021010.

79. *Progress, of Sorts; Argentina's Collapse,* Economist, Oct. 19, 2002 (mimeo).

80. Alan Beatie, *Argentina Plays Dangerous Game with the IMF,* Financial Times (Oct. 29, 2002) (mimeo).

81. *Argentina Hanging by a Thread,* Economist (Nov. 15, 2002) (mimeo); and Larry Rohter, *Argentina Defaults on Big Payment to World* Bank, N.Y. Times (Nov. 15,

2002), https://www.nytimes.com/2002/11/15/business/argentina-defaults-on-big-payment-to-world-bank.html.

82. IMF, *IMF Issues Press Statement on Argentina*, News Brief 02/114 (Nov. 14, 2002), https://www.imf.org/en/News/Articles/2015/09/29/18/03/nb02114 (first IMF quote).

83. Peter Hudson, *IMF Plays Down Argentine Default*, Financial Times (Nov. 15, 2002) (mimeo) (second IMF quote).

84. *Id.* (Lavagna quote).

85. *O'Neill: La Situación Argentina Merjoró*, La Nación (Nov. 16, 2002), https://www.lanacion.com.ar/politica/oneill-la-situacion-argentina-mejoro-nid450538/ (O'Neill quote).

86. IMF, *IMF Extends Argentina's SRF Repayment Expectation by One Year*, Press Release No. 02/51 (Nov. 20, 2002), https://www.imf.org/en/News/Articles/2015/09/14/01/49/pro251.

87. Lavagna, *El Desafío de la Voluntad*, at 187 (claiming that on November 13 a senior IMF official met with the head of the Inter-American Development Bank and assured him that Argentina would pay).

88. IMF, *IMF Approves Transitional Stand-By Credit Support for Argentina*, Press Release 03/09 (Jan. 24, 2003), https://www.imf.org/en/News/Articles/2015/09/14/01/49/pro309.

89. *Roberto Lavagna: Más que un Bombero*, Opinion, La Nación (Dec. 30, 2003), https://www.lanacion.com.ar/opinion/roberto-lavagna-mas-que-un-bombero-nid559530/.

90. David Cufré, *El Satanico Dr. No*, Página 12 (Jan. 16, 2003) (mimeo).

91. Lavagna, *El Desafío de la Voluntad*, (Lavagna asked to run for president).

92. Alan Beattie, *Argentina 'Blackmail' Tests IMF Credibility*, Financial Times (Jan. 20, 2003), http://ezproxy.nypl.org/login?url=https://search.proquest.com/docview/228715361?accountid=35635.

93. Alan Beattie, *Debt Deal for Argentina Provokes IMF Revolt*, Financial Times (Jan. 25, 2003) (mimeo).

94. Amadeo, *supra* at 339 (IMF softening tone in spring 2003).

95. Adam Thomson, *IMF's Medium-Term Deal Gives Boost to Argentina*, Financial Times (June 25, 2003) (mimeo).

2. The Three-Way War

1. David Haskel, *IMF Extends Argentina $6.78 Billion Loan; Duhalde Sets Target of 70% Debt Write-Off*, Bureau of National Affairs (Jan. 27, 2003).

2. Lex Rieffel, Restructuring Sovereign Debt: The Case for Ad Hoc Machinery 171 (2003).

3. For a detailed discussion of Argentina's stock of defaulted debt and distribution of investors, see World Bank, *Country Assistance Strategy for the Argentine Republic 2006–2008: Annex B Sovereign Debt Restructuring and Debt Profile*, Report No. 34015-AR (May 4, 2006) (mimeo); and República Argentina, *Oferta de Canje— Anuncio Final* (Mar. 18, 2005) (mimeo); International Centre for Settlement of Investment Disputes, *Decision on Jurisdiction and Admissibility, Abaclat and Others*, at 12–50, Case No. ARB/07/5 (2011) (mimeo); and GCAB, *Presentation on the Occasion of the IMF/World Bank Annual Meetings*, at 5 (Oct. 4, 2004) (mimeo).

4. For text and discussion of Kirchner's inaugural speech, see Néstor Kirchner, Inauguration Speech (in Spanish) (May 25, 2003), https://www.cfkargentina.com /discurso-de-asuncion-del-presidente-nestor-kirchner-a-la-asamblea-legislativa-el -25-de-mayo-del-2003/; *Excerpts: Kirchner's Inaugural Speech*, BBC News (May 26, 2003), http://news.bbc.co.uk/2/hi/americas/2938070.stm; *Kirchner Asumió con un Fuerte Mensaje de Cambio*, La Nación (May 26, 2003), https://www.lanacion.com.ar /politica/kirchner-asumio-con-un-fuerte-mensaje-de-cambio-nid499010; and David Haskel, *Poverty Alleviation More Important Than Honoring Debt, New Argentine Leader Says*, Bureau of National Affairs (May 28, 2003) (mimeo).

5. For diplomatic response and the Bush call with Kirchner, see *Argentina: Kirchner Takes Office with Predictable Speech but Purges Military Leadership*, Wikileaks (May 28, 2003), https://wikileaks.org/plusd/cables/03BUENOSAIRES1747_a.html; Jorge Rosales, *Para EE. UU., el Gobierno Tuvo un "Buen Comienzo,"* La Nación (May 30, 2003), https://www.lanacion.com.ar/politica/para-ee-uu-el-gobierno-tuvo-un -buen -comienzo-nid499903/; David Haskel, *Poverty Alleviation More Important Than Honoring Debt, New Argentine Leader Says,* Bureau of National Affairs (May 28, 2003) (mimeo) (call with Bush); *Excerpts: Kirchner's Inaugural Speech*, BBC News (May 26, 2003), http://news.bbc.co.uk/2/hi/americas/2938070.stm ("normal united Argentina" language separately reported to have been used on his call with Bush).

6. Jon Jeter, *Commanders Purged in Argentina*, Was. Post (May 29, 2003), https://www.washingtonpost.com/archive/politics/2003/05/29/commanders -purged-in-argentina/8c4c5406-e5bc-499b-9aba-2536143894a3/.

7. Adam Thomson, *Argentine Supreme Court Faces Shake-up*, Financial Times (June 5, 2003) (mimeo).

8. Larry Rohter, *In Patagonia, Sheep Ranches Get Another Chance*, N.Y. Times (July 23, 2003), https://www.nytimes.com/2003/07/23/business/in-patagonia -sheep-ranches-get-another-chance.html.

9. *Supra* note 4, Haskel (no automatic alignments).

10. *Supra* note 5, Wikileaks (Castro's second visit since 1959).

11. *Supra* note 4, Haskel (Mel Martínez, U.S. representative, at inauguration).

12. *US Prepared to Help Argentina: Powell*, ABC News (June 9, 2003), https://www .abc.net.au/news/2003-06-09/us-prepared-to-help-argentina-powell/1867396.

13. Larry Rohter, *Powell Visits Argentina and Finds It Wary on Foreign Policy*, N.Y. Times (June 11, 2003), https://www.nytimes.com/2003/06/11/world/powell-visits -argentina-and-finds-it-wary-on-foreign-policy.html.

14. Guillermo Nielsen, Description of the Process of Debt Restructuring, Address, New York, New York (Mar. 6, 2003), ¶18, Boccuzzi Affidavit Exhibit A, *Allan Applestein et al. v. Republic of Argentina* Case No. 02 Civ. 4124 (Apr. 7, 2003).

15. Guillermo Nielsen, Untitled, Remarks at Emerging Markets Traders Association Annual Meeting (Dec. 4, 2003) (mimeo). ("Earlier this year we put together Consultative Working Groups in Frankfurt, Rome, Zurich, Tokyo and New York.")

16. Republic of Argentina, *The Process of Debt Restructuring*, Communique (June 26, 2003) (mimeo). (Listing active team members Nielsen, Palla, and Madcur and noting the role of Lazard Frères in identifying bondholders.)

17. For a general discussion of the role of the IMF in sovereign debt restructurings, see Sean Hagan, *Sovereign Debt Restructuring: The Centrality of the IMF's Role*, Peterson Institute for International Economics Working Papers 20–13 (July 2020), https://www.piie.com/publications/working-papers/sovereign-debt-restructuring -centrality-imfs-role.

18. IMF, *Minutes of Executive Board Meeting 03/74*, at 23 (July 28, 2003).

19. See IMF, *Minutes of Executive Board Meeting 04/9-1*, at 48–52 (concerns of Mr. Yagi, Japan) and 46–48 (concerns of Mr. Padoan, Italy) (Jan. 28, 2004).

20. For a subsequent discussion of the IMF's approach to DSA, see IMF, *Modernizing the Framework for Fiscal Policy and Public Debt Sustainability Analysis* (Aug. 5, 2011), https://www.imf.org/external/np/pp/eng/2011/080511.pdf.

21. Rieffel at 171. (Poland's October 1994 Brady Plan incorporated an approximate discount of 52%.)

22. Eduardo Borensztein and Paolo Mauro, *Reviving the Case for GDP-Indexed Bonds*, IMF (Sept. 1, 2002), https://www.imf.org/en/Publications/IMF -Policy-Discussion-Papers/Issues/2016/12/30/Reviving-the-Case-for-GDP-Indexed -Bonds-16054.

23. As of December 2012, the total value paid on Argentina's U.S. dollar New York law GDP-linked securities issued in 2005 (CUSIP US040114GM64) was $0.1803974 per $1.0 face amount, or 18% of the nominal amount of bonds restructured in 2005, since $1.0 of such security was given to each participant per each $1 of old bonds tendered into the exchange. Republic of Argentina, Prospectus Supplement to prospectus dated Dec. 27, 2004 (Reg. No. 333-117111) at S-4 and S-66 (Jan. 12, 2005), https://www.sec.gov/Archives/edgar/data/914021

/000095012305000302/y04567e424b5.htm. (In addition to any bonds "you will receive GDP-linked Securities in a notional amount equal to the Eligible Amount of the Eligible Securities you tender that are accepted by Argentina.") (Holders were no longer entitled to payments if "the total amount paid, during the life of the GDP-linked Securities, per unit of GDP-linked Security exceeds 0.48." Payments were made on warrants in 2006, 2007, 2008, 2009, 2011, and 2012. The announcement of the 2012 payment indicated the maximum remaining payment of 0.2996026, implying payments to that date of 0.1803974 based on the 0.48 maximum payout amount specified in the contract. See Republic of Argentina, *Argentina Anuncia El Monto Por Unidad Correspondiente Al Sexto Pago de Los Valores Negociables Vinculados al PBI Emitidos en los Canjes de Deuda de 2005 y 2010*, Press Release (Dec. 2012), https://www.argentina.gob.ar/sites/default/files/comunicado_6to_pago_unidad _pbi.pdf. Ironically, Argentina is thought to have overpaid on these instruments as a result of misreporting of national accounts after 2006. See Ángel Ubide and Eduardo Levy Yeyati, *GDP-Linked Bonds: Can Argentina's Failure Become Greece's Success?*, Peterson Institute for International Economics (Feb. 19, 2015), https://www .piie.com/blogs/realtime-economic-issues-watch/gdp-linked-bonds-can-argentinas -failure-become-greeces-success. ("Inflation has been significantly understated for political reasons . . . but real GDP growth has been overstated. . . . Thus, short-term political incentives to exaggerate growth have led Argentina to overpay on its debt.")

24. While former Argentine officials have said in interviews that the U.S. government was supportive of their proposal, there is nothing in the public domain written by the U.S. Treasury saying it liked Argentina's GDP warrant solution. Suggestive, however, is a White House Council of Economic Advisors white paper trumpeting the benefits of GDP-indexed bonds: Council of Economic Advisors, *Growth-Indexed Bonds: A Primer* (July 8, 2004) (mimeo).

25. Interview with Guillermo Nielsen (various dates 2017–2022, Buenos Aires and New York) on Nielsen's background and hiring of team members.

26. *US President George W. Bush Welcomes Argentine President Nestor Kirchner, in the Oval Office of the White House, Washington, D.C.*, gettyimages (July 23, 2003), https://www.gettyimages.com/detail/news-photo/president-george-w-bush -welcomes-argentine-president-nestor-news-photo/2189281.

27. James Sterngold, *Volcker, the Deal-Making Professor*, N.Y. Times (Mar. 3, 1988), https://www.nytimes.com/1988/03/03/business/volcker-the-deal-making -professor.html.

28. U.S. Department of State, *Biographies of the Secretaries of State: George Pratt Schultz (1920–2021)*, https://history.state/gov/departmenthistory/people/Schultz -george-pratt (Secretary of Labor 1969–1970).

29. Board of Governors of the Federal Reserve System, *Randal K. Quarles Takes*

Oath of Office as Member of the Board of Governors of the Federal Reserve System and Vice Chair for Supervision, Press Release (Oct. 13, 2017), https://www.federalreserve .gov/newsevents/pressreleases/other20171013b.htm.

30. Randal Quarles, *Herding Cats: Collective-Action Clauses in Sovereign Debt— The Genesis of the Project to Change Market Practice in 2001 through 2003*, 73 Law and Contemporary Problems 4, 29, 32–35 (Fall 2010).

31. John Taylor, Undersecretary of Treasury for International Affairs, Prepared Remarks, Emerging Markets Traders Association Annual Meeting (Dec. 5, 2002), https://home.treasury.gov/news/press-releases/po3672.

32. IMF, *IMF Managing Director Issues Statement of Support for Argentina's New Medium-Term Program*, Press Release No. 03/154 (Sept. 10, 2003), https://www.imf .org/en/News/Articles/2015/09/14/01/49/pro3154.

33. For a discussion of the missed payment, see Jon Jeter, *Argentina Defaults on IMF Payment*, Was. Post (Sept. 10, 2003), https://www.washingtonpost.com/ar chive/politics/2003/09/10/argentina-defaults-on-imf-payment/1d278260-2a76 -41bb-a81d-53a094c222a2/; and Marcela Valente, *Economy-Argentina: IMF Deal a Close Victory*, Inter Press Service (Sept. 11, 2003), http://www.ipsnews.net/2003 /09/economy-argentina-imf-deal-a-close-victory/.

34. John Snow, Secretary of Treasury, Statement Regarding the Agreement by Argentina and IMF Management (Sept. 11, 2003), https://home.treasury.gov/news /press-releases/js724.

35. The White House, Press Gaggle by Scott McClellan (Sept. 12, 2003), https:// georgewbush-whitehouse.archives.gov/news/releases/2003/09/20030912-8.html.

36. David Haskel, *Bush Said to Back Tough Argentine Stance on Bondholder Debt Talks, Praise Kirchner*, Bureau of National Affairs (Sept. 25, 2003) (mimeo).

37. Republic of Argentina, to IMF, *Letter of Intent*, at 5 (Sept. 10, 2003), https:// www.imf.org/external/np/loi/2003/arg/03/091003.pdf.

38. *Supra* note 17, at 6 (saying that IMF models are used to determine the "re-structuring envelope").

39. IMF, *Transcript of Managing Director Horst Köhler's Briefing with the Press*, Sept. 12, 2003, https://www.imf.org/en/News/Articles/2015/09/28/04/54/tro30912.

40. The September 15 staff analysis was published later in IMF, *Request for Stand-By Arrangement and Request for Extension of Repurchase Expectation—Staff Report*, Country Report No. 03/392, Dec. 2003, at 57, https://www.imf.org/external /pubs/ft/scr/2003/cro3392.pdf.

41. *Supra* note 19, at 60 and 65 ("It appears the authorities see the Fund-supported program as containing a nominal value ceiling for the primary surplus based on growth assumptions made last September." and "The level of 3 percent is

a minimum and not a ceiling, and we expect the authorities to specify their intention on its increase.")

42. David Haskel, *Upbeat Argentina Warns Bondholders to Expect Unappealing Rescheduling Offer*, Bureau of National Affairs, Sept. 15, 2003 (mimeo).

43. Republic of Argentina, *Lineamientos de la Reestructuración de la Deuda Soberano* (Sept. 22, 2003), at 37, 38, http://cdi.mecon.gov.ar/bases/docelec/mm2291.pdf.

44. Tony Smith, *Holders of Argentine Bonds Reject 25% Redemption Offer*, N.Y. Times (Sept. 23, 2003), https://www.nytimes.com/2003/09/23/business/holders -of-argentine-bonds-reject-25-redemption-offer.html.

45. For example, Abigail McKenna, a portfolio manager at Morgan Stanley Asset Management, was listed as a director on the EMCA's website while also quoted in the financial press as being a member of the ABC. EMCA, *List of Directors 2002*, https://web.archive.org/web/20040401230905/http://emcreditors.com/list _directors_2002.html; and *Bondholder Suit Turns Up the Heat*, 1428 IFR, 77 (Apr. 6, 2002) (mimeo).

46. Argentina Bondholders Committee, Press Release (Sept. 24, 2003), in ¶41, Hranitzky declaration, *EM Ltd., v. Republic of Argentina*, No. 03 Civ. 2507 (S.D.N.Y. Oct. 27, 2003).

47. Argentina Bondholders Committee, Letter to Bondholders (Jan. 31, 2002), https://web.archive.org/web/20040401225351/http://emcreditors.com/list _defaulted_bonds_loans.html.

48. For the TFA's formation and membership, see *L'Associazione*, 2003, https:// web.archive.org/web/20030714182721/http://www.tfargentina.it/chisiamo.php; and list of 466 member bank members as of Feb. 27, 2006, downloaded from www .tfargentina.it (mimeo).

49. Elena Polidori, *Bond Argentini, Offerta Choc*, Repubblica (Sept. 23, 2003), https://ricerca.repubblica.it/repubblica/archivio/repubblica/2003/09/23/bond -argentini-offerta-choc.html.

50. For directors of the ABRA and their backgrounds, see Argentine Bond Restructuring Agency PLC, *Offering Circular* (Apr. 28, 2003), at 53–54 (mimeo). For position of Angel Gurría at the OECD, see *Angel Gurría, Former OECD Secretary-General (CV)*, OECD, https://www.oecd.org/about/secretary-general/former -oecd-secretary-general-angel-gurria-cv.htm. For a discussion of the rationale for the ABRA's formation and Hans Tietmeyer's involvement, see *Default Line*, Institutional Investor (June 30, 2003), at 4, https://www.institutionalinvestor.com /article/b15135sm7b99lp/default-line.

51. For details on how ABRA worked, supra note 50, *Offering Circular*, at 1–56.

52. For the estimated $1.2 billion aggregated holdings of the ABRA, see

Michael Casey, *Cross Interests in Argentina?*, Wall St. J. (Jan. 21, 2005), https://www.wsj.com/articles/SB110627007759432187. There is a discussion of ABRA's fixed fee of 1.6% of holdings (to which a performance fee would be added) in ABRA, *Performance of ABRA Bonds and Determination of ABRA Fees*, July 7, 2005 (mimeo).

53. Angela Pruitt and Michael Casey, *Argentine Bondholders to Face Larger Losses*, Wall St. J. (Oct. 24, 2003), https://www.wsj.com/articles/SB106695458146674300.

54. For a photo of a protestor waving a placard saying "Vulture Funds: Claws Off Argentina" outside of Elliott Associates' offices, see Austin Ryan, *vulture-unds-pro-testor-argentina*, The Globalist (Aug. 5, 2014), https://www.theglobalist.com/country-bankruptcies-and-the-shackles-of-us-law/vulture-funds-protestor-argentina/.

55. *Supra* note 45, IFR (Humes quote).

56. For personal information about Allan Applestein, see Deposition of Allan H. Applestein, Tr. at 3:13–15, 4:18–22, *Allan Applestein TTEE FBO D.C.A. Grantor Trust et al. v. Republic of Argentina*, No. 02 Civ. 4124 (Jan. 31, 2003); and Deepak Gopinath, *The Debt-Crisis Crisis*, Institutional Investor (Aug. 1, 2002), https://www.institutionalinvestor.com/article/b151353w9pfzno/the-debt-crisis-crisis.

57. For claims of Applestein and D.C.A. Grantor Trust, see ¶42, Judgment, *Allan Applestein TTEE FBO D.C.A. Grantor Trust et al. v. Republic of Argentina*, No. 02 Civ. 4124 (S.D.N.Y. Dec. 19, 2003); and Opinion, *Allan Applestein TTEE FBO D.C.A. Grantor Trust v. Prov. of Buenos Aires*, No. 02 Civ. 1773 (TPG) (S.D.N.Y. Apr. 25, 2003).

58. Zach Lowe, *The Death of the Dreier Model*, AM Law Daily (Dec. 9, 2008), https://amlawdaily.typepad.com/amlawdaily/2008/12/the-death-of-th.html.

59. ¶5, Statement of Material Undisputed Facts Pursuant to Local Civil Rule 56.1, *Lightwater Corp. Ltd. v. Republic of Argentina*, No. 02 Civ. 3804 (S.D.N.Y. Aug. 29, 2002); and ¶19, Judgment, *Old Castle Holdings, Ltd. v. Republic of Argentina*. No. 02 Civ. 3808 (S.D.N.Y. Apr. 16, 2003).

60. ¶1, Notice of Removal from Supreme State Court, County of New York, *Macrotecnic Int'l Corp. v. Republic of Argentina*, No. 02 Civ. 5932 (S.D.N.Y. July 26, 2002); and ¶20, Judgment, *Macrotecnic Int'l Corp. v. Republic of Argentina*, No. 02 Civ. 5932 (S.D.N.Y. May 27, 2003).

61. ¶11, Mark Vandevelde declaration, *EM Ltd. v. Republic of Argentina*, No. 03 Civ. 2507 (S.D.N.Y. May 19, 2003).

62. Elizabeth Lesly, *The Darts: Fear, Loathing, and Foam Cups*, Bloomberg (July 10, 1995), https://www.bloomberg.com/news/articles/1995-07-09/the-darts-fear-loathing-and-foam-cups.

63. For press coverage and Dart entities' account of the dispute, see Kenneth N. Gilpin, *Darts Clash with Brazil over Loans*, N.Y. Times (Oct. 23, 1993), https://www.nytimes.com/1993/10/23/business/darts-clash-with-brazil-over-loans.html;

and ¶23, Sharon M. Cornwell declaration, *EM Ltd. v. Republic of Argentina*, No. 03 Civ. 2507 (S.D.N.Y. Aug. 6, 2003).

64. Jane Bussey, *Ecuador Asks Creditors for 40 Percent Discount*, Miami Herald at 2C (Aug. 12, 2000) (mimeo).

65. Transcript, *Commemorating the Life and Service of Thomas P. Griesa*, Draft 2, at 4:23 (S.D.N.Y. Apr. 2, 2018). (Thomas P. Griesa born on Oct. 11, 1930.)

66. Arnold H. Lubasch, *U.S. Judge Finds Bell in Contempt in Informer Case*, N.Y. Times, July 7, 1978, https://www.nytimes.com/1978/07/07/archives/new-jersey -pages-us-judge-finds-bell-in-contempt-in-informer-case.html; *Id.* at 5:22 (Judge Griesa appointed by Nixon in 1972).

67. See generally William W. Buzbee, Fighting Westway (2014); specifically, see 34 (Clean Water Act), 200–203 (Griesa's rulings), 212–14 (New York City use it or lose it of funds for mass transport), and 228–34 (striped bass).

68. E. R. Shipp, *Man in the News; Meticulous Judge in Westway Case*, N.Y. Times (Apr. 22, 1982), https://www.nytimes.com/1982/04/22/nyregion/man-in-the-news -meticulous-judge-in-westway-case.html.

69. ¶27, Transcript of hearing held on Oct. 31, 2003, at 5–15, *Lightwater Corp. v. Republic of Argentina.* No. 02 Civ. 3804 (S.D.N.Y. Dec. 11, 2003) (Jonathan Black-man's argument).

70. *Id.* at 16–28, including quotes at 27:21–22 and 28:1–2 (creditor's counsel argument).

71. *Id.* at 15:22–23 and 16:1–6 (Judge Griesa's statement).

72. *Id.* at 9:16–22 (Roadshow dates and places).

73. Alan Beattie, *Creditors Lose Faith in Argentina's Plans over Debt*, Financial Times (Nov. 2, 2003), http://ezproxy.nypl.org/login?url=https://search.proquest .com/docview/228813289?ccounted=35635.

74. For Abigail McKenna's roles at the EMCA and the ABC, see Pamela Drucker-man, *Emerging Markets Creditors Association Continues Campaign for 'Creditor Rights,'* Wall St. J. (Oct. 31, 2001), https://www.wsj.com/articles/SB1004481596148606800 (citing McKenna as EMCA's chairman); and Pamela Druckerman, *Fed Up Argentine Bondholders Turn to Suing the Government*, Wall St. J. (Aug. 23, 2002), https://www .wsj.com/articles/SB1030052347862157475 (citing McKenna as a leader of the Argentina Bondholders Committee).

75. For policy change, see IMF, *IMF Board Discusses the Good-Faith Criterion under the Fund Policy on Lending into Arrears to Private Creditors*, Public Information Notice No. 02/107 (Sept. 24, 2002), at 3 ("[A] member in arrears would be expected to initiate a dialogue with its creditors prior to agreeing on a Fund-supported program consistent with the principles discussed above. In cases in which an organized negotiating framework is warranted by the complexity of the case and

by the fact that creditors have been able to form a representative committee on a timely basis, there would be an expectation that the member would enter into good faith negotiations with this committee."). For board discussion, see IMF, Minutes of Executive Board Meeting 02/92, Sept. 4, 2002, at 79–121 (mimeo). For staff paper, see IMF, *Fund Policy on Lending into Arrears to Private Creditors—Further Consideration of the Good Faith Criterion* (July 30, 2002), https://www.imf.org/external/pubs /ft/privcred/073002.pdf.

76. For public sources indicating pressure from the EMCA and others in favor of the adoption of bondholder committee prenegotiation of the terms of sovereign debt transactions, see Dow, El-Erian, Miller, McKenna, Siegel, et al., *Bondholder Roles in Sovereign Crisis Management and Prevention*, EMCA (undated), https:// web.archive.org/web/20030204183246/http://www.emcreditors.com/issues_and _initiatives.html (white paper outlining the rationale for and general procedures for setting up creditor committees); Chamberlin, Dallara, Gray, Green, Lackritz, and Mckenna, representing EMTA, the IIF, the IPMA, the BMA, the SIA, and the EMCA, Draft Letter to G7 Finance Ministers and Central Bank Governors (Aug. 13, 2002), https://web.archive.org/web/20030204183246/http://www.emcreditors.com /issues_an_initiatives.html (explaining how a standing creditor advisory group could assemble ad hoc creditor negotiating groups or formal committee when restructurings arise); and *Sovereign Bond Restructuring: The Buy Side Starts to Bite Back*, Euromoney (Apr. 1, 2001), https://www.euromoney.com/article/b1320lk k2jzjv8/sovereign-bond-restructuring-the-buy-side-starts-to-bite-back. ("The key event triggering EMCA's foundation came . . . when Ecuador actually when ahead and restructured its bonds, all by then in default, without any real input from bondholders.")

77. Anne Krueger, *A New Approach to Sovereign Debt Restructuring*, IMF, at 20 (2002), https://www.imf.org/external/pubs/ft/exrp/sdrm/eng/sdrm.pdf. ("To provide greater structure to the negotiating process, consideration could be given to designing the mechanism in a manner that gives a creditors' committee an explicit role in the restructuring process, as is the case in most modern insolvency laws.")

78. Argentina Bondholders Committee, *Restructuring Guidelines* (Dec. 3, 2003), at 12 (mimeo).

79. Approximate numbers calculated as follows: ~$100 billion of debt composed of ~$80 billion principal + ~$20 billion unpaid interest; Argentina proposal 25% of par and no interest implies issuances of $82 x 25% = $20 billion of new bonds; ABC proposal implies 65% of $80 new bonds = $52 billion new bonds + $20 billion new bonds for past due interest, for a total of $72 billion new bonds, over three times the $20 billion in new bonds Argentina was proposing to issue to settle the default.

80. *Supra* note 78, at 7 (Table of 11 restructuring from 1990, with eight Brady

transactions from the 1990s, including Russia 2000, Ecuador 2000, and Uruguay 2003).

81. Guillermo Nielsen, Untitled, Remarks at Emerging Markets Traders Association Annual Meeting (Dec. 4, 2003) (mimeo). (At 9, "We do not intend to impose a unilateral offer.")

82. Jenny Wiggins, *Argentina Finds Common Ground with Bond Holders*, Financial Times (Dec. 5, 2003), https://www.proquest.com/docview/228748078?accoun tid=35635&parentSessionId=Kn2CCH4pvJFhoph%2BIgzbtfX6PW9FmIhjtYUg4r 7AZRQ%3D.

83. The group was formally announced the following month. GCAB, *The Global Committee of Argentina Bondholders Was Formally Established Today in Rome*, Press Release (Jan. 12, 2004) (mimeo).

84. Richard Lapper, *Creditors Unite to Seek Better Deal on Argentine Debt*, Financial Times (Dec. 9, 2003), https://www-proquest-com.i.ezproxy.nypl.org/docview/2 2882356?accountid=35635.

85. Michael Casey, *Argentina's Lavagna, Nielsen Reiterate Tough Debt Stance*, Dow Jones International News (Dec. 12, 2003) (mimeo).

86. IMF, *Reviews of the Fund's Sovereign Arrears Policies and Perimeter* (May 18, 2022), at 22 ("Disagreements over the extent of Argentina's engagement with creditors under the [Good Faith Negotiations] policy delayed completion of that review."); and Guillermo Nielson, *Inside Argentina's Financial Crisis*, Euromoney (Mar. 1, 2006), at 5, https://www.euromoney.com/article/b1321wych2q36z/guillermo -nielsen-exclusive-inside-argentinas-financial-crisis ("The IMF management refused to present the review to the board meeting scheduled for December 2003, even though Argentina superseded most targets.").

87. *Argentine President Lashes Out against IMF*, Telam News Agency (Dec. 23, 2003) (as translated and published by BBC Monitoring International) (mimeo). (Kirchner saying he would not accept "pressures of any kind," "that Argentine[s] have entered a new period and we are no longer able to be chased by the Fund or friends of the Fund," and "We will build an Argentina with what we have . . . with the defenestration of the 'usual profits of doom' who intended to impose foreign remedies.")

88. Kevin Hall, *We Don't Take Orders from U.S., Kirchner Says*, Miami Herald (Jan. 8, 2004), at 11A (mimeo).

89. David Haskel, *World Bank Postpones Consideration of $5 Billion Loan Package to Argentina*, Bureau of National Affairs (Jan. 9, 2004) (mimeo).

90. David Haskel, *Köhler Tells Argentina's Kirchner Loan Review Now Has IMF Management Blessing*, Bureau of National Affairs (Jan. 12, 2004) (mimeo).

91. White House Photo by Eric Draper, *President George W. Bush Meets with President Nestor Kirchner of Argentina in Monterrey, Mexico* (Jan. 13, 2004), https://

georgewbush-whitehouse.archives.gov/news/releases/2004/01/images/20040113
-2_argentina-515h.html.

92. *Supra* note 19, at 2 (length of meeting three hours, thirty minutes).

93. *Id.*, at 1 (list of attendees).

94. *Id.*, at 80 (abstaining directors were "Messrs. Callaghan (AU) [Australia], Kiekens (BE) [Belgium], Kremers (NE) [Netherlands], Padoan (IT) [Italy], Scholar (UK) [United Kingdom], Solheim (NO) [Norway], Yagi (JA) [Japan], Zurbrügg (SZ) [Switzerland]"). The voting power of these countries can be found in IMF, *Appendix VII: Executive Directors and Voting Power on April 30, 2003*, Annual Report 2003 (2003), https://www.imf.org/en/Publications/AREB/Issues/2016/12/31/Annual -Report-of-the-Executive-Board-for-the-Financial-Year-Ended-April-30-2003.

95. *Supra* note 19, at 50 ("beyond mere formalities").

96. *Id.*, at 51 ("guardian of the international financial system").

97. *Id.*, at 47 (agreeing with Mr. Portugal's statement that "the way Argentina's relations with private creditors evolve in the near future will also have a material impact on the emerging markets asset class.")

98. *Argentine Bonds—Italian Bankers Take a Tough Stance*, Wikileaks (Feb. 4, 2004) (mimeo). ("Stock stated that Italian Banking Association (ABI) and its German, U.K., Japanese, and Austrian counterparts, individually and as members of GCAB, will continue to press their respective governments to oppose—as Italy has done—approval of the IMF's first-stage review of Argentina . . . Stock and his counterpart from the Argentine Bondholders Committee, Managing Director of Van Eck Capital Hans Humes, sent a letter two weeks ago to Treasury Secretary Snow requesting an appointment this month to seek U.S. agreement to: recognize GCAB as a legitimate representation of creditors; press the GOA to negotiate with GCAB in good faith; and lobby the GOA against any unilateral Argentine agreement in favor of Argentine domestic bondholders over its foreign bondholders.")

99. *IIF Says IMF Breaking Rules on Argentina*, Central Banking (Jan. 16, 2004), https://www.centralbanking.com/central-banking/news/1428033/iif-imf -breaking-rules-argentina; and Alan Beattie, *IMF Lending to Argentina 'Risks Breaking Rules*,' Financial Times (Jan. 15, 2004), http://ezproxy.nypl.org/login?url=https:// search.proquest.com/docview/228807940?accountid=35635. ("Mr. Dallara also stepped up the IIF's criticism of the International Monetary Fund for continuing to lend to Argentina despite its fractious negotiations with private bondholders who own its defaulted sovereign debt. . . . Mr. Dallara said the IMF was in danger of breaking its own rules about lending to governments in default to creditors, which say that such countries must be making an effort to negotiate in good faith.")

100. *Supra* note 19, at 31.

101. *Id.*, at 39 ("deeply concerned").

102. *Id.*, at 40 ("upward trend").

103. Roberto Lavagna, Construyendo la oportunidad, at 126–29 (1st Ed. Buenos Aires, Sudamericana, 2015).

104. *Supra* note 86, IMF, *Box 3*, at 22.

105. Telephone interview with Nicola Stock (Nov. 29, 2022).

106. Group of Seven, *Statement of G7 Finance Ministers and Central Bank Governors* (Feb. 7, 2004), http://www.g8.utoronto.ca/finance/fm040207.htm.

107. David Haskel, *Argentina Makes Last Minute IMF Payment; Krueger to Push Review of Lending Program*, Bureau of National Affairs (Mar. 10), 2004 (mimeo).

108. Adam Thomson, *Argentina on the Edge*, Financial Times (Mar. 7, 2004) http://ezproxy.nypl.org/login?url=https://search.proquest.com/docview/22888 7538?accountid=35635.

109. Andrew Balls, *Argentina Wins Approval for IMF Loan Payment*, Financial Times (Mar. 22, 2004), http://ezproxy.nypl.org/login?url=https://search.proquest .com/docview/228911854?accountid=35635.

110. For a discussion of Argentina's March 2004 compromise with the IMF, see Paul Blustein, *Argentina Agrees to Pay IMF; Pledge to Negotiate with Bondholders Keeps Loans Flowing to Argentina*, Was. Post (Mar. 10, 2004), https://www.washingtonpost.com/archive/business/2004/03/10/argentina-agrees-to-pay -imf/9967f607-96cd-4c9e-bde6-e5f68e730549/; and Republic of Argentina to IMF, *Letter of Intent* (Mar. 10, 2004), https://www.imf.org/external/np/loi/2004/arg/02/.

111. For the approximate calculation, see *supra* note 79.

112. Tony Smith, *Argentina Threatening to Default on Payment to I.M.F.*, N.Y. Times (Mar. 9, 2004), https://www.nytimes.com/2004/03/09/business/argentina -threatening-to-default-on-payment-to-imf.html.

113. Michael Mussa, *Statement*, Senate Banking Subcommittee on International Trade and Finance Hearing on the Argentine Financial Crisis (Mar. 10, 2004), at 14–15, https://www.banking.senate.gov/imo/media/doc/mussa.pdf (written statement); and *Argentina's Current Economic and Political Situation, Focusing on the Bilateral Relationship between the United States and Argentina: Hearing before the Subcommittee on International Trade and Finance of the Committee on Banking, Housing, and Urban Affairs, United States Senate*, 108th Cong. 23–27 (2004) (Statement of Michael Mussa, Senior Fellow, Institute for International Economics).

3. Kirchner's Triumph

1. Republic of Argentina to IMF, *Letter of Intent*, at 6 (Mar. 10, 2004), https://www.imf.org/External/NP/LOI/2004/arg/02/index.htm (list of investors invited to Buenos Aires).

2. Republic of Argentina, *La Argentina Anucia el Resultado Exitoso de la Oferta de Canje*, Press Release (Mar. 18, 2005), https://www.argentina.gob.ar/sites/default /files/mfin_comunicado_18_marzo_castellano.pdf (list of bank advisers).

3. Roberto Lavagna, Construyendo la oportunidad, at 149 (1st Ed. Buenos Aires, Sudamericana, 2015).

4. Telephone interviews with Stefan Engelsberger (Jan.–Feb. 2021) (hereinafter Engelsberger interview).

5. International Centre for Settlement of Investment Disputes, *Decision on Jurisdiction and Admissibility*, at 41, Case No. ARB/07/5 (2011) (date of Argentina– GCAB meeting in Buenos Aires) (hereinafter ICSID 2011).

6. This paragraph captures the events as described to the author by several participants in the meeting.

7. Interviews with officials and bankers involved with the transaction.

8. Engelsberger interview.

9. Martín Kanenguiser, *Críticas de los Bonistas Alemanes*, La Nación (Feb. 24, 2004) (mimeo).

10. Diego Dillenberger, *Engelsberger Superstar*, 67 Imagen 129–33 (2004) (mimeo); Sergio Langer and Rubén Mira, La Nelly Argentinísima, Vol. 1y2 (Del Nuevo Extremo, 2006); and Michael Casey, *Indebted Argentines Can Get Comic Relief*, Wall St. J. (June 24, 2004), https://www.wsj.com/articles/SB10880391341804666.

11. Cristina Fernández de Kirchner, Sinceramente 197 (Sudamericana 2019).

12. Interviews with Guillermo Nielsen (various dates 2017–2022, Buenos Aires and New York) on Nielsen's background and hiring of team members (hereinafter Nielsen interview).

13. David Cufré, *Gesto Para Seducir a los Bonistas*, Página 12 (June 2, 2004), https://www.pagina12.com.ar/diario/elpais/1-36162-2004-06-02.html.

14. Republic of Argentina, Form 18-K/A Amendment No. 1 (June 10, 2004), at 1–12, https://www.sec.gov/Archives/edgar/data/914021/000090342304000633 /repargentina-18ka1_0610.txt. (The 66% haircut in the discount offer is detailed on pages 7–8, the terms of the no-haircut, retail "par offer" is detailed on pages 6–7, and the terms of the GDP-warrant are detailed on pages 11–12).

15. *Argentina Offers Past-Due Bond Interest*, N.Y. Times (June 2, 2004), https:// www.nytimes.com/2004/06/02/business/argentina-offers-past-due-bond-interest .html.

16. *Dispar Reacción de Grupos de Bonistas*, La Nación (June 15, 2004), https:// www.lanacion.com.ar/economia/dispar-reaccion-de-grupos-de-bonistas-nid61 0332/.

17. *Duro Rechazo de los Bonistas Alemanes a la Oferta Argentina*, La Nación (June 14, 2004), https://www.lanacion.com.ar/economia/duro-rechazo-de-los-bonistas -alemanes-a-la-oferta-argentina-nid610239/.

18. Todd Benson, *Holders' Group Shuns Argentine Debt Plan*, N.Y. Times (June 9, 2004), https://www.nytimes.com/2004/06/09/business/holders-group-shuns-argentine-debt-plan.html.

19. ICSID 2011, at 41–42 (full account of correspondence between GCAB and Argentina).

20. GCAB, *Global Committee of Argentina Bondholders Announces Retention of Bear Stearns as Financial Advisor*, Press Release (June 21, 2004), https://web.archive.org/web/20051226170344/http://www.gcab.org/images/GCAB_-_Press_Release_-_6-21-2004.pdf.

21. Nielsen interview.

22. GCAB, *The Importance of and the Potential for the Expeditious Negotiation of a Consensual and Equitable Restructuring of Argentina's Defaulted Debt*, Position Paper (Aug. 3, 2004), at 5, https://web.archive.org/web/20051226040341/http://www.gcab.org/images/GCAB_White_Paper_Final.pdf (July 5 letter from Argentina saying it was "too late in the process").

23. Diana Gregg, *Taylor Says IMF's Third Review Will Show If Argentina Sticking to Plan*, Bureau of National Affairs (June 10, 2004).

24. Marcela Valente, *Economy-Argentina: Paying the IMF—and Ignoring Its Advice*, Inter Press Service (Aug. 9, 2004), http://www.ipsnews.net/2004/08/economy-argentina-paying-the-imf-and-ignoring-its-advice/; and Adam Thomson, *Argentina Aims to Go It Alone on Debt*, Financial Times (Aug. 12, 2004), https://www.ft.com/content/1d1b8822-ec97-11d8-b35c-00000e2511c8.

25. IMF, *IMF Executive Board Extends Argentina's Repayment Expectations*, Press Release 04/196 (Sept. 17, 2004), https://www.imf.org/en/News/Articles/2015/09/14/01/49/pr04196 (also mimeo of physical copy of actual press release).

26. GCAB, *GCAB Completes Global Road Show and Places Restructuring Framework on Website*, Press Release (Aug. 4, 2004), https://web.archive.org/web/20051226155215/http://www.gcab.org/images/GCAB_-_Press_Release_-_Presentation_on_Website_-_Final_Version_-_8-3-2004.pdf.

27. GCAB, *Global Road Show Presentation*, Presentation (July 30, 2004), at 20 and 40, https://web.archive.org/web/20041024120014/http://www.gcab.org/images/GCAB_Presentation_7.30.04.pdf.

28. Adam Thomson, *An 'Alternative View' on Argentina*, Financial Times (July 21, 2004) (mimeo).

29. Telephone interview with Vladimir Werning (Oct. 13, 2020).

30. Brad Setser, *Has Argentina Changed the Rules of the Sovereign Debt Game?*, Council on Foreign Relations (Feb. 26, 2005), https://www.cfr.org/blog/has-argentina-changed-rules-sovereign-debt-game.

31. Adam Thomson, *Argentina Aims to Go It Alone on Debt*, Financial Times (Aug. 12, 2004), https://www.ft.com/content/1d1b8822-ec97-11d8-b35c-00000e2511c8.

32. *Id.*

33. John Dizard, *Argentina on the Ropes over Bonds*, Financial Times (Sept. 10, 2004), https://www.ft.com/content/d83fed52-035b-11d9-aec4-00000e2511c8.

34. Adam Thomson, *Argentina's Creditors Talk of Legal Action*, Financial Times (Sept. 30, 2004), https://www.ft.com/content/186c11ba-1326-11d9-b869-00000e2511c8.

35. GCAB, *Global Committee of Argentina Bondholders Makes Presentation during IMF/World Bank Meetings*, Press Release (Oct. 7, 2004) (mimeo).

36. GCAB, Presentation on the Occasion of the IMF/World Bank Annual Meetings (Oct. 4, 2004), at 5, https://web.archive.org/web/20041024140227 /http://www.gcab.org/images/WB2004_Presentation_Final.pdf.

37. John Dizard, *Pre-match Bets against Argentina*, Financial Times (Jan. 10, 2005) (mimeo). (This author suggested that the IMF was the original source of the 70% participation rate target.)

38. Republic of Argentina, Prospectus Supplement to prospectus dated Dec. 27, 2004 (Reg. No. 333-117111), at cover page; and iii (Jan. 12, 2005) (listing countries where prospectuses were filed), https://www.sec.gov/Archives/edgar/data/914021/000095012305000302/y04567e424b5.htm.

39. *Argentina: Lavagna Considers Delay in Swap Operation*, COMTEX (Nov. 24, 2004) (mimeo).

40. Roberto Lavagna, Construyendo la oportunidad, at 266.

41. Nielsen interview.

42. *Supra* chapter 2, note 50, Institutional Investor. ("ABRA would vote the pooled bonds on behalf of retail investors, in theory counterbalancing the might of the institutions.")

43. Republic of Argentina, Prospectus Supplement of Jan. 12, 2005, at S-18 (Rights Upon Future Offers).

44. República Argentina, *Oferta de Canje* (roadshow kickoff date of Jan. 12, 2005) (mimeo); and Republic of Argentina, Prospectus Supplement of Jan. 12, 2005, at cover.

45. Roberto Lavagna, Minister of Economy and Production, Start of the Debt Restructuring Road Show, Speech, Buenos Aires (Jan. 12, 2005) (mimeo).

46. Notes from investor meetings (mimeo) (dates and locations of meetings).

47. *Id.* (frequently asked questions).

48. Adam Thomson, *Investor Road Show to Fight Argentine Settlement*, Financial Times (Jan. 16, 2005) (mimeo).

49. GCAB, *GCAB to Begin European Roadshow in Opposition of Argentina's Restructuring Offer*, Press Release (Jan. 21, 2005), https://web.archive.org /web /20051226170556/http://www.gcab.org/images/Press_Release_-_Roadshow_Europe_-_Jan_21_20052.pdf.

50. GCAB, *GCAB to Begin United States Roadshow in Opposition to Argentina's Restructuring Offer*, Press Release (Feb. 8, 2005), https://web.archive.org/web /20051226161813/http://www.gcab.org/images/GCAB_Shadow_Roadshow_US _-_Feb_8_2005.pdf.

51. *Offerta Sui Bond Argentini, la Protesta dei Risparmiatori*, Repubblica (Jan. 11, 2005), https://www.repubblica.it/2005/a/sezioni/economia/bondargentini/bond argentini/bondargentini.html (in English: Offer of Argentinian Bonds, the Savers' Protest).

52. *Tango Bond, Allarme dei Detentori; "Proposta Argentina è una Truffa,"* Repubblica (Jan. 12, 2005), https://www.repubblica.it/2005/a/sezioni/economia/bond argentini/bondstang/bondstang.html (in English: Tango Bond Offer, Alarm of the Holders; "Argentine Proposal Is a Scam").

53. Barbara Ardù, *Rivolta Contro i Tango-bond: l'Offerta è un Grande Imbroglio*, Repubblica (Jan. 13, 2005), https://ricerca.repubblica.it/repubblica/archivio/repub blica/2005/01/13/rivolta-contro-tango-bond-offerta-un-grande.html (in English: Revolt against Tango-Bonds: The Offer Is a Big Rip-off).

54. *Il Rifiuto*, Repubblica (Jan. 14, 2005), https://ricerca.repubblica.it/repubblica /archivio/repubblica/2005/01/14/il-rifiuto.html (in English: The Refusal).

55. *Supra* note 37. ("There is one good indication that the market believes Argentina will wind up having to sweeten the deal. The market price for Argentine debt is hovering around 34 cents on the dollar, above a generous valuation for the deal of 30 cents to 32 cents.")

56. Adam Thomson, *Creditors Cry Foul as Argentina Changes Rules*, Financial Times (Jan. 11, 2005), https://www.ft.com/content/990eebec-6409-11d9-b0ed-000 00e2511c8.

57. Adam Thomson, *Private Creditor to Reject Offer on Debt*, Financial Times (Jan. 20, 2005), https://www.ft.com/content/d24b572e-6b1b-11d9-9357-00000e2511c8.

58. Adam Thomson, *Argentine Swap Criticized by Bond Holders*, Financial Times (Feb. 1, 2005), https://www.ft.com/content/ed0e9ab0-748c-11d9-a769-0000 0e2511c8.

59. Adam Thomson, *Query on Argentine Debt Swap Clause*, Financial Times (Jan. 13, 2005), https://www.ft.com/content/1eefc5b4-65aa-11d9-8ff0-00000e2511c8.

60. *Id.* (Nielsen quote).

61. *Supra* note 46 (notes from meeting with Elliott on Jan. 28, 2005).

62. Lee C. Buchheit, *How Ecuador Escaped the Brady Bond Trap*, Int'l Fin. L. Rev., at 17 (2000); and Lee C. Buchheit and Jeremiah S. Pam, *Uruguay's Innovations*, 19 J. Int'l Banking L. and Reg. 28 (2004).

63. For a general discussion of the use of exit consents in sovereign and corporate bonds, see Lee C. Buchheit and G. Mitu Gulati, *Exit Consents in Sovereign Bond Exchanges*, 48 UCLA L. Rev. 59, 66 (2000). ("Through an exit amendment . . . the

specified majority or supermajority of bondholders exercises its power to amend the old bond—just before those creditors leave the old bond—as an incentive for all other holders to come along with them.")

64. Government of Ukraine, Offering Memorandum, at 5 (Feb. 9, 2000).

65. IMF, *IMF Managing Director Issues Statement on Uruguay*, Press Release 03/57 (Apr. 22, 2003), https://www.imf.org/en/News/Articles/2015/09/14/01/49/pr0357.

66. Republic of Argentina, Addendum to Prospectus Supplement dated Jan. 10, 2005 (Feb. 4, 2005) (mimeo) (announcing presentation to Argentine Congress of draft law later known as the Lock Law).

67. For English translation of the text of the Lock Law, see ¶231-6, Exhibit F at 1, Cohen declaration, *NML Capital, Ltd. v. Republic of Argentina*, No. 08 Civ. 6978 (S.D.N.Y. Oct. 20, 2010) (noting that the Senate and Chamber of Deputies passed the law on Feb. 9 and that it became effective on Feb. 10, 2005).

68. Adam Thomson, *Argentina Looks to Close Bond Loophole*, Financial Times (Feb. 3, 2005) (mimeo).

69. *Id.*

70. ICSID 2011, at 30 (text of TFA "Negotiating Mandate" says investors would be represented "free of charge.")

71. White & Case, *White & Case to Advise Global Committee of Argentina Bondholders in Landmark Restructuring*, Press Release (Aug. 23, 2004), https://web.archive.org/web/20051226171136/http://www.gcab.org/images/WC_Press_Release_8-23-04_3_.pdf.

72. GCAB, *GCAB Releases Legal Memorandum Summarizing Recent Argentine Legislation and Bondholder Remedies*, Press Release (Feb. 15, 2005), https://www.ots.at/presseaussendung/OTE_20050216_OTE0009/gcab-releases-legal-memorandum-summarizing-recent-argentine-legislation-and-bondholder-remedies. ("[T]he Argentine Legislation may well create opportunities for GCAB and its members to pursue a different and more efficient litigation path against Argentina. This path would be based on the possibility of binding arbitration proceedings against Argentina before the International Centre for the Settlement of Investment Disputes ('ICSID'). . . . The legislation specifically prohibits additional or extended versions of the Exchange Offer and also precludes other settlements or private transactions involving the Bonds. . . . [T]he Argentine government appears to be expropriating old debt in favor of new, less valuable, debt.")

73. Republic of Argentina, Prospectus Supplement of Jan. 12, 2005, at S-2.

74. Adam Thomson, *Argentine Growth Prompts New Creditor Demands*, Financial Times (Feb. 17, 2005) (mimeo).

75. Di Beppe Scienza, *Bond Argentini: Un Concambio de Valutare con*

Attenzione, analisiaziendale.it (Dec. 20, 2004), https://www.analisiaziendale.it/bond
_argentini_un_concambio_da_valutare_con_attenzione_1000529.html.

76. Elena Comelli, *Intervista a Giovanni Battista Ponzetto*, QN-Quotidiano Nazionale (Jan. 21, 2005), https://www.beppescienza.eu/documenti/QN-Quotidiano
-Nazionale-2005-01-21.htm.

77. Adam Thomson, *Argentine President Bullish on Debt Swap* (Feb. 25, 2005), https://www.ft.com/content/c3e47d8a-8765-11d9-84f3-00000e2511c8.

78. Adam Thomson, *Creditors Accept Argentina's Debt Offer* (Feb. 27, 2005), https://www.ft.com/content/168f3320-890c-11d9-b7ed-00000e2511c8; for the calculation of the overall participation rate, see note 81 below.

79. *Screeching to the Precipice*, Economist (Feb. 26, 2005), https://www
.economist.com/news/2005/02/28/screeching-to-the-precipice.

80. IMF, *Involving the Private Sector in the Resolution of Financial Crises—
Restructuring International Sovereign Bonds*, EBS/01/3, at 5, 32, 35 (Jan. 11, 2001), www.imf.org/external/pubs/ft/series/03/IPS.pdf (success rates for deals for Pakistan (99%), Ukraine (99%), Ecuador (97%); and Republic of Uruguay, *Prospectus Supplement to Prospectus Dated April 10, 2003, as amended on May 9, 2003* (Reg. No. 333-103739) at S-7 (May 29, 2003), https://www.sec.gov/Archives/edgar
/data/102385/000095012303006844/y87309b3e424b3.htm. (89.2% participation rate on International Offer, 92.6% overall participation).

81. World Bank, *Country Assistance Strategy for the Argentine Republic 2006–
2008: Annex B Sovereign Debt Restructuring and Debt Profile*, Report No. 34015-
AR, at 84 (May 4, 2006), https://web.worldbank.org/archive/website01249/WEB
/IMAGES/1CASAR.PDF ($19.587 billion = $81.835 billion eligible debt [nominal] less $62.248 participation; 76.1% participation rate).

82. República Argentina, *Oferta de Canje—Anuncio Final*, Presentation, at 14–
15 (Mar. 18, 2005) (mimeo). (Participation rates for bonds denominated are in euros, U.S. dollars, and Japanese yen.)

83. *Id.*, at 14 (participation rate for bonds originally denominated in Italian lira).

84. Oral argument hearing transcript, *NML Capital, Ltd. v. Republic of Argentina*, No. 03 Civ. 8845 (S.D.N.Y. Mar. 21, 2005).

85. Oral argument hearing transcript, at 48:24–25 and 49:1–3, *NML Capital, Ltd. v. Republic of Argentina*, No. 03 Civ. 8845 (S.D.N.Y. Mar. 29, 2005).

86. Summary Order, *EM Ltd. v. Republic of Argentina*, No. 05-1525 (2d. Cir. May 13, 2005).

87. ¶1, Complaint, *Capital Ventures Intl. v. Republic of Argentina*, No. 05 Civ. 4085 (S.D.N.Y. Apr. 25, 2005).

88. ¶26, Declaration of Eric S. Meyer, at 1, *Capital Ventures Intl. v. Republic of*

Argentina, No. 05 Civ. 4085 (S.D.N.Y. Apr. 25, 2005) (disclosing Susquehanna Advisors Group, Inc. as the authorized agent of plaintiff CVI).

89. ¶16, Transcript of hearing held on Apr. 25, 2005, at 4 and 39, *Capital Ventures Intl. v. Rep. of Argentina*, No. 05 Civ. 485 (S.D.N.Y. May, 24, 2005) (discussion of Brady collateral and denial of attachment).

90. Adam Thomson, *Argentina Closes Door on $100bn Debt Exchange*, Financial Times (June 3, 2005), https://www.ft.com/content/58e932ae-d3bf-11d9-ad4b-00000e2511c8.

91. Luca Pagni, *Tango Bond, Bufera Sulla Task Force*, Repubblica (Mar. 5, 2005) (in English: Tango Bond, Storm on the Task Force).

92. IMF, Statement by Group of Seven Finance Ministers and Central Bank Governors, EBD/05/39 (Apr. 16, 2005) (mimeo). ("Following the debt exchange, Argentina needs to address the remaining defaulted debt, in line with the lending into arrears policy of the IMF, and undertake structural reforms to ensure sustainable growth.")

93. Adam Thomson, *Argentina Rejects Negotiation with Hold-out Creditors*, Financial Times (Apr. 12, 2005), https://www.ft.com/content/d0aacc4e-ab5b-11d9-893c-00000e2511c8.

94. República Argentina, Boletin Fiscal Cuarto Trimestre de 2006, at cuadro 62.a (2006), https://www.economia.gob.ar/onp/documentos/boletin/2dotrim06/2dotrim06.pdf ($300.605 million outstanding FRANs as of Dec. 31, 2006; there were about $83 million more FRANs outstanding before the closing of Argentina's 2005 exchange offer according to Argentina's 2003 Boletin).

95. ¶24, Statement of Material Facts Pursuant to Local Rule 56.1, at 5, *Montreux Partners, L.P. v. Republic of Argentina*, No. 05 Civ. 4239 (S.D.N.Y. Apr. 10, 2008). ("By allowing Morgan Stanley's appointment to lapse, Argentina effectively froze the rate of interest on the FRANs at Morgan Stanley's last published rate of 50.526% per six-month period—or 101.52% per year.")

96. ¶1, Complaint, *NML Capital, Ltd. v. Republic of Argentina*, No. 05 Civ. 2434 (S.D.N.Y. Feb. 28, 2005).

97. As of 2006, soon after the suit was filed, FYI Ltd. reportedly was 100% owned by Yale University Endowment (Yale University IRS Form 990 2006 at Part IX), while later the university reported that it was an owner of New FYI Ltd., another Bracebridge fund (Yale University IRS Form 990 2012, Schedule R, Part IV). See also *Breaking Argentina*, http://www.33wallstreet.org/uploads/2/0/5/2/20520884/bracebridge_argentina.pdf (reporting that "Yale owns 100% of New FYI Ltd, a Cayman Islands hedge fund managed by Bracebridge Capital. New FYI Ltd in turn owns 97.87% of FYI Ltd., which makes Yale's share of the settlement $358.6 million, an estimated $315 million gain on its original investment"). Thomás Lukin, *Buitres*

con Título Universitario, Página 12 (Sept. 10, 2017), https://www.pagina12.com.ar /61998-buitres-con-titulo-universitario (reporting that FYI Ltd. was controlled by Yale). Generally, see also Sabrina Willmer and Tom Moroney, *The Secretive Hedge Fund That's Generating Huge Profits for Yale,* Bloomberg (Feb. 4, 2016). That Bracebridge manages FYI Ltd. and New FYI Ltd. is also evidenced in Bracebridge Capital LLC, Form ADV, Rev. 10/2017 filed with the SEC, accessed on Mar. 29, 2019 (mimeo). See also ¶1, Complaint, *FFI Fund Ltd., and FYI Ltd. v. Republic of Argentina,* No. 05 Civ. 3328 (S.D.N.Y. Mar. 29, 2005).

98. ¶44, Declaration of Michael Straus, at 1, *EM Ltd. v. Republic of Argentina,* No. 14 Civ. 8303 (S.D.N.Y. Feb. 11, 2016).

99. ¶1, Complaint, *Montreux Partners, L.P. v. Republic of Argentina,* No. 05 Civ. 4239 (S.D.N.Y. Apr. 28, 2005).

100. As of Aug. 30, 2007, Elliott, Bracebridge, and Montreux were listed members of American Task Force Argentina (ATFA), a group set up to lobby lawmakers for various measures to force Argentina pay its holdout creditors. See *About Us,* American Task Force Argentina, https://web.archive.org/web/20070830195022 /http://atfa.org/about/. For further discussion of ATFA, see chapters 7 and 9 in this volume.

101. See chapters 8 through 11, in which, inter alia, Bracebridge's Olifant Fund joins Elliott as an initial pari passu plaintiff, while Montreux files an amicus brief in favor of Elliott's position; the three firms also appeared to act jointly in the litigation of the value of the FRANs, particularly during 2008 and 2009.

102. ¶1, Complaint, at 2–9, *NML Capital, Ltd. v. Republic of Argentina,* No. 07 Civ. 1910 (S.D.N.Y. Mar. 5, 2007) (detailing dates and amounts of Elliott's global bond purchases in 2005).

103. Nouriel Roubini and Brad Setser, Bailouts or Bail-Ins?: Responding to Financial Crises in Emerging Economies (2004).

104. *Supra* note 30, at 5.

105. Nouriel Roubini, *The Successful End of the Argentine Debt Restructuring Saga . . . ,* EconoMonitor (Mar. 2, 2005), https://web.archive.org /web/201609 01181210/http://www.economonitor.com/nouriel/2005/03/02/the-successful-end -of-the-argentine-debt-restructuring-saga/.

106. Monte Reel and Michael A. Fletcher, *Anti-U.S. Protests Flare at Summit,* Was. Post (Nov. 5, 2005), https://www.washingtonpost.com/archive/politics/2005/11/05 /anti-us-protests-flare-at-summit/b98bec64-9009-4784-a568-fa3b8c16ea27/.

107. Larry Rohter, *Argentine President Ousts the Architect of the Country's Economic Recovery,* N.Y. Times (Nov. 29, 2005), https://www.nytimes.com/2005/11/29 /business/worldbusiness/argentine-president-ousts-the-architect-of-the.html.

108. IMF, *Argentina Announces Its Intention to Complete Early Repayment of Its*

Entire Outstanding Obligations to the IMF, Press Release 05/278 (Dec. 15, 2005) (corrected Dec. 16, 2005), https://www.imf.org/en/News/Articles/2015/09/14/01/49/pro5278.

109. Monte Reel, *Argentine Power Duo Taking a Defiant Tone President Kirchner and His Senator Wife Speak Their Minds at Home and Abroad,* Was. Post (Sept. 27, 2006), https://www.washingtonpost.com/archive/politics/2006/09/27/argentine-power-duo-taking-a-defiant-tone-span-classbankheadpresident-kirchner-and-his-senator-wife-speak-their-minds-at-home-and-abroadspan/423d963e-0742-4129-9013-d92e805aaaa2/.

4. Backstory

1. ¶100, Transcript of hearing held Mar. 17, 18, 19, 24, 25, at 728: 16–23, *Elliott Associates, L.P. v. The Republic of Peru,* No. 96 Civ. 7917 (S.D.N.Y. Apr. 14, 1998) (hereinafter *Elliott v. Peru Hearing Transcript*). (Transcript of hearings held on Mar. 17, 18, 19, 24, and 25, 1998.)

2. *Id.* 728:24–729:6.

3. *Elliott Assoc. L.P. v. Republic of Peru,* 12 F. Supp. 2d 328 (S.D.N.Y. 1998). (Noting that during January through March 1996 Elliott purchased $20,682,699.04 principal amount of defaulted Peruvian debt for a combined cost of $11,431,202.08.)

4. There is an elliptical reference to Elliott's role in Vietnam in Saskia Sassen, *A Short History of Vultures,* Foreign Policy (Aug. 3, 2014), https://foreignpolicy.com/2014/08/03/a-short-history-of-vultures/.

5. Pravin Banker, *About the Author,* Medium (Jan. 4, 2017), https://medium.com/@pravinbanker/about-the-author-e4a22a05280b. ("Pravin graduated from Columbia University with a master's degree in engineering and joined IBM Corporation, where he spent almost two decades. . . . On leaving IBM, he formed his own company, Pravin Banker Associates Ltd.")

6. *Pravin Banker Assoc. v. Banco Popular del Peru,* 165 B.R. 379 (S.D.N.Y. 1994).

7. *Pravin Banker Assoc. v. Banco Popular del Peru,* 9 F. Supp. 2d 300 (S.D.N.Y. 1998).

8. Letter from Mark A. Cymrot, to minister Carlos Boloña, on external debt litigation (Oct. 13, 2000), at 3, in Annexo No. 1, Republic of Peru, *Informe Decreto de Urgencia Nº 083-2000, Decreto Supreme Nº 106-2000-EF* (mimeo). ("In December 1998, unable to locate any Peruvian property, Pravin accepted a settlement equivalent to Brady terms.")

9. *Avoiding the Nightmare Scenario,* 11 Int'l Fin. L. Rev. 19 (1992). ("High on everyone's list of nightmares was the possibility that individual banks might ignore the requests for cooperation and begin commencing legal proceedings against their

respective borrowers, accompanied by attachments or similar seizures of the borrowers' property and external revenues. If the cry of *sauve qui peut* were to ring out, the resort to litigation might become infectious and unstoppable.")

10. Felix Salmon, *Elliott's Associates' Aggression Captures Low-Risk Returns*, Euromoney (Feb. 1, 2004), https://www.euromoney.com/article/b1320rn8zr43ws/elliott-associates-aggression-captures-low-risk-returns.

11. *Morgan Stanley Debt Group*, N.Y. Times (Sept. 26, 1990), https://www.nytimes.com/1990/09/26/business/morgan-stanley-debt-group.html.

12. Brief of the New York Clearing House Association as amicus curiae in support of the petition for rehearing, at cover, *Allied Bank International et al. v. Banco Credito Agricola de Cartago et al.*, No. 83-7714 (2d Cir. May 21, 1984).

13. Memorandum in Support of the Motion of Defendants-Appellees for an Order Dismissing the Appeal in This Action or, in the Alternative, Granting a Stay of the Appeal and Remanding to the District Court and Granting Attorneys' Fees and Costs, at 2, 3, and 8, *Allied Bank International et al. v. Banco Credito Agricola de Cartago et al.*, No. 83-7714 (2d Cir. Oct. 24, 1983) (170 banks overall and 39 banks in the particular facility subject to the suit; $50,000 of legal expenses).

14. *Allied Bank Int'l v. Banco Credito Agricola de Cartago*, 566 F. Supp. 1440 (S.D.N.Y. 1983). (Judge Griesa denies motion for summary judgment; amount in dispute is less than $5 million.)

15. *Supra* note 12.

16. Brief for the United States as amicus curiae in support of the petition for rehearing and suggestion for rehearing En Banc, at 4, *Allied Bank International et al. v. Banco Credito Agricola de Cartago et al.*, No. 83-7714 (2d. Cir. June 11, 1984). ("The policy of the United States with respect to private debt . . . places great weight upon the voluntary participation of private lenders in the debt restructuring process.")

17. *Allied Bank Int'l v. Banco Credito Agricola de Cartago*, 757 F.2d 516 (2d Cir. 1985).

18. See Lee C. Buchheit, *The Sharing Clause as a Litigation Shield*, 9 Int'l L. Rev. 15 (1990). (Regarding the effect of sharing clauses when included in syndicated loans, "By forcing a maverick litigant to share the proceeds of its recovery with other banks, sovereign borrowers and bank advisory committees have effectively replicated a protection from disruptive litigation which, in a domestic context, is usually conveyed by bankruptcy or insolvency laws.")

19. Joseph P. Fried, *Robert W. Sweet, Mayor's Deputy Turned Federal Judge, Is Dead at 96*, N.Y. Times (Mar. 25, 2019), https://www.nytimes.com/2019/03/25/obituaries/robert-w-sweet-dead.html.

20. *Pravin Banker Assoc. v. Banco Popular del Peru*, 165 B.R. 379 (S.D.N.Y. 1994).

21. *Elliott Assoc., L.P. v. Republic of Panama*, 975 F. Supp. 332 (S.D.N.Y. 1997).

22. *Elliott Assoc., L.P. v. Republic of Peru*, 961 F. Supp. 83 (S.D.N.Y. 1997).

23. *Id.* ("Some discovery in this action has been undertaken, and the defendants seek further discovery, principally relating to the role of Michael Straus, counsel to Elliott, pointing out that Straus has been involved in the following cases involving the collection of sovereign debt: [listing the Allied Bank case and cases against Paraguay, Ecuador, Congo, Ivory Coast, Poland, Panama, and Zaire].")

24. Deposition of Jay H. Newman, *Elliott Assoc., L.P. v. Republic of Peru*, No. 96 Civ. 7917 (S.D.N.Y. July 22, 1997).

25. ¶61, Declaration of Michael Straus, *Elliott Assoc., L.P. v. Republic of Peru*, No. 96 Civ. 7917 (S.D.N.Y. Sept. 25, 1997).

26. ¶46, Affidavit of Keith Fogerty, *Elliott Assoc., L.P. v. Republic of Peru*, No. 96 Civ. 7917 (S.D.N.Y. Sept. 2, 1997); and ¶46, Affidavit of Peter J. Grossman, *Elliott Assoc., L.P. v. Republic of Peru*, No. 96 Civ. 7917 (S.D.N.Y. Sept. 2, 1997).

27. Deposition of Timothy B. Web, *Elliott Assoc., L.P. v. Republic of Peru*, No. 96 Civ. 7917 (S.D.N.Y. July 7, 1997).

28. ¶81, Letter filed to Judge Sweet from Mark A. Cymrot, *Elliott Assoc., L.P. v. Republic of Peru*, No. 96 Civ. 7916 (S.D.N.Y. Oct. 24, 1997) (regarding testimony of Mr. Hermann and Mr. Wells).

29. *Elliott v. Peru Hearing Transcript*, at 1.

30. Richard Pérez-Peña, *U.S. Attorney Leaving Post In Manhattan*, N.Y. Times (Dec. 3, 1992), https://www.nytimes.com/1992/12/03/nyregion/us-attorney-leaving -post-in-manhattan.html.

31. *Elliott v. Peru Hearing Transcript*, at 15:16–23, 16:1–21, 17:1–13, 18:16–19:9, 20:18–21:1, and 21:12–15.

32. *Supra* note 11 (on Newman's Morgan Stanley team).

33. *Elliott v. Peru Hearing Transcript*, at 185:11–186:10 (on setting up Percheron with Biraben).

34. *Elliott v. Peru Hearing Transcript*, at 430:8–431:13 (on Newman setting up Romlease with Biraben).

35. *Elliott v. Peru Hearing Transcript*, at 398:16–22 (on Biraben organizing Water Street).

36. *Elliott v. Peru Hearing Transcript*, at 400:1–3 and 400:16–21; and Deposition of Jay Newman, at 405:13–406:10; and *Elliott Assoc., L.P. v. Republic of Peru*, No. 96 Civ. 7917, Sept. 3, 1997 (establishing that Newman had no official role with Water Street).

37. Cases filed by Water Street against sovereigns: ¶1, Complaint, *Water Street Bank & Trust v. People's Republic of Congo*, No. 93 Civ. 1894 (S.D.N.Y. Mar. 18, 1994); ¶1, Complaint, *Water Street Bank & Trust v. Republic of Ivory Coast*, No. 94 Civ. 2376 (S.D.N.Y. Apr. 4, 1994); ¶1, Complaint, *Water Street Bank & Trust v. Polish People's*

Republic et al., No. 94 Civ. 2428 (S.D.N.Y. Apr. 6, 1994); ¶1, Complaint, *Water Street Bank & Trust v. Republic of Poland et al.*, No. 95 Civ. 42 (S.D.N.Y. Jan. 4, 1995); ¶1, Complaint, *Water Street Bank & Trust v. Republic of Panama*, No. 94 Civ. 2609 (S.D.N.Y. Apr. 12, 1994); and ¶1, Complaint, *Water Street Bank & Trust v. Banco Central del Ecuador et al.*, No. 95 Civ. 5253 (S.D.N.Y. July 14, 1995).

38. ¶14, *Water Street Bank & Trust v. Republic of Panama*, No. 94 Civ. 2609 (S.D.N.Y. Dec. 22, 1994); and ¶29, *Water Street Bank & Trust v. Republic of Panama*, No. 94 Civ. 2609 (S.D.N.Y. Feb. 15, 1995). (Judge Baer's order to provide information on the owners of Water Street and dismissal of the suit when the information was not provided.)

39. *Elliott v. Peru Hearing Transcript*, at 412:9–11 (establishing that Water Street was liquidated after Judge Baer's decision).

40. *Elliott v. Peru Hearing Transcript*, at 254:19–21, 257:6–258:8 (on joining Elliott and meeting Michael Straus).

41. *Elliott v. Peru Hearing Transcript*, at 388:17–22, 398:8–15 (did not discuss litigation with Singer at first meeting, and suing was not a strategy).

42. *Elliott v. Peru Hearing Transcript*, at 402:16–21, 403:5–404:2, and 404:9–405:7 (regarding conversations with Christian Veilleux and Michael Straus while at Water Street about both investments and lawsuits).

43. *Elliott v. Peru Hearing Transcript*, at 739:5–17.

44. *Elliott Assoc. L.P. v. Republic of Peru*, 12 F. Supp. 2d 328 (S.D.N.Y. 1998).

45. *Id.*

46. ¶161, Notice of Appeal, *Elliott Assoc. v. Banco de la Nacion*, No. 96 Civ. 7916 (S.D.N.Y. Sept. 18, 1998).

47. Audio tape: Hearing, *Elliott Assoc. v. Banco de la Nacion*, No. 98-9268 and 98-9319 (2d Cir. May 5, 1999).

48. *Elliott Assoc., L.P. v. Banco de la Nacion*, 194 F.3d 363 (2d Cir. 1999).

49. *Elliott Assoc., L.P. v. Banco de la Nacion*, 194 F.R.D. 116 (S.D.N.Y. June 1, 2000). ("[D]uring 1997, Elliott, through its wholly-owned company Manchester Securities Corp., had retained a firm in Albany, New York, to lobby the New York State Legislature to amend [the relevant section of New York's General Obligations Law], allegedly in order to overcome a prior ruling of this Court in a separate case. . . . The lobbying materials submitted to the legislature in support of the amendment did not disclose the relationship of Manchester Securities to Elliott nor that Elliott was seeking a benefit in a pending lawsuit. The lobbying effort was successful and an amended version of that section of the General Obligations Law . . . was signed by Governor Pataki on July 29, 1997.")

50. ¶120, Judgment, *Elliott Assoc., L.P. v. Republic of Peru*, No. 96 Civ. 7916.

51. For further details on Elliott's four-prong attack, see ¶265, Supplemental Declaration by Mark A. Cymrot, at 4, *Elliott Assoc., L.P. v. Republic of Peru*, No. 96

Civ. 7917 (S.D.N.Y. Oct. 3, 2000); *First Affirmation of Andrew Elliot Tracey Hearn*, at 9, *Elliott Assoc., L.P. and (1) Banco de la Nacion (2) The Republic of Peru*, Folio 2000, No. 962 (High Court of Justice Queen's Bench Division Commercial Court Sept. 11, 2000), at 2, 8, 9; *supra* note 10, at 5–6; and ¶255 Declaration of Kirsten N. Geyer in Emergency Affidavit of James L. Kerr, at 8, *Elliott Assoc., L.P. v. Banco de la Nacion*, No. 96 Civ. 7916 (S.D.N.Y. Sept. 28, 2000) (details on blocked payment amount and relevant jurisdictions).

52. Jane Bussey, *Legal Fight with Hedge Fund Puts Peru on Brink of Default*, Miami Herald, at 1c (Sept. 28, 2000) (mimeo); and Felix Salmon, *Peru, Dodging Legal Restraint, Tries to Make Coupon Payments*, Bridge News (Sept. 13, 2000), https://www.felixsalmon.com/clips/perubrady.html (reporting that Peru delayed the coupon payment to buy time).

53. Elliott Assocs., L.P., General Docket No. 2000/QR/92 (Court of Appeals of Brussels, 8th. Section, Sept. 26, 2000).

54. Settlement agreement between the Republic of Peru, Banco de la Nacion, and Elliott Associates, L.P. (Sept. 29, 2000) (mimeo); and Philip S. Kaplan, *Memorandum to Minister Carlos Boloña* (Oct. 11, 2000), in Ministerio de Economía Y Finanzas del Perú, *Reporte Final Sobre el Caso Elliott Associates* (mimeo).

55. G. Mitu Gulati, and Kenneth N. Klee, *Sovereign Piracy*, 56 The Business Lawyer, 635, 638 (2001), https://www.jstor.org/stable/i40030151.

56. Declaration of Andreas F. Lowenfeld, at 11–12, *Elliott Assoc., L.P. v. Banco de la Nacion*, No. 96 Civ. 7916 (S.D.N.Y. Aug. 31, 2000), available in ¶10, Exhibit 43, Declaration of Robert Cohen, *NML Capital, Ltd. v. Republic of Argentina*, No. 14 Civ. 8601 (S.D.N.Y. Feb. 27, 2015).

57. Lee C. Buchheit and Jeremiah S. Pam, *The Pari Passu Clause in Sovereign Debt Instruments*, 53 Emory L. J., 871, 894–917, Special Edition (2004).

58. See chapter 10 for the outcome when the market eventually addressed the ambiguity of the meaning of the pari passu clause.

59. Anne Krueger, First Deputy Managing Director, IMF, *A New Approach to Sovereign Debt Restructuring*, Address given at the National Economists Club Annual Members' Dinner at the American Enterprise Institute, Washington, D.C. (Nov. 26, 2001), https://www.imf.org/en/News/Articles/2015/09/28/04/53/sp112601.

60. Michael M. Chamberlin, EMTA Executive Director, *The IMF's Sovereign Bankruptcy Proposal and the Quest for More Orderly Work-Outs*, Remarks at the UN Global Conference on Finance for Development Panel on Orderly Work-Outs (Jan. 23, 2002), at 3 (mimeo). ("[T]he danger of hold-out or 'rogue' creditors has been highly exaggerated.")

61. ¶49, *Exhibit A, Declaration of Dennis H. Hranitzky, EM Ltd. v. Republic of Argentina, No. 03 Civ. 2507 (S.D.N.Y. Jan. 5, 2004)* (Letter from Jonathan Blackman to David W. Rivkin dated Oct. 2, 2003).

62. *Id., Exhibit B* (Letter from David Rivkin to Jonathan Blackman dated Oct. 3, 2003).

63. *Id., Exhibit O* (Letter from Jonathan Blackman to Judge Thomas P. Griesa dated Oct. 14, 2003).

64. Hearing Transcript, at 1:15–22, *Allan Applestein v. Republic of Argentina*, No. 02 Civ. 1773 (S.D.N.Y. Jan. 15, 2004).

65. *State of Interest of the United States, Brief of the Federal Reserve Bank as Amicus Curiae, and Brief of the New York Clearing House Assoc.*, Jan. 12, 2004, in ¶271, Exhibits A, B, and C, Declaration of Carmine D. Boccuzzi, *NML Capital, Ltd. v. Republic of Argentina*, No. 08 Civ. 6978 (S.D.N.Y. Dec. 10, 2010).

66. ¶43, Letter from Kevin Reed to Judge Thomas P. Griesa, *Macrotecnic v. Republic of Argentina*, No. 02 Civ. 5932 (S.D.N.Y. Jan. 14, 2004).

67. ¶1 Complaint, *NML Capital, Ltd. v. Republic of Argentina*, No. 03 Civ. 8845 (S.D.N.Y. Nov. 7, 2003).

68. *Supra* note 64, at 14:10–11. ("It seems to me a very odd interpretation of the pari passu clause.")

5. Raid on the Argentine Central Bank

1. *Willie Sutton*, Wikipedia, https://en.wikipedia.org/wiki/Willie_Sutton.

2. *What We Do*, Federal Reserve Bank of New York, https://www.newyorkfed .org/aboutthefed/whatwedo.html; and Bob Eisenbeis, *Here's What We Know and Don't Know Yet about the Treasury Securities That Were Moved Out of the NY Fed*, Business Insider (Mar. 15, 2014), https://www.businessinsider.com/ny-fed-custody -104-billion-treasuries-2014-3.

3. IMF, *Argentina Announces Its Intention to Complete Early Repayment of Its Entire Outstanding Obligations to the IMF*, Press Release 05/278 (Dec. 15, 2005) (corrected Dec. 16, 2005), https://www.imf.org/en/News/Articles/2015/09/14/01/49 /pro 5278.

4. Republic of Argentina, Decree 1601/2005, "Dispónse la cancelación total de la dueda contraída con el fondo monetario internacional con reservas de libre disponibilidad que excedan el porcentaje establecido en el articulo 4⁰ de la ley N° 23.928 y sus modificaciones" (Dec. 15, 2005), http://servicios.infoleg.gob.ar/infolegInternet /anexos/110000-114999/112208/norma.htm (English: Decree 1601/2005, "The total cancellation of the debt contracted with the International Monetary Fund shall be made with freely available reserves that exceed the percentage established in Article 4 law No. 23,928 and its amendments").

5. The transcript of the hearing of the Southern District court on December 30, 2005, Judge Barbara Jones presiding, is not publicly available because it is still sealed by the court. However, the events that occurred are referred to in a

transcript of hearing, at 3:2–10, 17:16, *EM Ltd. v. Republic of Argentina*, No. 03 Civ. 2507 (S.D.N.Y. Jan. 12, 2006).

6. *EM Ltd. v. Rep. of Argentina*, 473 F.3d 463 (2d Cir. 2007) ($105 million attached amount).

7. *About BIS—Overview*, Bank for International Settlements, https://www .bis.org/about/index.htm?m=1%7C1; and *NML Capital, Ltd. v. BCRA*, 652 F.3d 172 (2d Cir. 2011) (regarding Argentina's shifting of assets to the Bank for International Settlements).

8. Transcript of hearing, at 3:24–4:3, *EM Ltd. v. Republic of Argentina*, No. 03 Civ. 2507 (S.D.N.Y. Jan. 12, 2006) (from "who wants to lead off" through "Let's hear from the affirmative in favor of attachment") (hereinafter January 12, 2006, Hearing).

9. *Id.*, at 4–15 (beginning of Rivkin's argument).

10. *Id.*, at 15:8–17:20 (from "textbook example" through "that is their assertion").

11. *Id.*, at 29:18–23 (Full text: "The Republic has irrevocably agreed not to claim and has irrevocably waived such immunity to the fullest extent permitted by the laws of such jurisdiction and consents generally for the purposes of the Foreign Sovereign Immunities Act to the giving of any relief or the issuance in any process in any proceeding or related judgment.")

12. *Id.*, at 35:2–43:5 (from "I was not planning on taking the floor" through "nor was it used").

13. *Id.*, at 43:6–9 ("And that money, as the Court noted, has been used, the amount has obviously ebbed and flowed over the years for central banking activities, buying and selling currencies, receiving reserve deposits of Argentine banks.")

14. *Id.*, at 45–49 (Neuhaus argument).

15. *Id.*, at 52:11–53:17 ("I found it amusing" through "Could I respond for two seconds to that, your Honor?").

16. *Id.*, at 58:4–7 ("What do you want to do about that" through "and not lose the benefit of that").

17. *Fontana v. Republic of Argentina*, 415 F.3d 238 (2d Cir. 2005). (This consolidation of two appeals dealt in essence with whether the plaintiffs needed to receive an authorization letter from the Depository Trust Company, the registered holder of the bonds, in order to have standing to sue; the case was remanded to Judge Griesa on technical grounds, and Argentina subsequently withdrew its demand for such authorization letters.)

18. One of the suits with fraudulent claims was filed in 2006 against Argentina was based on a falsified brokerage statement. See ¶44, Transcript of hearing held May 24, 2011, at 9:16–19, *Michelle Colella et al. v. Republic of Argentina*, No. 04 Civ. 2710 (S.D.N.Y. June 30, 2011) ("the bank states that the bank statements attached

to Mr. Forgione's declarations have been altered by changing the name and address on the statements"). In addition, in 2020 the court dismissed the cases brought by Michelle Colella et al. and by Marcelo Ruben Rigueiro et al. as fraudulent, as detailed in ¶96, Memorandum & Order, *Michelle Colella et al. v. Republic of Argentina*, No. 04 Civ. 2710 (S.D.N.Y. Aug. 13, 2020).

19. January 12, 2006, Hearing, at 58:8–59:19.

20. *Id.*, at 60:7–19.

21. For text of the act and the House report, see Foreign Sovereign Immunities Act, 28 U.S.C. §§ 1602–1611 (1976), https://www.govinfo.gov/content/pkg/USCODE -2011-title28/html/USCODE-2011-title28-partIV-chap97.htm; and United States: Congressional Committee Report of the Jurisdiction of the United States in Suits against Foreign States, in *International Legal Materials*, Vol. 15, No. 6 (Nov. 1976), at 1398–416, http://www.jstor.org/stable/20691670.

22. *Weltover, Inc. v. Republic of Argentina*, 941 F.2d 145, 149 (2d Cir. 1991). ("We have construed the FSIA to mean that 'if the activity is one in which a private person could engage, [the foreign sovereign] is not entitled to immunity," citing Texas Trading, 647 F.2d at 309.)

23. *EM Ltd. v. Republic of Argentina*, 473 F.3d 463 (2d Cir. 2007) (hearing date Aug. 29, 2006, and list of parties).

24. Audio Recording: Motion to Vacate Attachment, held by the Second Circuit Court of Appeals, *EM Ltd. v. Republic of Argentina*, No. 06-0403-cv (Aug. 29, 2006).

25. *Roy T. Englert Jr.*, Resume, Robbins Russell, https://www.robbinsrussell.com (accessed Apr. 21, 2020; similar information now available at Kramerlevin.com).

26. Transcript of motion to vacate attachment hearing, at 4:6–24, *EM Ltd. v. Republic of Argentina*, No. 06-403 (2d Cir. Aug. 29, 2006) (hereinafter August 29, 2006, Hearing).

27. *Id.*, at 9:10–11.

28. *Id.*, at 10:15–18. (Paraphrased, for clarity, from "Right, but why is the Republic of Argentina transacting business with the International Money Fund? Why isn't that a sovereign act opposed to a commercial act?")

29. *Id.*, 17:20–21.

30. *Id.*, at 29:25–30:2. (Paraphrased from "Didn't they release it? Or didn't it changed the character of the property, since it wasn't required to support the currency?")

31. *Id.*, at 30:20–22.

32. *Id.*, at 44:19–25.

33. *Id.*, at 45:1–4.

34. *Id.*, at 46:12–13.

35. *Id.*, at 47:8–20.

36. *Id.*, at 52:24–53:2.

37. *Id.*, at 55:24–56:3.

38. *Id.*, at 56:5–14.

39. *First Nat. City Bank v. Banco Para El Comercio Exterior de Cuba,* 462 U.S. 611 (1983).

40. ¶1, Complaint, *EM, Ltd. and NML Capital, Ltd. v. Banco Central de la Republica Argentina and the Republic of Argentina,* No. 06 Civ. 7792 (S.D.N.Y. Sept. 28, 2006).

41. ¶24, Transcript of hearing held on Nov. 3, 2006, at 19:10–15, *EM Ltd. et al. v. Banco Central de la Republica Argentina,* No. 06 Civ. 7792 (S.D.N.Y. Nov. 28, 2006). ("I would like to just take a minute to say that it has become a concern to me and in a broad sense where these cases are going. And I have asked to have a meeting of all the parties, the lawyers for all the parties in all the cases. And the reason for that is, I want to know what people have in mind.")

42. *Id.*, at 20:8–13.

43. *Id.*, at 20:14–24.

44. *Id.*, at 21:5–22:7.

45. *Id.*, at 22:8–9.

46. *Id.*, at 22:10–24.

47. *Id.*, at 22:25–23:5.

48. ¶23, Transcript of hearing held on Nov. 9, 2006, at 8:21–10:3, *EM Ltd. et al. v. Banco Central de la Republica Argentina,* No. 06 Civ. 7792 (S.D.N.Y. Nov. 27, 2006).

49. *Id.*, at 32:6–12.

50. *EM Ltd. v. Rep. of Argentina,* 473 F.3d 463 (2d Cir. 2007).

51. ¶133, Transcript of hearing held on Feb. 2, 2007, at 18:17–19:4, *EM Ltd. v. the Republic of Argentina,* No. 06 Civ. 2507 (S.D.N.Y. March 13, 2007).

52. While the funds continued to be subject to restraint, due to a stipulation signed by the parties in January 2006, the Central Bank of Argentina was allowed to use this $105 million for intraday transactions. See *supra* note 50.

6. All Plaintiffs Big and Small

1. Author's calculations. See also Gregory Makoff and Mark C. Weidemaier, *Mass Sovereign Debt Litigation: A Computer-Assisted Analysis of the Argentina Bond Litigation in the U.S. Federal Courts 2002–2016* (2022), U.C. Davis L. Rev. (Forthcoming), https://ssrn.com/abstract=4157688.

2. Telephone interview with Patricia Rosito Vago (Oct. 20, 2020) (regarding originating the cases and partnership with Dreier); and Testimony of Michael C.

Spencer of July 20, 2018, ¶4–5, Exhibit 3, at 5, *Milberg LLP v. Drawrah Ltd. et al.*, 19 Civ. 4058 (S.D.N.Y. May 6, 2019) (hereinafter Spencer testimony).

3. ¶1, Complaint, *Martinez et al. v. Republic of Argentina*, No. 05 Civ. 2521 (Mar. 3, 2005); ¶1, Complaint, *Ferri et al. v. Republic of Argentina*, No. 05 Civ. 2943 (Mar. 17, 2005); ¶1, Complaint, *Rigueiro et al. v. Republic of Argentina*, No. 05 Civ. 3089 (Mar. 22, 2005); ¶1, Complaint, *Sauco et al. v. Republic of Argentina*, No. 05 Civ. 3955 (Apr. 19, 2005); ¶1, Complaint, *Bettoni et al. v. Republic of Argentina*, No. 05 Civ. 4299 (May 2, 2005); ¶1, Complaint, *Fedocostante et al. v. Republic of Argentina*, No. 05 Civ. 4466 (May 6, 2005); ¶1, Complaint, *Lisi et al. v. Republic of Argentina*, No. 05 Civ. 6002 (June 28, 2005); ¶1, Complaint, *Rossini et al. v. Republic of Argentina*, No. 05 Civ. 6200 (July 5, 2005); ¶1, Complaint, *Klein et al. v. Republic of Argentina*, No. 05 Civ. 6599 (July 21, 2005); ¶1, Complaint, *Lovati et al. v. Republic of Argentina*, No. 05 Civ. 8195 (Sept. 23, 2005); ¶1, Complaint, *Botti et al. v. Republic of Argentina*, No. 05 Civ. 8687 (Oct. 12, 2005); and ¶1, Complaint, *Pasquali et al. v. Republic of Argentina*, No. 05 Civ. 10636 (Dec. 19, 2005).

4. ¶1, Complaint, *Prima et al. v. Republic of Argentina*, No. 04 Civ. 1077 (Feb. 2, 2004) (74 plaintiffs); and ¶1, Complaint, *Morata et al. v. Republic of Argentina*, No. 04 Civ. 3314 (Apr. 30, 2004) (109 plaintiffs).

5. See Spencer testimony, at 9, for the example fees paid by one such client.

6. ¶1, Complaint, *Andrarex, Ltd. v. Republic of Argentina*, No. 07 Civ. 5593 (S.D.N.Y. June 12, 2007).

7. According the author's database, the applicable district court hearing dates at which the class-action plaintiffs were primary participants included Dec. 9, 2003; Mar. 10, 2004; Nov. 16, 2004; Nov. 23, 2004; Nov. 24, 2004; Mar. 31, 2005; Sept. 13, 2005; Sept. 28, 2005; Sept. 14, 2007; Apr. 30, 2008; Nov. 12, 2008; Jan. 29, 2010; Apr. 15, 2010; Apr. 30, 2010; June 3, 2010; June 8, 2010; Oct. 19, 2010; Nov. 4, 2010; May 19, 2011; Mar. 27, 2012; June 8, 2012; Aug. 29, 2012; Feb. 21, 2014; and Nov. 10, 2016 (with appearance by the lawyers for the H. W. Urban, Seijas, Brecher, and Barboni class-action plaintiffs). The Second Circuit Court of Appeals case numbers for cases involving the class-action plaintiffs were 08-2847-cv, 09-0332-cv, 09-3888-cv, 11-3317-cv, 11-1714-cv, 14-2104-cv, and 14-4385-cv (four dealing with class-action case confirmation and certification and three dealing with attachment).

8. The class action cases that led to settlements included one case for the Brecher plaintiffs (with respect to one series of euro-denominated bonds) and eight jointly litigated cases for the so-called Seijas plaintiffs, each with respect to a different series of U.S. dollar–denominated global bonds: ¶1, Complaint, *Brecher et al. v. Republic of Argentina*, No. 06 Civ. 15297 (S.D.N.Y. Dec. 19, 2006); ¶1, Complaint, *Silvia Seijas et al. v. Republic of Argentina*, No. 04 Civ. 0400 (S.D.N.Y. Jan. 16, 2004); ¶1, Complaint, *Silvia Seijas et al. v. Republic of Argentina*, No. 04 Civ. 0401 (S.D.N.Y. Jan.

16, 2004); ¶1, Complaint, *Castro et al. v. Republic of Argentina*, No. 04 Civ. 00506 (S.D.N.Y. Jan. 22, 2004); ¶1, Complaint, *Hickory Securities et al. v. Republic of Argentina*, No. 04 Civ. 0936 (S.D.N.Y. Feb. 4, 2004); ¶1, Complaint, *Valls et al. v. Republic of Argentina*, No. 03 Civ. 0937 (S.D.N.Y. Filed Feb. 4, 2004); ¶1, Complaint, *Azza et al. v. Republic of Argentina*, No. 04 Civ. 1085 (S.D.N.Y. Feb. 10, 2004); ¶1, Complaint, *Puricelli et al. v. Republic of Argentina*, No. 04 Civ. 2117 (S.D.N.Y. Mar. 17, 2004); ¶1, Complaint, *Chorny et al. v. Republic of Argentina*, Case No. 04 Civ. 2118 (S.D.N.Y. Mar. 17, 2004). The total settlement amount of about $3 million for the Brecher case can be found in its docket at ¶150 (S.D.N.Y. May 24, 2017), and the settlement amounts for the various Seijas cases were posted to their dockets on Nov. 30, 2017, totaling about $24 million, altogether $27 million out of the roughly $9.3 billion settlement with plaintiffs during or after 2016, or 0.29% of the total.

9. See, for example, the Second Circuit's 2015 opinion in the Seijas cases: *Puricelli v. Republic of Argentina*, 797 F.3d 213 (2d Cir. 2015) ("After previous panels of this Court twice vacated aggregate judgments entered by the District Court in favor of plaintiff classes, we remanded with specific instructions. Rather than follow our instructions, the District Court certified expanded plaintiff classes. Because doing so was foreclosed by the mandate issued on the prior appeal, we VACATE and REMAND.")

10. ¶60, Order, *Macrotecnic Corp. v. Republic of Argentina*, No. 02 Civ. 5932 (S.D.N.Y. Mar. 18, 2004).

11. ¶61, Transcript of hearing held on March 1, 2007, at 2:6–24, 26:2–27:18, *Lightwater Corp. v. Republic of Argentina*, No. 02 Civ. 3804 (S.D.N.Y. Mar. 23, 2007).

12. ¶41, at 2:24–28, Order Granting Declaratory Relief, *Michele Colella and Denise Dussault v. Republic of Argentina*, No. C 07-80084 WHA (N.D. Cal. May 29, 2007).

13. Id., at 9–10 (finding of immunity based on diplomatic purpose and military character).

14. *Id.*, at 2:17–18 (pilots carrying cash).

15. ¶346, Opinion, *Aurelius Capital Partners, LP v. Republic of Argentina*, No. 07 Civ. 2715 (TPG), (S.D.N.Y. July 23, 2010). ("It is true that the Trust Bonds are not physical objects maintained in a physical location. But this does not take away from the fact that they were deposited, in an ordinary commercial sense, at Caja de Valores in Argentina. The court therefore holds that the situs of the Trust Bonds is Argentina.")

16. ¶137, Order, at 3, *Silvia Seijas et al. v. Republic of Argentina*, No. 04 Civ. 0400 (S.D.N.Y. Aug. 19, 2009).

17. ¶60, Transcript of hearing held on Dec. 19, 2006, at 2:12–20, *Lightwater Corp. v. Republic of Argentina*, No. 02 Civ. 3804 (S.D.N.Y. Mar. 16, 2007).

18. *Id.*, at 31:21–32:1.

19. ¶438, Transcript of hearing held on Dec. 17, 2010, at 10:18–23, *EM Ltd. v. Republic of Argentina*, No. 03 Civ. 2507 (S.D.N.Y. Jan. 19, 2011) (Robert Cohen: "We are now at the phase of this litigation, your Honor, where we need to understand the financial circulatory system of Argentina. This is a debtor that owes our client over $2 billion. We want to embark, with the help of this Court, on a forensic investigation of what it does with its money.")

20. ¶1, Complaint, *Agritech S.R.L. et al. v. Republic of Argentina*, No. 06 Civ. 15393 (Dec. 22, 2006); ¶1, Complaint, *A Gandola & C. S.P.A. v. Republic of Argentina*, No. 08 Civ. 9506 (Nov. 5, 2008); and ¶1, Complaint, *Diocesi Patriarcato Di Venezia, et al. v. Republic of Argentina*, No. 10 Civ. 1598 (Feb. 25, 2010).

21. GCAB, *GCAB Releases Legal Memorandum Summarizing Recent Argentine Legislation and Bondholder Remedies*, Press Release (Feb. 15, 2005), https://www.ots.at/presseaussendung/OTE_20050216_OTE0009/gcab-releases-legal-memorandum-summarizing-recent-argentine-legislation-and-bondholder-remedies.

22. International Centre for Settlement of Investment Disputes, *Decision on Jurisdiction and Admissibility, Abaclat and Others*, at 49, Case No. ARB/07/5 (2011), http://icsidfiles.worldbank.org/icsid/ICSIDBLOBS/OnlineAwards/C95/DS10925_En.pdf.

23. TFA, *Lettera Agli Obbligazionisti*, Feb. 7, 2007.

24. TFA, *Tango Bond: Pierre Tercier Nominato Nuovo Presidente del Collegio Arbitrale*, Press Release (Sept. 3, 2009) (mimeo).

25. Egidio Rolich, Tangobond: Chiuso Per Rapina (A.R.T. 2011).

26. E. Rolich, President A.R.T., Help! Help! Blog post on tangobond.it [no longer available] (mimeo).

27. Telephone interview with Nicola Stock (Nov. 29, 2022).

28. *Company Profile: Aurelius Capital Management LP*, Bloomberg, https://www.bloomberg.com/profile/company/0755347D:US; *Mark Brodsky, Chairman and Chief Investment Officer*, Aurelius Capital Management, https://www.aurelius-capital.com/team/mark-brodsky (accessed Aug. 19, 2023).

29. Spencer testimony, at 15, identifying the firms and managers behind several legal actions brought against Argentina. ("The hedge funds were: NML, which was part of Paul Singer's Elliott Management Corp.; . . . Aurelius Capital, led by Mark Brodsky, who was formerly at Elliott; Blue Angel and other funds related to Davidson Kempner Capital, represented by Avi Friedman and Ephraim Diamond; and funds related to Bracebridge Management, led by Nancy Zimmerman.")

30. The first suits by Aurelius and Blue Angel: ¶1, Complaint, *Aurelius Capital Partners, LP et al. v. Republic of Argentina*, No. 07 Civ. 2715 (S.D.N.Y. Apr. 3, 2007);

and ¶1, Complaint, *Blue Angel Capital I LLC v. Republic of Argentina*, No. 07 Civ. 2693 (S.D.N.Y. Apr. 2, 2007). Author's calculation of total based on all of the complaints filed by the parties.

31. *Capital Ventures Int'l v. Republic of Argentina* 443 F.3d 214 (2d Cir. 2006). (Vacating Judge Griesa's ruling on the topic of attachment of collateral at the New York Fed.)

32. ¶1, Complaint, at 3, *Capital Ventures Int'l v. Republic of Argentina*, 14 Civ. 7258 (S.D.N.Y. Sept. 8, 2014) ($52 million and $104 million judgments on U.S. dollar global bonds); and ¶197, Judgment, at 2, *Capital Ventures Int'l v. Republic of Argentina*, No. 05 Civ. 4085 (S.D.N.Y. Feb. 1, 2011) (€54 million judgment).

33. The appeals court reversed or vacated Judge Griesa's rulings a total of four times in the CVI cases: *supra* 31 (vacating ruling on initial attempt to attach Brady collateral); 280 F. App'x 14 (2d Cir. 2008) (affirming district court's denial of an attempt to garnish of excess interest collateral from an account at the New York Fed); 282 F. App'x 41 (2d Cir. 2008) (reversing the district court's denial of an attachment of certain accounts; affirm another matter); 552 F.3d 289 (2d Cir. 2009) (vacating the district court's dismissal of German bond claims; affirm remainder of the judgment); and 652 F.3d 266 (2d Cir. 2011) (reversing the district court's order to modify attachments to allow Brady bonds to participate in 2010 exchange offer).

34. ¶100, Transcript of hearing held on Apr. 30, 2008, *Silvia Seijas et al. v. Republic of Argentina*, at 33:8, No. 04 Civ. 400 (S.D.N.Y. May 2, 2008). (Judge Griesa: "The only thing I disagree with you, is that the argument made to the Court of Appeals was not even presented to me, but we won't get into that. We won't worry about that personal affront.")

35. ¶1, Complaint, *Teachers Insurance and Annuity Association of America v. Republic of Argentina*, No. 06 Civ. 6221 (S.D.N.Y. Aug. 16, 2006).

36. GMO filed complaints for one mutual fund, one hedge fund, and one U.K. entity: ¶1, Complaint, *GMO Emerging Country Debt L.P. v. Republic of Argentina*, No. 05 Civ. 10380 (S.D.N.Y. Dec. 12, 2005); ¶1, Complaint, *GMO Emerging Country Debt Investment Fund P.L.C. v. Republic of Argentina*, No. 05 Civ. 10382 (S.D.N.Y. Dec. 12, 2005); and ¶1, Complaint, *GMO Emerging Country Debt Fund. v. Republic of Argentina*, No. 05 Civ. 10383 (S.D.N.Y. Dec. 12, 2005).

37. See TIAA, *Who We Are*, https://www.tiaa.org/public/about-tiaa/why-tiaa /who-we-are (accessed Feb. 4, 2020).

38. GMO, *About GMO*, www.gmo.com/americas/about-gmo/ (accessed Jan. 13, 2020); GMO, *Emerging Country Debt Fund*, https://www.gmo.com/americas /product-index-page/fixed-income/emerging-country-debt-strategy/emerging -country-debt-fund---ecdf/?accept=Funds (accessed Apr. 20, 2020).

39. ¶37, Stipulation and Order for Dismissal with Prejudice, at 2, *Teachers*

Insurance and Annuity Association of America v. Republic of Argentina, No. 06 Civ. 6221 (S.D.N.Y. Aug. 18, 2010) ($104.757704 million judgment granted on May 14, 2007).

40. ¶24, Judgment, *GMO Emerging Country Debt L.P. v. Republic of Argentina*, No. 05 Civ. 10380 (S.D.N.Y. Sept. 24, 2007); ¶22, Judgment, *GMO Emerging Country Debt Investment Fund plc v. Republic of Argentina*, No. 05 Civ. 10382 (S.D.N.Y. Sept. 7, 2007); and ¶23, Judgment, *GMO Emerging Country Debt Fund v. Republic of Argentina*, No. 05 Civ. 10383 (S.D.N.Y. Sept. 24, 2007).

41. Elliott's holdings of FRANs are detailed in the following complaints: ¶1, Complaint, *NML Capital, Ltd. v. Republic of Argentina*, No. 05 Civ. 2434 (S.D.N.Y. Feb. 28, 2005); ¶1, Complaint, *NML Capital, Ltd. v. Republic of Argentina*, No. 06 Civ. 6466 (S.D.N.Y. Aug. 25, 2006); ¶1, Complaint, *NML Capital, Ltd. v. Republic of Argentina*, No. 07 Civ. 2690 (S.D.N.Y. Apr. 2, 2007); ¶1, *Complaint, NML Capital, Ltd. v. Republic of Argentina*, No. 08 Civ. 3302 (S.D.N.Y. Apr. 2, 2008); and ¶1, *Complaint, NML Capital, Ltd. v. Republic of Argentina*, No. 09 Civ. 1707 (S.D.N.Y. Feb. 24, 2009).

42. ¶1, Complaint, *FFI Fund Ltd and FYI Ltd. v. Republic of Argentina*, No. 05 Civ. 3328 (S.D.N.Y. Mar. 29, 2005). For the Yale relationship, *supra* chapter 3, note 97.

43. ¶1, Complaint, *Olifant Fund v. Republic of Argentina*, No. 10 Civ. 9587 (S.D.N.Y. Dec. 23, 2012). For evidence that Bracebridge manages the Olifant Fund, see Bracebridge Form ADV Rev. 10/2017 filed with the SEC (accessed Mar. 29, 2019).

44. For the Montreux group holdings, see ¶1, Complaint, *Montreux Partners L.P. v. Republic of Argentina*, No. 05 Civ. 4239 (S.D.N.Y. Apr. 28, 2005); ¶1, Complaint, *Los Angeles Capital v. Republic of Argentina*, No. 05 Civ. 10210 (S.D.N.Y. Dec. 5, 2005); ¶1, Complaint, *Cordoba Capital v. Republic of Argentina*, No. 06 Civ. 5887 (S.D.N.Y. Aug. 3, 2006); ¶1, Complaint, *Wilton Capital v. Republic of Argentina*, No. 07 Civ. 1797 (S.D.N.Y. Mar. 1, 2007); and ¶1, Complaint, *Wilton Capital, Ltd. v. Republic of Argentina*, No. 09 Civ. 401 (S.D.N.Y. Jan. 14, 2009).

45. Ahead of granting judgments on the FRANs, Judge Griesa ruled that the contractual terms of the bonds were binding even though the interest rate on the instrument had reset to an extraordinarily high level: ¶28, Opinion, *Montreux Partners, L.P. v. Republic of Argentina*, No. 05 Civ. 04239 TPG (S.D.N.Y. Mar. 18, 2009). (Judge Griesa: "There is no dispute as to the formula by which the FRAN interest rates were to be calculated, or as to the fact that 101.052% is currently the annual interest rate set by this formula. Rather, the Republic contends that the interest rate is too high to be enforced because (1) the rate is an unreasonable penalty barred by New York law governing liquidated damages clauses; (2) the rate is unconscionable; and (3) it would violate public policy to enforce such a high rate." Ruling: "Plaintiffs are entitled to receive contractual interest at the rate calculated according to the FRANs.")

46. For the full details of how the FRAN securities operate and Elliott's calculation of its judgment amount, see ¶24, Statement of Material Facts Pursuant to Local Rule 56.1, *Montreux Partners, L.P. v. Republic of Argentina*, at 3–4, No. 05 Civ. 4239 (S.D.N.Y. Apr. 10, 2008) (giving the history of FRAN index resets); and ¶202, Exhibit 2, Letter from Dennis H. Hranitzky to Judge Thomas P. Griesa dated May 12, 2009, at 2, *NML Capital, Ltd. v. Republic of Argentina*, No. 08 Civ. 3302 (S.D.N.Y. July 28, 2009) (claiming a 968% of par judgment).

47. *NML Capital, Ltd. v. Republic of Argentina*, 621 F.3d 230 (2d. Cir. 2010).

48. Jorge Rosales, *Inhibieron Más Bienes del País en los Estados Unidos*, Nación (Feb. 11, 2004), https://www.lanacion.com.ar/economia/inhibieron-mas-bienes-del -pais-en-los-estados-unidos-nid572186/.

49. Selected documents from Elliott's various attachments of Argentine diplomatic properties after removal of cases from state to federal courts: ¶2, Complaint, *NML Capital, Ltd. v. Republic of Argentina*, No. 04 Civ. 357 AW (D. Md. Feb. 11, 2004); ¶2, Complaint, *NML Capital, Ltd. v. Republic of Argentina*, No. 04 Civ. 358 AW (MD Feb. 11, 2004); ¶1, Notice of Removal, *NML Capital, Ltd. v. Republic of Argentina*, No. 04 Civ. 197 CKK (D.D.C. Feb. 10, 2004); ¶2-1, Declaration of (Ambassador) Jose Octavio Bordon, *NML Capital, Ltd. v. Republic of Argentina*, No. 04 Civ. 197 CKK (D.D.C. Feb. 17, 2004); ¶8-2, Declaration of (Air Attaché) Jorge Oscar Ratti, *NML Capital, Ltd. v. Republic of Argentina*, No. 04 Civ. 357 AW (D. Md. Feb. 17, 2004); and ¶8-5, Declaration of (Naval Attaché) Javier Armando Valladares, *NML Capital, Ltd. v. Republic of Argentina*, No. 04 Civ. 357 AW (D. Md. Feb. 17, 2004).

50. ¶33, Transcript of hearing held on Feb. 25, 2004, at 16:10–11, 17:14–15, 17:23–24, and 18:1–5, *NML Capital, Ltd. v. Republic of Argentina*, No. 03 Civ. 8845 (S.D.N.Y. Apr. 8, 2004).

51. For a discussion of the PNC bank rent attachment, see ¶19, Transcript of hearing held on Feb. 27, 2009, *NML Capital, Ltd. v. Republic of Argentina*, No. 08-00019-SJM (W.D. Pa. Mar. 11, 2009).

52. ¶280, Ex Parte Restraining Order, *EM Ltd. v. Republic of Argentina*, 03 Civ. 2507 (S.D.N.Y. May 22, 2007) (unsealed Aug. 18, 2009); and ¶301, at 2, Declaration of Estela Adriana Palomeque, *EM Ltd. v. Republic of Argentina*, 03 Civ. 2507 (S.D.N.Y. July 18, 2007) (unsealed Aug. 18, 2009) (detailing the number of shares and ownership thereof).

53. For two estimates of the value of the shares, see Hilary Burke, *Funds to Seize Argentine Assets Held in U.S.*, Reuters (July 20, 2012), https://www.reuters .com/article/argentina-debt-funds/funds-to-seize-argentine-assets-held-in-u-s -idUSL2E8IK8U920120720; and Michael D. Goldhaber, *Argentine Bond Litigation Wins Global Legal Awards for Disputes*, American Lawyer (Sept. 26, 2016), https:// www.law.com/americanlawyer/almID/1202767836946/.

54. ¶190, Opinion, *NML Capital, Ltd. v. Republic of Argentina*, 03 Civ. 8845 (S.D.N.Y. Aug. 18, 2009); and ¶253, Order, *EM Ltd. v. Republic of Argentina*, 03 Civ. 2507 (S.D.N.Y. Aug. 18, 2009).

55. *EM Ltd. v. Republic of Argentina*, 389 Fed. App'x. 38 (2d Cir. 2010).

56. Andrew Ross Sorkin, *Lehman Files for Bankruptcy; Merrill Is Sold*, N.Y. Times (Sept. 14, 2008), https://www.nytimes.com/2008/09/15/business/15lehman.html.

57. ¶110, Transcript of hearing held on Sept. 12, 2008, at 1:13–14, *NML Capital, Ltd. v. Republic of Argentina*, No. 03 Civ. 8845 (S.D.N.Y. Oct. 2, 2008).

58. *Id.*, at 3:2.

59. *Id.*, at 3:6–4:17.

60. *Id.*, at 4:18.

61. *Id.*, at 4:19–5:2.

62. *Id.*, at 6:15–16.

63. *Id.*, at 6:17–23.

64. *Id.*, at 6:24.

65. *Id.*, at 6:25–7:9.

66. ¶96, Opinion, *EM Ltd. and NML Capital, Ltd. v. Republic of Argentina and Banco de la Nacion Argentina*, No. 08 Civ. 7974 (S.D.N.Y. Sept. 30, 2009).

67. *NML Capital, Ltd. v. Republic of Argentina*, 680 F.3d 254 (2d Cir. 2012).

68. ¶532, Order, *NML Capital, Ltd. v. Republic of Argentina*, No. 03 Civ. 8845 (S.D.N.Y Nov. 26, 2012).

69. U.S. embassy officials in Argentina provide an interesting account of the pension takeover in the following leaked diplomatic cable: *Blow-by-Blow on Argentina's Nationalization of Pensions and Resulting Financial Panic*, Wikileaks (Oct. 27, 2008).

70. Jude Webber, *Pension Reform Plans Hit Argentine Markets*, Financial Times (Oct. 21, 2008), https://www.ft.com/content/7649a8c0-9fb2-11dd-a3fa-000077b07658.

71. ¶34, Order to Show Cause, *Aurelius Capital Partners L.P. et al. v. Republic of Argentina*, No. 07 Civ. 2715 (S.D.N.Y. Oct. 29, 2008); and ¶71, Transcript of hearing held on Oct. 29, 2008, *Aurelius Capital Partners L.P. et al. v. Republic of Argentina*, No. 07 Civ. 2715 (S.D.N.Y. Nov. 5, 2008).

72. ¶133, Notice of Appeal, *NML Capital, Ltd. v. Republic of Argentina*, No. 03 Civ. 8845 (S.D.N.Y. Oct. 31, 2008).

73. ¶16, Motion for Writ of Attachment, *Andrarex, Ltd. v. Republic of Argentina*, No. 07 Civ. 5593 (S.D.N.Y. Nov. 3, 2008).

74. ¶25, Order to Show Cause, *GMO Emerging Country Debt L.P. v. Republic of Argentina*, No. 05 Civ. 10380 LAP (S.D.N.Y. Nov. 5, 2008).

75. ¶95, Order to Show Cause, *Capital Ventures Int'l v. Republic of Argentina*, No.

05 Civ. 4085 (S.D.N.Y. Nov. 6, 2008); and one of the many Dreier LLP cases, ¶16, Order, *Allan Applestein TTEE FBO D.C.A. Grantor Trust et al. v. Republic of Argentina*, No. 02 Civ. 4124 (S.D.N.Y. Nov. 6, 2008).

76. ¶65, Order to Show Cause, *Lightwater Corp. v. Republic of Argentina*, No. 02 Civ. 3804 (S.D.N.Y. Nov. 12, 2008).

77. ¶14, Order to Show Cause, *Teachers Insurance and Annuity Association of America v. Republic of Argentina*, No. 06 Civ. 6221 (S.D.N.Y. Jan. 7, 2009).

78. ¶90, Plaintiff NML Capital, Ltd.'s Omnibus Memorandum of Law on Priority Issues, at 9–10, *Aurelius Capital Partners, L.P. et al. v. Republic of Argentina*, No. 07 Civ. 2715 (S.D.N.Y. Jan. 23, 2009). ("Upon publication of the nationalization legislation in the Official Gazette on December 9, 2008, NML's attorneys served the order and levied on the Argentine Property.")

79. ¶64, Opinion, at 38–39, *Aurelius Capital Partners, L.P. et al. v. Republic of Argentina*, No. 07 Civ. 2715 (S.D.N.Y. Dec. 11, 2008) ("[The state pension fund agency] is part of the Government of Argentina. The court has the direct authority to attach, execute upon, and restrain property in New York belonging to the Republic, which includes property of [the state pension fund agency]"); and ¶70, Memorandum of Law in Support of the Aurelius Plaintiffs' Motion to Confirm Priority, at 13–14, *Aurelius Capital Partners, L.P. et al. v. Republic of Argentina*, No. 07 Civ. 2715 (S.D.N.Y. Dec. 22, 2008). ("On December 12, 2008, consistent with the Court's December 11 Opinion, the Aurelius Plaintiffs submitted a proposed final order for the Court's consideration directing the U.S. Marshals to levy on the pension assets pursuant to the Aurelius Plaintiffs' outstanding writs of execution. . . . On December 16, 2008, the NML Plaintiffs submitted a letter to the Court contesting Aurelius Plaintiffs' priority on the theory that 'NML has already levied upon' the pension assets.")

80. ¶152, Transcript of hearing held on Apr. 6, 2009, at 22:3–10 and 22:24–23:1, *Aurelius Capital Partners, L.P. et al. v. Republic of Argentina*, No. 07 Civ. 2715. Doc. (S.D.N.Y. May 1, 2009).

81. *Id.*, at 16:8–11.

82. *Id.*, at 15:23–16:1.

83. *Id.*, at 23:4–22.

84. *Id.*, at 24:9–13.

85. ¶165, Transcript of hearing held on Apr. 24, 2009, at 2:7–15, *Aurelius Capital Partners, L.P. et al. v. Republic of Argentina*, No. 07 Civ. 2715. Doc. (S.D.N.Y. May 1, 2009). ("The article in La Nacion is included as an attachment. . . . According to the press reports in Argentina, [the state pension agency] has reportedly engaged in a transaction that was designed to liquidate assets, which presumptively are subject of your Honor's prior orders.")

86. Further details of Argentina's state pension agency's removal of assets from

the United States are in ¶179, Ostrager supplemental declaration, *Aurelius Capital Partners, L.P. v. Republic of Argentina*, No. 07 Civ. 2715. Doc. (S.D.N.Y. Apr. 30, 2009); and ¶180, Ostrager declaration, *Aurelius Capital Partners, L.P. et al. v. Republic of Argentina*, No. 07 Civ. 2715. Doc. (S.D.N.Y. Apr. 30, 2009).

87. ¶246, Order, *EM Ltd. v. Republic of Argentina*, No. 03 Civ. 2507 Doc. (S.D.N.Y. May 29, 2009). ("The Republic is held in civil contempt for its failure to comply with the Court's Opinion dated April 3, 2009, and the Court's Orders dated April 17, 2009 and May 6, 2009. IT IS FURTHER ORDERED that as a sanction for the Republic's contempt of Court, the Court will draw adverse inferences from the Republic's failure to comply with the Court's discovery orders that the Republic undertook the following transactions to remove funds improperly from the United States in violation of the order of the Court.")

88. ¶199, Transcript of hearing held on Aug. 7, 2009, *NML Capital, Ltd. v. Republic of Argentina*, No. 03 Civ. 8845 (S.D.N.Y. Aug. 27, 2009); and ¶198, Transcript of hearing held on Aug. 11, 2009, *NML Capital, Ltd. v. Republic of Argentina*, No. 03 Civ. 8845 (S.D.N.Y. Aug. 27, 2009).

89. *Id.*, hearing held on Aug. 7, 2009, at 3:3–5 and 4:25–5:7. ("The interest we are seeking to attach is in New York and it is the contract rights, your Honor, held by Morgan Stanley entity. . . . We do know that Morgan Stanley has been paid in whole or in part and under the contract if there is a force majeure, which includes an order of the Court, the contract could be voided. In that circumstance we are seeking to attach the money held by Morgan Stanley here in New York, which is the funds of Argentina. And then to protect Morgan Stanley, Morgan Stanley will be in a position to sell the cargo, make itself whole.")

90. *Supra* note 88. Hearing held on Aug. 11, 2009, at 49:14, 52:21–53:6,and 54:3–8. ("[T]he application is denied. . . . I could not grant an attachment without the certainty or at least the strong possibility that the attachment would frustrate the delivery of the natural gas and either frustrate or cloud Morgan Stanley's right to be paid the balance of what is due on the contract. . . . [T]hese are circumstances which would make it wholly improper for the court to grant the attachment requested. . . . [O]ne of the reasons I am declining the order of attachment is that this court believes it is inappropriate to interfere with the delivery of a commodity needed by the people of Argentina.")

91. *Aurelius Capital Partners, L.P. v. Republic of Argentina*, 584 F.3d 120 (2d Cir. 2009).

92. Nathan Koppel, Ashby Jones, and Peter Lattman, *Dreier Law Firm on the Brink After Founder's Arrest*, Wall St. J. (Dec. 8, 2008), https://www.wsj.com /articles/SB122869570778186741; *Elliott Management Bought Securities from Dreier*, N.Y. Times (Jan. 26, 2009), https://archive.nytimes.com/dealbook.nytimes

.com/2009/01/26/elliott-management-bought-securities-from-dreier/; and Chad Bray, *Dreier Is Sentenced to 20 Years for Fraud*, Wall St. J. (July 15, 2009), https://www.wsj.com/articles/SB124753190425836007.

93. ¶108, Transcript of hearing held on Apr. 30, 2008, at 47:23–48:7. *Seijas et al. v. Republic of Argentina*, No. 04 Civ. 400 (S.D.N.Y. May 16, 2008).

7. Turning Point

1. Interview with Marcelo Etchebarne (Apr. 24, 2018, New York) (hereinafter Etchebarne interview); and Marcelo Etchebarne, *Managing Partner*, DLA Piper, https://www.dlapiper.com/en/argentina/people/e/etchebarne-marcelo/?tab=credentials (accessed Jan. 25, 2020).

2. *The Road Ahead: An Examination of Argentina's Economic and Political Future*, Preliminary Conference Agenda, LatinFinance and Center for Hemispheric Policy, University of Miami (mimeo). (The author has been told that the final conference agenda included some changes in the order of panels and speakers.)

3. ATFA was incorporated in the Commonwealth of Virginia in January 2007. See American Task Force Argentina, *Certificate of Incorporation* (Jan. 11, 2007) (mimeo). ATFA's leadership included former assistant attorney general Robert Raben, former president Clinton adviser Robert J. Shapiro, and former ambassador Nancy Soderberg, as per *Leadership*, American Task Force Argentina, https://web.archive.org/web/20080422022522/http://atfa.org:80/leadership/.

4. ATFA's members as of Aug. 30, 2007, included Bracebridge Capital, LLC; Elliott Associates, L.P.; FH International Asset Management, LLC; Grantham, Mayo, Van Otterloo & Co. LLC; Greylock Capital Management; and Montreux Partners. As per *About Us*, American Task Force Argentina, https://web.archive.org/web/20070830195022/http://atfa.org/about/.

5. Lobbying Disclosure Act LD-2 Disclosure Form, The Raben Group, Q1 2008, https://lda.senate.gov/filings/public/filing/9073ff8d-8147-4116-8eeb-7e76a6830838/print/. ("16. Specific lobbying issues. Engage Congress in defending U.S. companies and organizations who invested in Argentine bonds and lost money when the country defaulted in 2001. Support Congress efforts to engage the Argentine government, state and treasury departments and the interamerican development bank with the goal of getting Argentina to pay its $3 billion debt.")

6. For information on Gramercy, see www.gramercy.com. For background on Koenigsberger, see Witness Statement of Robert S. Koenigsberger, at 1–6, *In the Arbitration under the Rules of the United Nations Commission on International Trade Law and the United States—Peru Trade Promotion Agreement* (June 2, 2016), http://www.perubonds.org/wpcontent/uploads/witness_statement_of_robert_s_koenigsberger.pdf (accessed Apr. 17, 2021; no longer available).

7. Etechebarne interview.

8. *Déjà vu All Over Again: Cristina's New Cabinet*, Wikileaks (Nov. 14, 2007) (mimeo).

9. *Argentina Boosts Export Taxes on Major Ag Commodities, Sector Responds with Strike*, Wikileaks, Mar. 14, 2008 (mimeo).

10. Argentina; *VP Cobos Votes Against Kirchner in Ag Export Tax Tiebreaker*, Wikileaks (July 18, 2008) (mimeo); and Vinod Sreeharsha and Alexei Barrionuevo, *President of Argentina Withdraws Tax Increase*, N.Y. Times (July 19, 2008), https:// www.nytimes.com/2008/07/19/world/americas/19argent.html.

11. *People Profile—Sergio Massa, Argentina*, LatinNews (Aug. 19, 2008), https:// www.latinnews.com/component/k2/item/37608-people-%20%20profile---sergio -massa,-argentina.html.

12. Barlcays Capital and Arcadia Advisors, Letter to President Cristina Fernández de Kirchner, *Plan Estratégico de Reinserción de la Argentina en los Mercados Financieros Internacionales y Apoyo Crediticio por hasta $2,500 Millones* (Aug. 12, 2008) (mimeo).

13. Etechebarne interview.

14. Republic of Argentina, Prospectus Supplement to Prospectus Dated April 13, 2010 (Reg. No. 333-163784), at S-1 (Apr. 28, 2010), https://www.sec.gov /Archives/edgar/data/914021/000090342310000252/roa-424b5_0428.htm (commencement of offer Apr. 30, 2010); and Republic of Argentina, *Completion of Final Settlement*, Press Release (Sept. 27, 2010), https://www.argentina.gob.ar/sites /default/files/culminacion_de_liquidacion_final_version_ingles_27092010.pdf (completion of offer on Sept. 27, 2010).

15. Republic of Argentina, Form 18-K, at 8, Sept. 30, 2011, https://www.sec .gov/Archives/edgar/data/914021/000090342311000486/roa-18k_0928.htm. ("As of December 31, 2010, Untendered Debt totaled U.S.$11.2 billion and consisted of U.S.$6.8 billion of past due principal amounts and principal that had not become due; and U.S.$4.4 billion of past due interest amounts.")

16. *Id.*, at 142. ("The aggregate eligible amount of securities in default tendered in the 2010 Debt Exchange . . . totaled approximately U.S.$12.4 billion, representing approximately 67.7% of the aggregate eligible amount of eligible securities. As a result of the 2005 and 2010 Debt Exchanges, Argentina succeeded in restructuring over 91% of the defaulted debt eligible for the 2005 and 2010 Debt Exchanges." The author calculates the aggregate success rate of the two transactions as 91.6%, so the text of this book cites the rounded 92% figure where applicable.)

17. ICSID 2011, at 75. ("On 5 October 2010, Claimants filed a letter submitting that certain Claimants, who tendered into the Exchange Offer 2010, would no longer participate in the present arbitration, thereby reducing the number of remaining Claimants to approximately 60,000.")

18. ¶37, Stipulation and Order for Dismissal with Prejudice, *Teachers Insurance*

and Annuity Association of America v. Republic of Argentina, 06 Civ. 6221 (S.D.N.Y. Aug. 18, 2010).

19. GMO put all its bonds into Argentina's 2010 exchange offer except its Brady bonds, which were excluded from the deal because of the block put on CVI's attachment of the associated collateral. See ¶72, Amended Judgment, *GMO Emerging Country Debt Investment Fund plc v. Republic of Argentina*, 05 Civ. 10382 (S.D.N.Y. Aug. 18, 2010); ¶75, Amended Judgment, *GMO Emerging Country Debt L.P. v. Republic of Argentina*, 05 Civ. 10380 (S.D.N.Y. Aug. 18, 2010); and ¶74, Stipulation and Order to Amend Judgment, *GMO Emerging Debt Fund v. Republic of Argentina*, 05 Civ. 10383 (S.D.N.Y. Aug. 25, 2010).

20. ¶253, Transcript of hearing held on Nov. 4, 2009, at 4:15–18, *NML Capital, Ltd. v. Republic of Argentina*, No. 03 Civ. 8845 (S.D.N.Y. Nov. 10, 2009). ("Your Honor, the subpoenas that we've served . . . relates to an exchange offer that Argentina has recently announced.")

21. ¶147, Opinion, *Silvia Seijas et al. v. Republic of Argentina*, No. 04 Civ. 400 (S.D.N.Y. Apr. 26, 2010) (Judge Griesa denies motions in ten cases to enjoin or restrain Argentina's 2010 exchange offer); and ¶157, Opinion, *Silvia Seijas et al. v. Republic of Argentina*, No. 04 Civ. 400 (S.D.N.Y. May 10, 2010) (Judge Griesa denies a motion for Argentina to maintain an escrow account in favor of plaintiffs in association with the exchange offer).

22. *Capital Ventures Int'l v. Republic of Argentina*, 652 F.3d 266 (2d Cir. 2011).

23. *Republic of Argentina v. NML Capital, Ltd.*, 573 U.S. 134 (2014).

24. For further details on subpoenas of BIS officers, see ¶422, Declaration of Jaime Caruana in Support of Motion to Quash the Plaintiffs' Subpoena Directed to Non-Parties Jaime Caruana and the Bank for International Settlements, *EM Ltd. v. Republic of Argentina*, No. 03 Civ. 2507 (S.D.N.Y. Oct. 21, 2010); ¶1, Non-Parties the Swiss National Bank and Philipp M. Hildebrand's Motion to Dismiss Discovery for Lack of Subject Matter Jurisdiction and to Quash Subpoenas, *Swiss Nat'l. Bank et al. v. NML Capital, Ltd. et al., Ltd.*, No. 10 MC 610 (D.D.C. Oct. 20, 2010); and ¶1, Motion by Non-Parties Banque de France and Christian Noyer to Dismiss Discovery for Lack of Subject Matter Jurisdiction and to Quash Subpoena, *Banque de France et al. v. NML Capital, Ltd.*, No. 10 MC 611 (D.D.C. Oct. 21, 2010).

25. *NML Capital, Ltd. v. Republic of Argentina*, 621 F.3d 230 (2d Cir. 2010). ("We conclude that Argentina's appeal is without merit insofar as it challenges the district court's refusal to reform the notes.")

26. ¶96, Opinion, *EM Ltd. and NML Capital, Ltd. v. Republic of Argentina*, 06 Civ. 7792 (S.D.N.Y. Apr. 7, 2010) (hereinafter 2010 Central Bank Opinion).

27. The Central Bank of Argentina alter ego case was discussed at hearings held on Nov. 3, 2006; Nov. 29, 2006; Feb. 2, 2007; Apr. 27, 2007; Oct. 26, 2007;

Dec. 17, 2007; May 6, 2008; May 30, 2008; Sept. 17, 2009; and Feb. 22, 2010. The case was also discussed at three hearings related to new attachments on the central bank in 2010 that were held on January 8, 13, and 15, 2010. (From author's database of transcripts for the cases.)

28. *Central Bank Robbery*, Economist (Feb. 6, 2010), https://www.economist .com/the-americas/2010/02/04/central-bank-robbery; and Jude Webber, *Argentina President Changes Tack to Tap Reserves*, Financial Times (Mar. 1, 2010) (mimeo).

29. 2010 Central Bank Opinion, at 71.

30. 2010 Central Bank Opinion, at 12.

31. 2010 Central Bank Opinion, at 70–71.

32. Elliott's pari passu related filings on Oct. 20, 2010: ¶226, Motion for Partial Summary Judgment and for Injunctive Relief Pursuant to the Equal Treatment Provision, *NML Capital, Ltd. v. Republic of Argentina*, No. 08 Civ. 6978 (S.D.N.Y. Oct. 20, 2010); ¶227, Declaration of Hal S. Scott, *NML Capital, Ltd. v. Republic of Argentina*, No. 08 Civ. 6978 (S.D.N.Y. Oct. 20, 2010); ¶230, Memorandum of Law, *NML Capital, Ltd. v. Republic of Argentina*, No. 08 Civ. 6978 (S.D.N.Y. Oct. 20, 2010); and ¶231, Declaration of Robert A. Cohen, *NML Capital, Ltd. v. Republic of Argentina*, No. 08 Civ. 6978 (S.D.N.Y. Oct. 20, 2010).

33. For 2010-era research on the origin of the pari passu clause, see Mark C. Weidemaier, Robert E. Scott, and G. Mitu Gulati, *Origin Myths, Contracts, and the Hunt for Pari Passu*, 38 Law & Social Inquiry, 72 (2013). For recent scholarship establishing an equal-ranking usage of the pari passu clause in bonds listed on the London Stock Exchange in the 1800s, see Marc Flandreau, *Pari Passu Lost and Found: The Origins of Sovereign Bankruptcy 1798–1873*, Institute for New Economic Thinking, Working Paper No. 186 (June 3, 2022), https://www.ineteconomics.org /uploads/papers/WP_186-Flandreau-Pari-Passu-Final.pdf.

34. Professor Anne Gelpern warned in 2005 that imposing a pari passu injunction on Argentina "would raise critical policy concerns—it could turn the world's largest payments system into collection agencies." See Anna Gelpern, *After Argentina*, Institute for International Economics, Policy Brief No. PB05-2 (2005), at 7, https://www.piie.com/sites/default/files/publications/pb/pb05-2.pdf.

35. See Rodrigo Olivares-Caminal, *To Rank Pari Passu or Not to Rank Pari Passu: That Is the Question in Sovereign Bonds after the Latest Episode of the Argentine Saga*, 15 L. & Bus. Rev. Am. 745, 777 (2009). ("Argentina not only closed the exchange offer tendering period but also 'locked-it' by passing the so-called Padlock Law. The fact that Argentina passed Law 26,017 prohibiting future offers to the holdout creditors could be interpreted as a formal subordination of creditors. The fact that these creditors [were] subordinated could be interpreted as a violation of the pari passu clause.")

8. Equal Treatment

1. *Pari Passu*, Wikipedia, https://en.wikipedia.org/wiki/Pari_passu.

2. Jonathan I. Blackman and Rahul Mukhi, *The Evolution of Modern Sovereign Debt Litigation: Vultures, Alter Egos, and Other Legal Fauna*, 73 Law and Contemporary Problems, 47, 56–57 (2010). (Claiming that the court in *Red Mountain Finance v. Democratic Republic of Congo* imposed an injunction but "appeared to reject" the equal payments interpretation of the clause, explaining that a Belgian court ruled in 2004 *Republic of Nicaragua v. LNC Investments LLC* against the imposition of an injunction irrespective of the construction of the contractual pari passu clause, citing the English case *Kensington International Ltd. v. Republic of the Congo* in which the judge denied an injunction on equitable grounds and called Elliott's interpretation "novel" and "unprecedented," and also noting that the Belgian parliament passed a law shielding Euroclear from injunctions.)

3. Robert A. Cohen, *"Sometimes a Cigar Is Just a Cigar": The Simple Story of Pari Passu*, 40 Hofstra L. Rev. 11, 15–17 (2011). ("[T]he only three courts to have interpreted *pari passu* covenants have consistently and uniformly mandated equal treatment of all creditors," citing the Belgian court ruling in Peru, a related ruling in Belgium in 2003 in *Republic of Nicaragua v. LNC Investments LLC*, and the imposition of a pari passu type of injunction in the Central District of California in *Red Mountain Finance, Inc. v. Democratic Republic of Congo* in 2002, a case brought by Michael Straus.)

4. ¶274, Memorandum of Law in Opposition to Plaintiff's Motions for Partial Summary Judgment and for Injunctive Relief Pursuant to the Pari Passu Clause, *NML Capital, Ltd. v. Republic of Argentina*, No. 08 Civ. 6978 (S.D.N.Y. Dec. 10, 2010).

5. ¶278, Reply in Support of the Motion by NML Capital, Ltd. for Partial Summary Judgment and for Injunction Relief Pursuant to the Equal Treatment Provision, *NML Capital, Ltd. v. Republic of Argentina*, No. 08 Civ. 6978 (S.D.N.Y. Jan. 14, 2011).

6. ¶230, Memorandum of Law in Support of the Motion by NML Capital, Ltd. for Partial Summary Judgment and for Injunction Relief Pursuant to the Equal Treatment Provision, at 1–2, *NML Capital, Ltd. v. Republic of Argentina*, No. 08 Civ. 6978 (S.D.N.Y. Oct. 20, 2010).

7. ¶227, Declaration of Hal S. Scott, at 1–2, *NML Capital, Ltd. v. Republic of Argentina*, No. 08 Civ. 6978 (S.D.N.Y. Oct. 20, 2010).

8. *Id.*, at 9 ("This clause includes Priority of Payment language and clearly provides that bondholders in these cases will have equal rights to payments as all other External Indebtedness.").

9. Republic of Argentina, Fiscal Agency Agreement between the Republic of Argentina and Bankers Trust Company, at 2 (Oct. 19, 1994).

10. *Supra* note 4, at 1–2.

11. *Id.*, at 2–3.

12. ¶272, Declaration of Stephen Choi, at 1–2, *NML Capital, Ltd. v. Republic of Argentina*, No. 08 Civ. 6978 (S.D.N.Y. Dec. 10, 2010).

13. *Id.*, at 5.

14. *Id.*, at 3.

15. ¶339, Transcript of hearing held on Sept. 28, 2011, at 3:6–10, 3:12, 8:7, 8:8–18, 8:19–9:1, 9:2, and 17:5–7, *NML Capital, Ltd. v. Republic of Argentina*, No. 08 Civ. 6978 (S.D.N.Y. Sept. 30, 2010).

16. *Id.*, at 30:7–8, 30:11–12, 30:13–14, 30:15, 30:16–17, 30:18–19, 30:20, 30:21–22, 30:23, 30:24–25, 31:1–2, 31:5–9, 41:17–20, 44:5–8, 45:3–7, 45:24–46:2, and 41:6–15.

17. ¶353, Order, at 4–5, *NML Capital, Ltd. v. Republic of Argentina*, No. 08 Civ. 6978 (S.D.N.Y. Dec. 7, 2011).

18. ¶453, Transcript of hearing held on Feb. 23, 2012, at 7:2–18:11, *NML Capital, Ltd. v. Republic of Argentina*, No. 03 Civ. 8845 (S.D.N.Y. Mar. 16, 2012).

19. *Id.*, at 28:5–32:7, 36:11–12, and 38:7–16.

20. *Id.*, at 43:7–8, 43:9–19, 44:2–4, and 45:11–23.

21. *Id.*, at 48:12–51:2.

22. ¶371, Order, *NML Capital, Ltd. v. Republic of Argentina*, No. 08 Civ. 6978 (S.D.N.Y. Feb. 23, 2012).

23. Emerging Markets Trading Association, *EMTA Special Seminar: Argentina and Its Pari Passu Clause* (Apr. 18, 2012), https://www.emta.org/new-developments /international-financial-architecture-and-debt-restructuring/.

24. Anna Gelpern, *Revival on the Head of a Pin: Do U Pari Passu?*, Credit Slips (Apr. 6, 2012), https://www.creditslips.org/creditslips/2012/04/revival-on-the-head -of-a-pin-do-u-pari-passu.html; Anna Gelpern, *Pari Passu: So Passe! (Extractive Edition)*, Credit Slips (Apr. 27, 2012), https://www.creditslips.org/creditslips/2012 /04/pari-passu-so-passe-extractive-edition.html; and Anna Gelpern, *Sovereign Restructuring after NML v. Argentina: CACs Don't Make Pari Passu Go Away*, Credit Slips (May 3, 2012), https://www.creditslips.org/creditslips/2012/05/sovereign -restructuring-after-nml-v-argentina-cacs-dont-make-pari-passu-go-away.html.

25. Felix Salmon, *Why Argentina's Likely to Beat Elliott Associates*, Reuters (July 25, 2012), https://www.reuters.com/article/idUK405107438020120725.

26. ¶1, Complaint *Pablo Alberto Varela et al. v. Republic of Argentina*, No. 10 Civ. 5338 (S.D.N.Y. July 13, 2010); and ¶24, Notice of Motion, *Pablo Alberto Varela et al. v. Republic of Argentina*, No. 10 Civ. 5338 (S.D.N.Y. Aug. 4, 2011) (notice of Varela's parri passu motion).

27. Testimony of Michael C. Spencer of July 20, 2018, ¶4–5, Exhibit 3, at 13, *Milberg LLP v. Drawrah Limited et al.*, 19 Civ. 4058 (S.D.N.Y. May 6, 2019). ("I do not exactly recall when I was approached by Robert Cohen, NML's lead lawyer at the

Dechert firm, about an Equal Treatment strategy. I see that he and I first had email contact about these cases in April 2010. . . . Mr. Cohen and I began discussing the possible utility of having an Equal Treatment motion initiated by non–hedge-fund plaintiffs—i.e., small or individual investors, who had bought their bonds at or near full price before the default, who ideally were from Argentina, and whose claims had not gone to money judgments. . . . Unlike the hedge funds, those investors could not easily be attacked by Argentina as foreign bond speculators who had purchased at large discounts but were litigating for full recoveries of principal and accrued interest.")

28. ¶147, Plaintiffs' Motion for Partial Summary Judgment with Respect to Their Claims for Breach of the Equal Treatment Provision, *Aurelius Capital Master, Ltd. et al. v. Republic of Argentina*, No. 09 Civ. 8757 (S.D.N.Y. Oct. 26, 2011).

29. ¶8, Notice of Motion for Partial Summary Judgment and for Injunctive Relief Pursuant to the Equal Treatment Provision, *Olifant Fund, Ltd. v. Republic of Argentina*, No. 10 Civ. 9587 (S.D.N.Y. Jan. 26, 2012).

30. David Boies and Theodore B. Olson, Redeeming the Dream: Proposition 8 and the Struggle for Marriage Equality, at 79 (2014). (The importance of keeping the number of plaintiffs small was emphasized by Boies and Olson with regard to their work on the marriage equality cases. They wrote, "[W]e were not enthusiastic about adding additional litigants. . . . We did not want to fight with other lawyers about the direction, timing, and strategy of the case, the identity of witnesses, and the way to express legal arguments. We did not want balkanized arguments, time-consuming debates about who would argue what. We wanted a controlled, coherent, and consistent message.")

31. Chapter 10 also resolves the additional mystery of why early pari passu plaintiffs Elliott, Bracebridge, Aurelius, and Blue Angel only moved to obtain pari passu injunctions with respect to a subset of their outstanding cases against Argentina.

32. Audio Recording: *NML Capital, Ltd. v. Republic of Argentina*, No. 12-105 (2d Cir. July 23, 2012).

33. *NML Capital, Ltd. v. Republic of Argentina*, 699 F.3d 246 (2d Cir. 2012).

34. Robin Wigglesworth, *Ruling Raises Fears of Argentine Default*, Financial Times (Oct. 30, 2012), https://www.ft.com/content/d0213464-22b5-11e2-938d-00144feabdc0.

35. ¶401, Notice of Motion to Vacate Injunction Pursuant to Rule 60(b), *NML Capital, Ltd. v. Republic of Argentina*, No. 08 Civ. 6978 (S.D.N.Y. Nov. 16, 2012).

36. ¶418, Opposition Brief of Interested Non-Party Fintech Advisory, Inc., *NML Capital, Ltd. v. Republic of Argentina*, No. 08 Civ. 6978 (S.D.N.Y. Nov. 19, 2012).

37. ¶702, Brief for Non-Party Intervenors Euro Bondholders, *NML Capital, Ltd. v. Republic of Argentina*, No. 12-105 (2d Cir. Jan. 4, 2013).

38. ¶698, Brief of Intervenor Ice Canyon LLC, *NML Capital, Ltd. v. Republic of Argentina*, No. 12-105 (2d Cir. Jan. 4, 2013).

39. ¶396, Brief of Non-Party Bank of New York Mellon, as Indenture Trustee, Addressing the Issues Raised on Remand from the Court of Appeals, *NML Capital, Ltd. v. Republic of Argentina*, No. 08 Civ. 6978 (S.D.N.Y. Nov. 16, 2012).

40. ¶778, Brief for *Amicus Curiae* Professor Anne Krueger in Support of the Republic of Argentina and Reversal, *NML Capital, Ltd. v. Republic of Argentina*, No. 12-105 (2d Cir. Jan. 10, 2013).

41. ¶780, Letter to the Second Circuit from Euroclear, *NML Capital, Ltd. v. Republic of Argentina*, No. 12-105 (2d Cir. Jan. 10, 2013).

42. ¶238, Brief for the United States of America as *Amicus Curiae* in Support of Reversal, *NML Capital, Ltd. v. Republic of Argentina*, No. 12-105 (2d Cir. Apr. 4, 2012).

43. ¶237, Brief for *Amicus Curiae* The Clearing House Association L.L.C. in Support of Reversal, *NML Capital, Ltd. v. Republic of Argentina*, No. 12-105 (2d Cir. Apr. 4, 2012).

44. ¶396, Brief of the Washington Legal Foundation as *Amicus Curiae* in Support of Plaintiffs/Appellees, Urging Affirmance, *NML Capital, Ltd. v. Republic of Argentina*, No. 12-105 (2d Cir. June 29, 2012).

45. ¶687, Brief for *Amicus Curiae* Kenneth W. Dam in Support of Affirmance, *NML Capital, Ltd. v. Republic of Argentina*, No.12-105 (2d Cir, Jan. 4, 2013).

46. ¶411, Transcript of hearing held on Nov. 9, 2012, *NML Capital, Ltd. v. Republic of Argentina*. No. 08 Civ. 6978 (S.D.N.Y. Nov. 19, 2012).

47. ¶410, Memorandum of Law of Exchange Bondholder Group Regarding Issues Remanded by the Second Circuit and in Support of Motion to Vacate Pursuant to Rule 60(b), at 20–21, *NML Capital, Ltd. v. Republic of Argentina*, No. 08 Civ. 6978 (S.D.N.Y. Nov. 16, 2012). ("Basic considerations of fairness and equity require rejecting Plaintiffs' proposal to enter an equitable remedy that requires the Republic immediately to pay 100% of the face value . . . before it can make payments . . . under the Exchange Bonds . . . [T]he Court should require a Ratable Payment to Plaintiffs.")

48. ¶425, Amended Feb. 23, 2012, Order, *NML Capital, Ltd. v. Republic of Argentina*, No. 08 Civ. 6978 (S.D.N.Y. Nov. 21, 2012).

49. *Supra* note 46, at 5:15–16.

50. ¶429, Order Concerning the Mar. 5, 2012 Order, at 1, *NML Capital, Ltd. v. Republic of Argentina*, No. 08 Civ. 6978 (S.D.N.Y. Nov. 26, 2012). ("[T]he February 23, 2012 Orders will be applicable to the interest payments made to exchange bondholders in December 2012. In order to avoid confusion and to give some reasonable time to arrange mechanics, the Court specifies that the precise interest payment involved will be that of December 15, 2012.")

51. ¶459, Emergency Motion by Defendant-Appellant the Republic of Argentina for Stay Pending Appeal, *NML Capital, Ltd. et al. v. Republic of Argentina*, No. 12-105 (2d Cir. Nov. 27, 2012); ¶491, Order, *NML Capital, Ltd. et al. v. Republic of Argentina*, No. 12-105 (2d Cir. Nov. 28, 2012). ("It is hereby ORDERED that the November 21, 2012 orders of the district court entered in relation to this matter are all stayed pending further order of this Court.")

52. Audio Recording: *NML Capital, Ltd. v. Republic of Argentina*, No. 12-105 (2d Cir. Feb. 27, 2013).

53. ¶903, Order, *NML Capital, Ltd. v. Republic of Argentina*, No. 12-105 (2d Cir. Mar. 1, 2013) (asking Argentina to propose an alternative payment formula).

54. ¶935, Letter from Argentina to Court in Response to Order of Mar. 1, 2013, *NML Capital, Ltd. v. Republic of Argentina*, No. 12-105 (2d Cir. Mar. 29, 2013). (Argentina reiterates its existing position.)

55. *NML Capital, Ltd. v. Republic of Argentina*, 727 F.3d 230 (2d Cir. 2013).

56. *Supra* note 32 (audio recording).

57. *Id.*

58. *Id.*

59. *Id.*

60. *Supra* note 52 (audio recording).

61. *Id.*

9. Argentina's Economic Stumbles and Elliott's Worldwide War

1. Helen Popper, *Argentina's Powerful Ex-President Kirchner Dies*, Reuters (Oct. 27, 2010), https://www.reuters.com/article/us-argentina-kirchner/argentinas-powerful-ex-president-kirchner-dies-idUSTRE69Q2TV20101027.

2. Alexei Barrionuevo, *Kirchner Achieves an Easy Victory in Argentina Presidential Election*, N.Y. Times (Oct. 23, 2011), https://www.nytimes.com/2011/10/24/world/americas/kirchner-appears-headed-to-second-term-as-argentinas-president.html.

3. *2011 Argentine General Election*, Wikipedia, https://en.wikipedia.org/wiki/2011_Argentine_general_election#:~:text=Incumbent%20president%20Cristina%20Fern%C3%A1ndez%20de,seats%20in%20the%20National%20Congress.

4. *ARA Libertad (Q-2)*, Wikipedia, https://en.wikipedia.org/wiki/ARA_Libertad_(Q-2).

5. Verbatim Record, Public Sitting Held on Thursday, Nov. 29, 2012, at 9:30 a.m., at 6:23 and 6:49, No. ITLOS/PV.12/C20/1/Rev.1, International Tribunal for the Law of the Sea (Nov. 29, 2012), https://www.itlos.org/fileadmin/itlos/documents/cases/case_no.20/Verbatim_Records/ITLOS_PV.12_C20_1_Rev.1.pdf (326 as sum of 281 and 45; "We had to evacuate 281 people" and "we had to support the 45 crew members remaining on board").

6. Request for the Prescription for Provisional Measures Submitted by Argentina, *Argentina v. Ghana*, at 3, International Tribunal for the Law of the Sea (Nov. 14, 2012), https://www.itlos.org/fileadmin/itlos/documents/cases/case_no.20/C20_Request_Argentina.pdf. ("The crew of the warship detained included guest officers from the Navies of Bolivia, Brazil, Chile, Paraguay, Peru, South Africa, Suriname, Uruguay, and Venezuela.")

7. *Id.*, at 3. ("Frigate ARA Libertad arrived on the scheduled date of 1 October, 2012, and on that same day a formal welcome ceremony was held on board the ship.")

8. *Id.*, at 3. ("At 8:00 pm on 2 October 2012, a person claiming to be an official for the Judicial Service of the Superior Court of Judicature of Ghana [Commercial Division] arrived at Frigate ARA Libertad, together with other persons, in order to deliver an official letter bearing the same date which contained an order by the Court, rendered by Judge Richard Adjei-Frimpong, requiring that Frigate ARA Libertad be held at the Tema Port.")

9. Superior Court of Judicature in the High Court of Justice (Commercial Division), Accra, Ghana, *Order for Interlocutory Injunction and Interim Preservation of the "ARA Libertad,"* Case No. MISC/58/12 (Oct. 2, 2012).

10. *Supra* note 5 (281 people evacuated).

11. *Supra* note 6, at 1. ("Argentina instituted proceedings against Ghana before an arbitral tribunal established under Annex VII of the Convention by a note dated 29 October 2012 and received on 30 October 2012.")

12. Verbatim Record, Public Sitting Held on Thursday, Nov. 29, 2012, at 3 p.m., at 4:47–48, No. ITLOS/PV.12/C20/1/Rev.1, International Tribunal for the Law of the Sea (Nov. 29, 2012), https://www.itlos.org/fileadmin/itlos/documents/cases/case_no.20/Verbatim_Records/ITLOS_PV.12_C20_2_Rev.1.pdf. ("It is estimated that for every day the *ARA Libertad* remains at berth 11, the Ports Authority is incurring a potential loss of $160,000 per day.")

13. *Los Marinos Impidieron con Armas el Traslado de la Frigata en Ghana*, Clarin (Nov. 10, 2012), https://www.clarin.com/politica/marinos-impidieron-traslado-fragata-ghana_0_HJog66psDQg.html.

14. International Tribunal for the Law of the Sea, *Tribunal Orders Release of Argentine Frigate* "ARA Libertad," ITLOS Press Release 188 (Dec. 15, 2012), https://www.itlos.org/fileadmin/itlos/documents/press_releases_english/PR_188_E.pdf. ("[O]n 14 November 2012, Argentina submitted a request for the prescription of provisional measures under article 290, paragraph 5, of the United Nations Convention on the Law of the Sea to the Tribunal.")

15. International Tribunal for the Law of the Sea, *Press Release: Public Hearing to Be Held in the "ARA Libertad" Case (Argentina v. Ghana) on 29 and 30 November 2012*, ITLOS Press Release 185 (Nov. 28, 2012), https://www.itlos.org/fileadmin/itlos

/documents/press_releases_english/PR_185_E_1.pdf.; and International Tribunal for the Law of the Sea, *Order of 15 December 2012*, at 338, *The "ARA Libertad" Case (Argentina v. Ghana)*, No. (Dec. 15, 2012), https://www.itlos.org/fileadmin/itlos /documents/cases/case_no.20/published/C20_Order_151212.pdf.

16. *Supra* note 14. ("Ghana shall forthwith and unconditionally release the frigate ARA Libertad, shall ensure the frigate ARA Libertad, its Commander and crew are able to leave the port of Tema and the maritime areas under the jurisdiction of Ghana, and shall ensure that the frigate ARA Libertad is resupplied to that end.")

17. James Kraska, *"ARA Libertad" (Argentina v. Ghana)*, 107 Am. J. Int'l L. 404, 408 (2013). ("The vessel departed from Ghana on December 19 and was welcomed back in Argentina on January 9, 2013.")

18. Permanent Court of Arbitration, Procedural Order No. 1, at 3, *The Argentine Republic and The Republic of Ghana* (July 31, 2013), https://jusmundi.com /en/document/other/en-the-ara-libertad-arbitration-argentina-v-ghana-procedural -order-no-1-wednesday-31st-july-2013. (Hearing scheduled for Oct. 27–31, 2014.)

19. The Supreme Court of Ghana, *In the Matter of an Application to Invoke the Supervisory Jurisdiction of the Supreme Court*, No. J5/10/2013, June 20, 2013, https:// pcacases.com/web/sendAttach/431; and Permanent Court of Arbitration, *The Arbitral Tribunal Issues a Termination Order in the ARA Libertad Arbitration*, Press Release (Nov. 13, 2013), https://pcacases.com/web/sendAttach/438.

20. Alejandro Rebossio, *Cristina Fernández de la Bienvenida a la Fragata Libertad*, EL País (Jan. 10, 2013), https://elpais.com/internacional/2013/01/10/actualidad /1357781261_811371.html.

21. Video of the homecoming athttps://www.youtube.com/watch?v=OdSKA KE8W-Q (accessed Aug. 19, 2023), translation by Carla Russo. See also Joseph Cotterill, *Fragata Libertad, the Movie*, Financial Times (Jan. 3, 2013), https:// www.ft.com/content/7bf5b9 3e-1017-3d43-ac93-5341593bcaec.

22. *Id.*

23. Republic of Argentina, Form 18-K, Annual Report, at D-7 (Sept. 23, 2016), https://www.sec.gov/Archives/edgar/data/914021/000090342316001278/ex99 -d.htm ("[A]n unofficial U.S. dollar trading market developed in which the peso–U.S. dollar exchange rate differed substantially from the official peso–U.S. dollar exchange rate"); and *id.*, at D-29 ("Between mid-2014 and March 2015, the premium for U.S. dollars offered in the unofficial market narrowed from approximately 80% to 55%. This premium reduction reflected the temporary boost provided by a U.S. $10.3 billion three-year currency-swap agreement between the Central Bank and the People's Bank of China, as well as the Central Bank's issuance of U.S. dollar-denominated local bonds.")

24. IMF, *Argentina: 2016 Article IV Staff Report*, at 25 (Nov. 2016), https://www

.imf.org/external/pubs/ft/scr/2016/cr16346.pdf. ("Energy subsidies have risen dramatically over the past decade and, at 4 percent of GDP in 2015, constitute the bulk of non-pension social transfers.")

25. Francisco Buera and Juan Pablo Nicolini, *The Monetary and Fiscal History of Argentina, 1960–2017*, Staff Report 580, at 19–20, Federal Reserve Bank of Minneapolis (Dec. 2019), https://www.minneapolisfed.org/research/staff-reports/the-monetary-and-fiscal-history-of-argentina-1960-2017. ("Things changed between 2008 and 2010. The healthy surpluses started to disappear and became a 2 percent fiscal deficit by 2013. The deficit then continued to increase, reaching a worrying value of close to 6 percent by 2017. Given the lack of access to foreign borrowing that lasted until 2016, the deficits had to be financed by seigniorage, and inflation rose again, to an average close to 25 percent a year, remaining around that value until the end of the sample. Not all the deficit was financed by the central bank during the period: domestic debt instruments were issued, explaining the upward trend in debt since 2010.")

26. Benedict Mander, *Argentina's Inflation Figures in Question*, Financial Times (Feb. 6, 2007), https://www.ft.com/content/f8691722-b630-11db-9ee-0000779e2340; and William Seltzer and Joseph B. Kadane, *Politics and Statistics Collide in Argentina*, AMSTAT News (Dec. 1, 2012), https://magazine.amstat.org/blog/2012/12/01/argentinastatistics/.

27. *List of Nationalizations by Country,* Wikipedia, https://en.wikipedia.org/wiki/List_of_nationalizations_by_country#Argentina; and Hilary Burke and Helen Popper, *Argentina Moves to Seize Control of Repsol's YPF,* Reuters (Apr. 17, 2012), https://www.reuters.com/article/uk-argentina-ypf/argentina-moves-to-seize-control-of-repsols-ypf-idUKBRE83F19420120417.

28. Mark Mulligan, *Chile-Argentine Links under Stress,* Financial Times (Apr. 29, 2004), (mimeo) and *Chronology-Argentine, Uruguay Dispute Pulp Mill,* Reuters (Apr. 20, 2010), https://www.reuters.com/article/argentina-uruguay /chronology-argentine-uruguay-dispute-pulp-mill-idUSN209920420100420.

29. Monte Reel, *Argentina Pursues Iran in '94 Blast as Neighbors Court Ahmadinejad,* Was. Post (Jan. 14, 2007), https://www.washingtonpost.com/wp-dyn/content/article/2007/01/13/AR2007011301253.html?tid=a_inl_manual.

30. Emily Schmall, *Deal Reached for Inquiry on Bombing in Argentina,* N.Y. Times (Jan. 27, 2013), https://www.nytimes.com/2013/01/28/world/americas/argentina-and-iran-to-investigate-jewish-center-bombing.html.

31. Fabián Bosoer and Federico Finchelstein, *Argentina's About-Face on Terror,* N.Y. Times (Mar. 1, 2013), https://www.nytimes.com/2013/03/02/opinion/why-is-argentinas-president-cozying-up-to-iran.html.

32. Marisa Lago, Asst. Sec'y for Int'l. Markets and Development, U.S. Dept.

of Treasury, *Statement*, Subcommittee on International Monetary Policy and Trade of the Committee on Financial Services U.S. House of Representatives, 112th Congress (Sept. 21, 2011), at 15–16, https://www.govinfo.gov/content/pkg/CHRG -112hhrg72605/html/CHRG-112hhrg72605.htm. ("We share the very serious concerns that you raised about Argentina's actions . . . including its failure to honor its ICSID awards. . . . In light of these concerns, the United States will oppose lending to Argentina in the two [Multilateral Development Banks] in which Argentina participates—that is, the World Bank and the Inter-American Development Bank.")

33. Doug Palmer, *Obama Says to Suspect Trade Benefits for Argentina*, Reuters (Mar. 26, 2012); (mimeo). and Theodore R. Posner, *Good Faith Recognition and Enforcement of Arbitral Awards as a Criteria under the United States Generalized System of Preferences*, 106 Am. Soc'y Int'l L. 125, 126 (2012).

34. IMF, *Statement by the IMF Executive Board on Argentina*, Press Release No. 13/33 (Feb. 1, 2013), https://www.imf.org/en/News/Articles/2015/09/14/01/49 /pr1333. ("The Board called on Argentina to adopt the remedial measures to address the inaccuracy of CPI-GBA and GDP data.")

35. ¶238, Brief for the United States of America as *Amicus Curia* in Support of Reversal, *NML Capital, Ltd. et al. v. Republic of Argentina*, No. 12-105 (2d Cir. Apr. 4, 2012) at 4, 7.

36. Daniel Bases, *IMF to File Brief with U.S. Supreme Court in Argentina Case*, Reuters (July 17, 2013), https://www.reuters.com/article/imf-argentina-bond holders/imf-to-file-brief-with-u-s-supreme-court-in-argentina-case-idUSL1 N0FN2JB20130718; Joseph Cotterill, *The IMF Won't Be Argentina's Pari Passu Frenemy. Why?*, Financial Times (July 23, 2013), https://www.ft.com/content/4157 080e-3ba9-3b0a-9f5b-0a8cf71058ad; Jude Webber, *IMF: Sorry Argentina, You Are on Your Own*, Financial Times (July 24, 2013), https://www.ft.com/content /57b65bb7-7a82-3224-a010-c9606df7b138; and IMF, *Transcript of Press Roundtable with IMF Managing Director* (Aug. 1, 2013), at 3, https://www.imf.org/en/News /Articles/2015/09/28/04/54/tr080113a. (Managing Director Christine Lagarde said, "The United States informed me that it would not support us filing an Amicus Curiae brief. Therefore, I decided to withdraw such proposal. But it doesn't affect or change our concern, which is high and which I think is shared by many.")

37. Jeromin Zettelmeyer, Christoph Trebesch, and Mitu Gulati, *The Greek Debt Restructuring: An Autopsy*, WP13-8, Peterson Inst. for Int'l Econ., at 53 (Aug. 2013), https://www.piie.com/publications/working-papers/greek-debt-restructuring -autopsy. (Noting "not passed" next to seventeen out of thirty-five listed bonds documented under English law.)

38. For two detailed accounts of the U.S. Treasury's working group on bond contracts, see Mark Sobel, *Strengthening Collective Action Clauses: Catalyzing*

Change—The Back Story, 11 Cap. Mkts. L.J. 1 (2016); and Alejandro Díaz de León, *Mexico's Adoption of New Standards in International Sovereign Debt Contracts: CACs, Pari Passu and a Trust Indenture*, 11 Cap. Mkts. L.J. 12 (2016).

39. Int'l Capital Mkt. Ass'n, Standard *Pari Passu* Provision for the Terms and Conditions of Sovereign Notes (2014), https://www.icmagroup.org/assets /documents/Resources/ICMA-Standard-Pari-Passu-Provision-August-2014.pdf. [https://perma.cc/FK9B-QY-JY].

40. Int'l Capital Mkt. Ass'n, Standard Aggregated Collective Action Clauses for the Terms and Conditions of Sovereign Notes (2014), https:// www.icmagroup.org/assets/documents/Resources/ICMA-Standard-CACs-August -2014.pdf.

41. Int'l Capital Mkt. Ass'n, ICMA Sovereign Bond Consultation Paper (Dec. 2013) (mimeo).

42. *Int'l Capital Mkt. Ass'n, ICMA Publishes Revised Collective Action Clauses (CACs) and a New Standard Pari Passu Clause to Facilitate Future Sovereign Debt Restructuring*, Press Release (Aug. 29, 2014), https://www.icmagroup.org/assets /documents/Media/Press-releases-2014/ICMA1406---ICMA-publishes-revised -collective-action-clauses.pdf.

43. The best overall summary of Argentina's offshore litigation can be found in the country's periodic 18-K Annual Report filings with the Securities and Exchange Commission. See Republic of Argentina, Annual Report (Form 18-K) (Sept. 30, 2011), 181–92, https://www.sec.gov/Archives/edgar/data/914021/000090342311000486 /roa-18k_0928.htm. The best summary of Elliott's successful attachments can be found in its 2016 settlement agreement with Argentina, which lists outstanding attachments. See Republic of Argentina, Agreement in Principal, at 14–20 (Feb. 29, 2016) (see specifically *Schedule 1: NML PENDING ACTIONS/ATTACHMENTS*), http://servicios.infoleg.gob.ar/infolegInternet/anexos/255000-259999/259940 /ley27249-2.pdf. For a detailed treatment of the Argentina bond litigation in Europe, see Sebastian Grund, Sovereign Debt Restructuring and the Law: The Holdout Creditor Problem in Argentina and Greece (2023), at 38–44.

44. ¶327, Opinion, *NML Capital, Ltd. v. Republic of Argentina*, No. 08 Civ. 6978 (S.D.N.Y. Apr. 22, 2011) ("On February 7, 2011, NML applied for, and the court signed, an *ex parte* order of attachment directed to assets of the Republic held at Honeywell International, Inc. in the name of Empressa Argentina de Soluciones Satelitales, S.A. ["AR-SAT"]. NML now moves to confirm the order of attachment. . . . NML's motion to confirm the attachment is denied.")

45. ¶61, Order Denying Plaintiff's Ex Parte Application for Temporary Protective Order, Temporary Restraining Order, and Order to Show Cause, at 4:18–22, *NML Capital, Ltd. v. Spaceport Sys. Int'l, Republic of Argentina*, No. CV 11-03507 SJO

(RZx) (C.D. Cal. May 25, 2011) ("On April 25, 2011 . . . Plaintiff asks the Court to place a temporary lien on the Aquarius/SAC-D Satellite and to prevent the Defendants and the United States from transferring or launching the Aquarius/SAC-D Satellite for at least 40 days.")

46. ¶51, Order Granting Defendants' Motion to Dismiss, *NML Capital, Ltd. v. Space Exploration Technologies Corp., et al.*, No. CV 14-02262 SVW (C.D. Cal. Mar. 6, 2015) at 13. ("Because the Launch Service Rights are immune from attachment and execution under the FSIA, the Court GRANTS Defendants' motion to dismiss the complaint.")

47. ¶1, NML Motion to Compel, *NML Capital, Ltd. v. Excelerate Energy, LLC*, No. 08 MC 574 (S.D. Tex. Nov. 19, 2008).

48. ¶41, Transcript of hearing held on Jan. 24, 2013, *NML Capital, Ltd. v. Republic of Argentina*, No. 3-12-mc-80 (N.D. Tex. Feb. 6, 2013) (regarding discovery on ExxonMobil, Apache Oil Corp., EOG Resources, Inc.).

49. For example ¶1, Motion to Quash of the Republic of Argentina, *NML Capital, Ltd. v. Republic of Argentina*, No. A12-mc-0745 (W.D. Tex. Aug. 17, 2012) (regarding subpoena served on ConocoPhillips on July 11, 2012).

50. ¶2, Amended Appendix of Exhibits to the Motion to Quash of the Republic of Argentina, *NML Capital, Ltd. v. Republic of Argentina*, No. 4:12-mc-00520 (S.D. Tex. Aug. 17, 2012) (includes copies of subpoenas or notices of intent to serve subpoenas to Petroleo Brasileiro S.A. in New York on Aug. 16, 2012; Petrobras America, Inc., in Texas on Aug. 16, 2012; ConocoPhillips in Texas on July 11, 2012; Chevron Corp. in California on July 26, 2012; ExxonMobil Corp. in Texas on July 11, 2012; Apache Oil Corp. in Texas on July 31, 2012; and EOG Resources, Inc., in Texas on Aug. 7, 2012).

51. ¶4, First Brief of Defendant-Appellant the Republic of Argentina, *NML Capital, Ltd. v. Republic of Argentina*, No. 12-17738 (9th Cir. Mar. 22, 2013). ("[T]he Republic of Argentina . . . appeals from two district court Orders . . . rejecting the Republic's motion to quash a post-judgment subpoena served on non-party Chevron Corporation.")

52. ¶37, Stipulation to Withdraw Motions to Quash and Close Case No. 13-MC-51030, *NML Capital, Ltd. v. Republic of Argentina*, No. 13-mc-51030 (E.D. Mich. Aug. 27, 2014). ("Plaintiff NML Capital, Ltd., Defendant The Republic of Argentina, and movant The Dow Chemical Company . . . stipulate that the subpoena . . . served on Dow on April 25, 2013 has been resolved and the Motions to Quash the Subpoena filed by Argentina and Dow are withdrawn.")

53. *Republic of Argentina v. NML Capital, Ltd.*, 573 U.S. 134 (2014) (decided on June 16, 2014).

54. *Supra* chapter 7, note 24.

55. *Supra* chapter 7, note 24.

56. ¶494, Transcript of hearing held on Nov. 15, 2013, at 19:20–22, *NML Capital, Ltd. v. Republic of Argentina*, No. 08 Civ. 6978 (S.D.N.Y. Nov. 26, 2013). ("[N]ow he just wants litigation about litigation, discovery about discovery, which is just a first step to further proceedings before your Honor.")

57. Form 990: Return of Organization Exempt from Income Tax: American Task Force Argentina (2010–2015), https://apps.irs.gov/pub/epostcard/cor/208233448 _201512_990O_2017041914300705.pdf (mimeo for years 2010, 2011, 2012, 2013, 2014, 2015, 2016; hyperlink above is to the 2015 form).

58. *Supra* chapter 7, note 3 (background on Raben, Soderberg, and Shapiro).

59. *Supra* note 57 (2015 tax returns).

60. *Supra* chapter 7, note 4 (initial members of ATFA according to website).

61. *About Us*, American Task Force Argentina, https://web.archive.org/web /20120209150433/http://www.atfa.org/about/ (ATFA members as of Feb. 9, 2012).

62. Ianthe Jeanne Dugan, *Argentine Lobby Mystifies 'Members,'* Wall St. J. (Oct. 15, 2012), https://www.wsj.com/articles/SB10000872396390444657804578057805092 3796499176.

63. Colin Wilhelm and Issac Arnsdorf, *Republicans Writing Puerto Rico Fix Face Attack Ads*, Politico (Apr. 13, 2016), https://www.politico.com/story/2016 /04/puerto-rico-debt-crisis-gop-attack-ads-221907; Jonathan Mahler and Nicholas Confessore, *Inside the Billion-Dollar Battle for Puerto Rico's Future*, N.Y. Times (Dec. 19, 2015), https://www.nytimes.com/2015/12/20/us/politics/puerto-rico-money -debt.html.

64. Robert J. Shapiro and Nam D. Pham, *Discredited—The Impact of Argentina's Sovereign Debt Default and Debt Restructuring on U.S. Taxpayers and Investors* (Oct. 2006), at 3, 24, 25, and 26, http://www.sonecon.com/docs/studies/studies /argentina_1006.pdf (accessed Aug. 19, 2023). ("This report was prepared with support from the American Task Force for Argentina.")

65. For example, Professor Scott's paper was prominently featured on ATFA's website on Jan. 5, 2007, at https://web.archive.org/web/20070105223204/http:// www.atfa.org/ and was still featured on its Resources page on February 15, 2010, at https://web.archive.org/web/20100215123433/http://atfa.org/resources/.

66. Hal S. Scott, *Sovereign Debt Default: Cry for the United States, Not Argentina*, Washington Legal Foundation, Critical Legal Issues Working Paper No. 140, at 1 (Sept. 2006), https://web.archive.org/web/20100714112211/http://www.atfa.org /resources/scott_wp.pdf.

67. *Id.*, at 10.

68. Transcript of Public Hearing Re: Argentine Bond Default, New York State Senate Standing Committee on Banking (Apr. 23, 2010), https://web.archive.org

/web/20100714115713/http://www.atfa.org/files/nytranscript.pdf; and information on event on ATFA website, https://web.archive.org/web/20100714110154 /http://www.atfa.org/nysenate/.

69. Supra note 57 (2015 Form 990, Part VII Section B, Independent Contractors, an entry for "ARKO, Ed Joao Carlos Saad 6th Floor Brasilia, BR, for Consultation Services, $360,000.")

70. Telephone interviews with Stefan Engelsberger (Jan.–Feb. 2021).

71. See, for example, *ATFA Denounces Christine Lagarde's Effort to Immerse the IMF in a U.S. Court Case between Argentina and Its U.S. Creditors*, Press Release (July 17, 2013), https://www.businesswire.com/news/home/20130717006371/en/ATFA-Denounces-Christine-Lagardes-Effort-to-Immerse-the-IMF-in-a-U.S.-Court-Case-Between-Argentina-and-Its-U.S.-Creditors (criticizing an announced intention to file an amicus brief in Argentina's favor, ATFA executive director Robert Raben said, "Were the IMF's Board to approve this request, informed IMF watchers assure me that it would represent an unprecedented power grab by the Fund—an attempt to end-run around the government of the United States in a domestic legal matter.")

72. Testimony of Michael C. Spencer of July 20, 2018, ¶4–5, Exhibit 3, at 16, *Milberg LLP v. Drawrah Limited et al.*, 19 Civ. 4058 (S.D.N.Y. May 6, 2019). ("As the Equal Treatment injunction strategy began to succeed, it attracted lots of public attention, particularly in Argentina, and soon enough not only Judge Griesa but the *Varela* plaintiffs themselves were featured in news articles and subject to a lot of criticism for supposedly being anti-Argentina. Eventually some of the plaintiffs were subject to harassment from the Argentine tax authorities as the Kirchner administration became more aggressive.")

73. ATFA, *ATFA Launches New "Fact Check" Website to Counter Argentine "Myths" on Debt Dispute*, Press Release (July 6, 2014), https://www.prnewswire.com/news-releases/atfa-launches-new-fact-check-website-to-counter-argentine-myths-on-debt-dispute-265969631.html.

74. *Players*, FactCheckArgentina.org (July 19, 2015), https://web.archive.org/web/20150719194018/http://factcheckargentina.org/followthemoney.

75. *The Kirchner Kickback Crew*, FactCheckArgentina.org (July 19, 2015), https://web.archive.org/web/20150915191349/http://factcheckargentina.org/the-kirchner-relationship; and *Báez-Kirchner Hotel Deals*, FactCheckArgentina.org (July 19, 2015), https://web.archive.org/web/20150719194018/http://factcheckargentina.org/followthemoney#baez-kirchner-hotel-deals.

76. ¶90-1, Transcript of videographed deposition of Patricia Amunategui taken on Sept. 11, 2014, *NML Capital, Ltd. v. Republic of Argentina*, No. 14-cv-492-RFB-VCF (Nevada Mar. 3, 2015).

77. *Nevada Shelters Offshore Shell Companies*, Times Record (Aug. 14, 2016),

https://www.swtimes.com/story/news/nation-world/2016/08/14/nevada-shelters -offshore-shell-companies/25851025007/.

78. See, for example, Bastian Obermayer and Frederik Obermaier, The Panama Papers: Breaking the Story of How the Rich and Powerful Hide Their Money (2016).

79. Felix Salmon, *Vulture Funds Exposed in Playboy*, Columbia J.R. (Feb. 24, 2011), https://archives.cjr.org/the_audit/vulture_funds_stripped_bare_in.php. (Quoting a December 2010 *Playboy* article by Aram Roston: "The vultures set up an intelligence operation to gather information and pursue allegations of corruption against the Congo. Newman supposedly set up an operation in London to conduct private investigations." Also quoting an investor who said, "They're all former spooks. . . . Senior guys, station chiefs.")

80. Tony Allen-Mills, *'Vultures' Expose Corruption*, Sunday Times (London) (June 15, 2008), https://www.thetimes.co.uk/article/vultures-expose-corruption -tm3h9nkwk0m.

81. *The Causes of Sovereign Defaults*, Moody's Investors Service (Aug. 13, 2020), at 5 (mimeo). (Stating Argentina's 2014 default applied to $29.43 billion of bonds.)

82. *Argentina Settles Five Outstanding Investment Treaty Arbitration Claims in Historic Break with Its Anti-Enforcement Stance*, Lexology (Oct. 14, 2013), https://hsfnotes.com/arbitration/2013/10/14/argentina-settles-five-outstanding-investment-treaty-arbitration-claims-in-historic-break-with-its-anti-enforcement -stance/; Jonathan Kandell, *Why Argentina Is Eager to Settle Its Financial Dispute with Repsol*, Institutional Investor (Dec. 5, 2013), https://www.institutionalinvestor .com/article/b14zbbk4xbchxx/why-argentina-is-eager-to-settle-its-financial-dispute -with-repsol; and Stanley Reed and Raphael Minder, *Repsol in $5 Billion Settlement with Argentina*, N.Y. Times (Feb. 25, 2014), https://www.nytimes.com/2014/02/26 /business/international/repsol-said-to-reach-settlement-with-argentina.html.

83. Paris Club, *The Paris Club and the Argentine Republic Agree to a Resumption of Payments and Clearance of All Arrears* (May 29, 2014), http://www.clubdeparis .org/en/traitements/argentina-29-05-2014/en; and Ken Parks, *Argentina Agrees to Pay US$9.7 Billion to Paris Club*, Wall St. J. (May 29, 2014), https://www.wsj.com /articles/argentina-strikes-deal-with-paris-club-to-clear-debt-arrears-1401348539.

10. It All Falls Apart

1. Mark Weidemaier, *Argentina's Cert Petition Denied*, Credit Slips (June 16, 2014), https://www.creditslips.org/creditslips/2014/06/argentinas-cert-petition-denied.html.

2. Mark Weidemaier, *A Quick One-Two Punch: Argentina Loses Discovery Case,*

Too, Credit Slips (June 16, 2014), https://www.creditslips.org/creditslips/2014/06 /a-quick-one-two-punch-argentina-loses-discovery-case-too.html.

3. ¶678, Exhibit 22, Message by National Broadcast, from President Cristina Fernández de Kirchner on June 16, 2014, *NML Capital, Ltd. v. Republic of Argentina*, No. 08 Civ. 6978 (S.D.N.Y. Sept. 24, 2014).

4. ¶678, Exhibit 23, Economy Ministry Press Announcement June 17, 2014, Press Conference, *NML Capital, Ltd. v. Republic of Argentina*, No. 08 Civ. 6978 (S.D.N.Y. Sept. 24, 2014).

5. ¶537, Transcript of hearing held on June 18, 2014, at 4:14–15, *NML Capital, Ltd. v. Republic of Argentina*, No. 08 Civ. 6978 (S.D.N.Y. June 26, 2014).

6. Transcript (Draft No. 2), *Commemorating the Life and Service of Judge Thomas P. Griesa* (S.D.N.Y. Apr. 2, 2018), at 52–53. (Daniel Pollack speaking about his relationship with Judge Griesa.)

7. Interview with Daniel Pollack (June 7, 2018, New York City) (hereinafter Pollack interview).

8. McCarter & English, *Pollack and Kaminsky to Join McCarter and English in New York*, Press Release (Oct. 1, 2009), https://www.globenewswire.com/news-release /2009/10/01/405752/174526/en/Pollack-Kaminsky-to-Join-McCarter-English-in -New-York.html. ("Mr. Pollack also successfully challenged New York Attorney General Eliot Spitzer . . . for exceeding his authority in the market-timing investigations. . . . Mr. Pollack first came to public notice early in his career in a lengthy trial on behalf of institutional commercial paper holders against Goldman Sachs arising out of the collapse of Penn Central.")

9. See Fed. R. Civ. P. Rule 53, Masters.

10. Pollack interview.

11. ¶530, Order for Appointment of Special Master, *NML Capital, Ltd. v. Republic of Argentina*, No. 08 Civ. 6978 (S.D.N.Y. June 23, 2014).

12. ¶622, Transcript of hearing held on June 27, 2014, at 26:16–17, *NML Capital, Ltd. v. Republic of Argentina*, No. 08 Civ. 6978 (S.D.N.Y. July 31, 2014).

13. *Id.*, at 33:1-9.

14. *Statement of Daniel A. Pollack, Special Master in Argentina Debt Litigation*, Press Release (July 3, 2014), https://www.prnewswire.com/news-releases/statement -of-daniel-a-pollack-special-master-in-argentina-debt-litigation-265760171.html.

15. Pollack interview; and Ken Parks, *Argentina Economy Minister Asks Mediator for More Time in Debt Dispute*, Wall St. J. (July 7, 2014), https://www.wsj.com/articles /argentina-economy-minister-asks-for-more-time-in-debt-dispute-1404779974.

16. Ken Parks, *Argentina to Continue Debt Talks Friday without Economy Minister*, Wall St. J. (July 10, 2014), https://www.wsj.com/articles/argentina-to-continue -debt-talks-friday-without-economy-minister-1405003094; and Maria Armental,

No Resolution in Argentina Bond Dispute, Wall St. J. (July 11, 2014), https://www.wsj
.com/articles/no-resolution-in-argentina-bond-dispute-1405118408. ("Government
representatives, bondholders meet separately with mediator to no avail.")

17. Jay Newman, *We Holdouts Are Open to Compromise but Argentina Has to
Talk*, Financial Times (July 7, 2014), https://www.ft.com/content/63cf7454-05be
-11e4-8b94-00144feab7de.

18. Axel Kicillof, *Vulture Funds Are Showing Their True Colors*, Financial
Times (July 9, 2014), https://www.ft.com/content/bf78b33a-0779-11e4-b1b0
-00144feab7de.

19. Nicola Stock, *Argentina Must Make Whole the Retail Bondholders Whom
It Once Targeted*, Financial Times (July 17, 2014) https://www.ft.com/content
/db675fd8-08eb-11e4-8d27-00144feab7de.

20. ¶619, Transcript of hearing held on July 22, 2014, at 44:4–16 and 49:6,
NML Capital, Ltd. v. Republic of Argentina, No. 08 Civ. 6978 (S.D.N.Y. July 30, 2014).

21. *Id.*, at 52:10–53:3.

22. *Statement of Daniel A. Pollack, Special Master in Argentina Debt Litigation*,
Press Release (July 24, 2014) (mimeo) ("After speaking with both sides . . . I proposed
direct, face-to-face talks between the parties. The representatives of the Bondholders
were agreeable to direct talks; the representatives of the Republic declined to engage
in direct talks."); and Ken Parks, *Argentine Delegation to Return Home after Debt Talks
Fail*, Wall St. J. (July 25, 2014), https://www.wsj.com/articles/BL-265B-988.

23. *Statement of Daniel A. Pollack, Special Master in Argentina Debt Litigation*,
Press Release (July 30, 2014 at 5:17 B.S.T.) (mimeo); Matt Day and Nicole Hong,
Argentina's Stocks, Debt Rally as Officials Negotiate to Avert a Default, Wall St. J. (July
29, 2014), https://www.wsj.com/articles/argentinas-stocks-debt-rally-as-officials-ne
gotiate-to-avert-a-default-1406670841?mod=europe_home; Pollack interview.

24. Taos Turner, Nicole Hong, and Matt Day, *Argentina Banks Preparing Bid to
Help Argentina Avoid Default*, Wall S. J. (July 30, 2014), https://www.wsj.com/articles
/argentina-banks-preparing-bid-to-help-argentina-avoid-default-1406692665.

25. Pollack interview.

26. *Argentine Economy Minister Kicillof Says Country Not in Default*, Reuters
(July 31, 2014), https://www.reuters.com/article/us-argentina-debt-kicillof/argen
tine-economy-minister-kicillof-says-country-not-in-default-idUSKBN0G02IV
20140731; Sarah Marsh and Richard Lough, *Argentine Markets Fall Post-Default,
NY Hearing on Friday*, Reuters (July 31, 2014), https://www .reuters.com/articl
e/argentina-debt/update-4-argentine-markets-fall-post-default-ny-hearing-on
-friday-idUSL6N0Q64AV20140731; and Video of Kicillof's New York consulate
press conference at *Argentina Heads into Default as Debt Talks End; Pro-Government
Demonstration*, AP Archive, https://www.youtube.com/watch?v=vP_nV6vSFfM.

27. Irene Caselli, *Argentina Defaults—But Isn't Using the 'D-Word,'* Christian Science Monitor (July 31, 2014), https://www.csmonitor.com/World/Americas /2014/0731/Argentina-defaults-but-isn-t-using-the-d-word. ("Argentina defaulted on its debt for the second time in little over a decade. But Argentina isn't calling it a 'default'. . . . The word 'default' carries bad memories for Argentines. . . . Last week, President Cristina Fernandez de Kirchner said a new term was needed to categorize what was happening in Argentina, since it wasn't a 'true' default. The hashtag #GrieFault started trending on Twitter soon after.")

28. ¶637, Transcript of hearing held on Aug. 1, 2014, at 4:24–25, *NML Capital, Ltd. v. Republic of Argentina*, No. 08 Civ. 6978 (S.D.N.Y. Aug. 13, 2014).

29. *Statement of Daniel A. Pollack, Special Master in Argentina Debt Litigation*, Press Release (July 30, 2014 6:43 ET), https://www.prnewswire.com/news-releases /daniel-a-pollack-special-master-in-argentina-debt-litigation-issues-the-following -statement-269292491.html.

30. ¶678, Exhibit 26, *NML Capital, Ltd. v. Republic of Argentina*, No. 08 Civ. 6978 (S.D.N.Y. Civ. Sept. 24, 2014). (Mimeo of Argentina's "Legal Notice" advert published in the *Washington Post* on Aug. 7, 2014).

31. ¶646, Transcript of hearing held on Aug. 8, 2014, at 4:2–3, *NML Capital, Ltd. v. Republic of Argentina*, No. 08 Civ. 6978 (S.D.N.Y. Aug. 20, 2014) (hereinafter Aug. 8 hearing).

32. *Id.*, at 10:8–11.

33. *Id.*, at 10:23–11:14. ("[S]hows me on the body of a vulture").

34. *Cleary's Default* (Aug. 4, 2014), Factcheckargentina.com, https:// web.archive.org/web/20140808062120/http://factcheckargentina.org/clearys -default/. See also *Riposte to Blackman* (Aug. 11, 2014), Factcheckargentina.com, https://web.archive.org/web/20140813081113/http://factcheckargentina.org/.

35. Aug. 8 hearing, at 11:18 through 12:3.

36. *Id.*, at 13:12–16.

37. *Id.*, at 15:14–18.

38. ¶693, Amended and Supplemental Order, *NML Capital, Ltd. v. Republic of Argentina*, No. 08 Civ. 6978 (S.D.N.Y. Oct. 3, 2014).

39. ¶694, Transcript of hearing held on Sept. 26, 2014, *NML Capital, Ltd. v. Republic of Argentina*, No. 08 Civ. 6978 (S.D.N.Y. Oct. 8, 2014).

40. Blocking payments on these Argentine law U.S. dollar–denominated securities was of particular interest to the plaintiffs. They were concerned that the government might later try to issue more of such bonds in an injunction-evading debt swap.

41. ¶696, Transcript of hearing held on Sept. 29, 2014, at 18:12–19:13, *NML Capital, Ltd. v. Republic of Argentina*, No. 08 Civ. 6978 (S.D.N.Y. Oct. 8, 2014).

42. International Capital Markets Association, *ICMA Publishes Revised Collective Action Clauses (CACs) and a New Standard Pari Passu Clause to Facilitate Future Sovereign Debt Restructurings*, Press Release (Aug. 29, 2014) (mimeo).

43. Elaine Moore, *Sovereign Debt Plan Takes on Holdouts*, Financial Times (Sept. 2, 2014), https://www.ft.com/content/05718380-2df4-11e4-b330-00144feabdco.

44. G20 Finance Ministers and Central Bank Governors, *Communiqué-Annex* (Sept. 21, 2014), http://www.g20.utoronto.ca/2014/2014-0921-finance.html.

45. IMF, *IMF Executive Board Discusses Strengthening the Contractual Framework in Sovereign Debt Restructuring*, Press Release 14/459 (Oct. 6, 2014), https://www.imf.org/en/News/Articles/2015/09/14/01/49/pr14459.

46. IMF, *Strengthening the Contractual Framework to Address Collective Action Problems in Sovereign Debt Restructuring*, Staff Report (Oct. 2014), https://www.imf.org/en/Publications/Policy-Papers/Issues/2016/12/31/Strengthening-the-Contractual-Framework-to-Address-Collective-Action-Problems-in-Sovereign-PP4911.

47. Gregory Makoff, *Email to Jeremey Pam Re: IIF Event* (Oct. 10, 2014) (mimeo). ("I went to IIF. Good IMF, UST, IIF line up—take icma and do it. No more changes. Consensus was reached. They almost sang cumbia.")

48. Jack Farchy and Elaine Moore, *Investors Snap Up Kazakhstan Dollar Bond*, Financial Times, Oct. 7, 2014, https://www.ft.com/content/4f4c0a82-4e21-11e4-bfda-00144feab7de.

49. G20 Leaders, *Communiqué* (Nov. 16, 2014), http://www.g20.utoronto.ca/2015/151116-communique.pdf. ("We welcome the progress achieved on the implementation of strengthened collective action and *pari passu* clauses in international sovereign bond contracts, which will contribute to the orderliness and predictability of sovereign debt restructuring processes. We ask the IMF, in consultation with other parties, to continue promoting the use of such clauses and to further explore market-based ways to speed up their incorporation in the outstanding stock of international sovereign debt.")

50. Davide Scigliuzzo, *Mexico Breaks New Ground with Issuer-Friendly Bond*, Reuters (Nov. 18, 2014), https://www.reuters.com/article/mexico-bondholders-cacs-idINL2N0T81DM20141118; and United Mexican States, Free Writing Prospectus (Reg. No. 333-185462) (Nov. 18, 2014), https://www.sec.gov/Archives/edgar/data/101368/000119312514417034/d824076dfwp.htm.

51. IMF, *Fourth Progress Report on Inclusion of Enhanced Contractual Provisions in International Sovereign Bond Contracts*, Staff Report (Mar. 2019) at 6, https://www.imf.org/en/Publications/Policy-Papers/Issues/2019/03/21/Fourth-Progress-Report-on-Inclusion-of-Enhanced-Contractual-Provisions-in-International-46671.

52. *Maurico Macri:"Ahora Hay Que ir, Sentarse en lo del Juez Griesa y Hacer*

lo que Diga," La Nación (June 19, 2014), https://www.lanacion.com.ar/economia /mauricio-macri-ahora-hay-que-ir-sentarse-en-lo-del-juez-griesa-y-hacer-lo-que -diga-nid1702716/.

53. *Supra* chapter 9, note 57 (ATFA's 2015 filing with the Internal Revenue Service).

54. Christina Fernández de Kirchner, Sinceramente, at 356–59 (2015). (She accuses the hedge funds of supporting a five-point plan developed by former Bush administration official Carlos Gutierrez to "attack and wear down the government." The plan included (1) "grinding and eroding the figure of the president of the nation," (2) "propitiate a wave of rumors to generate economic instability," (3) "prevent access to financing in the international capital markets," (4) "gain time to achieve a favorable agreement with a new government," and (5) "hire journalists, media outlets in Argentina and other countries to attack the government and directly or indirectly finance opposition politicians and trade unionists."); author's translation.

55. ¶756, Transcript of hearing held on Feb. 25, 2015, *NML Capital, Ltd. v. Republic of Argentina*, No. 08 Civ. 6978 (S.D.N.Y. Mar. 10, 2015); and ¶778, Transcript of hearing held on Apr. 22, 2015, *NML Capital, Ltd. v. Republic of Argentina*, No. 08 Civ. 6978 (S.D.N.Y. May 1, 2015), at 4:10–22.

56. Bob Van Voris, *Deutsche Bank Claims NML 'Harassment' over Argentine Bonds*, Bloomberg (July 6, 2015), https://www.bloomberg.com/news/articles/2015 -07-06/deutsche-bank-accuses-nml-aurelius-of-improper-tactics.

57. ¶773, Transcript of hearing held on Mar. 18, 2015, at 4:14–15, *NML Capital, Ltd. v. Republic of Argentina*, No. 08 Civ. 6978 (S.D.N.Y. Mar. 26, 2015) at 4:10–22.

58. ¶819, Transcript of hearing held on Aug. 12, 2015, at 19:4–6, *NML Capital, Ltd. v. Republic of Argentina*, No. 08 Civ. 6978 (S.D.N.Y. Aug. 28, 2015).

59. Testimony of Michael C. Spencer of July 20, 2018, ¶4–5, Exhibit 3, at 13, *Milberg LLP v. Drawrah Limited et al.*, 19 Civ. 4058 (S.D.N.Y. May 6, 2019).

60. ¶20, Opinion and Order, *NML Capital, Ltd. v. Republic of Argentina*, No. 14 Civ. 8601 (S.D.N.Y. June 5, 2015).

61. ¶1, Complaint, *Old Castle Holdings, Ltd. v. Republic of Argentina*, No. 14 Civ. 4091 (S.D.N.Y. June 5, 2014); and ¶1, Complaint, *Lightwater Corporation Limited v. Republic of Argentina*, No. 14 Civ. 4092 (S.D.N.Y. June 5, 2014).

62. Telephone interview with Mark Kalish (Sept. 29, 2022).

63. See the dockets in the following cases: ¶1, Complaint, *VR Global Partners, L.P. v. Republic of Argentina*, No. 11 Civ. 8817 (S.D.N.Y. Dec. 2, 2011); ¶1, Complaint, *Tortus Capital Master Fund, L.P. v. Republic of Argentina*, No. 14 Civ. 1109 (S.D.N.Y. Feb. 21, 2014); ¶1, Complaint, *Yellow Crane Holdings, LLC v. Republic of Argentina*, No. 14 Civ. 5675 (S.D.N.Y. July 24, 2014); ¶1, Complaint, *Attestor Master Value Fund LP v. Republic of Argentina*, No. 14 Civ. 5849 (S.D.N.Y. Civ. July 29, 2014); ¶1, Complaint,

MCHA Holdings, LLC v. Republic of Argentina, No. 14 Civ. 7637 (S.D.N.Y. Sept. 19, 2014); ¶1, Complaint, *Arag-A Limited et al. v. Republic of Argentina*, No. 14 Civ. 9855 (S.D.N.Y. Dec. 12, 2014); ¶1, Complaint, *Trinity Investments Limited v. Republic of Argentina*, No. 14 Civ. 10016 (S.D.N.Y. Dec. 18, 2014); ¶1, Complaint, *Procella Holdings L.P. v. Republic of Argentina*, No. 15 Civ. 3932 (S.D.N.Y. May 21, 2015); ¶1, Complaint, *White Hawthorne, LLC v. Republic of Argentina*, No. 15 Civ. 4767 (S.D.N.Y. June 18, 2015); ¶1, Complaint, *Honero Fund I, LLC v. Republic of Argentina*, No. 15 Civ. 1553 (S.D.N.Y. Mar. 3, 2015); and ¶1, Complaint, *Bybrook Capital Master Fund LP et al. v. Republic of Argentina*, No. 15 Civ. 2369 (S.D.N.Y. Mar. 30, 2015).

64. 28 U.S.C §1961(a), Post Judgment Interest Rates.

65. For details on the calculation, see Makoff and Weidemaier, *supra* chapter 6, note 1. However, in rough terms, a plaintiff asking for a judgment in 2003 on a 10% coupon bond obtained an amount of 1.2 times par, par plus two years of missed interest at 10%; this then accreted at about 1% a year for the next thirteen years, bringing its value to near 1.5 times par. In contrast, a plaintiff with the same bond holding off asking for a money judgment was owed in early 2016 par plus fifteen years of missed interest at 10%, or 2.5 times par, plus an additional amount for interest-on-interest at the New York statutory rate of 9%, which brought it up to 3.5 times par.

66. Benedict Mander, *Argentines Take to the Streets over Nisman's Mysterious Death*, Financial Times (Jan. 20, 2015), https://www.ft.com/content/6b850faa -a0bf-11e4-8ad8-00144feab7de.

67. Joshua Partlow and Irene Caselli, *Mauricio Macri Elected President of Argentina*, Was. Post (Nov. 23, 2015), https://www.washingtonpost.com/world/the_ameri cas/argentines-head-to-polls-to-choose-new-president--and-their-future-course /2015/11/22/0af46af9-fb32-424d-be46-70f61f62fcf9_story.html.

11. The Settlement

1. Interview with Luis Caputo (May 23, 2019, Buenos Aires) (hereinafter Caputo interview).

2. Interview with Daniel Pollack (June 7, 2018, New York City) (hereinafter Pollack interview).

3. ¶876, Declaration of Jay Newman, at 3, *NML Capital, Ltd. v. Republic of Argentina*, No. 08 Civ. 6978 (S.D.N.Y. Feb. 18, 2016) (hereinafter Newman declaration); and Pollack interview, Caputo interview..

4. Pollack interview; Paula Lugones, *Pollack Cuenta Todos los Secretos de la Negociación con los Fondoes Buitre*, Clarín (Apr. 30, 2016), https://www.clarin.com /economia/pollack-secretos-negociacion-fondos-buitre_0_4yIv5Ihgb.html.

5. Stephen Adler and Sujata Rao, *Argentina's Macri Hopes for Creditor Deal Early in 2016*, Reuters (Jan. 22, 2016), https://www.reuters.com/article/us-argen tina-president/argentinas-macri-hopes-for-creditor-deal-early-in-2016-idUSKCN 0V00UP; and Stephen Adler, *Interview of President Mauricio Macri*, Reuters, 2016, available at ¶222, Exhibit H, Joint Appendix Vol. III at A-623, *Aurelius Cap. Master et al. v. Republic of Argentina*, No. 16-628 (2d Cir. Mar. 14, 2016).

6. Chris Giles, Gillian Tett, Elaine Moore, and Benedict Mander, *Argentina Pledges to Honour Debts Owed to Holdout Creditors*, Financial Times (Jan. 22, 2016), https://www.ft.com/content/356cbbae-c0f1-11e5-9fdb-87b8d15baec2.

7. Lindsay Dunsmuir and Hugh Bronstein, *U.S. Ends Opposition to Multilateral Development Bank Loans to Argentina*, Reuters (Jan. 21, 2016), https://www .reuters.com/article/us-usa-argentina-loans/u-s-ends-opposition-to-multilateral -development-bank-loans-to-argentina-idUSKCN0UZ2H1.

8. Caputo interview.

9. Interview with Santiago Bausili (several dates in 2017, 2018, and 2019, Buenos Aires) (hereinafter Bausili interview).

10. Walter Bianchi and Sarah Marsh, *Argentina Seals $5 Bln Bank Loan as Heads into Holdout Talks*, Reuters (Jan. 29, 2016), https://www.reuters.com/article /argentina-cenbank/update-3-argentina-seals-5-bln-bank-loan-as-heads-into-hold out-talks-idUKL2N15D1TE.

11. Pollack interview.

12. Telephone interview with Nicola Stock (Nov. 29, 2022).

13. Caputo interview; and Bausili interview.

14. Republic of Argentina, Agreement in Principle Between the Republic of Argentina and Associazione per la Tutela degli Investitori in Titoli Argentini (Jan. 31, 2016), http://servicios.infoleg.gob.ar/infolegInternet/anexos/255000-259999 /259940/ley27249-1.pdf.

15. Newman declaration, at 4.

16. Caputo interview.

17. For example, a plaintiff holding a 10% coupon bond that sought a judgment in December 2006 would have been granted a judgment equal to about 1.73 times par that accreted to 1.89 times par as of the date of the settlement. However, because 70% of 1.89 equals 1.32 times par, less than the 1.5 times par available in the standard offer, the holder of that claim would have been better off accepting the standard offer rather than the pari passu offer. See calculations by Makoff and Weidemaier in *supra* chapter 6, note 1 at 1252–1256.

18. Pollack interview.

19. *Id.*

20. ¶872-2, Exhibit B, *NML Capital, Ltd. v. Republic of Argentina*, No. 08 Civ.

6978 (S.D.N.Y. Feb. 17, 2016) (EM Ltd. settlement terms): and ¶38, Amended Final Judgment, *EM Ltd. v. Republic of Argentina*, No. 03 Civ. 2507 (S.D.N.Y. Oct. 27, 2003).

21. ¶43-1, Exhibit A, Agreement in Principle, *Montreux Partners, L.P. v. Republic of Argentina*, No. 14 Civ. 7171 (S.D.N.Y. Feb. 17, 2016) (listing the Montreux group's settlement amount of $298,664,000, which corresponds to 72.5% of claim value); and Informe del Jefe de Gabinete de Ministros Licenciado D. Marcos Peña a la Honorable Cámara de Diputados de la Nación, Informe No. 95 (2016), at 15, https://www.diputados.gov.ar/export/hcdn/secparl/dgral_info_parlamentaria/dip/archivos/Informe-95-Diputados.pdf (listing amount paid to the Montreux group of $308,560,843, which corresponds to 75% of claim value post application of the agreed step-up).

22. The text of this book has only addressed the discount from full legal value Argentina negotiated with the large plaintiffs and provides no financial analysis of the savings achieved from other plaintiffs. However, a rough understanding of what was achieved can be estimated using Argentina's later disclosure that the country paid $9.3 billion to settle $4.2 billion in claims in the deal in 2016, or 2.21 times par; see the Argentina registration statement cited in note 29 below for aggregate settlement amounts. The legal maximum value Argentina could have been forced to pay (in a simplistic analysis) was 10 times par on the $0.3 billion of FRANs and 3.5 times par on the remaining $3.9 billion of bonds, or about $16.7 billion. Argentina's cash settlement was at 55.9% of the full maximum legal value, surprisingly close to what Argentina paid participants in the deal in 2005, when the value of the GDP warrants is included. Argentina paid much less than it could have been forced by the court to pay in accepting the deal in 2005 with only a 76% success rate, especially as the premium settlements were only applied to the last 9%. The various sources of this discount are hard to untangle, however. Some of the savings came from the negotiations described in the text, and other savings came from Argentina's recovery of some bonds from deal participants in 2016 at no cost because they had passed their statute of limitations, while still other savings derived from the many plaintiffs that sought judgments early, which cut the growth rate of the legal claims far below the maximum allowed under the law.

23. Pollack interview; *supra* note 4, Lugones, (regarding email from Paul Singer on Feb. 2).

24. *Supra* note 4, Lugones.

25. Newman declaration, at 4. (Note that Milberg's Michael Spencer represented the Varela plaintiffs.)

26. Caputo interview; and Bausili interview.

27. Caputo interview.

28. Pollack interview; Caputo interview; *supra* note 4, Lugones.

29. ¶864-1, Exhibit J from declaration of Michael Paskin, at 170, *NML Capital, Ltd. v. Republic of Argentina*, No. 08 Civ. 6978 (S.D.N.Y. Feb. 11, 2016) (text of la Propuesta); ¶865, Bausili declaration, at 17, *NML Capital, Ltd. v. Republic of Argentina*, No. 08 Civ. 6978 (S.D.N.Y. Feb. 11, 2016) (summary of timeline of events and of la Propuesta's terms and timeline); and Republic of Argentina, Registration Statement (Mar. 10, 2017), at 192–93, https://www.sec.gov/Archives/edgar/data/914021/000119312517078981/d314222dsb.htm (summary of events and results of the Propuesta).

30. ¶861, Order to Show Cause, *NML Capital, Ltd. v. Republic of Argentina*, No. 08 Civ. 6978 (Feb. 11, 2016).

31. *Statement of Daniel A. Pollack, Special Master in Argentina Debt Litigation*, Press Release (Feb. 5, 2016), https://www.prnewswire.com/news-releases/statement-of-daniel-a-pollack-special-master-in-argentina-debt-litigation-feb-5--2016-300216208.html.

32. Bausili interview.

33. U.S. Department of the Treasury, *Readout from a Treasury Spokesperson of Secretary Lew's Call with Argentine Finance Minister Alfonso Prat-Gay*, Press Release No. jl0339 (Feb. 7, 2016), https://home.treasury.gov/news/press-releases/jl0339.

34. Matt Levine, *Argentina's Bond Fight Comes Down to Its Worst Bonds*, Bloomberg (Feb. 8, 2016), https://www.bloomberg.com/opinion/articles/2016-02-08/argentina-s-bond-fight-comes-down-to-its-worst-bonds.

35. *Statement of Daniel A. Pollack, Special Master in Argentina Debt Litigation*, Press Release (Feb. 16, 2016) (mimeo).

36. ¶904-5, Exhibit 3, *NML Capital, Ltd. v. Republic of Argentina*, No. 08 Civ. 6978 (Feb. 29, 2016) (Clarex and Fiscella settlement agreement).

37. ¶904-6,7, Exhibits 4 and 5, *NML Capital, Ltd. v. Republic of Argentina*, No. 08 Civ. 6978 (Feb. 29, 2016) (Old Castle and Lightwater settlement agreements).

38. ¶904-8,9, 10, Exhibits 6, 7, 8, *NML Capital, Ltd. v. Republic of Argentina*, No. 08 Civ. 6978 (Feb. 29, 2016) (Capital Ventures International, VR Global Partners, and Procella Holdings settlement agreements); and *Statement of Daniel A. Pollack, Special Master in Argentina Debt Litigation*, Press Release (Feb. 22, 2016), https://en.prnasia.com/releases/apac/Statement_Of_Daniel_A_Pollack_Special_Master_In_Argentina_Debt_Litigation_Feb_22_2016-143054.shtml.

39. ¶59, Indicative Ruling, *NML Capital, Ltd. v. Republic of Argentina*, No. 14 Civ. 8601 (S.D.N.Y. Feb. 19, 2016).

40. ¶902-1, Exhibit A, Transcript of hearing held on Feb. 24, 2016, at the 2d. Cir., at 3:22–23 and 20:5–6, *NML Capital, Ltd. v. Republic of Argentina*, 08 Civ. 6978 (S.D.N.Y. Feb. 28, 2016). (McGill: "I'm here on behalf of appellees, NML Capital, The Aurelius appellees and the FFI and [FYI] Funds.... The three funds that I mentioned before, NML, the Aurelius Funds and FFI and [FYI], we're 65 percent.")

41. *Id.*, at 18:11–16, 19:10–11, 21:3–6, 21:7–11, 21:15–21, and 22:24–24:14.

42. ¶120, Order, *NML Capital, Ltd. v. Republic of Argentina*, No. 15-3675 (2d Cir. Feb. 24, 2016).

43. *Statement of Daniel A. Pollack, Special Master in Argentina Debt Litigation*, Press Release (Feb. 24, 2016), https://www.prnewswire.com/news-releases /statement-of-daniel-a-pollack-special-master-in-argentina-bonds-matter-feb-24 -2016-215-pm-est-300225624.html.

44. Pollack interview; and *supra* note 4, Lugones.

45. Pollack interview.

46. Caputo interview; and Pollack interview.

47. Pollack interview.

48. The full text of the deal was subsequently made public by the Republic of Argentina in the context of passing a law to validate the agreements. Republic of Argentina, Deuda Pública, Ley, 27249, Mar. 31, 2016, http://servicios.infoleg .gob.ar/infolegInternet/anexos/255000-259999/259940/norma.htm; and Republic of Argentina, Agreement in Principle, Feb. 26, 2016, http://servicios .infoleg.gob.ar/infolegInternet/anexos/255000-259999/259940/ley27249-3.pdf. ("Subject to the condition set forth in paragraph 5 below, the Republic of Argentina will pay, and the plaintiffs will accept, 75% of the face amount of their claims of $5,891,000,000 asserted in the U.S. District Court for the Southern District of New York on defaulted Argentine bonds, inclusive of all legal and statutory interest applicable to each such claim through February 29, 2016, which payment shall therefore be equal to $4,418,250,000.")

49. *Special Master Announces Settlement of 15-Year Battle Between Argentina And "Holdout" Hedge Funds*, Press Release (Feb. 29, 2016), https://www.prnewswire .com/news-releases/special-master-announces-settlement-of-15-year-battle-between -argentina-and-holdout-hedge-funds-300227673.html.

50. *Supra* note 48 (details of Settlement Agreement).

51. Pollack interview (fifty reporters showed up).

52. ¶919, Transcript of hearing held on Mar. 1, 2016, at 5:5–8, *NML Capital, Ltd. v. Republic of Argentina*, No. 08 Civ. 6978 (S.D.N.Y. Mar. 14, 2016) (hereinafter March 1 hearing).

53. *Michael B. Mukasey of Counsel*, Debevoise & Plimpton, https://www .debevoise.com/michaelmukasey.

54. March 1 hearing, at 9:14–16.

55. March 1 hearing, at 11:9–12:14.

56. March 1 hearing, at 51:4–20.

57. ¶912, Opinion and Order, *NML Capital, Ltd. v. Republic of Argentina*, No. 08 Civ. 6978 (S.D.N.Y. Mar. 2, 2016).

58. ¶914, Notice of Appeal, *NML Capital, Ltd. v. Republic of Argentina*, No. 08

Civ. 6978 (S.D.N.Y. Mar. 3, 2016); ¶66, Notice of Appeal, *FFI Fund Ltd. and FYI Ltd. v. Republic of Argentina*, No. 14 Civ. 8630 (S.D.N.Y. Mar. 3, 2016); ¶63, Notice of Appeal, *Aurelius Capital Partners, L.P. et al. v. Republic of Argentina*, No. 14 Civ. 8946 (S.D.N.Y. Mar. 3, 2016); ¶63, Notice of Appeal, *Blue Angel Capital I, LLC v. Republic of Argentina*, No. 14 Civ. 8947 (S.D.N.Y. Mar. 3, 2016); ¶54, Notice of Appeal, *Andrarex, Ltd. v. Republic of Argentina*, No. 14 Civ. 9093 (S.D.N.Y. Mar. 4, 2016), ¶49, Notice of Appeal (Milberg Plaintiffs), *Hector Perez et al. v. Republic of Argentina*, No. 14 Civ. 8242 (S.D.N.Y. Mar. 4, 2016); and ¶54, Notice of Appeal (Duane Morris Plaintiffs), *Adami et al. v. Republic of Argentina*, No. 14 Civ. 7739 (S.D.N.Y. Mar. 4, 2016).

59. *Court-Appointed Special Master*, Press Release (Mar. 4, 2016), https://www.prnewswire.co.uk/news-releases/statement-of-daniel-a-pollack-court-appointed-special-master-march-4-2016-571094251.html.

60. *Court-Appointed Special Master*, Press Release (Mar. 9, 2016), https://www.prnewswire.co.uk/news-releases/statement-of-daniel-a-pollack-court-appointed-special-master-march-9-2016-571562761.html.

61. Daniel Bases, Argentina, *Creditors Agree $155 Million More in Default Settlement: Mediator*, Reuters (Mar. 18, 2016), https://www.reuters.com/article/us-argentina-debt-idUKKCN0WK1TK.

62. ¶459, Brief for the United States of America as *Amicus Curiae, Aurelius Capital Master, Ltd. et al. v. Republic of Argentina* No. 16-628 (2d Cir. Mar. 23, 2016).

63. Republic of Argentina, Law 27249 (Mar. 31, 2016), http://servicios.infoleg.gob.ar/infolegInternet/anexos/255000-259999/259940/texact.htm.

64. Dan Bases, *Argentina, Creditors Agree $253 Million More in Default Settlement*, Reuters, Apr. 10, 2016, https://www.reuters.com/article/us-argentina-debt/argentina-creditors-agree-253-million-more-in-default-settlement-mediator-idUSKCN0X70UH.

65. *Arag-A Ltd. v. Republic of Argentina*, 178 F. Supp. 3d 192 (S.D.N.Y. 2016).

66. *Argentina Settles with Yellow Crane Holdings, LLC for $255 Million*, Press Release (Apr. 12, 2016), https://www.prnewswire.com/news-releases /argentina-settles-with-yellow-crane-holdings-llc-for-255-million-300250482.html.

67. ¶539-1, Letter from Alfonso Prat-Gay to the 2d Cir., *Aurelius Capital Master et al. v. Republic of Argentina*, 16-628 (2d Cir. Apr. 11, 2016). ("As the Finance Minister of the Republic of Argentina, I respectfully write to emphasize the sense of urgency that all of us entrusted with the public affairs of the Republic and our citizens feel as to the need for a prompt Decision of this appeal. . . . If at all feasible, we hope you will give consideration to announcing your Decision on the day of the oral argument. . . . As the Court will know from the briefs, one set of parties, with an agreed figure of $4.65 billion has a unilateral right to terminate their Agreement with us if they are not paid by April 14. Our capital-raise is poised and ready to go, globally, but cannot happen without swift clarity from this Court.")

68. Audio recording: Hearing held on Apr. 13, 2016, No 16-628 (2d Cir Apr. 13, 2016); and ¶928, Certified Copy of Order of the Second Circuit Court of Appeals, *NML Capital, Ltd. v. Republic of Argentina*, No. 08 Civ. 6978 (S.D.N.Y. Apr. 14, 2014). ("On April 13, 2016, the Court heard oral arguments in this consolidated expedited appeal taken from an order of the district order entered March 2, 2016. IT IS HEREBY ORDERED that the order of the district court is affirmed.")

69. *Julie Wernau and Carolyn Cui, Argentina Returns to Global Debt Markets with $16.5 Billion Bond Sale,* Wall St. J. (Apr. 19, 2016), https://www.wsj.com/articles /argentina-returns-to-global-debt-markets-with-16-5-billion-bond-sale-1461078033.

70. *Statement of Daniel A. Pollack, Special Master in Argentina Debt Litigation,* Press Release (Apr. 22, 2016), https://www.prnewswire.com/news-releases /statement-of-daniel-a-pollack-special-master-in-argentina-debt-litigation-apr-22 -2016-300256106.html.

71. See generally Testimony of Michael C. Spencer of July 20, 2018, ¶4–5, Exhibit 3, *Milberg LLP v. Drawrah Limited et al.*, 19 Civ. 4058 (S.D.N.Y. May 6, 2019) (hereinafter Spencer testimony).

72. Spencer testimony, at 55 ($162.5 million claim).

73. Spencer testimony, at 40 (hired new lawyers).

74. Spencer testimony, at 41 (tried to attach helicopter engines).

75. *Statement of Daniel A. Pollack, Court-Appointed Special Master,* Press Release (May 31, 2017), https://www.prnewswire.com/news-releases /statement-of -daniel-a-pollack-court-appointed-special-master-may-31-201-300466345.html (settled on the Propuesta's terms).

76. Bausili interview (not landing on the moon quote).

77. ¶49, Opinion, at 8, *White Hawthorne, LLC, et al. v. Republic of Argentina*, No. 16 Civ. 1042 (S.D.N.Y. Dec. 22, 2016).

Epilogue

1. ¶1, Complaint, at 1 and 3, *Aurelius Capital Master, Ltd. v. Republic of Argentina*, No. 19 Civ. 351 (S.D.N.Y. Jan. 14, 2019) ("This is an action for breach of contract brought to recover unpaid amounts due on. . . . U.S. Dollar–Denominated New York law GDP-linked Securities. . . . For Reference Year 2013 . . . actual real GDP exceeded the base case GDP, and actual real GDP growth exceeded base case GDP growth. . . . Plaintiff owns $797,159,198 notional amount of GDP warrants. . . . Argentina should therefore have paid $61,222,074 on December 15, 2014. . . . No part of this amount has been paid."); and ¶17, Defendant the Republic of Argentina's Memorandum of Law in Support of Its Motion to Dismiss the Complaint, *Aurelius Capital Master Ltd. v. Republic of Argentina*, at 1–2, No. 19 Civ. 351 (S.D.N.Y. Apr. 18, 2019) (in which Argentina accuses Aurelius of "second-guessing" Argentina's

calculation of amounts due, claiming that Argentina's calculations were of "binding effect," and explaining an overhaul in the government's calculation of its GDP growth and therefore that the way in which the GDP warrants were paid in 2014 was relative to how they had been paid before).

2. Scott Squires, *Argentine Warrants More Than Double after Ruling Favors Aurelius*, Bloomberg (Dec. 2, 2021), https://news.bloomberglaw.com/securities-law /aurelius-scores-win -in-fight-against-argentina-over-gdp-data; and *Argentina Fails in Bid to Halt 645 Mln Euro UK Lawsuit over GDP Warrants*, Reuters (July 22, 2020), https://www.reuters .com/article/britain-argentina-court/argentina-fails-in-bid-to-halt-645-mln-euro-uk-lawsuit-over-gdp-warrants-idUSL5N2ET61I.

3. IMF, *IMF Executive Board Approves US$50 Billion Stand-By Arrangement for Argentina*, Press Release No. 18/245 (June 20, 2018), https://www.imf.org /en/News/Articles/2018/06/20/pr18245-argentina-imf-executive-board-approves -us50-billion-stand-by-arrangement; and IMF, *IMF Executive Board Discusses the Ex- Post Evaluation of Argentina's Exceptional Access under the 2018 Stand-By Arrangement*, Press Release No. 21/401 (Dec. 22, 2021) https://www.imf.org/en/News/Articles /2021/12/22/pr21401-argentina. ("In support of an economic program, the Executive Board approved in June 2018 the largest stand-by arrangement in the Fund's history. After an augmentation in October 2018, access under the arrangement amounted to US$57 billion. . . . The program went off track in August 2019 with only four of the planned twelve reviews completed by the Executive Board.")

4. Benedict Mander and Michael Stott, *Argentina's Peronists Return to Power as Macri Concedes Defeat*, Financial Times (Oct. 27, 2019), https://www.ft.com/content /db72b3de-f921-11e9-98fd-4d6c20050229.

5. Walter Bianchi and Marc Jones, *Argentina's Old Bonds Wave Goodbye as Focus Turns to New Debt*, Reuters (Sept. 4, 2020), https://www.reuters.com/article/us -argentina-debt/argentinas-old-bonds-wave-goodbye-as-focus-turns-to-new -debt-idUSKBN25V2LQ. ("After months of tense negotiations, the country's center-left Peronist government reached a breakthrough accord with creditors at the start of August, which led to 99% of the eligible debt being restructured.") On use of enhanced CACs, see IMF, *International Architecture for Resolving Sovereign Debt Involving Private-Sector Creditors—Recent Developments, Challenges, and Reform Options* (Sept. 23, 2020), at 10 and 24–27, https://www.imf.org/en/Publications /Policy-Papers/Issues/2020/09/30/The-International-Architecture-for-Resolving -Sovereign-Debt-Involving-Private-Sector-49796.

6. Lucinda Elliott and Michael Stott, *Argentina's Crisis Deepens as Finance Minister Quits*, Financial Times (July 3, 2022), https://www.ft.com/content/cdf02358 -7ba8-4326-b1a5-66c7fffbf7ab; and IMF, *IMF Executive Board Completes Second Review of the Extended Arrangement under the Extended Fund Facility for Argentina*, Press

Release No. 22/344 (Oct. 7, 2022), https://www.imf.org/en/News/Articles/2022/10/07/pr22344-imf-executive-board-completes-second-review-argentina.

7. Jonathan Wheatley and Nikou Asgari, *Debt Sell-Off Intensifies Strains for More Than a Dozen Emerging Markets*, Financial Times (July 15, 2022), https://www.ft.com/content/5c948d5f-6822-4852-ac18-3fe24c6oeade. ("Markets suggest that Argentina's risk of another default is also high.")

Conclusion

1. Gregory Makoff, *Lending to Defaulters: The IMF Updates Its Lending into Arrears Policy*, CIGI Policy Brief No. 175 (Aug. 29, 2022), https://www.cigionline.org/publications/lending-to-defaulters-the-imf-updates-its-lending-into-arrears-policy/.

2. Ben Bartenstein, Sydney Maki, and Marisa Gertz, *One Country, Nine Defaults: Argentina Is Caught in a Vicious Cycle*, Bloomberg (Sept. 11, 2019), https://www.bloomberg.com/news/photo-essays/2019-09-11/one-country-eight-defaults-the-argentine-debacles.

3. The full story of these events is told in Sebastian Edwards, American Default: The Untold Story of FDR, the Supreme Court, and the Battle over Gold (2018).

4. Boies and Olson, at 28. ("For the marriage equality battle we would create a new organization, to be called the American Foundation for Equal Rights [AFER], that would become a hub of activity in support of the case.")

5. American Task Force Argentina, Certificate of Termination, June 7, 2016.

Index

Note: Information in figures is indicated by page numbers in *italics*.

About the Author

Gregory Makoff, a physicist by training, worked as a banker for twenty-one years. As a banker, he advised companies, financial institutions, and countries, including Jamaica, Colombia, the Philippines, and Turkey, regarding their debt. During 2015 and 2016, he worked as a senior policy adviser at the U.S. Department of the Treasury on the team that helped shepherd the Puerto Rico Oversight, Management, and Economic Stability Act through Congress. He is a senior fellow (nonresident) at the Centre for International Governance Innovation, a think tank based in Waterloo, Ontario, and holds a PhD in physics from the University of Chicago (1993) and a BSc in physics and political science from MIT (1986) and is a member of the CFA Institute. From 1993 through 2014, Makoff worked for Citigroup Global Markets and predecessor companies. As noted in chapter 7, Citigroup played a junior role in the reopening transaction completed by the Republic of Argentina in 2010.

About the Foreword Contributor

Lee C. Buchheit retired in 2019 after a forty-three-year career in private legal practice. For much of his career he specialized in sovereign debt management projects and has worked on over two dozen sovereign debt restructurings. Buchheit led the international legal teams advising the Hellenic Republic (2011–2012) and the Republic of Iraq (2005–2008) in their debt restructurings, the two largest sovereign debt workouts in history. He is the author of two books in the field of international law and over forty scholarly papers on sovereign debt matters. Buchheit holds academic appointments at several universities in Europe and the United States.